LEGAL FOUNDATIONS OF MACROPRUDENTIAL POLICY

LEGAL FOUNDATIONS OF MACROPRUDENTIAL POLICY

An Interdisciplinary Approach

Anat KELLER

Cambridge – Antwerp – Chicago

Intersentia Ltd
8 Wellington Mews
Wellington Street | Cambridge
CB1 1HW | United Kingdom
Tel: +44 1223 736 170
Email: mail@intersentia.co.uk
www.intersentia.com | www.intersentia.co.uk

Distribution for the UK and
Rest of the World (incl. Eastern Europe)
NBN International
1 Deltic Avenue, Rooksley
Milton Keynes MK13 8LD
United Kingdom
Tel: +44 1752 202 301 | Fax: +44 1752 202 331
Email: orders@nbninternational.com

Distribution for Europe
Intersentia Publishing nv
Groenstraat 31
2640 Mortsel
Belgium
Tel: +32 3 680 15 50
Email: mail@intersentia.be

Distribution for the USA and Canada
Independent Publishers Group
Order Department
814 North Franklin Street
Chicago, IL 60610
USA
Tel: +1 800 888 4741 (toll free) | Fax: +1 312 337 5985
Email: orders@ipgbook.com

Legal Foundations of Macroprudential Policy. An Interdisciplinary Approach
© Anat Keller 2020

Artwork on cover: Bruce Rolff / 123RF

ISBN 978-1-78068-787-2
D/2020/7849/32
NUR 820

British Library Cataloguing in Publication Data. A catalogue record for this book is available from the British Library.

Dedicated to my family and my colleagues at King's College London

CONTENTS

LIST OF CASES

LIST OF INSTRUMENTS

DECISIONS AND RECOMMENDATIONS

EU

Decision of the ESRB of 20 January 2011 Adopting the Rules of Procedure of the European Systemic Risk Board (ESRB/2011/1) OJ C 58/4.

Decision of the ESRB of 21 July 2015 on the Provision and Collection of Information for the Macro-prudential Oversight of the Financial System within the Union (ESRB/2015/2) OJ C 394/4.

Decision of the ESRB of 16 December 2015 on a Coordination Framework for the Notification of National Macroprudential Policy Measures by Relevant Authorities, the Issuing of Opinions and Recommendations by the ESRB (ESRB/2015/4) OJ C 97.

Decision of the EBA of 23 December 2016 Adopting Rules of Procedure for Investigation of Breach of Union Law (EBA/DC/2016/174).

Decision of the ECB of 24 February 2014 on the Organisation of Preparatory Measures for the Collection of Granular Credit Data by the European System of Central Banks ECB/2014/6 OJ L 104/72.

ESRB Recommendation of 21 September 2011 on Lending in Foreign Currencies (ESRB/2011/1) OJ C 342/1.

ESRB Recommendation of 22 December 2011 on US dollar Denominated Funding of Credit Institutions (ESRB/2011/2 OJ C 72/0.

ESRB Recommendation of 22 December 2011 on the Macroprudential Mandate of National Authorities (ESRB/2011/3) OJ C 41/01.

ESRB Recommendation of 20 December 2012 on Funding of Credit Institutions (ESRB/2012/2) OJ C 119/1).

ESRB Recommendations of 20 December 2012 on Money Market Funds (ESRB/2012/1) OJ C 146/01.

ESRB Recommendation of 4 April 2013 on Intermediate Objectives and Instruments of Macro-prudential Policy (ESRB/2013/1) OJ C 170/01.

ESRB Recommendation of 18 June 2014 on Guidance for Setting Countercyclical Buffer Rates (ESRB/2014/1) OJ C 293/1.

ESRB Recommendation of 11 December 2015 on Recognising and Setting Countercyclical Buffer Rates for Exposures to Third Countries (ESRB/2015/1) OJ C 97/1.

ESRB Recommendation of 15 December 2015 on the Assessment of Cross-border Effects of and Voluntary Reciprocity for Macroprudential Policy Measures (ESRB/2015/2) OJ C 97/9.

ESRB Recommendation of 21 March 2016 on Funding of Credit Institutions (ESRB/2016/2) OJ C140/1.

ESRB Recommendation of 31 October 2016 on Closing Real Estate Data Gaps (ESRB/2016/14) OJ C 31/1.

ESRB Recommendation of 20 October 2017 amending Recommendation ESRB/2015/2 on the Assessment of Cross-border Effects of and Voluntary Reciprocity for Macroprudential Policy Measures (ESRB/2017/4) OJ C 431/1.

UK

FPC Recommendation to the PRA and FCA on Loan-To-Income Ratios in Mortgage Lending, 25 June 2014.

GUIDANCE AND POLICY

UK

Communications Guidance for FPC Members, 28 April 2018.

US

FSOC, Authority to Require Supervision and Regulation of Certain Nonbank Financial Companies, Guidance, 84 Fed. No 249 Reg. 71740 (30 December 2019).
Transparency Policy for the Financial Stability Oversight Council (1 October 2010).

LEGISLATION AND REGULATIONS

EU

Directive 2013/36/EU of 26 June 2013 on Access to the Activity of Credit Institutions and the Prudential Supervision of Credit Institutions and Investment Firms OJ L 176 p 338.
Directive 2014/59/EU of 15 May 2014 Establishing a Framework for the Recovery and Resolution of Credit Institutions and Investment Firms OJ L 173 p 190.
Regulation (EU) No 1093/2010 Establishing a European Supervisory Authority (European Banking Authority) OJ L 331 p 12.
Regulation (EU) No 1094/2010 Establishing a European Supervisory Authority (European Insurance and Occupational Pensions Authority) OJ L 331 p 38.
Regulation (EU) No 1095/2010 Establishing a European Supervisory Authority (European Securities and Markets Authority) OJ L 331 p 84.
Regulation (EU) No 1092/2010 of 24 November 2010 on European Union Macro-prudential Oversight of the Financial System and Establishing a European Systemic Risk Board OJ L 331 p 1.
Regulation (EU) 1096/2010 of 17 November 2010 Conferring Specific Tasks upon the ECB concerning the Functioning of the ESRB OJ L 331 p 162.
Regulation (EU) 2019/2176 of 18 December 2019 Amending Regulation (EU) No 1092/2010 on European Union Macro-prudential Oversight of the Financial System and Establishing a European Systemic Risk Board OJ L 334 p 146.

Regulation (EU) 2019/2175 of 18 December 2019 amending Regulation (EU) No 1093/2010 Establishing a European Supervisory Authority (European Banking Authority), Regulation (EU) No 1094/2010 Establishing a European Supervisory Authority (European Insurance and Occupational Pensions Authority), Regulation (EU) No 1095/2010 Establishing a European Supervisory Authority (European Securities and Markets Authority), Regulation (EU) No 600/2014 on Markets in Financial Instruments, Regulation (EU) 2016/1011 on Indices used as Benchmarks in Financial Instruments and Financial Contracts or to Measure the Performance of Investment Funds, and Regulation (EU) 2015/847 on Information Accompanying Transfers of funds OJ L 334 p 1.

Regulation (EU) No 575/2013 of 26 June 2013 on Prudential Requirements for Credit Institutions and Investment Firms OJ L 176 p 1.

Regulation (EU) No 1024/2013 Conferring Specific Tasks on the European Central Bank Concerning Policies relating to the Prudential Supervision of Credit Institutions OJ L 287 p 63.

Regulation (EU) No 806/2014 of 15 July 2014 Establishing Uniform Rules and a Uniform Procedure for the Resolution of Credit Institutions and certain Investment Firms in the Framework of a Single Resolution Mechanism and a Single Resolution Fund OJ L 225 p 1.

Regulation of the ECB of 16 April 2014 Establishing the Framework for Cooperation within the Single Supervisory Mechanism between the European Central Bank and National Competent Authorities and with National Designated Authorities (ECB/2014/17) OJ L 141/1.

Regulation (EU) 2015/373 of 5 March 2015 amended Regulation (EC) No 2533/98 Concerning the Collection of Statistical Information by the ECB OJ L 64/6.

Regulation (EU) 2016/867 of the European Central Bank of 18 May 2016 on the Collection of Granular Credit and Credit Risk Data (ECB/2016/13) OJ L 144 p 44.

UK

Bank of England Act 1998 c 11.
Bank of England and Financial Services Act 2016 c 14.
Financial Services Act 2012 c 21.
Financial Services and Market Act 2000 c 8.

US

Dodd-Frank Wall Street Reform and Consumer Protection Act Public Law No 111–203, 21 July 2010, 124 STAT. 1376.

Economic, Growth Regulatory Relief and Consumer Protection Act Public Law No 115–174, 24 May 2018, 115th Congress.

CHAPTER 1

INTRODUCTION AND BACKGROUND

In 2009, Claudio Borio observed that "We are all macroprudentialists now".[1] The observation reflected the emergence of the term macroprudential policy as a true buzzword and its dominance in the post-crisis public discourse.[2] As the world was experiencing the long-lasting aftershock of the 2007–2009 financial crisis, macroprudential policy became to be the missing link that could rectify the failure to identify, in time, and prevent or mitigate systemic risks. This acknowledgement signified a major shift in the regulatory and supervisory thinking.[3] While micro-prudential regulation and supervision was still considered a necessary policy to maintaining the stability of the financial system, it was no longer viewed as a sufficient one. The reports that mushroomed following the financial crisis emphasised the importance of adding a macroprudential overlay to the existing concoctions of prudential and macroeconomic policy areas.[4] These reports were quickly followed by the design of national and regional macroprudential authorities, either by establishing new institutions for that purpose or providing new powers to existing institutions. In the UK, the Financial Policy Committee (FPC), a committee of the Bank of England, was established in 2013.[5] It is responsible for identifying, monitoring and taking action to remove or reduce systemic risks with a view to protecting

---

[1]   C Borio, "The Macroprudential Approach to Regulation and Supervision", VoxEU, 14 April 2009.
[2]   Ibid; P Clement, "The Term 'Macroprudential': Origins and Evolution" (2010) BIS Quarterly Review 59; G Galati and R Moessner, "Macroprudential Policy – A Literature Review" (2011) BIS Working Papers No 337.
[3]   Alan Greenspan, Former Federal Reserve Chairman, Evidence to the US House of Representatives, 23 October 2008, suggesting that the whole intellectual edifice collapsed following the 2007–2009 financial crisis.
[4]   The High-Level Group on Financial Supervision in the EU chaired by Jacques De Larosière Report Brussels, February 2009 (De Larosièr Report), 44; Financial Services Authority, *The Turner Review A Regulatory Response to the Global Banking Crisis* (March 2009), 83.
[5]   Section 4 of the Financial Services Act 2012 c 21 inserting Part 1A to the Bank of England Act 1998 (BEA 1998). The FPC was established as a sub-committee of the court and in 2016, the Bank of England and Financial Services Act 2016 c 14 made it a committee of the bank of England, This was part of the reform of the regulatory system in the UK and the establishment of the Prudential Regulation Authority (PRA) and the Financial Conduct Authority (FCA).

and enhancing the resilience of the UK financial system[6] and exercises its functions with a view to contributing to the achievement of the Bank's financial stability objective.[7] In the US, the Financial Stability Oversight Council (FSOC) is a collaborative body chaired by the Secretary of the Treasury that was established in 2010 under the Dodd-Frank Wall Street Reform and Consumer Protection Act, with a macroprudential mandate to identify risks and respond to emerging threats to the financial stability of the US.[8] In the EU, the European Systemic Risk Board (ESRB) became operational in 2011 as part of the new European System of Financial Supervision (ESFS)[9] and is responsible for the macroprudential oversight of the EU financial system and the prevention and mitigation of systemic risk.[10]

---

[6]   Section 9C(2) BEA. As shall be seen in Chapter 2, the FPC also has a secondary objective to support the Government's economic policies.

[7]   Section 9C(1) BEA 1998.

[8]   Dodd-Frank Wall Street Reform and Consumer Protection Act Public Law 111–203, 21 July 2010 124 STAT. 1376 (Dodd Frank Act), sections 111 and 112. For a comprehensive discussion of the FSOC's mandate, see Chapter 2.

[9]   Alongside three European Supervisory Authorities (ESAs) and national supervisors. The ESAs are the European Banking Authority (EBA), the European Insurance and Occupational Pensions Authority (EIOPA) and the European Securities and Markets Authority (ESMA), and they are responsible for micro-prudential supervision of their relevant sector.
In order, Regulation (EU) No 1093/2010 Establishing a European Supervisory Authority (European Banking Authority), OJ L 331 p 12 as amended; Regulation (EU) No 1094/2010 Establishing a European Supervisory Authority (European Insurance and Occupational Pensions Authority), OJ L 331 p 38 as amended; Regulation (EU) No 1095/2010 establishing a European Supervisory Authority (European Securities and Markets Authority), OJ L 331 p 84 as amended (hereinafter together: the ESAs Regulations).

[10]   Regulation (EU) No 1092/2010 of 24 November 2010 on European Union Macro-prudential Oversight of the Financial System and Establishing a European Systemic Risk Board OJ L 331 p 1 (ESRB Regulation), article 3. On 20 September 2017, the European Commission adopted a comprehensive package reviewing the ESFS and included a proposal amending the ESAs Regulation (COM (2017) 536 final) and a proposal amending the ESRB Regulation (COM (2017) 538 final). Regulation (EU) 2019/2176 of 18 December 2019 amending Regulation (EU) No 1092/2010 on European Union Macro-prudential Oversight of the Financial System and establishing a European Systemic Risk Board OJ L 334 p 146 (available at <https://eur-lex.europa.eu/legal-content/EN/TXT/PDF/?uri=CELEX:32019R2176&from=EN>) (hereinafter: "the Regulation amending the ESRB Regulation") entered into force on 30 December 2019; Regulation (EU) 2019/2175 of the European Parliament and of the Council of 18 December 2019 amending Regulation (EU) No 1093/2010 Establishing a European Supervisory Authority (European Banking Authority), Regulation (EU) No 1094/2010 Establishing a European Supervisory Authority (European Insurance and Occupational Pensions Authority), Regulation (EU) No 1095/2010 Establishing a European Supervisory Authority (European Securities and Markets Authority), Regulation (EU) No 600/2014 on Markets in Financial Instruments, Regulation (EU) 2016/1011 on Indices used as Benchmarks in Financial Instruments and Financial Contracts or to Measure the Performance of Investment Funds, and Regulation (EU) 2015/847 on Information Accompanying Transfers of funds OJ L 334 p 1 (hereinafter: "the Regulation amending the ESAs Regulations") entered into force on 30 December 2019.

The book offers a critical, contextual and comparative examination of the nature of macroprudential policy and exposes its conflictual elements and the unique challenges that macroprudential authorities must face. The book explores why macroprudential policy is needed and how to design tailored legal, institutional and governance frameworks that support the various supervisory stages in macroprudential regimes.

Framing macroprudential policy through the prisms of conflictual elements, trade-offs and asymmetries, assist in clarifying the legal, institutional and governance needs of macroprudential frameworks. Nonetheless, it is acknowledged that the elusive nature of systemic risks, the relative short experience in the conduct of macroprudential policy and its high dependency on national peculiarities and legal, political and social settings – all together, make it difficult for strong and decisive generalised contentions to surface. The book, therefore, borrows insights and notions from other disciplines to derive and capture the theoretical foundations of macroprudential policy to support high-level suggestions on how to operationalise macroprudential policymaking. In particular, it draws, where appropriate, on established scholarships from economics and international law as well as theories developed in the Organisational Behaviour field.

Theory, however, cannot be detached from practicalities. In order to ground the discussion in context, the book also explores macroprudential policy frameworks at the national level (UK and US), regional level (EU) and global level (FSB and IMF). In addition, the book explains the law in light of the most recent empirical research in economics literature, including research on the prevalent governance structure of macroprudential policy, its interaction with other policy areas and evidence of the effectiveness of particular macroprudential tools.

The book makes several key arguments.

First, the book argues in favour of tailored legal, institutional and governance frameworks in macroprudential regimes, which reflects the unique features of macroprudential policy, its asymmetries and pulling forces. Exploring the conflictual elements of macroprudential policy will counteract the natural tendency of legislators to borrow frameworks and mechanisms from monetary policy, without a thorough consideration of their relevance and applicability to the macroprudential sphere. Just like an axiom or a postulate, existing mechanisms and their supporting rationales are often accepted as a starting point of reasoning without needing to prove them. The book highlights the possible pitfalls in conducting such "theory transformation" and positions macroprudential policy as a distinctive policy area.

Second, macroprudential policy depends to a large extent on factors external to the macroprudential authorities. So much so that the causal link between the macroprudential authority's performance and the outcome (prevention or mitigation of systemic risks) is difficult to establish. It is therefore suggested to conceptualise the assessment of macroprudential authorities' performance and design their accountability mechanisms at the process level. The book reiterates the importance of the quality of governance processes, which hinges on clear procedural rules and the centrality of the accountability and transparency of those processes in forming effective macroprudential regimes.

Third, while macroprudential policy should be designed and implemented as a distinct policy area, it cannot be achieved in silos. Legal frameworks that support macroprudential authorities should be designed with a view to acknowledging potential trade-offs and facilitating interaction and exchange of information with other policy areas, without impinging on their respective independence.

Fourth, an open and inclusive regulatory and supervisory process, which is characterised by genuine depolarised and diversified deliberations, is critically important in macroprudential regimes. Diversity in the composition of the macroprudential authority through inclusion of external members and seeking external views are weighty factors in ameliorating inherent biases, such as groupthink and inaction bias, in the conduct of macroprudential policy and enhancing the democratic legitimacy of macroprudential authorities. The nature of the deliberations, the manner motions are presented, the transparency of the individual opinations, the role of the chair and the decision rule – may all have a significant effect on the quality of the macroprudential decision-making process. Moreover, opening up macroprudential policymaking to external counter views (experts and to some extent, non-experts) and to different perspectives of "financial stability" is key to identifying the next crisis. Therefore, it is suggested that viewing macroprudential policy through the prism of negative externalities and "fixing" failures in financial markets is unwarranted and can result in a narrow and ineffective policy conduct.

Fifth and more generally, normative judgments that often weigh conflicting public goods, are inherent in the macroprudential policymaking. Financial stability lies on a continuum rather than an approachable and static equilibrium point. Masking this normative nature of macroprudential policy is therefore a fruitless exercise. Instead, the legal framework should acknowledge and embrace it "out in the open" and address the consequent weakening of democratic legitimacy through a clear and operationalised mandate (Chapter 2); institutional models that enhance pluralism and inclusiveness (Chapter 3); having a set of powers that is adaptable and flexible to specificities and new developments but that is also enforceable and "can bite" (Chapter 4); a coherent and effective set of approaches to guide macroprudential decision-making process (Chapter 5); being cognisant of the challenges of designing, activating and calibrating tools and ways to address them (Chapter 6); designing independence, accountability and transparency arrangements that enhance legitimacy (Chapter 7); utilising complementarities with other policy areas (Chapter 8); understanding the complex nature of knowledge and expertise in the macroprudential context and utilising it in the data collection and analysis phase (Chapter 9); and, in the global architecture of systemic risk regulation and supervision, acknowledging the emergence of "new" market powers with perspectives on "financial stability" that may not be synonymous to the perspective of developed countries (Chapter 10).

Finally, looking at the international level, the book suggests that the dispersed and diffused architecture of global systemic risk regulation and supervision introduces pluralism and the "out of the box" thinking required in the macroprudential context. It is shown that the crux of the problem is that the view of "financial stability", particularly in relation to the oversight of shadow banking, is confined and does not adequately acknowledge competing considerations such as financial inclusion.

1. WHAT THIS BOOK IS ABOUT: MACROPRUDENTIAL POLICY AND ITS CONFLICTUAL ELEMENTS

There is a connecting thread that runs through all the chapters of the book. It is the contention that macroprudential policy is a "conflicted" policy area, which is subject to many pulling forces and asymmetries.

First and foremost, the macroprudential mandate can include conflicting objectives. While a macroprudential authority is tasked with preventing or mitigating systemic risks to financial stability, risks are still the lifeblood of financial systems. Being too cautious may stifle economic growth and inhibit innovation. One way to address this conflict is through a hierarchal mandate and inclusion of a secondary objective of "ensuring a sustainable contribution of the financial system to economic growth". These objectives, however, are not always aligned (at least in the short–medium term) and trade-offs can easily emerge.

Given the rather amorphic and largely untested nature of this policy area, there is also an inherent tension between the need to provide a macroprudential authority with a wide discretion in its mandate so as to enable it to adapt policy measures to changing risks and the need to restrict and limit its discretion so that its democratic legitimacy and accountability are preserved. A "constrained discretion" approach can provide a middle ground between a full-fledged discretion and a rule-based macroprudential policymaking that can balance these considerations, at least until there is more robust evidence that links indicators to tools.

In light of these considerations, the mandate and boundaries of macroprudential policy as a distinct policy area should be clear. But these boundaries cannot be hard. There is an urgent need to establish legal structures and mechanisms that facilitate exchange of information and coordination between macroprudential policy and other policy areas to smooth any potential conflicts and trade-offs. This should be done without blurring their respective objectives and diluting the accountability of the macroprudential authority.[11]

In addition, the very nature of systemic risk means that it has no borders and thus requires a coordinated global and reciprocal approach. However, the design and calibration of macroprudential tools cannot follow a "one size fits all" approach. Consideration of local factors, structural, economic, legal, social and political, cannot be left out of the equation. Hence, while macroprudential policy has to be addressed at the global level and ensure reciprocity and a level-playing field, it also requires a tailored approach that is fitted to specificities. Similarly, a macroprudential regime should be comprehensive and bring under its umbrella all sectors, financial institutions and products, regulated or unregulated, but its measures can be very much targeted in order to address the emergence of specific vulnerabilities in the financial system.

The prevalent use of semi-soft powers in macroprudential regimes also reflects these pulling forces. Semi-soft powers secure the flexibility, adaptability and ability of macroprudential authorities to adjust their policy to specificities and fast-moving market developments. Yet, it is also vital that these powers generate compliance. Therefore, various "hardening" mechanisms, such as "comply-or-explain", ensure that semi-soft powers have a discernible impact in terms of financial stability. On closer inspection, however, where semi-soft powers result in diffused and shared responsibility across many agencies, regulatory-turfs and misalignment between "financial stability" and other supervisory objectives may emerge.

Analysing the concepts of knowledge and expertise in the macroprudential sphere further validates this "conflicted" nature. In macroprudential policy, there is an urgent need to develop expertise, which is technical, evolving and non-dichotomous. Albeit, the need for specialisation and distance from day-to-day politics can also create a problem of "groupthink" that can inhibit the effectiveness of the macroprudential policymaking.

Another substantive conflict is revealed when exploring the design and calibration of macroprudential measures. Macroprudential measures are often designed to be implemented during the upswing stage when "everything is going well". Accordingly, policy measures can be unpopular and go against

---

[11]　This conflicted view of macroprudential policymaking as a way to organise the discussion of the pulling forces and "the play of power" in this policy area can be said to be firmly grounded in the "regulatory space" literature where space is composed of a cluster of regulation, decisions and policies that involves the interaction and competition between various interests. L Hancher and M Moran, "Organising Regulatory Space" in L Hancher and M Moran (eds), *Capitalism, Culture and Economic Regulation* (Oxford University Press, 1989), 272, 277; F Vibert, *The New Regulatory Space: Reframing Democratic Governance* (Edward Elgar, 2014).

the short-term interests of politicians, the financial industry and at times, the public at large. In addition, there is an asymmetry between the costs and benefits of macroprudential measures. The costs of macroprudential policy actions are often visible and can be felt in the short-term, however, the benefits are hard to quantify and can be appreciated (if at all) only in the long term. Independence of the macroprudential authority is therefore essential to the conduct of a timely and effective macroprudential policy. This insularity of the macroprudential authority can, nonetheless, destabilise its credibility, emphasising its "unelected bureaucrats" nature and diminished democratic legitimacy. The macroprudential authority is thus found, once again, amid conflicting forces. There is a pressure to exhibit more democratic legitimacy through enhanced accountability mechanisms and prominence of the Treasury or the fiscal authority in the governance of the macroprudential authority. Yet, enhancing democratic legitimacy through such representation might, in turn, impede on the independence of the macroprudential authority. This calls for a design of a tailored legal and institutional macroprudential framework that accentuates expertise and insularity from political and industry pressures but at the same time, enhances the democratic legitimacy of the macroprudential authority.

The vagueness of the mandate, the wide discretion of the macroprudential authority and the potential unpopularity of its policy decisions can result in an inherent tendency of macroprudential authorities to forbearance and inaction. Conversely, macroprudential authorities may instead follow a path of "better be safe than sorry" and be tempted to pre-emptively address a wide number of issues so as to avoid ex-post criticism of missing a problem that led to the build-up of systemic risk. As such, macroprudential authorities may take an over-active (and, in fact, over-cautious) approach and activate macroprudential tools through a "learning by doing" process. The danger, however, in doing so without a solid analytical grounding and rigorous analysis should not be underestimated. Again, such an over-active approach can result in real-economy costs and unnecessarily inhibit economic growth. It comes as no surprise, therefore, that often macroprudential authorities take a gradual approach to activating policy tools and incorporate a clear cost-benefit analysis in their decision-making process.

Finally, in communication, there is a clear tension between the need for macroprudential authorities to speak in one-voice but at the same time, internally, ensure deliberations are free and allow for differing or opposing views to be heard and considered. A communication strategy should also balance between transparency as a key accountability mechanism and the potential dangerous self-destructive effect of disclosing market-sensitive data.

These conflictual elements and others are at the core of this book. They provide a useful and powerful tool to explore the legal aspects of macroprudential policy.

2. THE STRUCTURE OF THE BOOK

Chapter 2 begins by exploring the nature of the ultimate objective of macroprudential policy – "financial stability". It suggests that, compared to the overarching "financial stability" objective, setting the macroprudential mandate in terms of "systemic risks" and "resilience" can bring the mandate focus and clarity and assist in making it more achievable and measurable. The chapter sketches the nature and key features of these terms to promote the refinement of macroprudential policy frameworks and analytical tools. It then analyses the effectiveness of intermediate objectives as a useful mechanism to operationalise macroprudential regimes and maintain their adaptability to reflect new risks to financial stability. The chapter advocates the inclusion of a secondary objective to financial stability in the macroprudential mandate in the form of "sustaining economic growth". While there is an intrinsic tension between these objectives, their open and clear hierarchical articulation in the legal framework is preferable to "masking" contested considerations. The chapter discusses how all these considerations come together in the legislative frameworks of the FPC, FSOC and ESRB and assesses the challenges that their implementation poses in practice.

Chapter 3 focuses on the main institutional models for macroprudential policymaking and analyses their strengths and weaknesses. It presents the rationales behind a committee structure becoming a popular institutional structure for macroprudential policymaking and the important role that external members can play in enhancing the quality of the macroprudential decision-making process. It suggests that in addition to diversity in composition, the way decisions are discussed, the nature of deliberations, the transparency of the individual opinations and the decision rule – are all key factors in strengthening the quality of the macroprudential decision-making process. The chapter looks at how the institutional structure of macroprudential authorities can significantly affect the level of resilience and ability to withstand political pressures and industry lobbying. As such, where central banks play a central role in macroprudential policymaking, their hard-won and long-standing independence can assist in weathering these pressures. In contrast, a dominant role of the finance ministry or treasury in a macroprudential committee could potentially inhibit its independence and insulation from political pressure and may result in a reduced willingness to take warranted pre-emptive measures to slow expansion that may lead to the build-up of systemic risk.[12] In addition, the choice of a particular institutional model may foster (or alternatively, inhibit) the much-needed coordination and flow of information between macroprudential

---

[12]   Though there are apparent benefits to the Treasury's participation in macroprudential committees in strengthening the democratic legitimacy of the macroprudential authority. See Chapter 7.

policy and other policy areas. More specifically, where the institutional setting is founded on cross-membership and representation of other policy areas in the macroprudential authority, coordination will be ingrained in the macroprudential decision-making process and exploit synergies across these policies.

Chapter 4 explores powers vested in macroprudential authorities that vary greatly across jurisdictions, ranging from hard to semi-soft and soft powers. The key takeaways from this chapter are threefold. First, the legal framework of the macroprudential regime should enable the macroprudential authority, where necessary, to expand the regulatory perimeter, close remaining data gaps and inject modalities in times of emergency. Second, drawing on literature from the international governance field and in particular, the legalisation theory, the chapter suggests that while softer powers allow for flexibility, there are key mechanisms that can assist in "hardening" the legal nature of these powers. These include precision of macroprudential authorities' outputs, a formal and clear decision-making process and pre-established procedures supported by a "comply-or-explain" mechanism. Yet, the effectiveness of these mechanisms is fraught with difficulties of regulatory-turf wars and the risk of "box-ticking" culture and ready-made justifications for non-compliance. Third, compliance can easily become the Achilles Heel of a macroprudential regime that is based on semi-soft powers. The chapter underlines the procedural quality of the decision-making process and the legitimacy that flows from it as a critical element in ensuring compliance with semi-soft powers.

Chapter 5 develops, for the first time, a comprehensive taxonomy of the potential approaches to guide the decision-making process in the macroprudential sphere to include: (1) A cost-benefit approach; (2) An entities-based approach that focuses on designation of individual institutions as systemically important and subjecting them to enhanced regulation and supervision and/or an entities based approach that focuses on regulating activities that could potentially result in the emergence of systemic risk; and (3) A rule-based approach; a discretionary approach or middle positioned approach that is based on "constrained discretion". The chapter explores the viability and desirability of these supervisory approaches and where appropriate, it identifies practical and legal obstacles in their implementation in the FSOC, FPC and ESRB's legal frameworks.

Chapter 6 analyses the challenges that macroprudential authorities face in activating, calibrating and deactivating macroprudential tools and seeks to bring greater clarity on the legal and practical ways to address these challenges. Accordingly, the chapter addresses the following questions: which macroprudential tools are currently available? Should combined tools be used? Should a gradual or more activist approach be taken when calibrating tools? How targeted should the tools be?

Chapter 7 offers a theoretical framework for the independence, accountability and transparency of macroprudential authorities by drawing parallels (alongside fundamental differences) with the burgeoning academic discussion of central banks' independence. The chapter assesses how specific accountability and transparency arrangements can be designed and implemented to improve the macroprudential authority's various forms of legitimacy. The transparency and accountability frameworks of the FPC, FSOC and ESRB are then used as a case study for that purpose.

The chapter concludes that accountability mechanisms, at least in the early stages of the policy development, should focus on the decision-making process of the macroprudential authority, to be differentiated from its policy results. Governance structure and decision-making procedures that enhance pluralism and inclusiveness through transparency and awareness of the rationales behind policy decisions can assist in bolstering the democratic legitimacy of the macroprudential authority. Moreover, the chapter suggests that overall, the current state of accountability in macroprudential regimes is troublesome and calls for further refinements.

Chapter 8 advances a holistic and non-dichotomous view of macroprudential policy and asserts that a frequent dialogue and suitable coordination mechanisms between macroprudential authorities and policymakers in other areas are essential to conducting effective macroprudential policy. In particular, it explores whether there should be a hierarchy between the "financial stability" objective and the objectives of other policy areas.

Chapter 9 deals with a paramount macroprudential supervisory stage – the data collection and analysis and explores both its institutional aspects and quality features. It discusses policy efforts to close remaining data gaps as well as emerging challenges that macroprudential authorities are facing at this supervisory stage: the use of big data and machine learning and the design and use of macro- stress tests to generate data. The chapter, however, advocates going beyond "data-driven" policymaking and highlights the importance of expertise and its inherent limitations in the macroprudential sphere. Drawing on insights from the knowledge literature, the chapter yields several suggestions including that the institutional and governance frameworks of the macroprudential authority should be designed and deployed to "favorably influence processes of transferring, sharing, integrating, using, and creating knowledge."[13] The dynamic expertise-accumulation process of the macroprudential authority could be achieved through coordination with other prudential regulators; designing a legal framework that incorporates

---

[13]   NJ Foss and S Michailova, "Knowledge Governance: Themes and Questions" in S Michailova and NJ Foss (eds), *Knowledge Governance: Processes and Perspectives* (Oxford Scholarship Online, 2009), 8 referring to the "knowledge governance approach" which advocates choosing governance structures to promote these aspects. According to this approach, governance structures include not only legal frameworks but also informal mechanisms such as trust, organisational cultures and communication flows.

and incentivises diversity in the decision-making process and viewing market players as partners, cautiously utilising their expertise. A macroprudential legal framework that favours expertise will not only close gaps in the evidence base but will also assist in identifying data gaps and resolving failures in interpretation and analysis of data.

Chapter 10 moves away from the domestic and regional legal and institutional macroprudential arrangements to the emerging global regulatory architecture for the regulation and supervision of systemic risk. Scholars often suggest that a more homogenised and centralised international regulatory order is needed to effectively prevent or mitigate systemic risk. This chapter suggests that, in fact, the incremental and depolarised structure of the global architecture of systemic risk regulation and supervision is not the crux of the problem. Its components of agenda setters, standards setters and institutions promoting compliance play complementary roles in the regulatory space and bring in the pluralism and "out of the box" thinking that is so vital in the macroprudential context. Still, there are areas that call for improvements such as enhancing inclusiveness, legitimacy and accountability of these international institutions. In particular, the political character of the FSB that is accountable to the G-20 does not go hand in hand with the nature of macroprudential policy that requires a high degree of autonomy to sound the sirens of systemic risk and fight inaction bias at the global level. The chapter dissects the interpretation of "financial stability" at the international level and critically analyses the challenges this (rather narrow) interpretation presents in addressing new forms of financial intermediation and the now, more than ever, diffused nature of market power of jurisdictions participating in the formation of international standards.

3. THE EMERGENCE OF MACROPRUDENTIAL POLICY: OLD CONCERNS, NEW TERM

The modest aim of this introduction is to set the scene. This feels a bit like putting the cart before the horse as many of the terms used here, such as systemic risk and macroprudential objectives and tools, require detailed dissecting and thoughtful analysis. It may be awkward but necessary.

With this in mind, the first appearance of the term macroprudential is attributed to the meeting of the Cooke Committee on 28–29 June 1979.[14] In 1986, the term surfaced, for the first time, in the public domain to describe a policy that promotes "the safety and soundness of the broad financial

---

[14]   Clement (2010) (n 2).

system and payments mechanism".[15] Following its first appearance, it largely remained outside the public sphere until, in 2000, it finally rose to prominence following Andrew Crockett's speech before the Eleventh International Conference of Banking Supervisors.[16] Crockett called for a strengthening of the macroprudential perspective to achieve financial stability, contrasting it with the micro-prudential perspective.[17] The objective of macroprudential supervision was accordingly defined as limiting the likelihood of the failure, and corresponding costs, of significant portions of the financial system.[18] Yet, it would be wrong to suggest that this was all novel. The underlying concerns of system-wide risks and the use of macroprudential tools to address these concerns predated the official coining of the term macroprudential policy. The US has a long history in implementing a variety of macroprudential tools going back as far as the 1930s.[19] Additionally, emerging market countries in Asia and Latin America have applied macroprudential policies since the aftermath of the 1997 Asian financial crisis and the 1998 Russian financial crisis.[20] While these historical accounts are important, there is no doubt that the 2007–2009 financial crisis ignited the interest in macroprudential policy and its tools, progressively gaining prominence in the years that followed.[21]

---

[15]   Cross Report on "Recent Innovations in International Banking" prepared by a study group of the central banks of the Group of Ten countries (April 1986).
       See also BL Smaghi, "Going Forward: Regulation and Supervision after the Financial Turmoil", speech at Bocconi University, Milano, Italy, 19 June 2009.

[16]   AD Crockett, "Marrying the Micro- and Macro-prudential Dimensions of Financial Stability" Remarks before the Eleventh International Conference of Banking Supervisors, Basel, 20–21 September 2000.
       See also I Maes, "The Origins of the BIS Macro-Prudential Approach to Financial Stability: Alexandre Lamfalussy and Financial Fragility" (2010) National Bank of Belgium Working Paper No 176.

[17]   Ibid.

[18]   Ibid.

[19]   DJ Elliott, G Feldberg and A Lehnert, "The History of Cyclical Macroprudential Policy in the United State" Finance and Economics Discussion Series 2013–29, Board of Governors of the Federal Reserve System (US).
       In other countries, macroprudential measures were taken in the 1960s and 1970s. See G Galati and R Moessner, "What Do We Know About the Effects of Macroprudential Policy?" (2014) DNB Working Paper No 440, 7.
       This is often overlooked, perhaps because the US has not actively used these macroprudential tools since the early 1990s.

[20]   BIS, "Macroprudential Instruments and Frameworks: A Stocktaking of Issues and Experiences" (2010) Committee on the Global Financial System Papers No 38; IMF, "Macroprudential Policy: An Organizing Framework" (2011) available at <https://www.imf.org/external/np/pp/eng/2011/031411.pdf>; IMF, "Macroprudential Policy: An Organizing Framework" (2011) available at <https://www.imf.org/en/Publications/Policy-Papers/Issues/2016/12/31/Macroprudential-Policy-An-Organizing-Framework-Background-Paper-PP4546>.
       See also Galati and Moessner (2014) (n 19), 7.

[21]   MD Knight, "Marrying the Micro- and Macroprudential Dimensions of Financial Stability: Six Years" (The 14th International Conference of Banking Supervisors, Mérida, 4–5 October 2006).

The macroprudential perspective focuses on the financial system as a whole as distinct from individual institutions and its objective is to limit the costs to the economy from financial distress.[22] In other words, it is aimed at limiting the likelihood of failure and corresponding costs of a significant portion of the financial system, often referred to as limiting systemic risks.[23]

The sources and the channels through which systemic risk is propagated will be discussed in length in Chapter 2. At this stage, it is sufficient to explain that the traditional classification of macroprudential policy is based on the distinction between two dimensions of systemic risk: the time-related (or cyclical) dimension and the cross-sectional (or structural) dimension.[24] The time-dimension deals with how systemic risk evolves over time and focuses on the pro-cyclicality of the financial system and the accumulation of risk over the business or financial cycle.[25] The cyclical dimension, therefore, originates from the tendency of financial institutions to assume excessive risks in the upswing and become excessively risk-averse in the downswing.[26] This tendency can promote the emergence of unsustainable boom which, when it turns to bust, magnifies the disruption and eventually, has the potential to cause a deep

---

[22]   Crockett (2000) (n 16).

[23]   Ibid; J Caruana, "Systemic Risk: How to Deal with It?" [2010] BIS Paper available at <http://www.bis.org/publ/othp08.htm>.

[24]   C Borio, "Implementing A Macroprudential Framework: Blending Boldness and Realism", a keynote address for the BIS-HKMA research conference on "Financial Stability: Towards a Macroprudential Approach", Hong Kong SAR, 5–6 July 2010; Clement (2010) (n 2); L Servén, "Macroprudential Policies in the Wake of the Global Financial Crisis" in O Canuto and M Giugale (eds), *The Day After Tomorrow, A Handbook on the Future of Economic Policy in the Developing World* (World Bank, 2010), 129; BIS (2010) (n 20); A Clark and A Large, "Macroprudential Policy: Addressing the Things We Don't Know" (2011) Group of Thirty Occasional Paper No 83.

[25]   Risks usually build up over the boom phase, when banks relax their credit standards; H Minsky, "The Financial Instability Hypothesis" (1992) Levy Economics Institute Working Paper 74; C Borio, C Furfine and P Lowe, "Procyclicality of the Financial System and Financial Stability: Issues and Policy Options" [2001] in "Marrying the Macro- and Micro-prudential Dimensions of Financial Stability" BIS Papers 1, 1–57; W White, "Procyclicality in the Financial System: Do We Need a New Macrofinancial Stabilisation Framework?" (2005) Kiel Economic Policy Papers 2; M Drehmann and others, "Countercyclical Capital Buffers: Exploring Options" (2010) BIS Working Papers 317; E Farhi and J Tirole, "Deadly Embrace: Sovereign and Financial Balance Sheets Doom Loops" (2015) Harvard University OpenScholar Working Paper 164, 191.
        See also M Schularick and A Taylor, "Credit Booms Gone Bust: Monetary Policy, Leverage Cycles and Financial Crises 1870–2008" [2009] NBER Working Paper 15512; H Ren, "Countercyclical Financial Regulation" [2011] World Bank Policy Research Working Paper 5823.

[26]   M Brunnermeier and others, *The Fundamental Principles of Financial Regulation* (2009) Geneva Papers on the World Economy No 11; Borio and Drehmann, "Assessing the Risk of Banking Crises-Revisited" (March 2009) BIS Quarterly Review.

economic recession.[27] Conversely, the cross-sectional dimension is related to the distribution of risks across the financial system at a given point in time. This dimension addresses cross-sectional systemic risks that originate generally from the structure of the financial system and in particular, from interconnectedness and/or common exposures of financial institutions.[28]

Reflecting these dimensions, macroprudential policy frameworks are often set in terms of the following interlocking objectives as a specification of the ultimate financial stability objective:

1. Contain the build-up of systemic vulnerabilities over time by reducing procyclicality and containing unsustainable increases in credit, debt and leverage;
2. Control structural vulnerabilities within the financial system that arise through interlinkages, common exposures, and the critical role of systemically important individual intermediaries.
3. Increase the resilience of the financial system to aggregate shocks by building and releasing buffers that help to maintain the ability of the financial system to function effectively, even under adverse conditions.[29]

Macroprudential policy should extend to any products, financial intermediaries, markets, infrastructures and their practice, whether regulated or not. As such, the shadow banking sector, broadly defined by the Financial Stability Board (FSB) as "credit intermediation involving entities and activities (fully or partially) outside the regular banking system" should fall within the remit of a macroprudential mandate. As shall be seen in Chapter 4, to ensure an all-encompassing mandate, powers of macroprudential authorities should include the ability to initiate any legislative changes to the regulatory perimeter, reporting perimeter or other deficiencies in supervisory powers needed to prevent or mitigate systemic risks to financial stability.

---

[27]   BIS, "Macro-prudential Policy and Addressing Procyclicality" (2010) BIS 80th Annual Report, Ch 7, 89; Report of the Financial Stability Forum on Addressing Procyclicality in the Financial System, Basel, April 2009; Borio, Furfine and Lowe, "Procyclicality of the Financial System" (2001) (n 25).

[28]   Developed by network theories such as F Allen and A Babus, "Networks in Finance" in PR Kleindorfer, Y Wind and R Gunther (eds), *The Network Challenge: Strategy, Profit and Risk in an Interlinked World* (Wharton School Publishing, 2009), 367; P Gai, A Haldane and S Kapadia, "Complexity, Concentration and Contagion" (2011) 58(5) Journal of Monetary Economics 453.

[29]   BIS-FSB-IMF, "Elements of Effective Macroprudential Policies Lessons from International Experience" (2016) available at <https://www.imf.org/external/np/g20/pdf/2016/083116.pdf>.

       The meaning of resilience and the importance of including it in a macroprudential mandate are discussed in Chapter 2.

4. THE RATIONALE FOR MACROPRUDENTIAL POLICY: THE NEGATIVE EXTERNALITIES VIEW AND ITS SHORTCOMINGS

While earlier scholarly and policy papers focused on the macroprudential perspective and the multifaceted nature of systemic risks, more recent papers focus on externalities as a key motivation to macroprudential policy.[30] A macroprudential perspective emphasises that actions that may seem reasonable or even desirable from the perspective of individual financial institutions can weaken system-wide stability and be unwelcome from a macroprudential perspective.[31] This tension can be attributed to the fact that risks that are taken by individual financial institutions may be ultimately borne by the system as a whole, i.e. they can create negative externalities.[32] A macroprudential regulatory and supervisory intervention is therefore needed to correct and ensure the internalisation of negative externalities that can lead to systemic risks.[33]

A classic example of negative externalities is of a factory that emits pollution. In its business decisions and pricing, the factory will only take into account its private production costs. It will, however, ignore the costs associated with health effects of the pollution on any citizens that live in proximity to the factory and costs associated with broader environmental implications. This negative externality will lead to a "market failure" as the factory is producing more pollution than is socially optimal. Regulatory intervention of mandating lower pollution levels or imposing tax will correct this market failure by ensuring that the factory internalises the social costs of its pollution.

Moreover, a clean environment and similarly, financial stability differ from conventional commodities in that they are both considered a public good. The two essential features of a public good are non-rivalrous consumption and non-excludability. The former means that the consumption by one consumer does not affect the potential benefits for other consumers; the latter means

---

[30] Brunnermeier and others (2009) (n 26); G De Nicolò, G Favara and L Ratnovski, "Externalities and Macroprudential Policy" (2012) IMF Staff Discussion Notes No 5; Bank of England, "Instruments of Macroprudential Policy" (December 2011) Discussion Paper; D Schoenmaker and PJ Wierts, "Macroprudential Policy: The Need for a Coherent Policy Framework" (2011) DSF Policy Paper 13 (Amsterdam, the Netherlands: Duisenberg School of Finance).
See also S Claessens, "An Overview of Macroprudential Policy Tools" (2014) IMF Working Paper 214.

[31] Brunnermeier and others (2009) (n 26), 6 known as the "fallacy of composition".

[32] Ibid, 20.

[33] C Goodhart and others, *Financial Regulation: Why How and Where Now?* (Oxford, Routledge, 1998); Brunnermeier and others (2009) (n 26), 28; S Hanson, A Kashyap and J Stein, "A Macroprudential Approach to Financial Regulation" (2011) 25 Journal of Economic Perspectives 3.

that the producer of the good does not have control over who benefits from its consumption and that it will be impossible, or at least very costly, to exclude anyone from using it.[34] Often externalities are associated with the acquisition of a public good. As such, the willingness of individual financial institutions (or more generally, investors) to pay for financial stability is less than its social value. Each financial institution or investor will want to free-ride on the willingness of others (the public at large) to pay for financial stability.[35]

The economics literature outlines several categories of externalities that can lead, at times simultaneously, to systemic risks.[36] These externalities assist in identifying market failures and guide macroprudential authorities in the activation of appropriate macroprudential tools to address these failures.

First is the externality related to the interconnectedness across financial markets and amongst financial intermediaries. Intermediaries in the financial system (banks, non-banks and institutions that support market infrastructure) are interconnected, for instance, through direct exposures and movement in asset prices.[37] Interconnectedness can amplify the propagation of shocks

---

[34]　P Samuelson, "The Pure Theory of Public Expenditure" (1954) 36 Review of Economics and Statistics 387; A Sandmo, "The Welfare Economics of Global Public Good" in *Providing Global Public Goods: Making Globalization Work for All* (Oxford University Press, 2002).
　　Though banking itself may not fit the definition of a pure public good particularly because of the non-rivalry requirement. C Lidgren and others, *Bank Soundness and Macroeconomic Policy* (Washington DC, IMF, 1996).
　　See also A Crockett, "Why Is Financial Stability a Goal of Public Policy?" ("Maintaining Financial Stability in a Global Economy", FRBKC, Wyoming, 1997), 7–36.

[35]　J Rochet, *Why Are There So Many Banking Crises? The Politics and Policy of Bank Regulation* (Princeton University Press, 2008), 4; P Fontaine, "Free Riding" (2014) 36(4) Journal of History of Economic Thought 359.

[36]　Brunnermeier and others (2009) (n 26); De Nicolò, Favara and Ratnovski (2012) (n 30); O De Bandt and P Hartmann, "Systemic Risk: A Survey" (2000) ECB Working Paper 35; E Nier, "Macroprudential Policy-Taxonomy and Challenges" (2011) 216(1) National Institute Economic Review 1; O De Bandt and others, "Systemic Risk in Banking: An Update" (2012) Oxford Handbook of Banking; F Allen and E Carletti, "What is Systemic Risk?" (2013) 45 Journal of Money, Credit and Banking 121.
　　The list of negative externalities is, of course, non-exhaustive. As empirical research advances, the list may be extended to include other forms.

[37]　For earlier papers, see F Allen and D Gale, "Financial Contagion" (2000) 108 Journal of Political Economy 1; P Gai and S Kapadia, "Contagion in Financial Networks" (2010) Bank of England Working Paper No 383. Available at SSRN: <https://ssrn.com/abstract=1577043>. More recently see, for instance, R Portes, "Interconnectedness: Mapping the Shadow Banking Sector" (April 2018) Banque de France European Stability Review.
　　A Kashyap and B King, "Why Better Measurement is Needed to Deliver Financial Stability" (28 October 2019) available at <https://voxeu.org/article/why-better-measurement-needed-deliver-financial-stability> argue that "We shouldn't assume interconnectedness will sit neatly within sectors" and accordingly, suggest that "there is a strong case for policymakers to think about the system as an interconnected whole, rather than as a set of distinct sectors to be regulated in isolation."
　　On the interconnectedness of the global financial system and its susceptibility to shocks see, for instance, Y Korniyneko and others, "Evolution of the Global Financial Network and Contagion: A New Approach" (2018) IMF Working Paper No 13.

through the system (contagion) and thus can threaten financial stability and heighten systemic risk.[38]

Second, correlations or common exposures of banks and other financial institutions to the same source of risk (indirect interconnectedness) amplify the credit and liquidity cycles and contribute to asset price volatility.[39] Liberalisation and internationalisation of financial markets have often made it possible for cross-market and cross-border correlations to arise.[40] Moreover, an increase in common exposures within financial systems can be attributed to the phenomenon of strategic behaviour of market participants.[41] "Strategic complementarities" behaviour means that where the benefit from a certain strategy increases with the number of other participants undertaking the same strategy all participants will choose to follow it (or more accurately, forced to follow it).[42] As such, investing ex-ante in correlated assets in financial markets maximises the probability that any failure will be a joint failure and hence will necessitate a government bailout. For instance, the penalty for poor credit standards is less noticeable when it is a widespread practise and bailout is perceived to be more likely when the failure is a joint one.

Third, the self-amplifying dynamic of fire sales can create externalities since individual financial institutions try to salvage their own balance sheet ignoring the potential system-wide impact.

Fire sales occur when a financial institution suffers large losses and is forced to sell assets at a distressed price under their fundamental value.[43] This brings

---

[38] Portes (2018) (n 37) refers to the other externalities listed below as indirect interconnectedness.

[39] H Scott, "Interconnectedness and Contagion" (2012) American Enterprise Institute Committee on Capital Market Regulation 17; W Wagner, "Diversification at Financial Institutions and Systemic Crises" (2010) 19(3) Journal of Financial Intermediation 373; V Acharya, "A Theory of Systemic Risk and Design of Prudential Bank Regulation" (2009) 5 Journal of Financial Stability 224; V Acharya and T Yorulmazer, "Information Contagion and Inter-Bank Correlation in a Theory of Systemic Risk" (2003) CEPR Discussion Paper 3473. More recently see, J Cai and others, "Syndication, Interconnectedness, and Systemic risk" (2018) 34 Journal of Financial Stability 105.
Correlations refer not only to risk exposure but also to similar business models and risk management procedures. A Persaud, "Sending the Herd off the Cliff Edge: The Disturbing Interaction between Herding and Market-Sensitive Risk Management Practices" (2000) BIS Papers 2, 233.

[40] K Alexander and others, "Financial Supervision and Crisis Management in the EU" (Study requested by the ECON, December 2007), Econ/ST/2007-26.

[41] Ibid, 7.

[42] V Acharya and T Yorulmazer, "Information Contagion and Bank Herding" (2008) 40(1) Journal of Money, Credit and Banking 215.

[43] A Shleifer and R Vishny, "Fire Sales in Finance and Macroeconomics" (1992) NBER Working Paper 16642; R Cifuentes, G Ferrucci and HS Shin, "Liquidity Risk and Contagion" (2005) 3(2–2) Journal of the European Economic Association and following the financial crisis; A Shleifer and R Vishny, "Fire sales in Finance and Macroeconomics" (2011) 25(1) Journal of Economic Perspectives 29; R Greenwood, A Landier and D Thesmar, "Vulnerable Banks"

loss to the financial institution but may also cause a decline in the value of similar assets held by other financial institutions. Those institutions may be forced to liquidate undervalued assets and trigger selling spirals. The first sale thus can set off a cascade of fire sales resulting in losses on many institutions and can eventually have a devastating impact on the real economy.[44]

The fourth externality and one that is intrinsically related to the preceding externalities is informational contagion.[45] Financial intermediaries with maturity mismatch between assets and liabilities are particularly exposed to this externality. It is commonly agreed that market participants are subject to asymmetric and incomplete information about their environment.[46] Therefore, a failure of one financial institution or the release of "bad news" about it may be read as a signal predicting weakness in other institutions. Those institutions may be perceived as being of the same type as the failed institution and accordingly, ones that the cause of failure applies to them as well.[47] This perception, wrongly formed at times, could trigger a chain reaction of loss of confidence and sudden withdrawal of funds in other institutions. In a self-fulfilling prophecy, those institutions may fail even though their fundamentals were actually strong.

It is suggested here, however, that viewing macroprudential policy only through the prism of externalities and the need to correct market failures is rather limiting.

First, the externalities view provides only a partial rationale to macroprudential policy intervention. The above-listed externalities relate to the structural dimension of systemic risk. But what about the cyclical dimension of systemic risk? As already explained, actors in the financial system are subject to

---

(2015) Journal of Financial Economics 115, 471 and more recently see M Brunnermeier and P Chridito, "Measuring and Allocating Systemic Risk" (2019) 7(2) Risks 46.

[44] Those spirals may lead banks to restrict their credit extension and in turn, weaken the economy resulting in more defaults and credit restrictions and so forth.
Shleifer and Vishny (2011) (n 43).

[45] Ibid; Y Chen, "Banking Panics: The Role of the First-come, First-served Rule and Information Externalities" (1999) 107(5) Journal of Political Economy 946.

[46] F Mishkin, "Anatomy of Financial Crises" (1992) 2 Journal of Evolutionary Economics 115; A Devenow and I Welch, "Rational Herding in Financial Economics" (1996) 40 European Economic Rev 603.

[47] J Aharony and I Swary, "Contagion Effects of Bank Failures: Evidence from Capital Markets" (1983) 56 Journal of Business 305 distinguish between pure contagion (negative information about one bank adversely affects others, even those that have nothing in common with it) and noisy contagion (failure of one bank reveals bad news about other banks that have common characteristics). For the former see T Ahnert and C Bertsch, "A Wake up Call: Information Contagion and Strategic Uncertainty" (2015) Sveriges Riksbank Working Paper Series 282; For the latter see T Ahnert and P Georg, "Information Contagion and Systemic Risk" (2015) <http://ssrn.com/abstract=2625575>.
On informational cascades across countries see M Cipriani and A Guarino, "Herd Behaviour and Contagion in Financial Markets" (2008) 8(1) B.E. Journal of Theoretical Economics 1.

a pro-cyclical collective behaviour. This is the tendency of financial institutions (as well as companies and households) to underestimate risks during booms, when conditions are favourable, and overestimate them when they materialise.[48] This gap can be rectified by viewing pro-cyclicality as a negative externality in its own right since it is a behaviour that is suboptimal from a system-wide perspective.[49]

Second, negative externalities are present in other economic sectors, not just in financial markets. However, financial markets present an additional complexity of powerful feedback and amplification mechanisms, which render any negative implications of initial shocks more severe and widespread.[50] While fire sales and contagion are often included in the list of negative externalities in the literature on macroprudential policy, the added self-amplifying feature is not inherent to the term "externalities". Accordingly, referring to externalities as a sole basis for macroprudential policymaking can be misleading when not accompanied by specific examples to signify the endogenous self-amplifying nature of financial markets.

Third, as shall be seen throughout the book, macroprudential policymaking should be adaptable, learn through experience and operate through a dynamic and transparent deliberative process. Macroprudential policymaking should also be legitimised via inclusiveness of the public and to some extent, partnership with the private sector. These contentions are largely aligned with a broader movement in economics discipline that suggests departing from the role of the state in the economy as a "fixer" of market failures and become more active and courageous. This relatively new strand of literature contends that in order to promote innovation, growth and development the state must go beyond weighing and balancing social and private returns. This can be achieved, inter alia, through collaboration between the "private" and the "public" sectors.[51]

---

[48]   Crockett (2000) (n 16); P Smaga, "The Concept of Systemic Risk" (August 2014) Systemic Risk Centre Special Paper 5, 7.
For an historical overview of this phenomenon, see CP Kindleberger and R Aliber, *Manias, Panics and Crises: A History of Financial Crises* (Palgrave Macmillan, New York, 2011), in particular on p 13.

[49]   Crockett (2000) (n 16), 3; BIS, "Macroprudential Policy and Addressing Procyclicality" (2010) *BIS 80th Annual Report.*
See also Borio, Furfine and Lowe (2001) (n 25). Systemic risks can generally be defined as potential for financial externalities while these externalities may have cyclical causes: T Adrian, D Covitz and N Liang, "Financial Stability Monitoring" (2014) Federal Reserve Bank of New York Staff Reports 601.

[50]   J Trichet, "Systemic Risk" (Clare Distinguished Lecture in Economics and Public Policy, Cambridge University, December 2009). These effects can be further amplified due to asymmetric information in financial markets.

[51]   M Mazzucato, *The Entrepreneurial State: Debunking Public v Sector* (Anthem Press, 2013), 3–4, 21–23.

Framing macroprudential policymaking in positive rather than negative; contesting the view that it is there just to fix failures in financial markets and force them to internalise negative externalities will result in a much broader framework than the one suggested by the externalities view. Opening up to external counter views (expert and non-expert) and to different perspectives of "financial stability" is perhaps the only way macroprudential authorities stand a chance to identify the next financial crisis and have the tools to take action.

CHAPTER 2

A MACROPRUDENTIAL MANDATE

How to Operationalise it

A clear and well-defined mandate is a *sine qua non* for good governance and a cornerstone of any public policy framework. It forms the basis for the delegation of macroprudential powers, secures the independence of the macroprudential authority and provides a benchmark for holding it accountable (Chapter 7).[1] However, the difficulty of encapsulating financial stability in a simple metric and the lack of an overall analytical framework to guide policy decisions mean that while the articulation of the macroprudential mandate is important it is also extremely challenging.

The aim of this chapter is to explore how to turn the amorphic concept of financial stability into a concrete, practical and achievable macroprudential mandate that can be used as a benchmark to assess the performance of macroprudential authorities and holding them, where necessary, accountable. The chapter thus analyses how the macroprudential mandates of the FPC, the FSOC, the ESRB and the national macroprudential authorities in the EU are articulated and whether there are any common essential ingredients that can be identified. It suggests that in order to operationalise a macroprudential mandate, legislators and macroprudential authorities often concretise the term financial stability through using the terms "systemic risks" and "resilience". These terms bring focus and clarity to the macroprudential mandate and assist in making it more achievable and measurable compared to the overarching notion of

---

[1]   A Alesina and G Tabellini, "Bureaucrats or Politicians? Part I: A Single Policy Task" (2007) 97(1) American Economic Review 169; A Alesina and G Tabellini, "Bureaucrats or Politicians? Part II: Multiple Policy Tasks" (2008) 92 Journal of Public Economics 426 outline the principles of delegation to a technocratic agency including that the policy goal and thus the performance criteria are well-defined and can be specified ex-ante.

It can be argued, however, that financial stability may fail this principle given that it is vague and non-observable and accordingly, is not possible to define ex-ante criteria of success. DG Demekas, "Building an Effective Financial Stability Policy Framework: Lessons from the Post-crisis Decade" (2019) The London School of Economics and Political Science available at <http://eprints.lse.ac.uk/100483/>.

financial stability. Identifying the nature of these terms and their key features will hopefully allow for the refinement of macroprudential policy frameworks and analytical tools. Another useful way to operationalise the macroprudential mandate is through the design and deployment of intermediate objectives that can be linked to specific indicators and tools and be periodically reviewed and adapted to reflect new risks to financial stability.

Following this introduction, the chapter proceeds as follows. Section 1 begins with outlining the mandates of the FPC, FSOC and the ESRB, laying the grounds for their normative assessment in the following sections. Section 2 explores the interpretation and articulation of financial stability as the ultimate objective of macroprudential policy and its comprising elements of strengthening the resilience of the financial system and decreasing the build-up of systemic risks. Section 3 then borrows from insights developed in economics discipline to interpret the meaning of resilience in the context of macroprudential policymaking. Section 4 analyses the prevalent definitions of systemic risk and identifies its core elements that should form part of a macroprudential mandate. Section 5 explores the design and deployment of intermediate objectives in macroprudential policymaking and analyses their added value in operationalising macroprudential policy as well as its potential drawbacks. Section 6 considers the inclusion of a secondary objective to financial stability in the macroprudential mandate in the form of "sustaining economic growth" and the emerging preference to put the potential trade-off between financial stability and economic growth "out in the open". Section 7 concludes.

1. THE ULTIMATE OBJECTIVE OF MACROPRUDENTIAL POLICY

Macroprudential policy aims at safeguarding the stability of the financial system as a whole as opposed to its individual components.[2] The ultimate

---

[2]   MD Knight, "Marrying the Micro- and Macroprudential Dimensions of Financial Stability: Six Years On" BIS, (The 14th International Conference of Banking Supervisors, Mérida, 4–5 October 2006); IMF-FSB-BIS, "Macroprudential Tools and Frameworks Progress Report to the G20" (2011) available at <https://www.imf.org/external/np/g20/pdf/102711.pdf and IMF-FSB-BIS>; "Elements of Effective Macroprudential Policies Lessons from International Experience" (2016) available at <https://www.imf.org/external/np/g20/pdf/2016/083116. pdf>; Report of the ESRB Advisory Scientific Committee, "Allocating Macro-prudential Powers" (November 2014); But see D Schoenmaker, "The ECB, Financial Supervision, and Financial Stability Management" in J de Haan and H Berger (eds), *The European Central Bank at Ten* (Heidelberg, Springer, 2010) who puts forward "stable economic growth" as the ultimate objective of both macroprudential policy and monetary policy.
        Clearly, a macroprudential mandate should cover the non-banking sectors of the financial system. This is indeed the case in all EU Member States. See, ESEB, "Review of Macroprudential Policy in 2017" (April 2018), 7.

macroprudential objective is, accordingly, financial stability.[3] Still, even a cursory view of mandates of various macroprudential authorities reveals substantive differences in the articulation of their mandate. For instance, the mandate of the FSOC has multiple primary objectives and does not refer to the terms, "resilience" or "systemic risks", which are often used interchangeably with financial stability. The FSOC is charged with the following purposes: (A) to identify risks to the financial stability of the US that could arise from the material financial distress or failure, or ongoing activities, of large, interconnected bank holding companies or non-bank financial companies, or that could arise outside the financial services marketplace; (B) to promote market discipline, by eliminating expectations on the part of shareholders, creditors, and counterparties of such companies that the Government will shield them from losses in the event of failure; and (C) to respond to emerging threats to the stability of the US financial system.[4]

In contrast, the mission of the ESRB refers to the term "systemic risks" and incorporates a secondary objective to the ultimate financial stability objective in the form of "ensuring a sustainable contribution of the financial sector to economic growth", as follows:

> The ESRB shall be responsible for the macro-prudential oversight of the financial system within the Union in order to contribute to the prevention or mitigation of systemic risks to financial stability in the Union that arise from developments within the financial system and taking into account macroeconomic developments, so as to avoid periods of widespread financial distress. It shall contribute to the smooth functioning of the internal market and thereby ensure a sustainable contribution of the financial sector to economic growth.[5]

Lastly, the mandate of the FPC combines all these ingredients. It refers to "systemic risks" as well as "resilience" and is lexicographic with "supporting economic growth objective" secondary to the primary financial stability objective.

The objectives of the FPC are as follows:

1. The Financial Policy Committee is to exercise its functions with a view to—
    a. contributing to the achievement by the Bank of the Financial Stability Objective, and
    b. subject to that, supporting the economic policy of Her Majesty's Government, including its objectives for growth and employment.

---

[3]   CGFS, "Objective Setting and Communication of Macroprudential Policies" (2016) CGFS Papers No 57 observe that all jurisdictions list financial stability as the key objective of macroprudential policy.
[4]   Section 112(a)(1) Dodd-Frank Act.
[5]   Article 3(1) ESRB Regulation.

2. The responsibility of the Committee in relation to the achievement by
    the Bank of the Financial Stability Objective relates primarily to the
    identification of, monitoring of, and taking of action to remove or reduce,
    systemic risks with a view to protecting and enhancing the resilience of the
    UK financial system ...[6]

2. WHAT IS FINANCIAL STABILITY?

2.1. FINANCIAL STABILITY IS HARD TO DEFINE

While financial stability is predominantly the ultimate macroprudential
objective,[7] its definitions are as varied as the sources of risks that could
materialise and lead to instability. Several definitions focus on the orderly
performance of functionalities of the financial system in the face of shocks or its
resilience to shocks.[8] Schinasi, for instance, suggests that "a financial system is in
a range of stability when it is able to facilitate (rather than impeding) economic
performance and to remove any financial imbalances that arise from within or
as a result of adverse and unanticipated events".[9] Other scholars define financial
instability and emphasise the impact on the real economy.[10]

---

[6]   Section 9C(1) and (2) BEA 1998.

[7]   Though within the FSOC's mandate there is also the requirement to promote market
discipline as well (section 112(a)(1)(B) Dodd-Frank Act).

[8]   L Svensson, "The Relation between Monetary Policy and Financial Policy" (2012) 8
International Journal of Central Banking 294 defines financial stability as "a situation where
the financial system can fulfil its main functions (of sub-mitting payments, transforming
saving into financing, and providing risk management) with sufficient resilience to
disruptions that threaten these functions".

[9]   GJ Schinasi, "Defining Financial Stability" (2004) IMF Working Paper 187.
See also T Padoa-Schioppa, "Central Banks and Financial Stability: Exploring a Land in
Between" in V Gaspar, P Hartmann and O Sleijpen, *The Transformation of European Financial
System*, Second ECB Central Banking Conference, May 2003, 287 defines financial stability as
"a condition of the financial system, when it is able to withstand shocks without giving rise to
cumulative dynamics impairing its proper role in the allocation of resources in the economy".

[10]   For instance, IMF, "Financial Asset Price Volatility: A Source of Instability?", Chapter 3 of the
IMF Global Financial Stability Report (September 2003), 62, 63 defines financial instability
(rather than stability) as "Periods of financial system instability entail severe market disruptions
that – by impairing the system's ability to provide payment services, to price and transfer risks,
and/or to allocate credit and liquidity – have the potential to cause a reduction in real activity."
See also C Borio and M Drehmann, "Towards an Operational Framework for Financial
Stability: 'Fuzzy' Measurements and its Consequences" (2009) BIS Working Papers No 284
who define "financial instability" as "a set of conditions that is sufficient to result in the
emergence of financial distress/crises in response to normal-sized shocks. These shocks
could originate either in the real economy or the financial system itself." Financial distress
is defined as "an event in which substantial losses at financial institutions and/or the failure
of these institutions cause, or threaten to cause, serious dislocations to the real economy,
measured in terms of output foregone".

An overview of financial stability definitions in the founding legislation of macroprudential authorities also fails to reveal a clearer common picture. The Dodd-Frank Act, as well as the FSOC Final Rule and Interpretive Guidance for its authority to designating non-bank financial companies as systemically important,[11] do not define financial stability or risk to financial stability and the FSOC 2011 annual report vaguely suggests that "A stable financial system can continue to provide financial services while absorbing a range of shocks. A stable financial system should not be the source of, nor amplify the impact of, shocks."[12] More recently, the FSOC put forward a new Guidance to its designation authority (discussed in length in Chapter 5) that defines risk to financial stability as "a risk of an event or development that could impair financial intermediation or financial market functioning to a degree that would be sufficient to inflict *significant damage* on the broader economy."[13] Further down the FSOC's Guidance, however, the FSOC clarifies that "threat to the financial stability of the United States" will be defined by reference to the potential for a "*severe* damage on the broader economy" [author's emphasis],[14] a higher threshold to financial instability or threat to stability. Interestingly, while the connection between financial stability and the state of the underlying economy forms part of the definition in the FSOC's Guidance, it is absent from the Dodd-Frank Act itself.

The FPC views financial stability as "the consistent supply of the vital services that the real economy demands from the financial system".[15] While the European Central Bank emphasises resistance to shocks and defines financial stability as

> … a condition in which the financial system – comprising of financial intermediaries, markets and market infrastructures – is capable of withstanding shocks and the

---

[11] FSOC, "Authority to Require Supervision and Regulation of Certain Nonbank Financial Companies" 77 Fed Reg 21, 637 (11 April 2012). On the designation authority under section 113 of the Dodd-Frank Act see Chapter 4. This is not to be confused with section 121 Dodd-Frank Act that authorises the Federal Reserve Board, and a two-thirds majority of the voting members of the FSOC to take various actions with respect to a bank holding company with assets of $250 billion or more or a non-bank financial company supervised by the Federal Reserve Board. This will apply if it is determined that the company poses a grave threat to the financial stability of the US. Note that effective from 24 November 2019, pursuant to section 401(c)(1)(C) and (d)(1) of Public Law 115–174, section 121(a) has been amended by striking $50 billion and inserting $250 billion.

[12] FSOC Annual Report 2011, available at <https://www.treasury.gov/initiatives/fsoc/studies-reports/Pages/2011-Annual-Report.aspx>, 3.

[13] FSOC, Authority to Require Supervision and Regulation of Certain Nonbank Financial Companies, Guidance, 84 Fed. No 249 Reg. 71740 (30 December 2019), available at <https://www.govinfo.gov/content/pkg/FR-2019-12-30/pdf/2019-27108.pdf> (hereinafter: "the FSOC's Guidance"), 71745.

[14] The FSOC's Guidance (n 13), 71751.

[15] FPC Financial Stability Report, June 2018, 40.

unravelling of financial imbalances, thereby mitigating the likelihood of disruptions in the financial intermediation process which are severe enough to significantly impair the allocation of savings to profitable investment opportunities.[16]

Whichever definition is followed, it is clear that financial stability is a vague goal that is hard to define[17] and achieve.[18] To operationalise the macroprudential mandate, financial stability has to be interpreted and broken down into more specific and achievable objective(s). Thus, often safeguarding the stability of the financial system as a whole is articulated in terms of strengthening the resilience of the financial system and decreasing the build-up of systemic risks.[19] In addition, a key foundation for understanding financial stability is that it is not a single and sustainable position. Rather, it lies on a continuum frame within a set of tolerable boundaries.[20] The role of the macroprudential authority (and depending on the institutional setting, other authorities or policymakers involved) is to ensure that the financial system stays within these accepted stable boundaries.

2.2. RESILIENCE AND DECREASING THE BUILD-UP OF SYSTEMIC RISKS

Strengthening resilience and decreasing the build-up of systemic risks are elemental in operationalising a macroprudential mandate. But what do they mean in practical terms?

---

[16] For instance, ECB Financial Stability Review, December 2008, 9, available at <https://www.ecb.europa.eu/pub/fsr/html/index.en.html>.

[17] BIS, "Moving Forward with Macroprudential Frameworks", Chapter 4 in Annual Economic Report, 17 June 2018, available at <https://www.bis.org/publ/arpdf/ar2018e4.htm>.

[18] ES Rosengren, "Defining Financial Stability and Some Policy Implications of Applying the Definition" (The Stanford Finance Forum Graduate School of Business, 3 June 2011); WA Allen and G Wood, "Defining and Achieving Financial Stability" (2005) LSE Financial Markets Group Special Paper Series No 160; GJ Schinasi, "Understanding Financial Stability: Towards a Practical Framework" ("Law And Financial Stability" IMF Seminar, Washington DC, 23–26 October 2006); B Gadanecz and K Jayaram, "Measures of Financial Stability– A Review" (2009) IFC Bulletins Volume 31 in BIS (ed.), Proceedings of the IFC Conference on "Measuring Financial Innovation and its Impact", Basel, 26–27 August 2008), 365–380.

[19] BIS (June 2018) (n 17); CGFS, "Objective Setting and Communication of Macroprudential Policies" (November 2016) CGFS Papers No 57 Table 1 on p 43; CGFS, "Macroprudential Instruments and Frameworks: A Stocktaking of Issues and Experiences" (May 2010) CGFS Papers No 38, 2; The ESRB Handbook on Operationalising Macroprudential Policy in the Banking Sector (2017); JL Yellen, "Monetary Policy and Financial Stability", The 2014 Michel Camdessus Central Banking Lecture, IMF, Washington, DC, 2 July 2014, available at <https://www.federalreserve.gov/newsevents/speech/yellen20140702a.htm>; JH Powell, "The Federal Reserve's Framework for Monitoring Financial Stability" at The Economic Club of New York, New York, 28 November 2018.
See also ECB, "Financial Stability Review" (June 2010), 131.

[20] Schinasi (2004) (n 9), 7.

Strengthening resilience refers to increasing the resilience of the financial system to aggregate shocks by building and releasing buffers that help maintain the ability of the financial system to function effectively even under adverse conditions. Decreasing the build-up of systemic risks refers to containing the build-up of vulnerabilities over time by reducing procyclical feedback between asset prices and credit and containing unsustainable increases in leverage debt shocks and volatile funding.[21] In addition, the macroprudential mandate should also address the cross-sectional dimension of systemic risks by controlling structural vulnerabilities within the financial system that arise through interlinkages, common exposures and the critical role of individual intermediaries in key markets that can render individual institutions "too-big-to-fail".[22]

However, in practice, these elements of financial stability may not be of equal bearing. The objective of decreasing the build-up of systemic risks is considered much more ambitious than "strengthening resilience".[23] Borio, for instance, observed that:

> In order to increase the financial system's resilience, it is sufficient to build up adequate buffers in good times for the system to withstand a bust. In effect, all macroprudential tools do precisely that – provided, of course, they are vigorously deployed. By contrast, when it comes to constraining financial booms, the build-up of the buffers should also succeed in reining in the growth of credit and asset prices as well as risk-taking.[24]

Therefore and as can be expected, countries differ in the formulation of macroprudential policy objectives with some countries focusing on limiting the build-up of systemic risks, while others emphasise adequate resilience in the financial sector.[25] Overall, however, it seems that, to date, the focus of

---

21 CGFS (2016) (n 19), Table 1 shows that macroprudential authorities typically aim for building resilience but that a substantial number of macroprudential authorities also aim to lean against the build-up of financial imbalances.

22 IMF-FSB-BIS, "Elements of Effective Macroprudential Policies Lessons from International Experience" (2016), available at <https://www.imf.org/external/np/g20/pdf/2016/083116. pdf>, 4; IMF, "Key Aspects of Macroprudential Policy" (2013), available at <https://www.imf. org/external/np/pp/eng/20s13/061013b.pdf>, 7; G Kaufman, "Too Big To Fail in Banking: What Does It Mean?" (2013) LSE Financial Markets Special Paper Series No 222 explaining that the TBTF frequently also goes by other names, including, "too big to unwind", "too big to liquidate", "too important to fail", "too complex to fail" or "too interconnected to fail".

23 C Borio, "Macroprudential Frameworks: (Too) Great Expectations?" (August 2014) 41 Central Banking Journal 79, 81.

24 Ibid.

25 ESRB, "Features of Macroprudential Stance: Initial Considerations" (April 2019), available at <https://www.esrb.europa.eu/pub/pdf/reports/esrb.report190408_features_ macroprudential_stance_initial_considerations~f9cc4c05f4.en.pdf>, 11.
Similarly, when examining the objective of the Countercyclical Buffer (CCyB) it is (1) building resilience during the upswing of the financial cycle and (2) dampening the financial cycle. In their frameworks and analyses, Member States in the EU differ on the weight they put on these two objectives. ESRB, "Review of Macroprudential Policy in the EU in 2017" (April 2018), 71.

national and international macroprudential regimes and the activated tools is on increasing the resilience of the system rather than intervening in the build-up of systemic risks during the upswing of the financial cycle.[26] The reluctance of policymakers to utilise anti-cyclical macroprudential measures, particularly in the US and the UK,[27] can be attributed to the dearth in scientific evidence on the reliability of these policy measures. It may also originate from reputational concerns immanent in the implementation of unpopular anti-cyclical measures that could ultimately endanger the legitimacy of central banks where they play a key role in the macroprudential authority.[28]

As pointed out in Section 1, the ESRB and the FSOC's mandates, to be differentiated from the FPC's mandate, do not contain the component of resilience. Recently, however, the ESRB published a report highlighting the distinction as well as the interlinks between resilience and systemic risk.[29] The report develops a conceptual framework to guide the discussion on macroprudential policies and in particular, the link between macroprudential policies and the objective of financial stability.[30] It puts forward a "risk-resilience framework" which entails

> assessing the balance between systemic risk and resilience relative to financial stability objectives given implemented macroprudential policies … If macroprudential policies permanently reduce the build-up of systemic risk, less resilience would be needed as the level of systemic risk would be contained before its potential materialisation … In turn, an increase in the resilience of the financial system also affects the response to shocks and might prevent the amplification of specific shocks, dampening thereby the amplitude of financial cycles.[31]

The ESRB risk-resilience framework, therefore, emphasises that while the concepts of resilience and build-up of systemic risks are distinct, they are inherently interlinked and should both form part of a macroprudential mandate. The ESRB further explains that "Comparing systemic risk with the level of

---

[26]   M Thiemann, "Is Resilience Enough? The Macroprudential Reform Agenda and the Lack of Smoothing of the Cycle" (2018) 97(3) Public Administration 561 <https://doi.org/10.1111/padm.12551> observed that "even the most prominent counter-cyclical measure, the counter-cyclical capital buffer, primarily seeks to increase the resilience of the financial system, although it 'may also help to lean against the build-up phase of the credit cycle in the first place'". See also Basel Committee on Banking Supervision, "Frequently Asked Questions on Basel 3 Countercyclical Buffer" (2015). According to RM Edge and N Liang, "New Financial Stability Governance Structures and Central Banks" (2017) Hutchins Center Working Paper No 32, 3 only two financial stability committees (out of 41 countries that have a financial stability committee) can directly implement countercyclical policies.

[27]   Thiemann (2018) (n 26), 568–570. To be contrasted with the ECB approach, with its Vice-President Constâncio as a strong advocate of anti-cyclical measures.

[28]   Ibid. On the institutional structure of macroprudential authorities see Chapter 3.

[29]   ESRB, "Features of Macroprudential Stance: Initial Considerations" (2019) (n 25).

[30]   Ibid.

[31]   Ibid 11.

resilience in the system could provide an overall measure of the macroprudential stance or the residual level of systemic risk. A higher level of residual systemic risk indicates that systemic risks substantially exceed the prevailing resilience."[32] Based on this stance, and its relativity to the neutral level (the level of overall risks that the policymaker has tended to accept according to his/her preferences) the macroprudential authority determines whether the currently implemented macroprudential policies need to be adjusted.[33]

Several observations with regard to the emerging concept of the macroprudential stance are warranted. First, the macroprudential stance links between macroprudential policy actions and the ultimate objective of financial stability that macroprudential authorities are set to achieve.[34] The stance is defined at the level of intermediate objectives (resilience and systemic risks) rather than the ultimate objective of financial stability. Second, the preferences and specific risk tolerance of macroprudential authorities is an integral part of the macroprudential stance. This reflects the idea that "financial stability" lies on a continuum and its boundaries are determined according to risk tolerance and are thus specificities dependent.

3. RESILIENCE: AN ADAPTIVE CONCEPTION IN THE MACROPRUDENTIAL CONTEXT

Traditionally, resilience is conceptualised through three dimensions: the first is the ability to withstand the impact of a shock or reduction of the probability of a shock ("shock absorption" aspect); the second is the reduced consequences of the shock and lastly, the ability to recover quickly from a shock (reduced time to recovery).[35] Elsewhere this author has argued that,

---

[32] Ibid 5.

[33] Ibid 6.

[34] F Mazzaferro and T Peltonen, "Macroprudential Policy Implementation in Europe" (ESRB-ECB Conference "Macroprudential Policy – Intermediate Objectives and Instruments", Session 2, 17–19 October 2018).

[35] AG Haldane, "Rethinking the Financial Network" speech at The Financial Student Association, Amsterdam, 28 April 2009. On resilience of ecological systems see CS Holling, "Resilience and Stability of Ecological Systems" (1973) 4 Annual Review of Ecology and Systematics 1; CS Holling, "Engineering Resilience Versus Ecological Resilience" in P Schulze (ed), *Engineering within Ecological Constraints* (Washington DC: National Academy, 1996); L Briguglio and others, "Economic Vulnerability and Resilience: Concepts and Measurements" (2008), United Nations University, World Institute for Development Economics Research Working Paper No 55, available at <http://www.econstor.eu/bitstream/10419/45146/1/571437761.pdf>. On the origins of the concept of "resilience" see Torrens Resilience Institute at <http://www.torrensresilience.org>. Resilience has footing in many domains such as ecology, engineering, organisational behaviour and psychology. For an overview of the meaning of resilience in other disciplines see YT Maru, "Resilient Regions: Clarity of Concepts and Challenges to Systemic Measurement" (2010) Socio-Economics and the Environment in Discussion

---

given the complex[36] and adaptive[37] nature of financial systems, macroprudential authorities should conceptualise resilience of financial markets based on an adaptive approach that regards resilience as the capacity to support a process of evolution of a system over time.[38] Borrowing from theories of resilience developed for economic regions,[39] this author has previously suggested that an adaptive approach supports the ability of the financial system to "bounce forward", i.e. adapt to shocks in a way that maintains its core functionality and performance rather than merely quickly re-bounce to its previous state.[40]

Working Paper Series, No 4 from CSIRO Sustainable Ecosystems; AZ Rose, "Economic Resilience to Disasters" (2009) Community and Regional Resilience Institute Research Report No 8, available at <https://create.usc.edu>.

See also H Thorén, "Resilience as a Unifying Concept" (2014) 28(3) International Studies in the Philosophy of Science 303. But J Joseph, "Resilience as Embedded Neoliberalism: A Governmentality Approach" (2013) 1(1) Resilience 38–52 contends that the concept of resilience does not mean very much.

[36] I.e. it is difficult or impossible to predict accurately the overall system-level behaviour even when data is available on individual components. On complexity of systems see HA Simon, *The Science of Artificial* (Cambridge: MIT Press, 1981). On the complexity of modern financial markets see NF Johnson, P Jefferies and PM Hui, *Financial Market Complexity* (Oxford University Press, 2003); MA Utset, "Complex Financial Institutions and Systemic Risk" (2011) 45 Georgia Law Review 779; JP Zigrand, "Systems and Systemic Risk in Finance and Economics" (2014) Systemic Risk Centre Special Papers No 1. On complexity at the transactions level in financial markets see SL Schwarcz, "Regulating Complexity in Financial Markets" (2009) 87(2) Washington University Law Review 211.

[37] I.e. it derives not only from economic factors but also from social ones and, therefore, is dynamic, learns from experience, adjusts and evolves its response over time. AG Haldane, "On Microscopes and Telescopes", Lorentz Centre Workshop on Socio-Economic Complexity, Leiden, 27 March 2015; Haldane, "Rethinking the Financial Network" (2009) (n 35).

See also A Lo, "The Adaptive Markets Hypothesis: Market Efficiency from an Evolutionary Perspective" (2004) 30 J of Portfolio Management 15; A Lo, "Reconciling Efficient Markets with Behavioral Finance: The Adaptive Markets Hypothesis" (2005) 7(2) Journal of Investment Consulting 21.

[38] A Keller, "The Mandate of the European Systemic Risk Board and Resilience as an Essential Component: Part 2" (2015) 32(2) JIBLR 65.

[39] For instance, J Simmie and R Martin, "The Economic Resilience of Regions: Towards an Evolutionary Approach" (2009) Cambridge Journal of Regions, Economy and Society 1–17; S Christopherson, J Michie and P Tyler, "Regional Resilience: Theoretical and Empirical Perspectives" (2010) 3(1) Cambridge Journal of Regions, Economy and Society 3.

See also T Greenham, E Cox and JR Collins, "Mapping Economic Resilience Literature Review" (2013) The New Economics Foundation at <http://www.friendsprovidentfoundation. org>; A Pike, S Dawley and J Tomaney, "Resilience, Adaptation and Adaptability" (2010) 3 Cambridge Journal of Regions, Economy and Society 59.

[40] Keller (2015) (n 38), 69. Drawing on insights from R Martin and P Sunley, "On the Notion of Regional Economic Resilience: Conceptualisation and Explanation" (2014) Journal of Economic Geography; J Simmie and R Martin, "The Economic Resilience of Regions: Towards a Revolutionary Approach" (2010) 3 Cambridge Journal of Regions, Economy and Society 27; S Davoudi and others, "Resilience: A Bridging Concept or a Dead End?" (2012) 13(2) Planning Theory and Practice 299. Any other understanding of resilience will reinforce the preservation of inefficient financial systems.

Resilience, accordingly, means that, in the face of shocks (whatever their nature and origin may be), the financial system would continue to assess, price, allocate, and manage financial risks while facilitating the performance of an economy.[41]

While the core functionality of the financial system should be maintained in the face of shocks, the structure of the financial system and its modes of operation may adapt and change over time. This process takes place primarily through innovation in the form of new financial products, new practices or new forms of intermediation.[42] It can also take place through self-corrective or market disciplining changes or alternatively, via external changes facilitated by legislators or regulators.

Recently, the Bank of England has adopted this conception of resilience of firms, financial market infrastructures and the system as a whole, explaining that "operational resilience" means:

"prevent disruption occurring to the extent practicable; adapt systems and processes to continue to provide services and functions in the event of an incident; return to normal running promptly when the disruption is over; and learn and evolve from both incidents and near misses."[43] This dynamic view of resilience is welcome. It enables the financial system to evolve over time through innovation and changes to its structure and operations, adapt rapidly to unknown[44] and unpredictable events[45] and learn from experience.

To be differentiated from the Bank of England, the ESRB follows a more traditional view of resilience being "the ability of the financial system and the economy to absorb adverse shocks, while continuing to provide products and

---

[41]   Building upon the definition of financial stability. See Schinasi (2004) (n 9), 6. The system's adaptability also enhances its ability to withstand or cope with future shocks. See Keller (2015) (n 38), 68.

[42]   W Silber, "The Process of Financial Innovation" (1983) 73(2) American Economic Review 89. On the positive and dark side of financial innovation see F Allen, "Trends in Financial Innovation and Their Welfare Impact An Overview", "Welfare Effects of Financial Innovation" in honour of N Wellink, 11 November 2011; T Geithner, "Risk Management Challenges in the U.S. Financial System", Global Association of Risk Professionals 7th Annual Risk Management Convention, NY, 28 February 2006.

[43]   Bank of England, "Building the UK Financial Sector's Operational Resilience" (July 2018) Discussion Paper 1, 39 defines operational risk as "the risk of loss from inadequate or failed processes, people or systems or from external events."

[44]   CSB Holling, "Resilience Dynamics" (Seminar at the Swedish Academy of Sciences, November 2008), available at <https://www.stockholmresilience.org/research/research-news/2019-08-23-pioneering-the-science-of-surprise-.html>, in particular minute 23 into the speech.

[45]   See, for instance, R Sharp, "Financial stability in an Unpredictable World", Nottingham Trent University, 12 October 2015, available at <https://www.bankofengland.co.uk/-/media/boe/files/speech/2015/financial-stability-in-an-unpredictable-world.pdf> who observes that "… whilst, I'm content that the FPC should take account of its indicators and its forecasts, it must always provide for resilience and capital strength that takes account of the reality of unpredictable events." On the nature of risks and the various "types" of unknowns see Chapter 9.

services to the real economy".[46] This narrow approach can have two important ramifications. The first, such interpretation of resilience focuses on the prevention of crises and essentially means that macroprudential authorities do not have a role to play once a crisis erupted in minimising the potential adverse impact. Second, the financial system is viewed as static and one that has a clear and single state of stability (or "equilibrium"). This conception does not fit well with the view of financial stability as a continuum within acceptable boundaries that vary according to national specificities. A broader interpretation of resilience, which incorporates the inherent nature of financial systems to bounce-forward and adapt, is preferable.

4. WHAT IS SYSTEMIC RISK?: DEFINITIONS AND CORE ELEMENTS

As noted above, a macroprudential mandate is often articulated in terms of systemic risks rather than the overarching notion of financial (in)stability.[47] Systemic risks offer a relatively observable feature of widespread instability that can be captured by various indicators. It allows the macroprudential authority to assess the movement along the "financial stability continuum" and ensure that the financial system stays within the accepted stable boundaries.[48] Systemic risk, therefore, brings focus, clarity and achievability to the macroprudential mandate and creates a measurable benchmark for the purposes of holding the macroprudential authority accountable.

The advantages of articulating financial instability in terms of systemic risks can only be utilised where systemic risk is appropriately defined. A definition of systemic risk that forms a comprehensive, clear and effective mandate for macroprudential authorities requires heavy lifting. Currently, there is still confusion about what types of risks are truly systemic and there is no commonly agreed definition of systemic risks.[49] Indeed, the ESRB Vice-Chair correctly

---

[46]   ESRB, "Features of Macroprudential Stance" (2019) (n 25), 5.

[47]   JL Yellen, "Pursuing Financial Stability" at the Fourteenth Annual International Banking Conference, Federal Reserve Bank of Chicago, Chicago 11 November 2011, available at   <https://www.federalreserve.gov/newsevents/speech/yellen20111111a.htm>;   CGFS, "Macroprudential Instruments and Frameworks: A Stocktaking of Issues and Experiences" (2010) CGFS Publications No 38; CGFS, "Operationalising the Selection and Application of Macroprudential Instruments" (2012) CGFS Papers No 48.

[48]   A Keller, "The ESRB Mandate and Resilience as An Essential Component: Part 1" (2016) 31(1) JIBLR 13, 19.

[49]   J Caruana, "Measuring Systemic Risk" in A Dmobert and O Lucius (eds), *Stability of the Financial System Illusion or Feasible Concept?* (Edward Elgar, 2013), 216; L Schwarcz, "Systemic Risk" (2008) Georgetown Law Journal 193; P Smaga, "The Concept of Systemic

observed that "systemic risk can mean almost anything (or nothing), depending on whom you ask".[50]

Reflecting on these difficulties, the FSOC's mandate does not refer to systemic risks and offers only a vague explanation of systemic risks in its 2011 Annual Report: "Although there is no one way to define systemic risk, all definitions attempt to capture risks to the stability of the financial system as a whole, as opposed to the risk facing individual financial institutions or market participants."[51]

While the FPC mandate is set in terms of systemic risks to financial stability, the BEA 1998 is similarly unhelpful and does not offer much in terms of concretising the term. It states that systemic risk "means a risk to the stability of the UK financial system as a whole or of a significant part of that system".[52] In addition, the BEA 1998 provides an indication for sources of systemic risks that include, in particular: (a) systemic risks attributable to structural features of financial markets, such as connections between financial institutions, (b) systemic risks attributable to the distribution of risk within the financial sector, and (c) unsustainable levels of leverage, debt or credit growth.[53]

In contrast, the ESRB Regulation sets a more detailed and concrete definition of systemic risk as "a risk of disruption in the financial system with the potential to have serious negative consequences for the real economy of the Union or one or more of it Member States and for the functioning of the internal market …".[54] This definition also resembles the definition adopted by the IMF-BIS-FSB[55] and will be used as a case study in the ensuing discussion to identify the core and necessary ingredients of a systemic risk definition in the macroprudential mandate.

It is important to note that this section does not seek to reach a universal definition of systemic risk or to provide a comprehensive overview of its modes or propagation. Rather, its modest (though important) contribution is

Risk" (2014) Systemic Risk Centre Paper No 5, available at <http://eprints.lse.ac.uk/61214/1/sp-5.pdf>.

50   S Cecchetti, "Measuring Systemic Risk" in S Gerlac, E Gnan and J Ulbrich (eds), *The ESRB at 1*, SUERF-The European Money and Finance Forum, Vienna, December 2012, 25.

51   FSOC Annual Report 2011, 132.

52   Section 9C(5) BEA 1998.

53   Section 9C(3) BEA 1998.

54   Regulation amending the ESRB Regulation replacing article 2(c).

55   IMF-BIS-FSB IMF, "Guidance to Assess the Systemic Importance of Financial Institutions, Markets and Instruments: Initial considerations" (2009) Report to the G20, 5–6 define systemic event as "the disruption to the flow of financial services that is (i) caused by an impairment of all or parts of the financial system and (ii) has the potential to have serious negative consequences for the real economy."

in identifying a "common ground" of multiple definitions that were identified in academic literature and policy documents so as to form a clear conceptual framework for defining systemic risks. The analysis is based on a myriad of definitions of systemic risk that appeared in academic and policy literature (Table 1, see below).[56] The apparent diversity of definitions reflects the complexity of financial systems, their market participants and the wide scope of the endogenous and exogenous factors that are driving it. Furthermore, the relative infrequency of crises caused by the materialisation of systemic risks makes it difficult to form and test its definition.[57]

At its core, systemic risk is no different from any other risk, be it the risk of a stigma propagated through the media or an industrial accident. It can be conceptualised in the form of three consecutive elements: a triggering event, prorogation of such an event through the financial sector and consequent significant financial disruption to the macro-economy.[58] The section, accordingly, begins with examining the nature and magnitude of the triggering event, then moves on to discuss the key propagation channels of systemic risks and finally, whether the impact on the real economy is a necessary component for defining systemic risk.

---

[56] Smaga (2014) (n 49).

[57] C Borio and M Drehmann "Towards an Operational Framework for Financial Stability: 'Fuzzy' Measurements and its Consequences" (2009) BIS Working Paper 284. However, the number of banking crises is still substantial. For instance, according to L Laeven and F Valencia, "Systemic Banking Crises Database" (2012) IMF Working Paper 163 between 1970 and 2011 there were 147 banking crises; L Laeven and F Valencia, "Systemic Banking Crises Database revisited" (2018) IMF Working Paper 206 between 1970 and 2017 there were 151 systemic banking crises around the globe. According to S Cecchetti, M Kohler and C Upper, "Financial Crises and Economic Activity" (2009) NEBR Working Paper 15379, on average, there have been between three and four systemic banking crises per year for the past quarter century.

[58] O De Bandt and P Hartmann, "Systemic Risk: A Survey" (2000) ECB Working Paper 35; J Taylor, "Defining Systemic Risk Operationally" in G Shultz, K Scott and J Taylor (eds), *Ending Government Bailouts As We Know Them* (Hoover Press, Stanford University, 2009); OECD, "Emerging Risks in the 21st Century an Agenda for Action" (2003).
The FSOC's Guidance (2019) (n 13), 71746 offers a risk-analysis process which follows these ingredients, focusing on four framing questions: "(1) Triggers of potential risks (for example, sharp reductions in the valuation of particular classes of financial assets or significant credit losses); (2) how adverse effects of the potential risk may be transmitted to financial markets or market participants …; (3) the effects the potential risk could have on the U.S. financial system (for example, the scale and magnitude of adverse effects on other companies and markets, and whether such effects could be concentrated or diffused among market participants); and (4) whether the adverse effects of the potential risk could impair the U.S. financial system in a manner that could harm the nonfinancial sector of the U.S. economy (for example, through curtailed or interrupted provision of credit to nonfinancial companies)."

4.1. TRIGGERING EVENT: FROM WITHIN OR OUTSIDE, SINGLE, LARGE, STRONG?

Similarly to other risks, the spark that ignites the fire or the triggering event/s should also be the starting point of any study of systemic risk. Surprisingly, however, the majority of the definitions in Table 1, as well as the ESRB definition of systemic risks, do not refer to a triggering event(s).[59] What is the rationale behind the exclusion of the "triggering event" elements from systemic risk definitions?

Often, it is not a single triggering event that can be identified but rather several events or imbalances that have built up slowly in the background over time.[60] The 2007–2009 global financial crisis aptly illustrated the difficulty in identifying, even with hindsight, a single triggering event.[61] In addition, definitions that do include a triggering event differ in the reference to the magnitude or other descriptive words of the event. As such, an earlier line of scholars defined systemic risk as a *big* shock that has an adverse effect on the entire banking, financial, or economic system, as opposed to just individual or a few institutions.[62] Nonetheless, experience has suggested that a triggering event does not necessarily have to be big. Where financial imbalances have been building up over time and a bubble forms, it could just be a small event that gives the little push required to tip the system over the cliff.[63] Under certain market conditions, such as when global liquidity is constrained or the risk-appetite

---

[59] According to the survey of systemic risks definitions in Smaga (2014) (n 49) only 16 out of 59 definitions refer to a sudden occurrence or disturbance or shock.

[60] Referring to the time-dimension of systemic risk that could be indicated by excessive leverage, credit expansion or an asset bubble. N Kiyotaki and J Moore, "Credit Cycles" (1997) 105(2) Journal of Political Economy 211 show that even small, temporary shocks to technology or income distribution can ignite a crisis; C Borio and P Lowe, "Assessing the Risk of Banking Crises" (2002) BIS Quarterly Review 43; C Borio and M Drehmann, "Assessing the Risk of Banking Crises – Revisited" (March 2009) BIS Quarterly Review 29; C Borio, "Macroprudential Policy and the Financial Cycle: Some Stylized Facts and Policy Suggestions", IMF Rethinking Macro Policy II Conference, First Steps and Early Lessons, 16–17 April 2013.

[61] E.g. The High-Level Group on Financial Supervision in the EU Chaired by Jacques De Larosière Report Brussels, February 2009 (De Larosière Report).

[62] These definitions commonly appeared before 2000. G Kaufman and K Scott, "What is Systemic Risk and Do Bank Regulators Retard or Contribute to it?" (2003) 7(3) Independent Review 371.
On inconsistencies between the various "systemic risk" definitions (for instance, the trigger event in one definition is an "event" and in other definitions – a "modest economic shock" or a "default by one market participant"). S Schwarcz, "Systemic Risk" (2008) 97 Georgetown Law Journal 193.

[63] Often referred to as "Minsky moment". H Minsky, *The Financial Instability Hypothesis* (1992) Jerome Levy Economics Institute Working Paper 74; G Magnus, "What this Minsky Moment Means", *FT*, 23 August 2007.

of investors is low even a small shock can have a systemic effect on financial markets.[64]

As such, the IOSCO definition of systemic risks reiterates that in securities markets systemic risk "is not limited to sudden catastrophic events" and that "it may also take the form of a more gradual erosion of market trust."[65] In the same vein, the ESRB mandate refers to risks arising from "developments" (to be differentiated from a triggering event) without hinting on their magnitude or their nature. These "developments" can encompass all kinds of "fire igniters": abrupt, slow-forming developments, single, multiple events, small or big. Nevertheless, the ESRB mandate falls short in its restrictive identification of the origin of these developments – *within the financial system*. This erroneous reference should be rectified given that systemic risks could emerge not only endogenously (from within the financial system) but also as a result of an exogenous shock/s, outside the financial system.[66]

4.2. PROPAGATION OF A SYSTEMIC EVENT

The triggering event(s) or imbalances, whatever their nature, are propagated in the financial system through transmission mechanisms. To use the fire analogy, those mechanisms would be the trees through which the initial spark spreads and gets hold of the whole forest. Several definitions in Table 1 include propagation channels, in various forms, as a component to define systemic risks.[67] Two preliminary observations should be made regarding these definitions.

First, the typical forms of propagation are (1) contagion, i.e. the failure of one financial institution can lead to failures of other financial institutions, even when the latter have not invested in the same risks and are not subject to the same original shock as the former,[68] (2) aggregate exogenous shocks that

---

See also Haldane (2009) (n 35) stating that in hindsight the triggering event to the financial crisis was modest; M Brunnermeier, "Deciphering Liquidity and Credit Crunch 2007–2008" (2009) 23(1) Journal of Economic Perspectives 77.

[64] IMF, "Detecting Systemic Risk", Chapter 3 in the Global Financial Stability Report 2009 111, 114.

[65] IOSCO, Risk Identification and Assessment Methodologies for Securities Regulators, June 2014, available at <https://www.iosco.org/library/pubdocs/pdf/IOSCOPD443.pdf>, 9.

[66] H Minsky and H Kaufman, *Stabilizing an Unstable Economy* (McGraw-Hill, 2008); "Systemic Risk Cube" in the ECB Financial Stability Review (June 2010), 139; ECB, "The Concept of Systemic Risk" Financial Stability Review (December 2009). Nonetheless, it can be argued that monitoring systemic risks originating from monetary or fiscal policies could fall within "taking into account macroeconomic developments". Ideally, the ESRB Regulation should state that the ESRB is tasked with analysing and monitoring all risks, whatever their source is, either originating from inside or outside the financial system.

[67] For instance, 24 definitions out of the 59 listed in Table 1 refer to contagion.

[68] J Trichet, "Systemic Risk" (Clare Distinguished Lecture in Economics and Public Policy, Cambridge University, December 2009); M Dijman, "A Framework for Assessing Systemic

negatively affects simultaneously a range of intermediaries and/or markets,[69] and (3) unravelling of endogenous imbalances that have built up over time.[70] These propagation channels reflect the various negative externalities already identified in Chapter 1 as a rationale for macroprudential policy. The propagation channels are not mutually exclusive and hence can materialise independently or in conjunction with other channels of risks.[71] Most of the time, they will be mutually reinforcing.[72]

A distinctive line of definitions relies on the concept of contagion to convey how systemic risk is propagated through the system though they differ in the way the contagion is manifested.[73] The contagion could be a result of the direct connections amongst institutions and markets and the transmission of shocks from one unit to the rest of the system. In the so-called domino effect, the initial failure of a financial intermediary could set a chain reaction of falling interconnected dominos. This could happen even though the subsequent failing intermediaries were not exposed to the same risks or subject to the initial triggering shock.[74] Bank runs are another example of a contagion risk, where the decision of depositors of one bank to withdraw their money results in large-scale withdrawals and liquidity shortage.[75]

The definition of systemic risk could potentially refer to the other two channels of propagation as well:[76] exogenous shocks causing simultaneous

---

Risk" (2010) World Bank Policy Research Working Paper 5282, 2 clarifies that "A distinction needs to be made between real and information contagion channels. The former refers to the knock-on effects on other parts of the financial system and the real economy through direct exposures. The latter refers to behavioral changes by economic agents in response to a specific crisis event."

[69]   Trichet (2009) (n 68), 2–3.
[70]   P Hartmann, O de Bandt and J Peydró, "Systemic Risk in Banking After the Great Financial Crisis" in A Berger, P Molyneux, and J Wilson (eds), *Oxford Handbook of Banking*, 2nd edn (Oxford University Press, 2014); ECB (2009) (n 66), 135.
[71]   ECB (2009) (n 66), 135.
[72]   J Trichet, "Intellectual Challenges to Financial Stability Analysis in the Era of Macroprudential Oversight" (February 2011) Banque de France Financial Stability Review 15 139, 141.
[73]   K Forbes, "'Big C': Identifying and Mitigating Contagion" (Jackson Hole Symposium hosted by the FRBKC, 31 August to 1 September 2012); Kaufman and Scott (2003) (n 62); P Hartmann, S Straetmans and C de Vries, "Banking System Stability: A Cross-Atlantic Perspective" in M Carey and R Stulz (eds), *The Risks of Financial Institutions* (NBER and Chicago UP, 2006). See also De Bandt and P Hartmann, "Systemic Risk: A Survey" (2000) (n 58); ECB (2009) (n 66), 135 suggest that contagion usually refers to "a supposedly idiosyncratic problem that becomes more widespread in the cross-sectional dimension, often in a sequential fashion"; ECB, "Financial Market Contagion" Financial Stability Review (December 2005), 142.
[74]   Via the informational channel. F Allen and D Gale, "Financial Contagion" (2000) 108(1) Journal of Political Economy 1; Y Chen, "Banking Panics: The Rule of First Come First Served" (1999) 107(5) Journal of Political Economy 946; V Costancio, "Contagion and the European Debt Crisis" (April 2012) Banque de France Financial Stability Review 16, 109.
[75]   C Calomiris and G Gorton, "The Origins of Banking Panics: Models, Facts, and Bank Regulation" in R Hubbard (ed), *Financial Markets and Financial Crises* (University of Chicago Press, 1991), 109.
[76]   Kaufman and Scott (2003) (n 62), 372–373.

failures or endogenous imbalances that build up over time. The former focuses on spill-overs from an initial shock to the rest of the financial system through common exposures. To be differentiated from the "domino effect" definition, there is no direct causation between the triggering event and the impact. Rather, the propagation and accordingly, the definitions rely on more indirect and weaker connections between the institutions that result in a simultaneous reaction and wider impact on the financial system and the economy at large.[77] In contrast, endogenous imbalances particularly refer to asset price bubbles or excessive credit expansion and leverage, which unravel abruptly when a breaking point is reached.[78] The unravelling can be triggered by a small event (sometimes even undetectable) that results in an adjustment of expectations and re-pricing of risks and in turn, may have simultaneous adverse effects on financial intermediaries and markets.

Furthermore, systemic risks can be propagated not only through "real" channels (i.e. domino effects through real exposures in the interbank markets and/or in payment systems) but also through the less predictable information channel (i.e. rational revisions of depositor or investor expectations, including potential losses of confidence).[79]

Overall, it is questionable whether the various channels through which systemic risk can propagate should be a component of its definition. The propagation channels differ widely and choosing to point out one channel

---

[77]   G Co-Pierre, "The Effect of the Interbank Network Structure on Contagion and Common Shocks" (2011) Deutsche Bundesbank Discussion Paper 12 suggests that common shocks pose a greater threat to financial stability than contagion in the interbank market.

[78]   HP Minsky, "The Financial Instability Hypothesis" (1992) The Levy Economics Institute Working Paper No 4; G Kaminsky and CM Reinhart, "The Twin Crises: The Causes of Banking and Balance of Payment Problems" (1999) 89(3) American Economic Review 473; C Reinhart and K Rogoff, *This Time is Different: Eight Centuries of Financial Folly* (PUP, 2011), 157.
On leverage cycles see A Fostel and J Geanakoplos, "Reviewing the Leverage Cycle" (2013) Cowles Foundation Yale University Discussion Paper No 1918.

[79]   O De Bandt and P Hartmann, "What is Systemic Risk Today?", Risk Measurement and Systemic Risk, Proceedings of the Second Joint Central Bank Research Conference, Bank of Japan, 1998, 37.
F Mishkin defines systemic risk as "The likelihood of a sudden, usually unexpected, event *that disrupts information* in financial markets, making them unable to effectively channel funds to those parties with the most productive investment opportunities"[author's emphasis]. F Mishkin, "Comment on Systemic Risk" (1995) in G Kaufman, *Research in Financial Services: Banking, Financial Markets and Systemic Risk* Vol 7 (JAI Press, 1995), 31, 32 (the definition does not appear in Table 1).
On the various forms of information channels (herd behaviour; information cascades or "sunspots") see M Dijkman, "A Framework for Assessing Systemic Risk" (2010) World Bank Policy Research Working Paper 5282.
See also Y Chen, "Banking Panics: The Rule of First Come First Served" (1999) 107(5) Journal of Political Economy 946; M McAleer and K Radalj, "Herding, Information Cascades and Volatility Spillovers in Future Markets" (2013) 2 Journal of Review on Global Economics 307.

constrains the breadth of the definition and inhibits its comprehensiveness. Only when put together may these channels reflect the full spectrum of systemic risk and its dimensions. For instance, while the first two channels refer to the cross-sectional dimension, the last one essentially forms the time-varying dimension. It may also be that, in the future as empirical research develops, new channels will be identified. In that case, inclusion of propagation channels as part of a systemic risk definition can become a "Maginot line" to inclusion of unforeseen and new propagation channels. This undesirable scenario can be prevented by omitting altogether channels of propagation from systemic risk definition, as is the case in the ESRB Regulation.

4.3. THE IMPACT OF SYSTEMIC RISK: SHOULD IT BE A NECESSARY COMPONENT OF SYSTEMIC RISK DEFINITION?

The nature of systemic risk is that it has a low probability of materialising but high impact if it does.[80] The majority of the definitions emphasise the magnitude of the impact (i.e. large social costs) as a key characteristic of systemic risk.[81] In the same vein, the ESRB Regulation emphasises this aspect twice: once within the definition of systemic risk as resulting in *"serious* negative consequences for the *real economy* of the Union or one or more of its Member States and for the functioning of the internal market" and once again within its mandate "so as to avoid periods of *widespread* financial distress".[82]

The severe costs of systemic financial crises to the real economy are indeed unquestionable. Crockett suggested that "the direct losses to shareholders, creditors, uninsured depositors, insurance funds and employees [from systemic financial crisis] would be enormous. But they would be the tip of a very large iceberg".[83] The deep recessions and slow recoveries following the financial turmoil, supported by empirical evidence of past systemic crises, are indisputable evidence of these costs.[84]

---

[80] The impact can be simultaneous or sequential. ECB (2009) (n 66).

[81] 23 out of the 59 definitions listed in Table 1 refer to the impact on real economy (particularly in more recent definitions following the financial crisis). Other impacts, such as insolvency or defaults, are also frequently found in systemic risk definitions (19 out of 59 definitions).

[82] Emphasis added. Articles 2(c) as amended by the Regulation amending the ESRB Regulation and 3(1), ESRB Regulation, respectively.

[83] A Crockett, "Dealing with Stress at Large and Complex Financial Institutions" in D Evanoff and G Kaufman (eds), *Systemic Financial Crises Resolving Large Bank Insolvencies* (World Scientific Pub Co, 2005), 17.

[84] On estimate of the costs of the 2007–2009 financial crisis on US output see, for instance, R Barnichon, C Matthes and A Ziegenbein, "The Financial Crisis at 10: Will We Ever Recover?" (August 2018) Federal Reserve Bank of San Francisco Economic, Letter available at

The materialisation of systemic risk, accordingly, needs to be distinguished from welcome developments in the financial system. The failure of a financial institution or the sudden rise in asset-price volatility could be a result of healthy and desirable competition, new information or self-correcting market mechanisms.[85] The distinguishing factor here is the devastating impact or more accurately, the potential for such an impact, on the financial system and the real economy. As such, developments will not be considered systemic risk to financial stability if they are not expected to have a negative impact on the real economy.[86]

To highlight the possible devastating impact of systemic risks beyond the financial system scholars have distinguished between a "horizontal" and a "vertical" perspective of systemic risk. In the horizontal perspective, the attention is confined to the financial system, where all its components (financial intermediaries, financial markets and market infrastructures) can be involved. In the vertical perspective, a two-way relationship between the financial system and the economy is taken into account.[87] Systemic risk can emerge from sources outside the financial system, including the real economy and systemic risk could have a grave negative on the real economy.[88] For instance, systemic risk could result in a decline in the availability of credit and ultimately, in a constrained funding of productive activity.[89] In addition, systemic risk

---

<https://www.frbsf.org/economic-research/files/el2018-19.pdf>; Reinhart and Rogoff (2011) (n 78), 224 suggest the aftermath of a banking crisis is associated with profound declines in output (more than 9 per cent on average) and unemployment.

[85] If financial markets do not react to changing conditions in the markets, misallocation of financial resources will occur. IMF, "Financial Asset Price Volatility: A Source of Instability?" in *IMF GFSR: Market Developments and Issues* (September 2003), Chapter 3, 62.

[86] Whether the requirement is "expected", "likely expected" or "highly likely expected" depends on the social choice of the place on the continuum that is considered stable. This will always depend on a case-by-case judgment and balancing between wide range of interests and policies. See Schinasi (2004) (n 9).

[87] De Bandt and Hartmann (2000) (n 58); ECB (2009) (n 66).

[88] M Bjellerup and H Shahnazarian, "The Interaction Between the Financial System and the Real Economy" (2012) Report from the Economic Affairs Department, Government of Sweden.
On the relationship between economic growth and the financial system see F Allen and H Oura, "Sustained Economic Growth and the Financial System" (2004) Institute for Monetary and Economic Studies, Bank of Japan Discussion Paper 17.
See also S Cecchetti, M Kohler and C Upper, "Financial Crises and Economic Activity" (Economic Policy Symposium, Jackson Hole FRBKC, 2009), 89; G Kenny and J Morgan, "Some Lessons from the Financial Crisis for Economic Analysis" (2011) ECB Occasional Paper Series 130, 10–11.

[89] D Jacob and V Rayner, "The Role of Credit Supply in the Australian Economy" (May 2012) Reserve Bank of Australia Research Discussion Paper No 2.

manifested through assets decline could have a significant negative effect on the consumption of households.[90] It is suggested that the vertical perspective should be a key component of a definition of systemic risk. This element requires the materialisation of risks to induce or to be likely to induce significant adverse effects on the real economy.[91]

To conclude, the definition of systemic risk should capture the breadth of the responsibilities that macroprudential authorities are expected to assume. It should cast the net wide and avoid referring to the initial triggering event and its nature or to the channels through which systemic risks can be propagated thus conforming to the findings in this section that no single event and/ or single channel can be identified to encompass all forms of systemic risks. Conversely, the definition of systemic risk should point to the possible negative impact on the real economy as a key ingredient of systemic risk. The impact element distinguishes systemic risks from other market imperfections and risks. Understanding this distinction lies at the heart of macroprudential policy. Risk and volatility are essential elements of a properly functioning financial system.[92] Their absence would entail ossified financial markets that fail to provide investment capital to the real economy.[93] Therefore, the aim of macroprudential policy is not to eliminate risk and volatility entirely but rather to prevent risk and volatility from reaching the point where they may potentially result in a costly financial crisis.[94] This balance also allows macroprudential authorities to reconcile the possible conflict between financial stability and economic growth, as discussed in Section 6 below.

---

[90] M Gertler and N Kiyotaki, "Financial Intermediation and Credit Policy in Business Cycle Analysis" in BM Friedman and M Woodford (eds), *Handbook of Monetary Economics* (Elsevier, 2010), Vol 3 Chapter 11; P Gerlach-Kristen, B O'Connell and C O'Toole, "How do Banking Crises Affect Consumption? Evidence from International Crisis Episodes" (2013) Economic and Social Research Institute Working Paper 464.
See also C Hewett, "The Role of Household Savings and Debt in a Sustainable Economy" (Multinational Knowledge Brokerage Event on Household Finance and Sustainable Economy, London, 24–25 May 2012); D Christelis, D Georgarakos and T Jappelli, "Wealth Shocks, Unemployment Shocks and Consumption in the Wake of the Great Recession" (2015) 72 Journal of Monetary Economics, available at <https://ssrn.com/abstract=2607726>.

[91] G10 Report on Consolidation in Financial Sector (2001), Chapter 3(2), 125 defines systemic risk as "the risk that an event will trigger a loss of economic value or confidence in, and attendant increases in uncertainly about, a substantial portion of the financial system that is serious enough to quite probably have significant adverse effects on the real economy". Note the strict requirement of "quite probable" in this definition.

[92] Group of Thirty, "Enhancing Financial Stability and Resilience: Macro-prudential Policy, Tools and Systems for the Future" (October 2010), available at <http://group30.org/images/uploads/publications/G30_EnhancingFinancialStabilityResilience.pdf>, 21.

[93] Ibid 23.

[94] Ibid.

Table 1. Comparison of systemic risk definitions

Author / Feature	Sudden occurence/disturbance/shock	Disturbance of financial system functions (e.g. financial intermediation)	Significant (systemic) scale	Probability (chance of) occurence	Evolving nature of the phenomenon	Contagion (chain reaction/domino effect)	Interconnectedness between financial system elements	Insolvency/defaults	Impact on the real economy	Loss of confidence
BIS (1994)			X			X		X		
Kaufmann (1995)				X		X	X			
Bartholomew and Whalen (1995)	X		X	X					X	X
Davis (1995)		X				X				
Rochet and Tirole (1996)						X	X			
G-30 (1997)	X		X						X	
De Bandt and Hartmann (1998)			X		X	X				
Lacker (1998)	X	X								
Staub (1998)	X	X		X		X	X			
G-10 (2001)	X		X	X	X				X	X
De Nicol'o and Kwast (2001)	X		X	X					X	X
Kaufman and Scott (2003)			X	X	X	X	X	X		
Cifuentes (2003)			X	X				X		
Minderhound (2003)	X	X	X							
Boss (et al., 2004)		X	X			X	X	X		
Andersen (2004)						X	X			
ECB (2004)		X				X				X
Kupiec and Nickerson (2004)	X	X	X					X		
Schinasi (2005)			X						X	X
Chan (et al., 2005)	X			X		X		X		
Bancarewicz (2005)		X		X		X	X			
EFDI (2006)			X					X		

continued

Table 1 *continued*

Author / Feature	Sudden occurence/disturbance/shock	Disturbance of financial system functions (e.g. financial intermediation)	Significant (systemic) scale	Probability (chance of) occurence	Evolving nature of the phenomenon	Contagion (chain reaction/domino effect)	Interconnectedness between financial system elements	Insolvency/defaults	Impact on the real economy	Loss of confidence
Mishkin (2007)	X	X	X						X	
Ryan (2007)					X	X	X			
Kotyński (2007)		X				X		X	X	
Jurkowska-Zeidler (2008)			X			X				
Schwarcz (2008)	X					X	X	X		
Martínez-Jaramillo (et al., 2008)		X		X						
Solarz (2008)	X		X	X						X
IMF (2009)		X	X						X	
Huang (et al., 2009)	X		X						X	
IMF/BIS/FSB (2009)		X	X		X			X	X	
Adrian and Brunnermeier (2009)		X				X			X	
Korinek (2009)		X	X							
Kayne (2009)			X		X	X	X	X	X	
Summer (2009)						X		X		
Perotti and Suarez (2009)	X					X			X	
Acharya (et al., 2010)		X	X					X	X	
IMF (2010)			X				X	X		
Billio (et al., 2011)						X	X	X		
Moussa (2011)			X	X					X	
Giesecke and Kim (2011)			X	X		X	X	X		
Hautsch (et al., 2011)		X	X				X		X	

continued

Table 1 *continued*

Author / Feature	Sudden occurence/disturbance/shock	Disturbance of financial system functions (e.g. financial intermediation)	Significant (systemic) scale	Probability (chance of) occurence	Evolving nature of the phenomenon	Contagion (chain reaction/domino effect)	Interconnectedness between financial system elements	Insolvency/defaults	Impact on the real economy	Loss of confidence
Selody (2011)		X		X	X				X	
Beau (et al., 2011)		X	X						X	
Tucker (2011)						X	X			
ESRB (2011)		X							X	
BIS (2011)		X				X	X		X	
Niedziółka (2011)							X	X		
Szpunar (2012)			X	X	X				X	
Maino (2012)			X		X					
Patro (et al., 2012)	X		X	X				X	X	
De Nicolò (et al., 2012)			X						X	
Zigrand (2014)			X	X	X		X			
Smaga (2014)	X	X	X	X		X			X	
Total	16	22	34	18	11	24	17	19	23	6

Source: Smaga (2014).

5. INTERMEDIATE MACROPRUDENTIAL OBJECTIVES

Another way to ensure the operationalisation of financial stability is via defining and pursuing intermediate objectives.[95] Intermediate objectives are essentially operational specifications of the ultimate macroprudential objective.[96] They can

---

[95] D Schoenmaker and P Wierts, "Macroprudential Policy: The Need for a Coherent Policy Framework" (2011) Duisenberg School of Finance Policy Paper, No 13; ESRB Flagship Report on Macro-prudential Policy 2014, available at <https://www.esrb.europa.eu/pub/pdf/other/140303_flagship_report.pdf>; The ESRB Handbook on Operationalising Macro-prudential Policy in the Banking Sector 2014, available at <https://www.esrb.europa.eu/pub/pdf/other/140303_esrb_handbook_mp.en.pdf>.

[96] ESRB Recommendation of 4 April 2013 on Intermediate Objectives and Instruments of Macro-prudential Policy ESRB/2013/1 OJ C 170/01 Recommendation A.

be closely linked to indicators and individual policy instruments thus making macroprudential policy more concrete and quantifiable.[97]

Intermediate objectives are particularly useful in counteracting the macroprudential authority's inherent inaction bias, incentivising the macroprudential authority to act when risks are identified or otherwise explain the rationale behind no action. By being verifiable within a reasonable time, intermediate objectives can enhance the accountability of macroprudential authorities[98] and enable closer monitoring of policy action or inaction.[99] Intermediate objectives can also facilitate smoother coordination with other policy areas overcoming the challenge of differing interpretations of financial stability.[100] These benefits, however, should be weighed against the risk of setting too narrow and partial objectives that do not necessarily achieve the ultimate financial stability objective.[101] Moreover, the weighted importance of these benefits will gradually diminish as macroprudential regimes gain track and knowledge gaps close (Chapter 9).

Macroprudential authorities already utilise intermediate objectives as a key tool to make macroprudential policy more operational, transparent, accountable and to provide an economic basis for the selection of instruments.[102] For instance, the ESRB recommends that EU Member States define and pursue five intermediate objectives based on specific market failures relevant to macroprudential policy and linking them to appropriate tools.[103] The recommended intermediate objectives include: (a) to mitigate and prevent excessive credit growth and leverage; (b) to mitigate and prevent excessive maturity mismatch and market illiquidity; (c) to limit direct and indirect exposure concentrations; (d) to limit the systemic impact of misaligned incentives with a view to reducing moral hazard; and (e) to strengthen the resilience of financial infrastructures.[104]

---

[97] Ibid, Annex para 2, Recommendation B.

[98] CGFS (2016) (n 19), 16.

[99] A Duncan and C Nolan, "Objectives and Challenges of Macroprudential Policy" (2015) Business School – Economics, University of Glasgow Working Papers, available at <https://www.gla.ac.uk/media/media_427189_en.pdf>.

[100] CGFS (2016) (n 19), 37.

[101] Ibid.

[102] ESRB Recommendation on Intermediate Objectives (2013) (n 96), para 4.

[103] ESRB Recommendation on Intermediate Objectives (2013) (n 96). In relation to linking intermediate objectives to macroprudential tools, Countercyclical buffer or caps on Loan-to-Value ratio, for instance, can be used to address excessive credit growth and leverage and liquidity surcharges and other liquidity buffers can address excessive maturity mismatch and market illiquidity.

[104] Ibid, Recommendation A. It is to be noted that a later ESRB report identifies only four intermediate objectives and omit the fifth one "because it does not fall within the scope of the macro-prudential framework for the banking sector, as provided under the CRD/CRR". ESRB, "The ESRB Handbook on Operationalising Macro-prudential Policy in the Banking Sector" (2015), available at <https://www.esrb.europa.eu/pub/pdf/other/140303_esrb_handbook_mp.en.pdf>.

Similarly, several other policy documents refer to underlying market failures or drivers of systemic risks[105] and converge on intermediate objectives that correspond to macroprudential tools, which can address these failures. These are:

1. Tools geared towards credit, leverage and asset price booms;
2. Tools that address liquidity or market risk and finally;
3. Tools which address vulnerabilities that originate in financial infrastructures or arise from market structure (i.e. interconnectedness, size, position in the market).[106]

The performance of the macroprudential authority can be assessed against these intermediate objectives and their corresponding indicators.[107] Where ex-post evaluation of policy measures reveals that specific targets were not met, it should be considered whether it was due to an intermediate policy objective that is insufficiently linked to financial stability or whether it was due to a missing conceptual link between intermediate objectives and the instruments.[108]

Intermediate objectives must be subject to review and, where appropriate, should be revised to ensure that they reflect potential new risks to financial stability.[109] Furthermore, there may be a need to add other intermediate objectives so as to reflect other underlying market failures as well as country-specific structural characteristics of the financial system and overall economic conditions.[110] An alternative approach, taken by several advanced economies such as the UK,[111] articulates intermediate objectives when specific tools are

---

[105] C Buch, E Vogel and B Weigert, "Evaluating Macroprudential Policies" (2018) ESRB Working Paper Series No 76, 4 also highlight that, in many cases, it is impossible to specify "a direct, simple, and linear relationship between intermediate objectives and financial stability".

[106] IMF, "Macroprudential Policy: An Organizing Framework. Background Paper" (2011). Category 3 corresponds with the ESRB intermediate objectives 3–5.

[107] Buch and others (2018) (n 105), 10.

[108] Buch and others (2018) (n 105), 7.

[109] Ibid. ESRB Recommendation on Intermediate Objectives (n 96), Recommendation D.

[110] Other intermediate objectives can include improving lending or risk management standards and limiting direct exposures among banks. This is the case in Austria where the macroprudential authority pursues six intermediate objectives including minimising information deficits. The Financial Markets Stability Board, The Macroprudential Policy Strategy for Austria, available at <https://fmsg.at/en/publications/strategy.html>.

[111] For instance, for Loan-to-Income (LTI) instrument (Chapter 6) the intermediate objective set is: enhance financial stability by limiting household indebtedness. The FPC's Powers over Housing Tools A policy Statement July 2015, available at <https://www.bankofengland.co.uk/-/media/boe/files/statement/2015/the-financial-policy-committees-powers-over-housing-tools>, 10.
For CCyB, the intermediate objective is to ensure the ability of banking system to withstand stress without restricting essential services, such as the supply of credit, to the real economy. FPC Policy Statement on Approach to Setting Countercyclical Capital Buffer, April 2016, 5,

implemented rather than ex-ante.[112] While this ad-hoc approach resolves the risk that the relevance of intermediate objectives may diminish over time, it suffers from reduced accountability of the macroprudential authority[113] given that it does not provide an ex-ante benchmark for assessing policy actions or inactions.

6. TRADE-OFFS WITHIN A MACROPRUDENTIAL MANDATE: FINANCIAL STABILITY V ECONOMIC GROWTH

Economic growth is the quantitative change or expansion in a country, group of countries or a region's economy and is conventionally measured as the percentage increase in gross domestic product ("GDP") or gross national product ("GNP") during one year.[114] In the long-term, financial stability is a prerequisite for sustainable economic growth.[115] In turn, subdued economic growth may amplify major risks and have negative implications for the stability of the financial sector.[116] It is, therefore, no surprise that credit-to-GDP gap is

---

available at <https://www.bankofengland.co.uk/-/media/boe/files/statement/2016/the-financial-policy-committees-approach-to-setting-the-countercyclical-capital-buffer.pdf>.

[112] CGFS (2016) (n 19), 6.

[113] P Gai, "The Design, Implementation and Governance of Macroprudential Policy" (2017) Report to the New Zealand Treasury, 27.

[114] Available at <http://ec.europa.eu/eurostat>.

[115] On the vital role that a well-functioning stable financial sector plays in supporting a nation's economic growth and development see DW Arner (ed), *Financial Stability, Economic Growth, and the Role of Law* (CUP, 2007), 35–46; HM Treasury, "A New Approach to Financial Regulation: Building a Stronger System", CM 8012 (2011), para 2.13; A Clark, "What's the FPC For?" (Speech at the Society of Business Economists Annual Conference, 24 May 2012), available at <https://www.bankofengland.co.uk/-/media/boe/files/speech/2012/what-is-the-fpc-for>; WC Dudley, "Financial Stability and Economic Growth" (Speech at the Bretton Woods Committee International Council Meeting, Washington DC, 23 September 2011), available at <https://www.newyorkfed.org/newsevents/speeches/2011/dud110923.html>.
See also S Carbó-Valverde and L Pedauga Sánchez, "Financial Stability and Economic Growth" Chapter 1 in J Radoselovics and J Monsálvez, *Crisis, Risk and Stability in Financial Markets* (London: Palgrave Macmillan, 2012), 8–23; and for empirical evidence on the negative effect of financial instability on economic growth see T Sotiropoulou, SG Giakoumatos and DP Petropoulos, "Financial Development, Financial Stability and Economic growth in European Union: A Panel Data Approach" (2019) 9(3) Advances in Management and Applied Economics 1–4.

[116] For instance, ECB Press Release 28 May 2015, "Growing Financial Risk Appetite within a Gradual Economic Recovery – Financial Stability Review", available at <https://www.ecb.europa.eu/press/pr/date/2015/html/pr150528.en.html> and, more recently, ECB Press Conference, "Challenges to Financial Stability Increase Amid Downside Risks to the Economic Outlook" 29 May 2019, available at <https://www.ecb.europa.eu/press/pr/date/2019/html/ecb.pr190529~127c30e3c4.en.html> point out that "materialisation of downside risks to economic growth could spark greater financial market volatility".

used as an indicator to gauge risks to financial stability.[117] Yet, there is an intrinsic tension and, on occasions, even trade-offs between enhancing financial stability and economic growth.[118] After all, risk-taking, to a certain level, is necessary for stimulating economic growth.[119] As such, preventing or mitigating systemic risks to financial stability may stifle economic growth by reducing the flow of credit to the economy.[120]

In order to resolve this potential tension, it may be appropriate to include within the mandate of the macroprudential authority, a secondary aim of "ensuring the financial system supports long-term economic growth" subject to ensuring the ultimate objective of financial stability.[121] The FPC mandate is an example of the internalisation of the potential trade-off between financial stability and economic growth. As mentioned in Section 1, the FPC is mandated to exercise its functions with a view to contributing to the achievement of the financial stability objective and, subject to that, supporting the Government's economic policy, including its objectives for growth and employment.[122]

---

[117]   Basel III uses the Credit-to-GDP gap (the difference between the Credit-to-GDP ratio and its long-term trend) as a guide for setting countercyclical capital buffers. M Drehmann and K Tsatsaronis, "The Credit-to-GDP Gap and Countercyclical Capital Buffers: Questions and Answers" BIS Quarterly Review (March 2014), available at <https://www.bis.org/publ/qtrpdf/r_qt1403g.htm>.
        See also N Lian and T Adrian, "How Growth-At-Risk Can Help Central Banks Gauge Risks to Financial Stability" (11 April 2019), Brookings, available at <https://www.brookings.edu/blog/up-front/2019/04/11/how-growth-at-risk-can-help-central-bankers-gauge-financial-stability-risks/>. See also Chapter 6.

[118]   FPC's Formal Response on 26 June 2013 to the Remit and Recommendations set out by HM Treasury on 30 April 2013 regarding the Responsibility of the FPC in relation to Support for the Government's Economic Policy and Matters to Which it Should have Regard in Exercising its Functions, available at <https://www.gov.uk/government/uploads/system / uploads/attachment_data/file/208945/Govs_letter_-_George_Osborne_Chancellor_-_FPC_remit.pdf>.
        See also A Popov and F Smets, "On the Tradeoff between Growth and Stability: The Role of Financial Markets" VoxEU (November 2011), available at <https://voxeu.org/article/tradeoff-between-growth-and-stability>.

[119]   OECD Report, *Bank Competition and Financial Stability* (2011), available at <http://www.oecd.org/daf/financialmarketsinsuranceandpensions/financialmarkets/48501035.pdf>.

[120]   The ESRB Handbook on Operationalising Macro-prudential Policy in the Banking Sector, A Report by the ESRB Instruments Working Group Chaired by A Houben, available at <https://www.esrb.europa.eu/pub/pdf/other/140303_esrb_handbook_mp.en.pdf>.
        On the trade-off between regulatory capital and liquidity requirements and economic growth see BCBS, "The Policy Implications of Transmission Channels between the Financial System and the Real Economy" (May 2012), available at <https://www.bis.org/publ/bcbs_wp20.htm>, 7.

[121]   IMF Staff Guidance Note on Macroprudential Policy (December 2014), available at <https://www.imf.org/external/np/pp/eng/2014/110614.pdf>, 36.

[122]   Section 9C(1) BEA 1998.
        But CGFS (2016) (n 19), 5 suggests that explicit ranking of objectives for the macroprudential authority is surprisingly considered rare perhaps leaving it more flexibility to determine the optimal balance between conflicting objectives depending on the specific circumstances at the time.

The FPC is neither required nor authorised to exercise its functions in a way that would in its opinion be likely to have a significant adverse effect on the capacity of the financial sector to contribute to the growth of the UK economy in the medium or long term.[123] For that purpose, the Bank of England Act 1998 requires that the Treasury specify what the economic policy of the Government is to be taken to be at least once in every calendar year (remit) and make recommendations to the FPC about matters that the FPC should regard as relevant to its understanding of the Bank's Financial Stability Objective; the responsibility of the FPC in relation to the achievement of that objective; the responsibility of the FPC in relation to support for the economic policy of the Government, including its objectives for growth and employment and matters to which the Committee should have regard in exercising its functions.[124] The FPC's response to the Treasury's recommendations follows a "comply or explain" mechanism, i.e. the FPC must respond to the recommendation by notifying the Treasury on its actions or intention to act or alternatively, give its reasons for not intending to act.[125] The FPC is also required to prepare an explanation on the compatibility of its recommendations and directions with both financial stability and economic growth.[126]

In practice, the prioritisation of objectives in the FPC's mandate means that when faced with an immediate or incipient threat to stability, the FPC has to find a solution that avoids damage to long-term growth.[127] This formulation places a considerably higher priority to safeguarding growth compared to the MPC formulation.[128] In the former, growth can only be considered subject to having

---

[123] Section 9C(4) BEA 1998.

[124] Section 9D and 9E(1) BEA 1998. According to section 9E(2) the FPC must make recommendations about the objective at least once a year.

[125] Section 9E(3) BEA 1998.

[126] And compatible with other general duties under section 9F of BEA 1998. Section 9S(1)(b) BEA 1998.

[127] P Tucker, "Macroprudential Policy: Building Financial Stability Institutions", Speech at the 20th Annual Hyman P Minsky Conference, New York Thursday 14 April 2011, available at <https://www.bankofengland.co.uk/-/media/boe/files/speech/2011/macroprudential-policy-building-financial-stability-institutions-speech-by-paul-tucker.pdf>.
See also A Formal Response of Mark Carney, Governor of the Bank of England at the time, dated 11 August 2015 to the Treasury Remit and Recommendations Set Out on the 8 July 2015, available at <https://www.bankofengland.co.uk/-/media/boe/files/letter/2015/governor-letter-110815>, 2 explaining that managing this trade-off will be done in three ways: (1) the FPC will take account of the costs and benefits of its actions to both its primary and secondary objectives; (2) design carefully its policies in pursuit of its primary objective in ways that as far as possible contribute to its secondary objective; and (3) assess its work programme to consider the extent to which policies in pursuit of its primary objective can also support its secondary objective directly.

[128] Joint Committee House of Lords House of Commons on the Draft Financial Services Bill Session 2010–12, report, paras 41–44.

delivered price stability while the latter means that the FPC will not be able to take decisions to promote financial stability if it believes those decisions risk medium- to long-term economic growth.[129]

Aside from being embedded in the legislative framework of the FPC, the short-term trade-offs between financial stability and the secondary objective of sustaining economic growth is openly acknowledged in the Treasury remits.[130] The 2018 remit, for instance, recommends the FPC to manage and communicate this trade-off transparently and consistently with its assessment of the costs and benefits of its actions.[131]

The ESRB's mandate also includes a secondary economic growth objective and similarly recommends Member States in the EU to include economic growth in the mandate of the national macroprudential authority.[132] With regard to the FSOC, while "consideration of economic growth" is not included in its mandate, the Dodd-Frank Act calls on the FSOC's chairperson to carry out a study, issued at least every five years, on the impact on long-term growth of potential regulatory actions that are intended to reduce systemic risk.[133] The chairperson is then required to issue a report to the Congress containing any findings and determinations made in carrying out the study.[134]

A mandate that combines financial stability and economic growth is proportionate and keeps any potential trade-offs "out in the open".[135]

---

[129]   Ibid.
[130]   For instance, HM Treasury Remit and Recommendations for the FPC, 29 October 2018, available at <https://www.bankofengland.co.uk/-/media/boe/files/letter/2018/chancellor-letter-291018-fpc>.
[131]   Ibid.
[132]   ESRB Recommendation of 22 December 2011 on the Macroprudential Mandate of National Authorities ESRB/2011/3, OJ 2012/C 41/01, Recommendation A.
[133]   Section 123(a) Dodd-Frank Act. According to this section: "Such study shall estimate the benefits and costs on the efficiency of capital markets, on the financial sector, and on national economic growth, of – (A) explicit or implicit limits on the maximum size of banks, bank holding companies, and other large financial institutions; (B) limits on the organizational complexity and diversification of large financial institutions; (C) requirements for operational separation between business units of large financial institutions in order to expedite resolution in case of failure; (D) limits on risk transfer between business units of large financial institutions; (E) requirements to carry contingent capital or similar mechanisms; (F) limits on commingling of commercial and financial activities by large financial institutions; (G) segregation requirements between traditional financial activities and trading or other high-risk operations in large financial institutions; and (H) other limitations on the activities or structure of large financial institutions that may be useful to limit systemic risk." In addition, (1) the impact on the real economy is considered in "systemic risk" definition in the FSOC proposed Guidance on its designation authority. See Section 2.1 above. (2) when using its power under section 120 of the Dodd-Frank Act the FSOC must take costs to long-term economic growth into account (section 120(b)(2)(A) Dodd-Frank Act).
[134]   Section 123(b) Dodd-Frank Act.
[135]   C Jones and B Masters, "FPC Growth Objective Supported by Sants" (*Financial Times*, 18 June 2012).

Nonetheless, legislators should be cognisant of the risks in a multi-lexicographic macroprudential mandate as it may introduce lack of clarity of the macroprudential objective and correspondingly, weaken the accountability of the macroprudential authority. Indeed, social research suggests that in a multi-task environment, the focus may shift to those tasks that are easily measurable and away from those tasks that are more difficult to measure (but are nevertheless valuable).[136] Where the priority of the objectives are not set clearly in statute, it may result in financial stability "taking the back seat" and giving way to popular economic growth considerations.[137] Taking economic growth into account within the macroprudential mandate may also subject the macroprudential authority to political pressure potentially compromising its independence and can be used as a strong and "ready to use" excuse for inaction.[138]

7.   CONCLUSION

The role of a macroprudential authority can be captured as a balancing act. A balance between the ultimate objective of financial stability and its interpretation through preventing systemic risk build-up and enhancing resilience; between the design and deployment of intermediate objectives and their corresponding indicators and instruments as well as a possible balance between financial stability and economic growth.

This chapter explored how these considerations come together in the legislative frameworks of FPC, FSOC and ESRB and assessed the challenges their implementation poses in practice. There is a risk that macroprudential authorities that are guided by a mandate which acknowledges the trade-off between stability and economic growth and requires its management will be subject to political pressure to subdue distant and unmeasurable risks of financial instability to economic growth. The challenge to overcome is a real one. The FPC, for instance, which was forced to operate within an uncertain environment pre-Brexit, faced demands to "encourage long-term investment"; "promoting a dynamic economy that encourages innovation" and ensuring competitiveness

---

[136]   B Holmstrom and P Milgrom, "Multitask Principal-Agent Analyses: Incentive Contracts, Asset Ownership, and Job Design" (1991) 7 Journal of Law, Economics and Organization 24; B Holmstrom and P Milgrom, "The Firm as an Incentive System" (1994) 84 American Economic Review 972.

[137]   Keller (2016) (n 48), 20 suggesting that economic growth will be easier to measure than financial stability.

[138]   Thus, exacerbating the inherent inaction bias of the macroprudential authority (particularly when implementing any-cyclical measures). Discussion in UK Parliament on the Draft Financial Services Bill, December 2011, Chapter 3, available at <http://www.publications.parliament.uk/pa/jt201012/jtselect/jtdraftfin/236/23606.htm>.

where "the UK remains an attractive domicile for internationally active financial institutions and that London retains its position as the leading international financial centre …".[139] As shall be seen in Chapter 7, solid transparency and accountability mechanisms can act as a counterbalance to these strong forces and prevent drifting away from the ultimate objective of financial stability.

---

[139]   HM Treasury Remit and Recommendations for the FPC, 29 October 2018 (n 130).

CHAPTER 3

INSTITUTIONAL AND PROCEDURAL DESIGN FOR MACROPRUDENTIAL REGIMES

Institutional Models and the Nature of the Decision-Making Process

As will be discussed in length in Chapter 7, macroprudential authorities may be subject to strong political pressure and demands from the financial industry and/or the public at large to tone down or even delay the implementation of macroprudential tools. The institutional structure of macroprudential authorities can significantly affect their level of resilience and ability to withstand these pressures and make unpopular policy decisions. As such, where central banks play a central role in macroprudential policymaking, their hard-won and long-standing independence can provide a solid ground to resisting these pressures and lobbying. In contrast, a dominant role of the ministry of finance in a macroprudential committee could potentially inhibit the independence of the committee and may result in a reduced willingness to take pre-emptive measures, for example, to slow expansion.[1] Furthermore, the choice of an institutional structure can exacerbate or alternatively, ameliorate biases in the macroprudential decision-making process, such as inaction bias[2] and groupthink,[3] and thus affect its quality and effectiveness. For instance,

---

[1] Though there are apparent benefits to the Treasury or Ministry of Finance's participation in macroprudential committees, as will be discussed below.

[2] For instance, ESRB, "The ESRB Handbook on Operationalising Macroprudential Policy in the Banking Sector", available at <https://www.esrb.europa.eu/pub/pdf/reports/esrb.report180115_handbook~c9160ed5b1.en.pdf>. The inherent inaction bias in macroprudential policymaking is often explained on the basis that "the costs of activating macroprudential instruments are felt in the short term and are immediately visible, while the benefits are long-term and less obvious" (p 21); "… Faced with public pressure in response to the short-term costs, a natural bias might exist against tightening macroprudential policy or in favour of premature deactivation" (p 200).

[3] See, for instance, A Keller, "Debiasing Macroprudential Policy: Part 1: An Evidence-based Approach and the Precautionary Principle" (2018) 34(1) JIBLR 5 analysing other prevalent cognitive biases in the decision-making process of macroprudential authorities, such as issue

---

as will be discussed in subsequent sections, diversity in the composition of a macroprudential committee via inclusion of external members can act as an antidote to groupthink in the macroprudential decision-making process.

The choice of a particular institutional model may foster (or alternatively, inhibit) the much-needed coordination and flow of information between macroprudential policy and other policy areas. More specifically, where the institutional setting is founded on cross-membership and representation of other policy areas, coordination will be ingrained in the macroprudential decision-making process and exploit synergies across these policies. Conversely, an institutional model that does not acknowledge these interlinks may result in a confined, insular and perhaps even entrenched decision-making process and further deepen potential trade-offs and conflicts between macroprudential policy and other policy areas. Nevertheless, the significance of institutional models and their impact on the effectiveness of macroprudential authorities in achieving their mandate present two limitations. First, and a recurrent theme in this book, the design and conduct of macroprudential policy cannot follow a one-size-fits-all approach. Governance is no exception as evident from the considerable differences in macroprudential institutional settings across countries. Therefore, a "right", "wrong" or superior structure cannot be identified[4] and will differ in accordance with local conditions and the environment within which the macroprudential authority operates in, including existing institutional arrangements.[5] Second, an institutional structure is effective in ameliorating biases and enhancing coordination of macroprudential policy with other policy areas only to the extent that is complemented by solid independence, accountability and transparency arrangements, as discussed in Chapter 7.

---

bias and the tendency of macroprudential authorities to focus, so far, in their data collection and implemented measures on the banking sector. The issue of biases will be returned to in Chapter 7.

[4] Similar to financial regulation, see E Ferran, "Institutional Design for Financial Market Supervision: The Choice for National Systems" (2014) University of Cambridge Faculty of Law Research Paper No 28, available at SSRN: <https://ssrn.com/abstract=2425177> or <http://dx.doi.org/10.2139/ssrn.2425177>.
See also A Prasad, HA Monem and PG Martinez, "Macroprudential Policy and Financial Stability in the Arab Region" (2016) IMF Working Paper 98.

[5] IMF-BIS-FSB, "Macroprudential Policy Tools and Frameworks" Progress Report to G20 (October 2011), 17; J Osinski, K Seal and L Hoogduin, "Macroprudential and Micro prudential Policies: Toward Cohabitation" (2013) IMF Discussion Note, 19.
See also E Egawa, A Otani and T Sakiyama, "What Determines Institutional Arrangements for Macroprudential Policy?" (2015) Institute for Monetary and Economic Studies Bank of Japan Discussion Paper No 3, available at <https://www.ies.boj.or.jp/research/papers/english/15-E-03.pdf>; CH Lim, R Ramchand, H Wang and X Wu, "Institutional Arrangements for Macroprudential Policy in Asia" (2013) IMF Working Paper 165, Appendix on how Asia's institutional arrangements have been partially shaped by countries' political and legal environment and historical events.

Following this introduction, the chapter proceeds as follows. Section 1 summarises the current main institutional models for macroprudential policymaking. Section 2 focuses on the rationales behind a committee structure becoming a popular institutional structure for macroprudential policymaking. Sections 3 and 4 discuss the role that the central bank and ministry of finance play in prevalent macroprudential settings and the strengths and weaknesses of these models. Section 5 critically analyses the important role that external members can play in a macroprudential authority and the manner in which they can enhance the quality of the decision-making process. Section 6 suggests that in addition to diversity in composition, the way decisions are discussed, the nature of the deliberation, the transparency of the individual opinations and the decision rule – may all have a significant effect on the quality of the macroprudential decision-making process. In light of the preceding discussion, Section 7 critically analyses the institutional structures of the FPC, FSOC and ESRB, and Section 8 concludes.

1. KEY INSTITUTIONAL MODELS FOR MACROPRUDENTIAL POLICYMAKING

An institutional model should be conducive to the achievement of the macroprudential mandate through effective identification, analysis and monitoring of systemic risk; timely and effective use of macroprudential policy tools and effective coordination with other policy areas.[6] The analysis of the strengths and weaknesses of the various institutional models should be, therefore, conducted against these elements.

In broad terms, there are four main institutional models for macroprudential authorities.[7]

---

[6]   E Nier and others, "Institutional Models for Macroprudential Policy" (2011) IMF Staff Discussion Note SDN/11/18, available at <https://www.imf.org/external/pubs/ft/sdn/2011/sdn1118.pdf>, 9; E Nier and others, "The IMF Staff Guidance Note on Macroprudential Policy" (2014), available at <https://www.imf.org/external/np/pp/eng/2014/110614.pdf>, 34–35 refer to the need to facilitate the following elements in macroprudential frameworks: "willingness to act", "ability to act" and "effective cooperation".

[7]   Adapted from IMF-FSB-BIS, "Elements of Effective Macroprudential Policies: Lessons from International Experience" (2016) Report to G20 Leaders, available at <https://www.imf.org/external/np/g20/pdf/2016/083116.pdf>.
     See also M Edge and N Liang, "New Financial Stability Governance Structures and Central Banks" (2017) Hutchins Center Working Paper 32; Nier and others (2011) (n 6), 7; S Jeanneau, "Financial Stability Objectives and Arrangements – What's New?" (2012) BIS Papers 76.
     In the EU, see Reports of the Advisory Scientific Committee, "Allocating Macro-prudential Powers", November 2014, available at <https://www.esrb.europa.eu/pub/pdf/asc/Reports_ASC_5_1411.pdf>.

The macroprudential mandate can rest with the board or governor of the central bank (either also being the micro-prudential supervisor or with a separate micro-prudential supervisor). Similarly, the mandate can rest with a policymaking committee related to the central bank that is legally part of the central bank and chaired by its governor. This committee can allow the participation of external authorities and/or external experts. Alternatively, the macroprudential mandate can be vested in an independent macroprudential policymaking committee with multiple agencies membership. This model can take the form of a formal committee created by legislation or a de facto committee. Finally, macroprudential oversight can be conducted by an informal inter-agency arrangement to facilitate coordination and information sharing amongst the various agencies responsible for financial stability.

Recent studies suggest that a macroprudential committee (sometimes also termed a financial stability committee) structure is gaining ascendency, most likely borrowing from the prevailing institutional arrangement for monetary policymaking.[8] Members of macroprudential committees[9] often include representatives from other policy areas, most frequently central banks, minister of finance, bank prudential regulators, securities regulators and deposit insurance authority.[10] Surprisingly, only in a small number of cases, financial stability committees include independent external experts.[11]

In the real world, the term "financial stability committee" is far from signifying a monolithic structure. Considerable variations exist across countries as to the

---

[8]   Edge and Liang (2017) (n 7). With 41 out of 58 countries surveyed having a formal financial stability committee. The authors also show that larger countries set up financial stability committees, while smaller countries rely on the central bank to be the single macroprudential authority.
        A more recent study, which covers 82 jurisdictions worldwide, found that "a dedicated committee is the primary entity responsible for macroprudential supervision in close to a third of the jurisdictions included in our sample", D Calvo and others, "Financial Supervisory Architecture – What has Changed After the Crisis?" (April 2018) Financial Stability Institute Insights on Policy Implementation No 8, available at <https://www.bis.org/fsi/publ/insights8. pdf>, 19.
        This is to be contrasted with an earlier study from 2011 that surveyed 50 countries and showed that "although the majority of countries have multi-agency set ups less than one third have committees that play a coordinating role among the central bank and other regulatory authorities". Nier and others, "Towards Effective Macroprudential Policy Frameworks: An Assessment of Stylized Institutional Models" (2011) IMF Working Paper 250.
[9]   These members can be with or without a voting right or act solely as observers. See Calvo and others (2018) (n 8), 19 and Table 14.
[10]   Ibid, also show that the most common size in the surveyed countries was four voting agencies (17 countries). In some cases, other representatives may also be involved in the committee, for instance, resolution agency or accounting body. This is the case in several Member States in the EU. See ESRB, "A Review of Macroprudential Policy in the EU in 2017" (April 2018), available at <https://www.esrb.europa.eu/pub/pdf/reports/esrb.report180425_review_of_ macroprudential_policy.en.pdf>, 6.
[11]   Calvo and others (2018) (n 8), 19. See also IMF-FSB-BIS (2016) (n 7).

institutional design within these general models and divergence is apparent, inter alia, in relation to its location (related to the central bank or independent), the size of the committee, its composition and the voting or non-voting rights of its members. Furthermore, in many cases, a macroprudential mandate is assigned to more than one entity (e.g. to the central bank and to an additional committee) making the discussion of the strengths and weaknesses of the institutional models even more complex.[12]

2. WHY A COMMITTEE STRUCTURE IS A POPULAR INSTITUTIONAL SETTING IN MACROPRUDENTIAL POLICYMAKING

Tracing the trends in the institutional structure of monetary policy can assist in understanding the background and rationale behind the independent policymaking committee becoming a prominent institutional model for macroprudential policymaking. While now a much-faded phenomenon, more than a decade ago, monetary policy decisions were made by a single governor.[13] Not surprisingly, the global shift that followed towards collective decision-making in monetary policy was viewed as "a quiet revolution in central banking practice".[14] Now, there seems to be a consensus amongst practitioners and scholars that collective decision-making is international best practice for monetary policy.[15]

This is hardly surprising. Group decision-making is generally thought to be superior to individual decision-making, ultimately leading to better decisions.[16] For instance, the strength of a committee in monetary policymaking was primarily attributed to the virtues of committee members having different preferences, different views on the models of the economy and forecasts and

---

[12]   IMF, "Macroprudential Policy Survey: Objectives, Design, and Country Responses" April 2018, 5, available at <https://www.imf.org/en/Publications/Policy-Papers/Issues/2018/04/30/pp043018-imf-annual-macroprudential-policy-survey>.

[13]   AS Blinder, "Ex Uno Plures: Central Banking by Committee", Chapter 2 in *The Quiet Revolution: Central Banking Goes Modern* (New Haven: Yale University Press, 2004), 34–64.

[14]   Ibid; A Blinder and J Morgan, "Are Two Heads Better than One: Monetary Policy by Committee" (2005) 37(5) Journal of Money, Credit and Banking 789.

[15]   J Vandenbussche, "Elements of Optimal Monetary Policy Committee Design" (2006) IMF Working Paper 277; Blinder (2004) (n 13).

[16]   For an experimental evidence on the superiority of group decision-making over individuals in monetary policy see AS Blinder and K Morgan, "Leadership in Groups: A Monetary Policy Experiment" (2008) International Journal of Central Banking 117; C Lombardelli, J Proudman and J Talbot, "Committees versus Individuals: An Experimental Analysis of Monetary Policy" (2015) 1(1) International Journal of Central Banking 181.
See also NRF Maier, "Assets and Liabilities in Groups Problem Solving: The Need for an Integrative Function" (1967) 74(4) Psychological Review 239.

different decision-making heroics.[17] In an uncertain environment, pooling together knowledge and factoring in all these differences are believed to lead to better decisions that are more precise than any individual's (even a highly skilled one). Group decision-making with a spectrum of opinions could also provide some insurance against the possibility of extreme preferences of an individual central banker.[18]

These arguments draw heavily upon the burgeoning scholarship on group decision-making in the organisational behaviour discipline. Empirical research in that field shows that the quality of decisions on complex and ambiguous problems can be improved through the expression of alternative views and consideration of multiple perspectives.[19] In particular, a key stream in the behavioural strategy field highlights the importance of diverse groups in reducing cognitive biases by fostering information sharing and introducing new perspectives in the decision-making process.[20]

The arguments in support of a committee structure in monetary policymaking apply equally (perhaps even more forcefully) in the macroprudential domain. Indeed, macroprudential policy decisions are taken in a complex, uncertain and evolving environment and require an even wider spectrum of knowledge and understanding than monetary policymaking. The expertise required for data analysis and selection of suitable macroprudential tools is unlikely to exist within one agency let alone an individual.[21] It "shares characteristics with analysis used for microprudential policy (to understand the risk characteristics of systemically important institutions), for monetary and fiscal policy

---

17   AS Blinder, "Making Monetary Policy by Committee" (2008) Princeton University Center for Economic Policy Studies Working Paper No 167, 15; L Hong and S Page, "Groups of Diverse Problem Solvers Can Outperform Groups of High-ability Problem Solvers" (2004) 121(46) Proceedings of the National Academy of Sciences of the US 16385.
      See also Blinder and Morgan (2005) (n 16); Vandenbussche (2006) (n 15).
18   AS Blinder, "Monetary Policy by Committee: Why and How?" (2005) Princeton University CEPS Working Paper No 118, 8.
19   LR Hoffman, E Harburg and N Maier, "Differences and Disagreement as Factors in Creative Group Problem Solving" (1962) 64 Journal of Abnormal and Social Psychology 206; HC Triandis, ER Hall and RB Ewen, "Member Homogeneity and Dyadic Creativity" (1965) 18 Human Relations 33; C Nemeth, "Differential Contributions of Majority and Minority Influence" (1986) 93 Psychological Review 23.
20   RP Larrick, "Debiasing", Chapter 16 in DJ Koehler and N Harvey (eds), Blackwell Handbook of Judgment and Decision Making (Oxford: Blackwell Publishing, 2004), 316, especially 326–327.
      See also P Meissner and W Torsten, "The Effect of Cognitive Diversity on the Illusion of Control Bias in Strategic Decisions: An Experimental Investigation" (2017) 35 European Management Journal 430.
21   CGFS, "Experiences with the Ex Ante Appraisal of Macroprudential Instruments" (2016) CGFS Papers No 56, available at <https://www.bis.org/publ/cgfs56.pdf>, 1. For instance, "ex ante appraisals of macroprudential instruments require expertise in a number of areas: how regulation impacts financial institutions, how financial markets react to structural changes, how monetary and microprudential policy may interact with macroprudential policy, how the real and financial sectors interact, etc."

(for macroeconomic dimensions, and systems analysis), and for financial policy (to understand the implications of different financial structures) ...".[22] A committee structure, thus, supports expertise and information sharing amongst the various policy areas under a single roof.[23]

Moreover, while on the face of it, macroprudential policymaking necessitates a technical ability to identify the build-up of systemic risk (i.e. read heat maps; identify asset bubbles and assess cyclicality), it is far from being just a simple implementation of indicators achieving a single numerical target; it often requires decisions that may dampen economic growth and potentially have immediate and tangible distributional effects. Therefore, as shall be seen in Chapter 7, democratic legitimacy is of critical importance for a macroprudential authority. A committee structure that involves multiple agencies is associated with stronger legitimacy compared to a single decision-maker (be it a single authority or an individual) and is thus, in that respect, a preferable institutional model.[24]

3. THE CENTRAL ROLE OF CENTRAL BANKS

Central banks are the lead authority for macroprudential policy in most jurisdictions[25] either as a single agency or chair or co-chair in a financial stability committee.[26] The IMF's 2018 Annual Macroprudential Policy Survey noted that:

> Most jurisdictions (80 out of 111) indicated that the central bank played an important role in macroprudential policy. Indeed, 39 countries (about 35 per cent of all

---

[22]   BIS, *Central Bank Governance and Financial Stability*, A Report by a BIS Study Group chaired by S Ingves, June 2011, 55.
       See also P Tucker, "The Design and Governance of Financial Stability Regimes" in *The Design and Governance of Financial Stability Regimes* (September 2016) Vol 3 Centre for International Governance Innovation Essays on International Finance, at 55.

[23]   See, for instance, M Bodenstein, L Guerrieri and J LaBriola, "Macroeconomic Policy Games" (2014) FEDS Working Paper No 87, available at SSRN <https://ssrn.com/abstract=2520201>.

[24]   Still, as will be discussed in the following section, a committee structure may introduce to the decision-making process a plethora of biases, such as groupthink, that can have a detrimental effect on the quality of its decisions and thus require tailored mechanisms to ameliorate them.

[25]   Calvo and others (2018) (n 8), 6 show that this is the case in close to 60 per cent of the surveyed jurisdictions. Edge and Lian (2017) (n 7), 16 also show that in more than half of the sample (32 countries), the central bank is the lead macroprudential authority. Interestingly, D Masciandaro and A Volpicella, "Macroprudential Governance and Central Banks: Facts and Drivers" (2016) 61 Journal of International Money and Finance 101, 114 conclude in their study of 31 advanced and emerging market economies that central banks already in charge of micro-prudential supervision and less politically independent are more likely to have extended macroprudential powers. The authors explain these results based on political economy considerations including the information advantages of a central bank as a micro-prudential supervisor.

[26]   Edge and Lian (2017) (n 7), 16 show that in more than half of the sampled jurisdictions, the central bank is the lead macroprudential authority. A central role to central banks can

countries with a macroprudential authority) reported that the central bank is the sole macroprudential authority. An additional ten countries reported that both the central bank and a committee within the central bank were being jointly responsible for macroprudential policy, while seven more (including the UK) reported that a committee within the central bank was the sole authority.[27]

Moreover, evidence suggests that macroprudential responsibilities are more likely to be given to the central bank when it is also the micro-prudential supervisor for banking.[28] A similar picture is found in the EU, where in most of the Member States, the macroprudential authority "is either the central bank or an interinstitutional cooperation structure, with a leading role for the central bank".[29]

The dominance of central banks in macroprudential policymaking is not surprising.[30] First and foremost, it ensures that information synergies are utilised, particularly where the central bank is also the micro-prudential supervisor[31] and it can enhance coordination between macroprudential and monetary

---

also mean that the central bank provides the Secretariat, and/or supply analysis in the macroprudential committee.

In Asia, in a Central Bank model (where bank supervision is inside the central bank), the principal agency in charge of macroprudential policy is typically the central bank while in the Separate Authority model (where banking supervision is outside the central bank) the executive branch is usually the principal agency making macroprudential decisions. The prominent role of the government in the latter can be attributed to the good position of the government in those countries compared to the other agencies to coordinate in a multiple agency setting. Lim and others (2013) (n 5), 12.

[27] The IMF's Annual Macroprudential Policy Survey Objectives, Design, and Country Responses (April 2018), available at <https://www.imf.org/en/Publications/Policy-Papers/Issues/2018/04/30/pp043018-imf-annual-macroprudential-policy-survey>, 5.

[28] Calvo and others (2018) (n 8), 2.

See also Lim and others (2013) (n 5), 12–13; D Masciandaro, "Central Banks and Macroprudential Policies: Economics and Politics" (2018) Bocconi University Working Paper No 78 shows that that the central bank's role as a micro-prudential supervisor is a significant driver of its macroprudential involvement.

[29] ESRB (2018) (n 10), 6. The central bank generally plays a central role in the working of the macroprudential committee, for instance by chairing it and/or providing the secretariat and/or supplying analysis.

[30] IMF, Key Aspects of Macroprudential Policy 2013, available at <https://www.imf.org/external/np/pp/eng/2013/061013b.pdf>, 1; The High-Level Group on Financial Supervision in the EU, chaired by J de Larosière (Brussels, 25 February 2009), paras 174–178.

See also S Mckphilmey, "Integrating Macro-prudential Policy: Central Banks as the 'Third Force' in EU Financial Reform" (2016) 39(3) West European Politics 526.

[31] Nier and others (2011) (n 6), 9. However, in that case, the risk of capture by banks may be of a concern. See PC Boyer and J Ponce, "Regulatory Capture and Banking Supervision Reform" (2012) 8(3) Journal of Financial Stability 206.

But see D Masciandaro, R Pansini and M Quintyn, "The Economic Crisis: Did Financial Supervision Matter" (2011) IMF Working Paper 261 on the advantage of having separate institutions for micro and macroprudential supervision and introducing a layer of checks and balances in the supervisory process.

policies.[32] Giving a prominent role to central banks in macroprudential policy enables the harnessing of the central banks' expertise and technical skills that are already being utilised in their monetary policymaking, oversight of payment systems and their role as the lender-of-last-resort.[33] Moreover, as monetary policy setters, central banks often enjoy a high level of independence and credibility that is so valuable in mitigating the risk of political pressure and lobbying when making macroprudential policy decisions.[34] Finally, central banks have essential skills in communicating risks to the markets and the general public that could be garnered to enhance transparency in macroprudential policymaking.[35]

Notwithstanding these heavy-weighted considerations, assigning a macroprudential mandate to a central bank as a single agency can generate conflicts of interest as between setting monetary policy and macroprudential oversight.[36] The potential conflict between low-interest rates and the build-up of systemic risk is frequently provided as a key example for this potential conflict. It has been acknowledged that prolonged periods of low-interest rates may contribute to the build-up of financial imbalances via the so-called "risk-taking channel".[37] Periods of very low-interest rates can stimulate excessive

---

[32]   See Chapter 8; D Schoenmaker, D Gros, S Langfield and M Pagano, "Allocating Macro-prudential Powers" (2014) Report of the ESRB Advisory Scientific Committee No 5. There is evidence to suggest that giving the central bank an important role is conductive to reducing macroprudential policy response-time. CH Lim and others, "The Macroprudential Framework: Policy Responsiveness and Institutional Arrangements" (2013) IMF Working Paper 166.

[33]   Nier and others (2011) (n 6), 9.
       See also Chairman BS Bernanke, "The Effects of the Great Recession on Central Bank Doctrine and Practice", Speech at the Federal Reserve Bank of Boston 56th Economic Conference, Boston, Massachusetts, 18 October 2011; in the UK, see George Osborne MP, Speech given at the Lord Mayor's dinner for bankers and merchants of the City of London, Mansion House, June 2010, available at <https://www.gov.uk/government/speeches/speech-by-the-chancellor-of-the-exchequer-rt-hon-george-osborne-mp-at-mansion-house>.

[34]   BIS (2011) (n 22); J Klomp and J de Haan, "Central Bank Independence and Financial Instability" (2009) 5(4) Journal of Financial Stability 321–338.

[35]   Ibid 10.

[36]   In the EU, for instance, W Buiter highlighted the potential problems with assigning a leading role to the ECB in the governance of the ESRB, such as potential conflict of interests between the monetary and macroprudential supervision role and undermining the independence of the ECB. W Buiter, "The Proposed European Systemic Risk Board is Overweight by Central Banks" in Willem Buiter's Maverecon (28 October 2009), available at <http://blogs.ft.com/maverecon/2009/10/>. In the UK, see discussion in UK Joint Committee House of Commons and House of Lords on the Draft Financial Services Bill, Session 2010–12, HL Paper 236/HC, paras 59–70.

[37]   As discussed in length in Chapter 8. C Borio and H Zhu, "Capital Regulation, Risk-taking and Monetary Policy: A Missing Link in the Transmission Mechanism?" (2008) BIS Working Paper 268; Y Altunbas, L Gambacorta and D Marques-Ibanez, "Does Monetary Policy Affect Bank Risk Taking?" (2010) BIS Working Paper 298; De Nicolò and others, "Monetary Policy and Bank Risk-Taking" (2010) IMF Staff Position Note 9; T Adrian and H Shin, "Capital Flows and Risk-Taking Channel of Monetary Policy" (11th BIS Annual Conference, 22–23 June 2012).

risk-taking by banks, which, in turn, increases systemic fragility.[38] Combining the two policies under the same roof makes it more difficult to observe the relative weight that central banks give to each set of responsibilities (monetary policy, macroprudential policy and perhaps even micro-prudential policy). This, in turn, can result in diluted accountability and potentially undermine the credibility and effectiveness of monetary policy.[39] Positioning macroprudential policy within a central bank can also result in institutional overburdening,[40] and bring about concerns of excess power and barriers to challenging "house views".[41] Excessive insularity within a homogenous and cohesive group of central banks can increase groupthink, i.e. the tendency to consider issues only within a certain paradigm and not challenge its basic premises.[42] Groupthink mentality can result in self-censuring and discourage consideration of alternative and differing views.[43] In the macroprudential sphere, this concern is far from being theoretical. The Financial Stability Board, for instance, has warned that, in the UK, centralising supervisory and systemic roles within the Bank of England increases the potential of creating a groupthink mentality.[44]

Loose monetary policy may encourage a "search for yield". See, for instance, R Rajan, "Has Financial Development Made the World Riskier?" (Greenspan Era: Lessons for the Future, Jackson Hole, 27 August 2005), 313.

[38] CGFS, "Financial Stability Implications of a Prolonged Period of Low Interest Rates" Report of the CGFS Working Group co-chaired by U Bindseil (ECB) and SB Kamin (Board of Governors of the Federal Reserve System) CGFS Paper No 61, July 2018, available at <https://www.bis.org/publ/cgfs61.pdf>, 48.

[39] F Smets, "Financial Stability and Monetary Policy: How Closely Interlinked?" (2014) 10(2) International Journal of Central Banking 263, 277.
See also J Chwieroth and J Danielsson, "Political Challenges of the Macroprudential Agenda", VoxEU.org, 6 September 2013, available at <https://voxeu.org/article/political-challenges-macroprudential-agenda>.

[40] A Orphanides, "Is Monetary Policy Overburdened" (2013) BIS Working Paper No 435.
See also UK Joint Committee House of Commons and House of Lords on the Draft Financial Services Bill, Session 2010–12, HL Paper 236/HC, paras 329–321.

[41] Nier and others (2011) (n 6), 13.

[42] IL Janis, "Groupthink" (1971) Psychology Today Magazine 84; IL Janis, Groupthink: Psychological Studies of Policy Decisions and Fiascos (Boston, Massachusetts: Houghton Mifflin, 1982). In monetary policy see A Sibert, "Central Banking by Committee" (2006) De Nederlandsche Bank Working Paper 91 identified the following factors as leading to groupthink: insulation from outsiders; lack of diversity in viewpoints and leaders actively advocating solutions.
See also IMF, "IMF Performance in the Run-Up to the Financial and Economic Crisis: IMF Surveillance in 2004–07 – Evaluation Report" (2011), 17.

[43] This is not just a theoretical phenomenon See, for instance, LM Ball, "Ben Bernanke and the Zero Bound" (2012) NBER Working Papers Series 17836, 22–27.

[44] FSB, Peer-Review of the UK (September 2013), available at <https://www.fsb.org/2013/09/r_130910/>, 18.
See also A Spicer and others, "Cultural Change in the FCA, PRA and Bank of England Practising What They Preach?" Report of New City Agency and Cass Business (October 2016), available at <https://newcityagenda.co.uk/wp-content/uploads/2016/10/NCA-Cultural-change-in-regulators-report_embargoed.pdf>, 57. But see M Taylor, "The Committee of Public Safety"

4. PARTICIPATION OF MINISTRY OF FINANCE/ TREASURY

As will be seen in Chapter 8, there are synergies and potential trade-offs between macroprudential policy and fiscal policy. Participation of the ministry of finance in the macroprudential committee can advance coordination and exchange of information across these policies. In addition, the ministry of finance has a direct democratic authority (rather than a delegated authority) and it represents elected officials. Therefore, its participation enhances the legitimacy of the macroprudential authority and garners the much-needed political support for its policy decisions.[45] This is particularly important where fiscal resources or legislative changes are needed to support and complement macroprudential policy measures.[46] The risks, however, involved in handing a voting right to finance minister in a macroprudential committee, are self-evident (and perhaps, intractable). Participation of the executive branch can jeopardise the independence of the macroprudential authority[47] and may increase its tendency to succumb to short-term political considerations, avoid making unpopular choices and thus delay pre-emptive and timely policy action.

While cognisance of these risks is important in order to foster transparency and accountability of a macroprudential committee, the reality is that a representative of fiscal authorities often has a leading role in the financial stability committee, most commonly as a chairperson.[48] This is also the case

---

speech at the Institute of International Monetary Research, 7 November 2017, available at <https://www.bankofengland.co.uk/-/media/boe/files/speech/2017/martin-taylor-speech-at-the-institute-of-international-monetary-research>.

[45] A Clark and A Large, "Macroprudential Policy: Addressing the Things We don't Know", Group of 30 Occasional Paper 83 (Washington DC, 2011).

[46] This is particularly the case in small and open economies where there may be a need to use fiscal tools for macroprudential purposes. In addition, if fiscal and macroprudential policies conflict, the effectiveness of the latter could be substantially impaired. Coordination and common understanding are therefore vital. P Szpunar, "Institutional and Operational Aspects of Macroprudential Policy in Central and Eastern European EU Member States in Macroprudential Frameworks, Implementation and Relationship with other Policies" (December 2017) BIS Paper No 94, 289, 296–297.

[47] Nier and others (2011) (n 6), 14.
A Duncan and C Nolan, "Objectives and Challenges of Macroprudential Policy" (2015) 22 University of Glasgow Working Paper 25 suggest that costs associated with the coordination of time varying macroprudential policy interventions with tax policy may well be greater than the associated benefits.

[48] Nier and others, (2011) (n 6), 8.
Nier and others (2011) (n 6), 14. Finance ministries are more likely to be the sole chair of a financial stability committee than is the central bank; in addition, Edge and Liang (2017) (n 7) suggest that countries that have a greater number of financial crises and thus anticipate that fiscal expenditure is more likely to be needed during a crisis will be more keen to have their finance ministry represented on the committee. In contrast, in the EU, there are only a few Member States where the Ministry of Finance representative acts as chair, ESRB (2018) (n 10), 6.

in Asia, where the executive branch is perceived to be in a better position than other agencies to ensure coordination in a multiple agency setting.[49]

A middle-ground institutional model may offer a sensible solution for the tension between the added benefits of a government agency's involvement and the need to maintain the independence of the macroprudential authority. This model grants a passive role to the ministry of finance that participates in the committee without a voting right and facilitates the exchange of information and coordination across macroprudential and fiscal policies. In Section 7 below, it will be seen that this is the model adopted in the UK.

5. EXTERNAL EXPERTS AND EXTERNAL MEMBERS AS A DEBIASING MECHANISM

Arrangements in a macroprudential committee structure could include the participation of independent external experts with voting rights. Alternatively, the committee could seek the views of external stakeholders who are not its members on an *ad hoc* basis.[50] This could take the form of a legal requirement to seek such views as part of the macroprudential authority's tasks or as an informal framework of deliberation with the relevant stakeholders. Another option is to establish an advisory committee to the main body composed of external members. This is the model adopted in the ESRB, which its internal structure includes an Advisory Scientific Committee (ASC) consisting of 15 experts representing a wide range of skills, experience and knowledge pertaining to all relevant financial market sectors.[51]

---

[49] Particularly in countries that have the Central Bank model (central bank is responsible also for the supervision of banks). Lim and others (2013) (n 5), 12–13.

[50] IMF-FSB-BIS (2016) (n 5), 6. In Germany and the Netherlands, for instance, the macroprudential authority can invite, as required, external experts on an *ad hoc* basis. IMF, Germany: Financial Sector Assessment Program (June 2016) IMF Country Report No 196, available at <https://www.imf.org/external/pubs/ft/scr/2016/cr16196.pdf>; FSB, Netherlands Peer Review (November 2014), 14, available at <http://www.fsb.org/wp-content/uploads/Netherlands-peer-review-report.pdf>.

[51] In addition to the Chair of the Advisory Technical Committee. Articles 4(1) and 12 of the ESRB Regulation, as amended. Article 12 was amended by the Regulation amending the ESRB Regulation and inserted in addition to the requirement for the experts to represent a wide range of skills and experience a requirement for "knowledge" and that all these to be "pertaining to all relevant financial market sectors". A 2018 call for expression of interest for members of the ASC included a requirement for background from academic fields or other sectors, in particular in small and medium-sized enterprises or trade unions, or as providers or consumers of financial services. Calls for Expression of Interest for Members of the ESRB's Advisory Scientific Committee, available at <https://www.esrb.europa.eu/news/pr/date/2018/html/esrb.pr180502.en.html>. This is particularly important since the ESRB (and the FPC) do not have specific representation of consumers on their board in contrast to the FSOC that includes the Director of the Bureau of Consumer Financial Protection as a voting member.

External members can break down groupthink through depolarising and diversifying the deliberations of the macroprudential authority. This was indeed the rationale behind the inclusion of five external members in the FPC, who are selected from outside the Bank of England.[52] These members are expected to bring a different range of knowledge and insights to the FPC and make room for a "creative tension".[53] External members are also a salient element in the accountability framework of the FPC. As a practice, the Treasury Select Committee takes, from time to time, views from the external members without the presence of the FPC internal members.[54] As shall be seen in Chapter 7, the Treasury Committee uses these hearings to conduct rigorous and meaningful "checks and balances" on the FPC decision-making process. A recurrent theme, advanced in a pertinent manner during those hearings, is whether FPC members feel that they co-operate in the desire to achieve a consensus; are guided by the chair of the meeting; or subject to political or other pressure to conform with the majority.[55]

While the involvement of external experts in the macroprudential decision-making can be a useful antidote to groupthink, it remains a strong

---

[52] Section 9B(1)(e) BEA 1998, as amended by section 6 Bank of England and Financial Services Act 2016 which increased the number of members of the FPC appointed by the Chancellor of the Exchequer from four to five in order to maintain the balance between external members and officers of the Bank following the addition of the Deputy Governor for markets and banking as a member of the FPC.

[53] HM Treasury, "A New Approach to Financial Regulation: Securing Stability, Protecting Consumers" (January 2012) Cm.8268, paras B.16–B.17; HM Treasury, "A New Approach to Financial Regulation: Judgment, Focus and Stability" (July 2010), Cm.7874, para 3.19; HM Treasury, "A New Approach to Financial Regulation: Building a Stronger System" (February 2011), Cm.8012, paras 2.78–2.79; R. Sharp, "The Financial Policy Committee of the Bank of England: An Experiment in Macroprudential Management – The View of an External Member" (London: London School of Economics, 4 June 2014), available at <http://www.lse.ac.uk/assets/richmedia/channels/publicLecturesAndEvents/transcripts/20140604_1830_boeFinancialPolicyCommittee_tr.pdf>.
On the contribution of external members to the Monetary Policy Committee, see S Hansen and M McMahon, "What Do Outside Experts Bring to a Committee? Evidence from the Bank of England" (2010) Barcelona Economics Working Paper Series No 512.
Whilst there is no statutory requirement for the FPC to consult external experts, the *Communications Guidance for FPC members* encourages members to make contact, subject to certain limitations, with financial market participants. Bank of England, Communications Guidance for FPC Members (28 April 2018), available at <https://www.bankofengland.co.uk/-/media/boe/files/about/fpc/fpccoc>.

[54] As shall be seen in Chapter 7, the Treasury Committee is particularly "keen to take individual views notwithstanding the desire to, as far as possible, to speak in consensus". FPC External Members Hearing in the Treasury Select Committee (24 May 2016) attending Richard Sharp, Donald Kohen and Martin Taylor.

[55] See, for instance, FPC External Members Hearing in the Treasury Select Committee (24 May 2016), question posed 14.35 minutes into the hearing on the possibility that the view of external members on Brexit being a risk to financial stability conforms with the FPC chair and Governor of the Bank of England, Mark Carney.

---

force that is hard to overcome. There is a real danger that external members will also succumb to groupthink, as evidenced in the following self-reflective comment of one of the FPC external members – "the trouble is the more time you stay there [i.e. Bank of England, author's addition], the more you become imbued in its atmosphere and tend to agree with it …".[56] The length of the term that external members serve on the macroprudential committee may, therefore, be a key factor in their ability to bring to the table a fresh and different view.

Another hurdle that could negatively affect the effectiveness of external members as a debiasing mechanism is the difficulty to balance between expertise and distance from a homogenised view. Finding external members that would meet both requirements can prove to be a difficult task.[57]

6. GOING BEYOND STRUCTURE: THE DECISION-MAKING PROCESS OF A MACROPRUDENTIAL COMMITTEE

Diversity in the composition of the macroprudential authority through the inclusion of external members or seeking external views is a weighty factor in minimising the degree of groupthink and other inherent biases in macroprudential policymaking. However, to reap the full benefits of a collective decision-making process and encourage genuine deliberation, several other determinants, which go beyond composition, should be carefully considered.

It is important to emphasise that the use of the term "deliberation" in the context of a macroprudential decision-making process is of critical importance. Deliberation, to be differentiated from an ordinary discussion, is "an enlightened and open-minded search for consensus amid diverse participants".[58] It is an open process designed to encourage exchange of ideas, consideration of alternatives and encouragement of dissension.[59] But how to encourage such genuine deliberation in the macroprudential policymaking and what are the key

---

[56] M Taylor in FPC Hearing before the Select Committee on 18 April 2018, at approximately 16:18 minutes into the hearing.

[57] Therefore, Professor Charles Goodhart has brought up this concern during the legislative process and suggested that it will be difficult to recruit commercially savvy people for the FPC (more than the MPC): House of Lords and House of Commons, Joint Committee on the Draft Financial Services Bill, HL Paper No 236, HC Paper No 1447 (Session 2010–12), paras 323–324.
See also A Keller, "Debiasing Macroprudential Policy: Part 2: Designing a New Diversity Criterion for Macroprudential Policy" (2018) 34(2) JIBLR 37.

[58] J Barabas, "How Deliberation Affects Policy Opinions" (2004) 98(4) American Political Science Review 687, 699.

[59] KM Warsh, "Institutional Design: Deliberations, Decisions and Committee Dynamics" in KM Warsh (ed), *Central Bank Governance and Oversight Reform* (Hoover Institution, Stanford University, 2016), 173 at 178–179.

determinants affecting it? It is suggested here that the manner in which motions are presented, the transparency of the individual opinations, the role and style of the chair and the decision rule – may all have a significant effect on the quality of the macroprudential decision-making process.[60]

6.1. STYLE OF THE CHAIR

To begin with, the chair of the macroprudential committee has a key role to play in creating suitable conditions for a deliberative process and ensuring that individual members' views are voiced freely and considered. Drawing on monetary policy literature, it can be observed that a "genuinely-collegial" committee, where members do not hesitate to voice their opinion (which may be different) but ultimately reach a group decision, is preferable to an "autocratically-collegial" committee, where decisions are largely dictated by the chair.[61] To avoid dangerously slipping into a culture of "groupthink", the chair should strive to encourage members to express heterogeneous policy views and discuss alternatives rather than strongly promote its own personal preferences or even dictate them.[62]

6.2. DECISION RULE

At the time of writing, there is yet no empirical evidence on the dominant decision rule adopted in macroprudential committees around the globe.[63]

---

[60] Other factors include the size of the committee and whether there is individual accountability of committee members. DG Mayes, PL Siklos and J Strum, "Central Banking Long March over the Decades", Chapter 1 in DG Mayes, PL Siklos and J Strum (eds), *Oxford Handbook of The Economic of Central Banking* (OUP 2019), 4.
In the context of monetary policy see, for instance P Maier, "How Central Banks Take Decisions: An Analysis of Monetary Policy Meetings" in PL Siklos, MT Bohl and ME Wohar (eds), *Challenges in Central Banking: The Current Institutional Environment and Forces Affecting Monetary Policy* (New York: Cambridge University Press, 2010), 320–356.
For a detailed discussion in the context of the FPC, see Keller (2018) (Part 2) (n 57).

[61] AS Blinder and S Alan, "Monetary Policy by Committee: Why and How?" (2007) 23(1) European Journal of Political Economy 106.
See also H Chappell and others, *Committee Decisions on Monetary Policy Evidence from Historical Records of the Federal Open Market Committee* (Cambridge: MIT Press, 2005); LH Meyer, *A Term at the Fed* (New York: Harper Collins, 2004).

[62] The latter is known as a promotional leader to be contrasted with a participative leader. See NR Ahlfinger and JK Esser, "Testing the Groupthink Model: Effects of Promotional Leadership and Conformity Predisposition" (2001) 29(1) Social Behaviour and Personality 31; CR Leana, "A Partial Test of Janis' Groupthink Model: Effects of Group Cohesiveness and Leader Behavior on Defective Decision Making" (1985) 11(1) Journal of Management 5.

[63] See a brief comment in IMF FSB BIS (2016) (n 5), 12 that normally it would be a majority rule though in practise, the macroprudential authority will strive for consensus.

In the UK, the BEA 1998 requires the chair of the FPC meeting[64] to seek to secure a decision by consensus, wherever possible.[65] Where consensus cannot be reached, a vote is taken and, in the event of a tied vote, the chair has a second casting vote.[66] Regrettably, the rationale behind the choice of this particular decision rule was not reported during the legislative process. Nonetheless, evidence from the Organisational Behaviour field reveals the positive effect of a unanimous decision rule on the dynamics of deliberation:

> with unanimous decision schemes, group members often run into difficulty in deciding upon a course of action, forcing a group to move beyond a discussion of preferences to a discussion of the reasons underlying the preferences ... more systematic processing of information because attention must be paid to all members' perspectives ... unanimity encourages the sharing of minority points of view and the questioning of assumptions than majority rule.[67]

Reaching a consensus for policy measures can also facilitate their successful implementation[68] and make it easier to project a clear message when addressing the public.[69]

These considerations fit well in the macroprudential sphere. The internal policymaking process requires plurality of views and diversity. In contrast, in the external presentation of policy decisions to stakeholders and the public, speaking in one voice is vital, particularly given the potential unpopularity of policy measures. Yet, there is a real concern that a unanimous decision rule may, in fact, foster cohesiveness and expose the group to a risk of groupthink.[70] In order to alleviate such risk, the FPC model offers a middle ground and utilises,

---

64   BEA 1998 Sch 2A para 11(3). The chair is to be taken by the Governor of the Bank or, if the Governor is not present, by the Bank's Deputy Governor for financial stability.

65   BEA 1998 Sch 2A para 11(4).

66   BEA 1998 Sch 2A para 11(5). This can be contrasted with the MPC decision rule. BEA 1998 Sch 3 para 11.

67   S Mohammed and E Ringseis, "Cognitive Diversity and Consensus in Group Decision Making: The Role of Inputs Processes and Outcomes" (2001) 85(2) Organisational Behaviour and Human Decision Processes 310.

68   DR Brodwin and LJ Bourgeois, "Five Steps to Strategic Action" (1984) 26 California Management Review 176.

69   The House of Commons Treasury Committee 8th Report of Session 2012/13 Appointment of Dr Mark Carney as Governor of the Bank of England, Answer to question No 22 on p 12. On the challenges of communication in macroprudential policy see Chapter 7.

70   KC Rumison, "Unanimity as a Rule for Group Consensus: A Review of the Theoretical and Experimental Literature on the Use of Unanimity in Group Decision Making" (1998) 6(1) Modern Psychological Studies 9, 20; D Frey, S Schulz-Hardt and D Stahlberg, "Information Seeking Amongst Individuals and Groups and Possible Consequences for Decision Making in Business and Politics" in RH Witte and JH Davis (eds), *Understanding Group Behaviour: Small Group Processes and Interpersonal Relations* (Abingdon: Psychology Press, 2009), Vol 2, Ch 8, 211, 220.

where possible, the virtues of a consensus rule whilst maintaining the option to revert to a majority rule. This model also removes the risk of paralysis when consensus cannot be reached.[71]

Given the complexity of macroprudential policy decisions and the variety of policy alternatives, it is, therefore, somewhat surprising that, to date, the FPC's decisions have all been reached by consensus.[72] The reasons behind this overwhelming uniformity are of essence: is the consensus a result of deliberation and consideration of minority views? Alternatively, are decisions dictated by pressure to conform with an overpowering chair or with the majority of members and points to strong groupthink in the decision-making process?

The FSOC's decision rule offers an alternative model to the FPC model. Generally and unless otherwise specified, the FSOC's decisions follow a majority vote of the voting members and there is no requirement to reach consensus where possible.[73] Certain decisions, however, require a two-thirds majority of the voting members of the FSOC[74] and other decisions require a majority of two-thirds with the Secretary of the Treasury as the chair of the FSOC having veto power.[75] The Treasury's veto right may subject those decisions to a significant political influence[76] but it can also provide an important source of legitimacy to the macroprudential authority.[77]

Regarding the ESRB and as shall be seen below, in light of the size of its decision-making body, the ESRB generally acts by a simple majority of members present with voting rights and in the event of a tie, the chair of the ESRB has a casting voice.[78] However, to adopt a recommendation or to make a warning or recommendation public, which could potentially have more far-reaching

---

[71] On the benefits of a majority rule that "supports robust adaptively viable decisions under uncertainty" see, for instance, R Hastie and T Kameda, "The robust beauty of majority rules in group decisions" (2005) 112(2) Psychological Review 494–508.

[72] Keller – Part 2 (2018) (n 57). This may be attributed, at least in part, to the preliminary meetings. See Written Evidence submitted by Donald Kohn (DKF0002): Responses to Questionnaire from Treasury Committee (21 March 2018), available at <http://data.parliament. uk/writtenevidence/committeeevidence.svc/evidencedocument/treasury-committee/ reappointment-of-donald-kohn-to-the-financial-policy-committee/written/81464.pdf>, para 14 who explains that "Preliminary meetings have been used to narrow options and identify areas for the staff to explore with additional data and analytics. This process has helped to shape a consensus about the actions themselves and about the descriptions of current and possible future actions."

[73] Section 111(f) Dodd-Frank Act.

[74] Sections 119(c)(3) and 121(a) Dodd-Frank Act.

[75] Sections 113(a)(1), 113(b)(1), 113(d)(2), 113(f)(1) and 117(c)(2)(A) Dodd-Frank Act.

[76] A Duff, "Central Bank Independence and Macroprudential Policy: A Critical Look at the U.S. Financial Stability Framework" (2014) 11(1) Berkley Business Law Journal 183, 213.

[77] D Schwarcz and D Zaring, "Regulation by Threat: Understanding Dodd Frank's Regulation of Systemically Significant Non-Bank Financial Companies" (2017) 84 The University of Chicago Law Review 1811, 1873. See also the discussion in Chapter 7

[78] Article 10(2) ESRB Regulation.

implications on specific countries within the EU, a majority of two-thirds is required.[79]

6.3. TRANSPARENCY OF DIFFERING AND DISSENTING VIEWS

Transparency of the decision-making process of the macroprudential authority and presenting the rationales behind policy decisions, the balance of views and consideration of alternatives enable scrutiny of the process and accordingly strengthen the accountability of its members. This comes, however, with a cost. It has been suggested that the transparency of the monetary policy decision process may result in conformism, stifling of the discussion[80] and reluctance of members to dissent.[81] While this concern could, on principle, be carried over to the macroprudential domain, a more perennial concern is the potential for transparency to result in weakening of a strong and unified "front line". Where policy measures may result in political, public or industry pressure, as is the case in macroprudential policymaking, speaking in "one voice" can strengthen the implementation of the measures. Yet, when weighing this concern against the associated benefits of accountability, the balance is most likely to tip over the latter, subject to certain exceptions. This is indeed, by and large, reflected in the transparency frameworks of both the FPC and the FSOC.

The FPC is required to publish in the records of its meetings a summary of the deliberations that were considered in reaching any decision without identifying particular members.[82] The Chancellor's Remit and Recommendations to the FPC further clarify that, where decisions are reached by consensus, the arguments considered in reaching that consensus are to be reflected in the record of the meeting and where a vote is taken, the balance of arguments advanced for each position should be reflected in the record of the meeting.[83] It was also acknowledged that, at this stage, going beyond a summary of deliberation may destabilise the delicate balance between accountability and an "unconstrained space for open discussion and deliberation".[84]

---

[79]   Article 10(3) ESRB Regulation.

[80]   S Hansen, M McMahon and A Prat, "Transparency and Deliberation within the FOMC: A Computational Linguistics Approach" (2017) 133(2) Quarterly Journal of Economics 801.

[81]   E Meade and D Stasavage, "Publicity of Debate and the Incentive to Dissent: Evidence from the US Federal Reserve" (2008) 118 Economic Journal 695–717.

[82]   Section 9U(1)–(2) and (7) BEA 1998 but see section 9U(8) BEA and in particular, section 9U(8)(b) BEA 1998.

[83]   HM Treasury, "Remit and Recommendations for the FPC" (8 March 2017), available at <https://www.bankofengland.co.uk/-/media/boe/files/letter/2017/chancellor-letter-080317-fpc.pdf>.

[84]   The Warsaw Review, *Transparency and the Bank of England's Monetary Policy Committee*, December 2014, 11–12 concludes, in contrast to its recommendations with regard to the MPC, that making sound policy decisions could be impaired if FPC discussions were made public through transcript release.

The FSOC also releases minutes of its meetings and records the votes of its members.[85] However, in contrast to the FPC, specific comments made during the deliberation are often attributed to individual members.[86] Minutes may be subject to redactions, as determined by the FSOC's chairperson.[87] The level of transparency of the FSOC's minutes has been subject to heavy criticism, suggesting that the minutes largely describe general agenda items for the meetings and information on presenters with no additional detail even when the information is not market sensitive or may limit the quality of deliberations.[88] The US Government Accountability Office suggested that a similar deliberative body

> … the Federal Reserve's Federal Open Market Committee, keeps transcripts of its meetings and voluntarily releases these transcripts to the public after 5 years. Releasing the transcripts after a period of time should allow the members of the committee to talk freely and provides documentation that can be used to assess the entity's performance and monitor their decision-making process.[89]

In recent years, there has been an apparent improvement of transparency in the FSOC's minutes and they are substantially more detailed compared to its early years. In particular, the minutes now provide more information on questions asked during the meetings and on the presentations and the discussion that took place.[90]

The ESRB, as a regional macroprudential authority, presents further layers of complexity. Being a large body, there is a natural difficulty to speak in one voice. In addition, there is an inherent reticence of Member States to disclose data,

---

[85] Transparency Policy for the Financial Stability Oversight Council (1 October 2010), available at <http://www.treasury.gov/initiatives/Documents/FSOCtransparencypolicy.pdf>.

[86] For instance, Minutes of the FSOC, 29 September 2017. But see section 9U(7) BEA 1998.

[87] Transparency Policy for the FSOC (n 85) commits the FSOC to holding at least two open meetings per year but there is an extensive list of disclosure restrictions where a meeting or a portion thereof will be closed, such as where it "would lead to significant financial speculation, significantly endanger the stability of any financial market or financial institution, or significantly frustrate implementation of a proposed agency action".

[88] US Government Accountability Office, Report to Congressional Requesters, Financial Stability New Council Strengthen the Accountability and Transparency of Their Decisions, September 2012, available at <https://www.gao.gov/assets/650/648064.pdf>, 27.

[89] Ibid 20.

[90] For instance, when comparing the minutes of the FSOC meeting on 6 March 2019 with the FSOC meeting on 11 March 2015, the latter includes the expression "Council members asked questions and had a discussion" but the more recent meeting outlines a long list of issues that were discussed and compared minutes. Similarly, when comparing the FSOC meeting on 6 March 2019 with the FSOC meeting on the 3 April 2012 they both make a reference to a presentation that was given during the meeting, but the more recent meeting also includes key points from the presentation. The FSOC meeting minutes are available at <https://www.treasury.gov/initiatives/fsoc/council-meetings/Pages/meeting-minutes.aspx>.

particularly disaggregated, that can impinge on national interests.[91] Following the conclusion of the quarterly General Board meeting, the ESRB publishes a one-page press release with the key issues discussed in the meeting, assessment of the current key risks and ESRB activities.[92] Here, the merits of the transparency of views may be outweighed by the need to encourage the free flow of discussion amongst the Members States.[93]

6.4. STAKEHOLDERS' COLLABORATION AND INCLUSIVENESS

Taking an inclusive approach that incorporates the views of relevant stakeholders, who are not members of the macroprudential authority, is vital to ensuring effective macroprudential policymaking. Seeking input from industry participants and other relevant stakeholders (expert and non-expert) enhances the transparency of the supervisory process and accordingly, can strengthen its legitimacy and support existing accountability mechanisms. These issues will be further explored in Chapter 7.

The FPC is under no legislative requirement to consult stakeholders, however, the *Communications Guidance for FPC members* encourages FPC members to make contact, subject to certain limitations, with financial market participants.[94] The FPC also seeks input from informed stakeholders as well as risk specialists from across the financial sector, climate scientists and other industry experts on the design, coverage and nature of scenarios of future stress tests of the UK financial system's resilience to the physical and transition risks of climate change.[95] Similarly, the FSOC seeks input from a wide array of

---

91 Commission Staff Working Document Accompanying the Document Report to the European Parliament and the Council on the Mission and Organisation of the ESRB COM (2014) 508 final, 23.

92 ESRB Decision of 20 January 2011 Adopting the Rules of Procedure of the European Systemic Risk Board (ESRB/2011/1) OJ C 58/4.
According to Article 9(6) ESRB Regulation, as amended by the Regulation amending the ESRB Regulation the proceeding of the ESRB General Board meetings are confidential but "The General Board may decide to make an account of its deliberation public, subject to applicable confidentiality requirements and in a manner that does not allow for the identification of individual members of the General Board or of individual institutions. The General Board may decide to hold press conference after its meetings".

93 Nevertheless, there are ways to overcome these limitations, for instance by having a mechanism in place to reassess the need to maintain confidentiality of the discussion with a view to publishing it at an opportune time.

94 Treasury Remit and Recommendations for the FPC, 16 March 2016 Recommendations as to engagement with financial sector participants and other external experts to seek the views of industry participants, academics, other regulators and the public, as appropriate to supplement its own expertise.

95 Summary and Record of the FPC Meetings on 13 June and 4 July 2019, available at <https://www.bankofengland.co.uk/-/media/boe/files/financial-policy-summary-and-record/2019/july-2019.pdf>.

stakeholders through public comments on its policy analysis[96] as well as on its rules and guidance.[97]

In the EU, in performing its tasks, the ESRB is required, where appropriate, to seek the views of relevant private sector stakeholders.[98] In addition, the ESRB's ASC and Advisory Technical Committee (ATC) are required, where appropriate, to organise consultations with stakeholders such as market participants, consumer bodies and academic experts, at an early stage and in an open and transparent manner while taking into account confidentiality requirements.[99]

7. TAILORED INSTITUTIONAL MODELS FOR MACROPRUDENTIAL POLICY IN SELECTED JURISDICTIONS

7.1. INSTITUTIONAL STRUCTURE OF THE FPC

The FPC was originally set up as a statutory subcommittee of the Bank of England's Court[100] but in 2016, it became a policy committee of the Bank of England alongside the Monetary Policy Committee (MPC) and the Prudential Regulation Committee (PRC).[101] The FPC is composed of the Governor of the Bank of England,[102] four Deputy Governors of the Bank of England[103] and

---

96　For instance, FSOC, Notice Seeking Comment on Asset Management Products and Activities, 80 FR 7595 7595, available at <http://www.federalregister.gov/documents/2015/02/11/2015-02813/notice-seeking-comment-onasset-management-products-and-activities>.

97　On 6 March 2019, the FSOC adopted a final rule that requires it to seek public comment before adopting any future amendments to its non-bank financial company designations guidance. FSOC Final Rule Authority to Require Supervision and Regulation of Certain Nonbank Financial Companies 12 CFR Part 1310 FR Vol 84, No 49 8958. Contemporaneous with the publication of the final rule, the FSOC published proposed interpretive guidance that would replace the 2012 Interpretive Guidance and the proposal included a request for public comment. FSOC Notification of Proposed Interpretive Guidance; Request for Public Comment 84 FR 9028–9048.

98　Article 14 ESRB Regulation, as amended. The Regulation amending the ESRB Regulation adds that "such consultations shall be conducted as widely as possible to ensure an inclusive approach towards all interested parties and relevant financial sectors and shall allow reasonable time for stakeholders to respond".

99　Article 12(5) and Article 13 (4a) ESRB Regulation, as amended. It is to be noted that the Regulation amending the ESRB Regulation added the requirement that "Such consultations shall be conducted as widely as possible to ensure an inclusive approach towards all interested parties and relevant financial sectors and shall allow reasonable time for stakeholder to respond".

100　Financial Services Act 2012 c 21, section 4 inserting section 9B(1) to the BEA 1998.

101　Bank of England and Financial Services Act 2016 section 6(2) amending section 9B(1) BEA 1998. On the PRC see chapter 8.

102　Section 9B(1)(a) BEA 1998 as amended by section 6 Bank of England and Financial Services Act 2016.

the Executive Director for Financial Stability Strategy and Risk at the Bank of England,[104] five external members who are selected from outside the Bank of England for their knowledge and experience relevant to the FPC's functions[105] and the Chief Executive of the Financial Conduct Authority.[106] There is also a member from HM Treasury without a voting right who is expected to contribute to the debate, shape the views of the FPC and, where appropriate, challenge the proceedings.[107] The external members do not, therefore, have a majority on the FPC, even if allied with the FCA Chief Executive who is also a non-Bank member.[108] While there were concerns, voiced during the legislative process, that this imbalance between 'insiders' and 'outsiders' might exacerbate groupthink,[109] the UK Government was of the view that it provides the optimal balance between, on the one hand, harnessing the expertise of the Bank of England and on the other hand, inclusion of external challenge.[110]

The FPC's institutional structure and decision-making process are in many respects attractive, however, its de facto diversity may be called into question. To date, decisions have been reached by consensus and evidence of differing views before a consensus was reached is rare.[111] The role of the Governor of the Bank of England as a facilitator rather than an autocratic chair is another thorny matter, particularly where the responsibility to facilitate consensus is vested on the chair.[112]

---

[103] Section 9B(1)(b); 9B(1)(ba); 9B(1)(bb); 9B(1)(bc) BEA 1998 responsible for financial stability, markets and banking, monetary policy and prudential regulation. The Deputy Governor for prudential regulation is also the Chief Executive Officer for Prudential Regulation Authority, the authority responsible for micro-prudential supervision with the bank of England.

[104] According to section 9B(1)(d) BEA 1998 appointed by the Governor of the Bank of England after consultation with the Chancellor of Exchequer.

[105] Section 9B(1)(e) BEA 1998 as amended by section 6 Bank of England and Financial Services Act 2016.

[106] Section 9B(1)(c) BEA 1998 as amended by section 6 Bank of England and Financial Services Act 2016.

[107] Section 9B(1)(f) BEA 1998; House of Commons, Treasury Committee, Accountability of the Bank of England, Twenty-First Report of Session 2010–12, para.102, available at <https://publications.parliament.uk/pa/cm201012/cmselect/cmtreasy/874/874.pdf>.
See also remarks by Mark Hoban, House of Commons Public Bill Committee, Financial Services Bill, Hansard, col 206 (28 February 2012).

[108] The FPC normally has 13 members, six of them are from the Bank of England staff.

[109] The Joint Committee on the Draft Financial Services Bill, HC Paper No 1447 (Session 2010–12), para 325; The Treasury White Paper, "A New Approach to Financial Regulation" (June 2011), Cm.8083, para 2.18.

[110] HM Treasury, "A New Approach to Financial Regulation: Securing Stability, Protecting Consumers" (January 2012) Cm.8268, para B.17.

[111] The record of the 23 March 2016 FPC meeting suggests that initially there was a disagreement amongst members about the level of the countercyclical buffer rate but that later, those members were happy to join a consensus. However, the reasons why those members changed their view was not communicated in the record.

[112] This was a concern during the legislative process see, for instance, George Kerevan, Bank of England and Financial Services Bill, Hansard, col 19 (Session 2015–16, 9 February 2016)

7.2. INSTITUTIONAL STRUCTURE OF THE FSOC

In contrast to the UK centralised structure that puts all the eggs in one basket, the macroprudential institutional design in the US can be seen as more diffused and fragmented. This can be largely attributed to the fact that following the global financial crisis, the UK has overhauled the supervisory system[113] while the US left in place the regulatory structure that existed at the time and "grafted the macroprudential authority on top of it."[114] Nevertheless, the heterogeneous membership within the FSOC and the FPC is their common ground.

The FSOC is composed of 15 members, ten with voting rights and five members without voting rights. The voting members include the Secretary of the Treasury, who serves as the Chairperson of the FSOC; eight regulatory agency heads[115] and an independent member with insurance expertise who is appointed by the President, upon advice and consent of the US Senate.[116] In addition, there are five non-voting members, who serve in an advisory capacity: the Director of the Office of Financial Research (OFR);[117] the Director of the Federal Insurance Office; a state insurance commissioner designated by the state insurance commissioners; a state banking supervisor designated by the state banking supervisors; and a state securities commissioner (or officer performing like functions) designated by the state securities commissioners.[118]

---

and is also a continuous concern during hearing of the FPC in the Treasury Committee. For instance, during the FCP Hearing before the Treasury Committee (12 July 2016) at 10:24 minutes into the hearing the Governor of the Bank of England, Mark Carney was queried about his response to the allegation that, following a discussion with the Chancellor of Exchequer, he guided the decision of the FPC in relation to the assessment that Brexit poses risks to financial stability.

[113] HM Treasury, "A New Approach to Financial Regulation: The Blueprint for Reform" June 2011 Cm 8083; following two consultations: HM Treasury, "A New Approach to Financial Regulation: Building a Stronger System", February 2011; HM Treasury, "A New Approach to Financial Regulation: Judgment, Focus and Stability", July 2010.

[114] D Kohn, "Institutions for Macroprudential regulation: The UK and the US" speech at the Kennedy School of Government, Harvard University, 17 April 2014, available at <https://www.bankofengland.co.uk/-/media/boe/files/speech/2014/institutions-for-macroprudential-regulation-the-uk-and-the-us>.

Though initially the plan was much more ambitious see LA Cunningham and D Zaring, "The Three or Four Approaches to Financial Regulation: A Cautionary Analysis Against Exuberance in Crisis Response" (2009) 78 George Washington Law Review 39.

[115] The Chairman of the Board of Governors of the Federal Reserve System; the Comptroller of the Currency (OCC); the Director of the Bureau of Consumer Financial Protection (CFPB); the Chairman of the Securities and Exchange Commission (SEC); the Chairperson of the Federal Deposit Insurance Corporation (FDIC); the Chairperson of the Commodity Futures Trading Commission (CFTC); the Director of the Federal Housing Finance Agency (FHFA); and the Chairman of the National Credit Union Administration (NCUA).

[116] Section 111(b)(1)(J) Dodd-Frank Act.

[117] Housed within the Treasury and supports the FSOC inter alia in data collection analysis and systemic risk identification. See Chapter 9

[118] Section 111(b)(2) Dodd-Frank Act.

Non-voting members, however, may be excluded, upon an affirmative vote of the member agencies, from proceedings, meetings, discussions, deliberations when necessary to safeguard and promote the exchange of confidential information.[119]

In contrast to the FPC, the FSOC governance provides a leading role to the Treasury and a minimal one to central banks. The dominance of the US Treasury in the governance of the FSOC goes beyond chairmanship and extends to veto rights in certain decisions,[120] providing administrative support through the FSOC's Secretariat[121] and housing the OFR.[122] It is to be differentiated from the FPC that puts central banks at the centre and represents a more arm's length approach relationship between macroprudential policy setting and the political process.[123] The difference between these governance structures is understandable. In the UK, regulatory mistakes were attributed to the FSA (rather than central banks) and to the lack of coordination amongst financial regulators.[124] Conversely, in the US, while initial reform proposals intended to vest the overall responsibility for a macroprudential oversight on the Federal Reserve,[125] the adopted reform accorded with the post-crisis dented credibility of central banks.[126] Naturally, the dominance of the US Treasury in the FSOC's

---

[119]   Section 111(b)(3) Dodd-Frank Act.

[120]   Section 6.2 above. See United States: Financial Sector Assessment Program-Systemic Risk Oversight and Management IMF Country Reports 15/172, 14 observing that such a prominent role is relatively unusual in terms of international practice.

[121]   The FSOC Secretariat staff is drawn almost entirely from the US Treasury. See GAO Report to the Ranking Member, Committee on Banking, Housing, and Urban Affairs, US Senate, FSOC Further Actions Could Improve the Nonbank Designation, November 2014, 20.

[122]   Section 152(a) Dodd-Frank Act.
        See also S Johnson, "The Disappointing Office of Financial Research" (NY Times, 30 January 2014), available at <https://economix.blogs.nytimes.com/2014/01/30/the-disappointing-office-of-financial-research/>.

[123]   Though the FPC financial stability primary objective is subject to taking into account the Government's economic policy as specified in the "remit letter". See Chapter 2.
        See also Kohn (2014) (n 114).

[124]   Financial Services Authority, "The Supervision of Northern Rock: A Lessons Learned Review" (March 2008); Treasury Committee, The Run on the Rock (Fifth Report of Session 2007–08); The Turner Review: A Regulatory Response to the Global Financial Crisis (London, FSA, March 2009).

[125]   The Department of Treasury, "Blueprint for a Modernised Financial Regulatory Structure", March 2008, available at <https://www.treasury.gov/press-center/press-releases/Documents/Blueprint.pdf>, 15 and 147.

[126]   On the motivations behind regulatory reforms establishing macroprudential authorities and their institutional structures see D Lombardi and M Moschella, "The Symbolic Politics of Delegation: Macroprudential Policy and Independent Regulatory Authorities" (2017) 22(1) New Political Economy 92. On the dented credibility of central banks in the US, see for instance, J Zumbrun, "More than Half of U.S. Wants Fed Curbed or Abolished", Bloomberg Business (9 December 2010), available at <http://www.bloomberg.com/news/articles/2010-12-09/more-than-half-of-americans-want-fed-reined-in-or-abolished>.

governance raises the concern that it may be more susceptible to political pressure and lobbying.[127] This will be further discussed in Chapter 7.

7.3. INSTITUTIONAL STRUCTURE OF THE EUROPEAN SYSTEMIC RISK BOARD

The ESRB was established as an independent body with no legal personality or independent budget.[128] It is comprised of a General Board, a Steering Committee, a Secretariat, an ASC and an ATC.[129] The General Board is the decision-making body of the ESRB;[130] the Steering Committee assists in the decision-making process of the ESRB by preparing the meetings of the General Board, reviewing the documents to be discussed and monitoring the progress of the ESRB's ongoing work;[131] the ASC, composed of the Chair of the ATC and 15 experts representing a wide range of skills and experience and knowledge, provides external expertise to the General Board[132] and the ATC provides advice and assistance on issues relevant to the ESRB work and at the request of the Chair of the ESRB General Board or the General Board.[133] Finally, the Secretariat is responsible for the day-to-day business of the ESRB and provides a high-quality analytical, statistical, administrative and logistical support to the ESRB.[134]

---

[127]   S Gadinis, "From Independence to Politics in Financial Regulation" (2013) 101 (2) California Law Review 327, 369–370.

[128]   Recitals 6 and 15 of the ESRB Regulation. The reform proposal in the de Larosiere Report recommended entrusting macroprudential responsibilities on the ESRC, a newly established body under the auspices and with the logistical support of the ECB. The High-level Group on Financial Supervision in the EU chaired by J de Larosiere 25 February 2009, para 177.

[129]   Article 4(1) ESRB Regulation.

[130]   Article 4(2) and 10 ESRB Regulation.

[131]   Articles 4(3) and 11 ESRB Regulation.

[132]   Article 12 (1) and (3) ESRB Regulation, as amended.

[133]   Article 13(3) of the ESRB Regulation, as amended. The ATC is composed of: (a) a representative of each national central bank and a representative of the ECB; (b) one representative per Member State of the competent national supervisory authorities, in accordance with the second subparagraph; (c) a representative of the European Supervisory Authority (European Banking Authority); (d) a representative of the European Supervisory Authority (European Insurance and Occupational Pensions Authority); (e) a representative of the European Supervisory Authority (European Securities and Markets Authority); (f) a representative of the Commission; (fa) a representative of the Supervisory Board of the ECB; (fb) a representative of the Single Resolution Board; (g) a representative of the EFC; and (h) a representative of the Advisory Scientific Committee. Article 13(1) ESRB Regulation, as amended.

It is to be noted that Regulation Amending the ESRB Regulation reduced the number of representatives of the Commission in the ATC from two representatives to one representative and added a representative of the Supervisory Board of the ECB and a representative of the Single Resolution Board.

[134]   Article 4(4) ESRB Regulation.

Similar to the FPC, the dominance of central banks in the governance of the ESRB is apparent. The ties with the ECB, alongside the associated benefits of expertise, access to data and existing connections to national central banks and EU supervisors, are widely enshrined in the governance of the ESRB.[135] The ESRB is chaired by the President of the ECB;[136] the first Vice-Chair is elected by and from the national members of the General Board with voting rights for a term of five years;[137] both the President and the Vice-President of the ECB are members of the ESRB General Board with voting rights;[138] the chair of the ESRB (who is also the President of the ECB) and the member of the Executive Board of the ECB responsible for financial stability and macroprudential policy are members of the Steering Committee;[139] and finally, a representative of the ECB sits in the ATC.[140] The ties are most tangible in the ECB's role of ensuring the provision of a Secretariat for the ESRB, thereby providing it with analytical, statistical, logistical and administrative support.[141]

---

[135]   The ESRB Regulation Preamble (para 24) points out that the ECB and the national central banks should have a leading role in macroprudential oversight given their expertise and existing responsibilities in the area of financial stability; The de Larosière Report, paras 174–178.
See also S Mckphilmey, "Integrating Macro-prudential Policy: Central Banks as the 'Third force' in EU Financial Reform" (2016) 39(3) West European Politics 526.

[136]   Article 5(1) ESRB Regulation, as amended. The ESRB Regulation stated that this was to be for a five-year term following the entry into force of the ESRB Regulation. After that, the ECB President has continued to chair the ESRB on an interim basis. Following the review in accordance with Article 20 of the ESRB Regulation, it was decided that it is appropriate that the President of the ECB chair the ESRB on a permanent basis. This was light of the fact that during the five year term and the interim period "the President of the ECB has conferred authority and credibility on the ESRB and ensured that it can effectively build and rely on the expertise of the ECB in the area of financial stability". Regulation amending the ESRB Regulation, paragraph 5 Preamble. To strengthen the visibility of the ESRB, the Chair of the ESRB is able to delegate tasks, including tasks related to the external representation of the ESRB to the first Vice-Chair and if unavailable and where appropriate to the second Vice-Chair or to the head of the Secretariat. But "Such delegation should not extend to participation in public hearings and in discussions behind closed doors at the European Parliament." Regulation amending the ESRB Regulation, paragraph 8 Preamble, amending article 5(8) ESRB Regulation.

[137]   Article 5(2) ESRB Regulation, as amended.

[138]   Article 6(1)(a) ESRB Regulation.

[139]   Article 11(1)(a)–(c) ESRB Regulation, as amended. The Regulation amending the ESRB Regulation amended article 11 by replacing the Vice-President of the ECB as a member of the Steering Committee with the member of the Executive Board of the ECB responsible for financial stability and macroprudential policy and replaced four other members of the General Board who are also members of the General Council of the ECB as members of the Steering Committee with four national members of the General Board with voting rights. These changes result in slightly weakened ties between the ESRB and the ECB.

[140]   Article 13(1)(a) ESRB Regulation.

[141]   ESRB Regulation, Preamble para 6 and article 4(1); Council Regulation (EU) 1096/2010 of 17 November 2010 Conferring Specific Tasks Upon the ECB Concerning the Functioning of the ESRB L331/163, article 2.

The members of the General Board with voting rights are the President and the Vice-President of the ECB; the Governors of the national central banks of the Member States but Member States in which the national central bank is not a designated authority pursuant to Directive 2013/36/EU (CRD) or Regulation (EU) No 575/2013 (CRR) and in which that designated authority has the leading role in financial stability in its area of competence may alternatively nominate a high-level representative of a designated authority;[142] a representative of the Commission[143] and the Chairpersons of the three ESAs (EBA, EIOPA and ESMA); the Chair and the two Vice-Chairs of the ASC and the Chair of the ATC.[144] The Regulation amending the ESRB Regulation adds the Chair of the Supervisory Board of the ECB and the Chair of the Single Resolution Board as members of the General Board without voting rights.[145]

The General Board also consist of numerous members without voting rights: a high-level representative per Member State of the national supervisory authorities of a national authority entrusted with the conduct of macroprudential policy or of the national central bank; unless the Governor of the national central bank is not a member of the General Board with voting rights in which case a high-level representative of the national central bank will be the member of the General Board without voting rights;[146] the President of the Economic and Financial Committee (EFC) and the Governor of the national central bank of Iceland; the Governor of the national central bank of Norway; a high-level representative of the Ministry of Finance of Liechtenstein; a high-level representative of the competent national supervisory authority of the above-mentioned European Free Trade Association (EFTA) States; a college member of the EFTA Surveillance Authority may participate in meetings of the General Board, whenever relevant to its tasks.

---

[142] Article 6(1)(b) ESRB Regulation, as amended. Directive 2013/36/EU of 26 June 2013 on Access to the Activity of Credit Institutions and the Prudential Supervision of Credit Institutions and Investment Firms OJ L 176 p 338 and Regulation (EU) No 575/2013 of 26 June 2013 on Prudential Requirements for Credit Institutions and Investment Firms OJ L 176 p 1.

The Regulation amending the ESRB Regulation, paragraph 9 Preamble explains that this change is "In order to provide for flexibility as regards the selection of the member of the General Board with voting rights" and that this flexibility "does not affect Member States where the national central bank is a designated authority pursuant to Directive 2013/36/EU or Regulation (EU) No 575/2013." It also clarifies that "In order to avoid political influence, no member of the General Board should have a function in the central government of a Member State". Article 7(b) ESRB Regulation, as amended.

[143] The Regulation amending the ESRB Regulation replacing it from 'one member of the European Commission'.

[144] Article 6(1) ESRB Regulation, as amended.

[145] Article 6(2)(c) and (d) ESRB Regulation, as amended.

[146] Article 6(2)(a) ESRB Regulation, as amended. The high-level representatives will rotate depending on the item discussed, unless the national authorities of a particular Member State have agreed on a common representative (article 6(3) ESRB Regulation, as amended.

Three observations can be made here with regard to the governance of the ESRB.

First, the ESRB General Board is a very large body that consists of more than 60 members comprising a broad set of institutions including central banks, supervisors, supranational institutions and academic advisors.[147] With such a large body there were doubts as to its ability to make effective[148] and swift decisions.[149] Nonetheless, the size of the ESRB appears to fit the cross-country and cross-sectoral needs of the macroprudential framework in the EU and proved "to be a major strength, as it has made the ESRB a platform on which to foster dialogue, benchmarking and mutual learning, as well as to build trust among institutions."[150]

Second, the governance of the ESRB is characterised by the dominance of central banks[151] and has been subject to vociferous criticism,[152] suggesting that it may contribute to conflicting objectives and result in a banking bias.[153] Overall, however, this structure remains a favourable model for the conduct of macroprudential policy in the EU.[154] The idea of having a full-time managing

---

[147] Commission Staff Working Document Effect Analysis Accompanying the document Proposal for a Regulation of the European Parliament and the Council amending Regulation (EU) No 1092/2010 on European Union macro-prudential oversight of the financial system and establishing a European Systemic Risk Board SWD (2017) 313 final, 5.

[148] The Treasury Committee's Opinion on Proposals for European Financial Supervision, The European Systemic Risk Board, November 2009, para 39: "Buiter described the total membership as 'enough to run a small football league' and concluded that with such a large membership this was not 'a body that will do anything useful.'"

[149] Commission Staff Working Paper (2017) (n 147), 6 though pointing out that, to date, it has not been a major impediment.

[150] Commission Staff Working Paper (2017) (n 147), 5; Commission Proposal for Regulation amending the ESRB Regulation of 20 September 2017 COM/2017/0538 final, preamble para 3.

[151] Article 10(3) ESRB Regulation; M Goldby and A Keller, "Oversight of Systemically Relevant Insurance Practices within the EU: The role of Macro-prudential Supervision" in A Georgosouli and M Goldby (eds), *Systemic Risk and the Future of Insurance Regulation* (Informa, 2015).

[152] Professor Buiter described the ESRB as being "ludicrously lopsided in favour of central banks in general and of the ECB in particular". He argued that it was difficult to see why central banks should be given such a prominent role given that "the ECB, the Eurosystem NCBs and the rest of the EU NCBs have not exactly covered themselves with glory in the area of macro-prudential supervision and regulation during the past decade". Treasury Committee's Opinion (n 146), para 35.

[153] Commission Staff Working Paper (2017) (n 147), 7; Commission Staff Working Document Accompanying the Report to the European Parliament and the Council on the mission and organisation of the European Systemic Risk Board (ESRB) SWD (2014) 260 final, 14–15. See also Goldby and Keller (2015) (n 151).

[154] See, for instance, Summary of Responses to the European Commission Consultation on the Proposed Review of the EU Macro-prudential Framework that closed on the 24 October 2019, 19 highlighting that "most respondents believed that central banks should continue to play key role."

director to enhance visibility and autonomy of the ESRB did not find its way to the Regulation amending the ESRB Regulation.[155] Instead, the suggested mechanisms that can loosen the ties between the ECB and the ESRB are rather modest. The ECB is required to consider systematically opening the selection procedure of the ESRB Head of Secretariat to external candidates.[156] In addition, Member States will have a choice for their voting representative in the ESRB General Board between the Governor of the national central bank and a high-level representative of a designated authority according to CRD or CRR where it has the leading role in financial stability in its area of competence.[157] Finally, in the Steering Committee the requirement for its four members of the General Board also to be members of the General Council of the ECB is replaced with a requirement for these members to be members of the General Board with voting rights.[158]

Third, it is to be noted that compared to the ties with the ECB, the fiscal ties within the ESRB's governance are looser and includes the President of the EFC as a non-voting member of the ESRB General Board; a representative of the EFC in the ATC and the President of the EFC as a member of the Steering Committee. The structure of the ESRB is in many respects closer to the FPC model as it forms an arms-length relationship between macroprudential and fiscal policies whilst still enabling coordination and exchange of information. These issues will be discussed in length in Chapter 8.

8. CONCLUSION

It may be too early to detect a *sine qua non* of good institutional structure in macroprudential regimes, particularly considering the dearth of empirical research and experience. A tailored approach that recognises country-specific factors is thus warranted. Accordingly, the focus of this chapter was on exploring trade-offs associated with different structures and identifying "clear messages"[159] about the optimal institutional design and decision-making process in the macroprudential sphere. Moreover, a full picture of deliberations and their

---

[155] Report from the Commission to the European Parliament and the Council on the Mission and Organisation of ESRB COM (2014) 508 final, 8.

[156] Regulation Amending the ESRB Regulation, Preamble 11. According to article 3(2) ECB Regulation, the head of the ESRB Secretariat is to be appointed by the ECB, in consultation with the General Board.

[157] Ibid, para 4; article 6(1)(b) ESRB Regulation, as amended.

[158] Ibid, para 8; article 11(1)(c) ESRB Regulation, as amended.

[159] This term was used by R Reis, "Central Bank Design" (2013) NBER Working Paper 19187, available at <http://www.nber.org/papers/w19187> to describe his attempt to establish a design for a central bank in the US.

nature is hard to attain given limits on disclosure of market-sensitive data and strict confidentiality rules in the macroprudential policy domain. Whilst these restrictions remove any concerns of inhibiting free flow of views, they make it all the more difficult to subject the macroprudential decision-making process to scrutiny.

Despite these challenges, the chapter lays out the foundations for future research and presents key aspects of the decision-making process as powerful mechanisms for improving the effectiveness of macroprudential policy. It suggests that heterogeneity in the governance of the macroprudential authority which brings in a diversity of views and perspectives (sectoral, national, supervisory, industry and market) is a necessary but not a sufficient ingredient in the governance of macroprudential policymakers. In the popular committee structure for macroprudential policymaking, the nature of deliberation and the transparency of dissenting views, the decision rule, the role of the chair and the inclusiveness of external stakeholders in the decision-making process could have a determinative effect on the quality of policy decisions.

Still, this structure comes in a variety of forms. The role of central banks in the institutional structure of macroprudential authorities and the degree of their dominance; the involvement of fiscal authorities and the inclusion of external experts may entail advantages of pooling of opinions, informational synergies and coordination but may also affect the degree of autonomy and independence of the macroprudential authority and its incentives to act in a timely manner.

CHAPTER 4

POWERS OF MACROPRUDENTIAL
AUTHORITIES AND THE USE
OF SOFT LAW

This chapter explores the nature of powers vested in macroprudential authorities and suggests a benchmark to assessing their effectiveness in achieving a macroprudential mandate. It does so by drawing on the literature on hard and soft law in the international governance field and in particular, the legalisation theory.

Two key observations emerge from the analysis. The first is that macroprudential authorities should have powers that are adaptable to ensure that the regulatory and supervisory perimeter and the set of macroprudential tools can, where necessary, be adjusted and expanded and that data gaps can be addressed. Second, while the "comply-or-explain" can provide a reinforcement mechanism to soft powers in the macroprudential sphere, its effectiveness largely depends on the institutional setting supporting it. Third, the precision of macroprudential authorities' outputs alongside a formal and clear decision-making process and pre-established procedures can harden the legal nature of soft macroprudential powers. Furthermore, legitimacy has a key role to play in enhancing compliance with macroprudential measures.

The chapter is organised as follows. Section 1 examines the types of powers that macroprudential policy requires and the current state of powers in macroprudential frameworks around the globe. Section 2 outlines the supervisory powers of the FPC, the FSOC and the ESRB. Section 3 draws on theories developed in international law to conceptualise the legal nature of macroprudential powers and explores legitimacy as a key factor in enhancing compliance and implementation in the macroprudential setting. Section 4 takes the ESRB powers as a case study and analyses the nature of its powers through the prism of the legalisation theory. It analyses the various legal mechanisms that were put in place to reinforce the effectiveness of the ESRB soft powers and the role they play in "hardening" these powers. Section 5 concedes that there are limitations to what can be achieved through softer macroprudential supervisory powers; the weaknesses of the "comply-or-explain" mechanism and regulatory turf wars are provided as examples for prominent (and far from being theoretical) hurdles.

In the absence of a "standalone" international best practice of macroprudential conduct, Section 6 offers a benchmark to assessing the effectiveness of soft/ semi-soft powers. Section 7 then highlights the importance of ensuring the adaptability of the macroprudential legal framework, through empowering the macroprudential authority to request expansion of the regulatory perimeter and through flexibility in times of emergency, when procedures can become an impediment to the delivery of a swift response and expediated action. Section 8 concludes.

1. PRIMARY POWERS OF MACROPRUDENTIAL AUTHORITIES

In general terms, macroprudential authorities should have the power to: (1) obtain information from other authorities and where necessary, fill in any data gaps (information powers); (2) activate or influence the activation and calibration of a range of macroprudential tools that can address the main sources of systemic risks (calibration powers); (3) determine or influence the designation of individual institutions as systemically important (designation powers); and (4) initiate any legislative changes to the regulatory perimeter, reporting perimeter or other deficiencies in supervisory powers needed to achieve the macroprudential mandate.[1]

The "strength" of these powers vary greatly across jurisdictions and may range from: (1) hard powers that provide macroprudential authorities with a direct control over a set of macroprudential tools or the ability to direct other regulatory authorities; (2) semi-soft powers that enable the macroprudential authority to issue warnings, recommendations or opinions to other authorities supported by reinforcing mechanisms such as the "comply-or-explain"; or (3) soft powers that are not supported by any reinforcing mechanisms.[2]

---

[1]   These powers should expand to non-bank institutions and other financial infrastructure providers such as central counterparties. IMF, "Macroprudential Policy: An Organizing Framework" 2011, 39; CGFS, "Operationalising the Selection and Application of Macroprudential Instruments" (2012) CGFS Papers No 48, available at <https://www.bis.org/publ/cgfs48.pdf>, 42; IMF-FSB-BIS, "Elements of Effective Macroprudential Policies Lessons from International Experience" (2016), available at <https://www.imf.org/external/np/g20/pdf/2016/083116.pdf>, 7.

[2]   On the categorisation of macroprudential powers as soft, hard and semi-hard see IMF, "Key Aspects of Macroprudential Policy" (2013), available at <https://www.imf.org/external/np/pp/eng/2013/061013b.pdf>, 28–27; G Napoletano, "Legal Aspect of Macro-prudential Policy in the United States and in the EU" (2014) Banca D'Italia Legal Aspects Papers 76.
   In the international context see C Menkel-Meadow, "Why and How to Study 'Transnational' Law'" (2011) 1(1) UC Irvine Law Review 97.

Macroprudential frameworks may include a mix of these powers, as is the case in the UK, where the FPC is empowered with soft, semi-soft and hard powers.

The IMF's Annual Macroprudential Policy 2018 Survey of 111 jurisdictions suggests that the strength of the powers assigned to the macroprudential authority depends, to some extent, on the institutional set-up.[3] As such, where the macroprudential mandate resides with the central bank or a committee within a central bank, it is more likely to have hard powers but a committee outside the central bank is more likely to have soft powers or semi-soft powers.[4] Furthermore, recent empirical evidence suggests that, where the macroprudential mandate resides with a macroprudential committee, powers are more likely to be soft (rather than hard or semi-soft) or arguably, have an even softer power that solely entails an information sharing.[5]

Soft powers mean that action can be undertaken quickly and efficiently.[6] The flexibility of soft powers also means that there is an opportunity for supervisory authorities and addressees to learn about the impact of policy choices over time and adapt it accordingly.[7] This fits in well in the macroprudential sphere and allows for a process of "learning by experience" to take place and adapt macroprudential policymaking when new information emerges or new challenges to financial stability arise (Chapter 9). In addition, soft law is "not coercive; instead, it is an expression of cooperation",[8] matching well the dynamic nature of the macroprudential mandate (Chapter 2) and the need to facilitate coordination with other policy areas (Chapter 8).

---

[3]   IMF, "Annual Macroprudential Policy Survey 2018 Objectives, Design, and Country Responses", available at <https://www.imf.org/en/Publications/Policy-Papers/Issues/2018/04/30/pp043018-imf-annual-macroprudential-policy-survey>, 5.

[4]   Ibid. The existence of hard powers was reported by 80 jurisdictions, where hard powers were assigned to a total of 91 bodies (committees or agencies). In 66 of these cases hard powers rested with the central bank of a committee within the central bank, while only five cases a committee outside the central bank was assigned hard powers. 31 jurisdictions reported semi-hard powers, of which just over a third (11) were reported by jurisdictions that indicated that the macroprudential authority was vested in a committee outside the central bank. Soft powers were reported by over a quarter of the respondents (39 and vested in 42 authorities), but these jurisdictions reported hard powers too.

[5]   Reviewing 58 countries, only 11 of the 41 countries with a macroprudential committee have hard or semi-soft powers to direct countercyclical measures. R Edge and N Liang, "New Financial Stability Structures and Central Banks" (2017) Hutchins Center Working Paper No 32, 12.
      See also BIS, "Moving Forward with Macroprudential Frameworks" (2018) BIS Annual Economic Report 63, 71.

[6]   KW Abbott and D Snidal, "Hard and Soft Law in International Governance" (2000) 54 International Organisation 421; C Lipson, "Why Are Some International Agreements Informal?" (1991) 45 International Organization 495.

[7]   Abbott and Snidal (2000) (n 6), 412.

[8]   C Brummer, *Soft Law and Global Financial System* (Cambridge University Press, 2015), 128.

Under closer inspection, however, these comparative advantages of soft powers are met with potential risks. Such is the risk that policy outcomes will not commensurate with policy needs and financial instability concerns. Decoupling the macroprudential mandate from a hard authority to implement macroprudential policy resembles, in many respects, the ineffectiveness of financial stability reports prior to the 2007–2009 global financial crisis.[9] The ability to foresee risks to financial stability absent the power to link it to a timely supervisory policy action may result in modest gains in terms of financial stability outcomes.[10] It is therefore not surprising that the IMF observed that "soft powers alone are unlikely to be sufficient to ensure the effectiveness of the overall policy framework."[11]

On the other end of the spectrum, hard powers "avoid delay and other frictions that may arise when implementation relies on other policymakers."[12] Indeed, most macroprudential authorities have some hard powers.[13] Hard powers require strong accountability mechanisms, whatever the institutional structure is. As shall be seen in Chapter 7, where central banks have a key role in the macroprudential authority, legitimacy is a key concern and therefore, hard powers should be strengthened by a clear transparency strategy and solid accountability mechanisms.[14] Similarly, where the Treasury has a prominent role in macroprudential policymaking (for instance, through chairing the macroprudential committee, framing its remit or deciding on expanding macroprudential tools), independence and succumbing to political pressures become a concern and any hard powers should be supported by a due process to making macroprudential decisions and scrutinising them.

Lastly, "middle ground" powers or semi-soft powers and their reinforcing mechanisms present the most intriguing questions as to their legal nature and effectiveness in achieving the macroprudential mandate. These powers will be the focus of this chapter.[15]

---

[9]   Ibid, 13; J Christensson, K Spong and J Wilkinson, "What Can Financial Stability Reports Tell Us About Macroprudential Supervision?" (2011) The Federal Reserve Bank of Kansas City Research Working Papers 11.

[10] Brummer (2015) (n 8), 13. Though pointing out that soft powers "may be useful to extend the influence of macroprudential policymakers beyond prudential tools or the existing regulatory perimeter."

[11] IMF (2013) (n 2), 28.

[12] IMF, FSB and BIS (2016) (n 1), 8.

[13] IMF, "Regulatory Reform 10 Years After the Global Financial Crisis: Looking Back, Looking Forward", Chapter 2 in IMF Global Financial Stability Report – A Decade After the Global Financial Crisis: Are We Safer?, October 2018, 55, 71.

[14] Questionnaire to Alex Brazier, Executive Director for Financial Stability Strategy and Risk, Bank of England, available at <https://www.bankofengland.co.uk/-/media/boe/files/about/people/alex-brazier/alex-brazier-questionnaire-2018>.

[15] Data collection powers will be discussed in Chapter 9.

2. THE FPC, THE FSOC AND THE ESRB'S SUPERVISORY POWERS

2.1. SUPERVISORY POWERS OF THE FPC: DIRECTIONS AND RECOMMENDATIONS

The FPC has a full range of supervisory powers: hard, soft and semi-soft.[16]

First, the FPC is empowered to issue a direction addressed to the regulators (PRA and/or FCA) to exercise their powers to ensure implementation of a macroprudential policy measure described in the direction (hard powers).[17] The "macroprudential measures" that are within the FPC's power of direction are measures prescribed by the Treasury by order and approved by Parliament.[18] To date, HM Treasury has given the FPC power of direction over an impressive list of tools: a countercyclical capital buffer rate, sectoral capital requirements, a leverage ratio requirement, loan-to-value and debt-to-income limits on owner-occupied properties and buy-to-let properties.[19] Following the issuance of a direction, the PRA and/or FCA are required to comply with an FPC's direction as soon as reasonably practicable[20] and give the FPC one or more reports on how it is complying or has complied with the direction.[21]

Second, the FPC has the power to issue recommendations (soft powers) to: (1) the Bank of England (for instance, in relation to the provision of liquidity to financial institutions or its oversight of payments systems, settlement systems and clearing houses);[22] (2) HM Treasury (including changes to the scope of regulated activities, the allocation of regulated activities between the PRA and FCA or additional or revised power of direction);[23] and, more broadly,

---

[16]   Section 9G BEA 1998.

[17]   Section 9H BEA 1998.

[18]   Sections 9L and 9N BEA 1998. An order under section 9L may be made without a draft if the order contains a statement that the Treasury are of the opinion that, by reason of urgency, it is necessary to make the order without a draft being so laid and approved. Section 9N(2) BEA 1998.
See also section 9M BEA 1998 requiring the FPC in relation to each macroprudential measure prescribed under section 9L to prepare and maintain a written statement of the general policy that it proposes to follow in relation to the exercise of its power of direction under section 9H so far as it relates to that measure.

[19]   The direction may relate to all regulated persons or to regulated persons of a specified description, but may not relate to a specified regulated person (section 9H(4) BEA 1998) and may not require the regulator to do anything that it has no power to do (section 9H(8) BEA 1998); The direction may not require its provisions to be implemented by specified means or within a specified period but may include recommendations as to the means to be used and the timing of implementation (section 9H(6) BEA 1998)and these may include a requirement to comply or explain (section 9H(7) BEA 1998).

[20]   Section 9I(1) BEA 1998 but see section 9I(1A)–(2) BEA 1998.

[21]   Section 9(I)(3) BEA 1998.

[22]   Section 9O BEA 1998.

[23]   Section 9P BEA 1998.

(3) other persons.[24] The latter allows the FPC to make recommendations, for instance, directly to the industry or to independent bodies such as the Financial Reporting Council.[25]

Third, the FPC has the power to issue recommendations to the FCA and/or PRA about the exercise of their respective functions.[26] Recommendations to the FCA and PRA are unique as they are subject to the "comply or explain" mechanism and are therefore of a semi-soft nature.[27]

The FPC's power to give direction to the FCA or PRA as well as power to make recommendation within the Bank of England relating to the exercise of its functions in relation to payment systems, settlement systems, clearing houses and central securities depositories; to the Treasury and to the PRA and/or FCA[28] are subject to a procedural explanation requirement.[29] The FPC is required to give reasons for exercising the power and for believing the exercise of the power is compatible with its objectives and matters to which it is to have regard.[30] In discharging this requirement, the FPC is required to "set out publicly how its actions are assessed to contribute to its objectives, including its judgement as to the balance of risks to those objectives, how those risks are judged to have evolved and how they are expected to evolve."[31] The explanation must include an estimate of the costs and benefits that would arise from compliance with the direction or recommendation, unless the FPC considers that it is not reasonably practicable to do so.[32]

2.2. SUPERVISORY POWERS OF THE FSOC: DESIGNATION, RECOMMENDATIONS AND RESOLVING DISPUTES

The FSOC's hard power to designate a nonbank financial company as a systemically important financial institution under section 113 of the Dodd-Frank

---

[24]   Section 9R BEA 1998.
[25]   The Financial Policy Committee's Housing Market Tools October 2014, available at <https://assets.publishing.service.gov.uk/government/uploads/system/uploads/attachment_data/file/368614/FPC_Housing_Consultation.pdf>, para 2.13.
[26]   Section 9Q(1) BEA 1998. The recommendations may relate to all regulated persons or to regulated persons of a specified description, but they may not relate to the exercise of the functions of the FCA or the PRA in relation to a specified regulated person. See section 9Q(2) BEA 1998.
[27]   Section 9Q(3) BEA 1998.
[28]   Section 9S(2) BEA 1998.
[29]   Section 9S(1) BEA 1998.
[30]   Ibid.
[31]   HM Treasury, Remit and Recommendations for the FPC, 29 October 2018, available at <https://www.bankofengland.co.uk/-/media/boe/files/letter/2018/chancellor-letter-291018-fpc.pdf>.
[32]   Section 9S(3) BEA 1998. According to section 9W(5) BEA 1998, the explanation must be published in the next financial stability report published by the Bank of England.

Act and thus, subject it to the supervision of the Federal Reserve and enhanced prudential standards will be discussed in length in Chapter 5.[33]

The FSOC is also armoured with semi-soft powers and under section 120 of the Dodd-Frank Act can issue non-binding recommendations to the primary federal regulatory agencies to apply new or heightened standards and safeguards under their respective jurisdictions for a financial activity or practice conducted by bank holding companies or non-bank financial companies.[34] The FSOC will use its recommendation power when an "activity or practice could create or increase the risk of significant liquidity, credit, or other problems spreading among bank holding companies and nonbank financial companies, financial markets of the United States, or low-income, minority, or underserved communities".[35] The relevant primary regulatory agency is then required to comply with the recommendation (and thus impose the recommended standards or similar standards approved by the FSOC) or explain to the FSOC, in writing and within 90 days after the recommendation was issued, why it determined not to follow the recommendation.[36]

Before proceeding with a proposed recommendation, there are certain procedural requirements that need to be met in the form of a consultation with the primary financial regulatory agencies and providing the public with notice and opportunity to comment.[37] No legislative mechanism is provided, however, to fast-tracking this period in urgent cases.[38] In addition, recommendations must take costs to long-term economic growth into account and may include prescribing the conduct of the activity or practice in specific ways or prohibiting the activity or practice entirely.[39] When making a proposed recommendation, there is no explicit requirement to provide an explanation,[40] however, in practice, the FSOC provides a detailed explanation.[41]

The FSOC is required to report to Congress on any recommendation, its implementation or failure to implement and where there is no primary regulatory agency that can implement the recommendation, to report on

---

[33] See also the FSOC power to designate Financial Market Utilities under section 804 Dodd Frank Act.

[34] Section 120(a) Dodd-Frank Act.

[35] Ibid.

[36] Section 120(c)(2) Dodd-Frank Act.

[37] Section 120(b)(1) Dodd-Frank Act.

[38] D Kohn, "Institutions for Macroprudential Regulation: The U.K. and the U.S.", Speech at the Kennedy School of Government, Harvard University, Cambridge, Massachusetts, April 2014.

[39] Section 120(b)(2) Dodd Frank Act.

[40] To be differentiated from the designation power that requires the FSOC to provide an explanation of the basis of the proposed determination. Section 113(e)(1) Dodd Frank Act.

[41] For instance, FSOC, Proposed Recommendations for Money Market Mutual Funds Reform, 77 FR 69455 (19 November 2012) provided a detailed explanation on the use of its power and applied the systemic criteria set in its mandate to the MMF's sector (including, size, scale, concentration and interconnectedness).

recommendations for legislation that would prevent such activities or practices from threatening the stability of the financial system of the US.[42] This may result in the relevant agency being called before Congress to explain its position. If this threat is insufficient to force individual agencies to comply with FSOC's recommendations, then the FSOC can trigger its designation authority thus shifting the supervision of a US non-bank financial company to the Federal Reserve.[43] The substantive narrowing of the scope of the designation authority (Chapter 5) means, however, that deterrence through the FSOC's hard powers has become limited.

In addition, the FSOC has soft-power to resolve supervisory jurisdictional disputes amongst its member agencies.[44] Where the FSOC determines that the disputing agencies cannot, after a demonstrated good faith effort, resolve the dispute and a member agency requests in writing, after providing notice to all other disputants, the intervention of the FSOC and provides notice to the other agencies,[45] the FSOC must issue a non-binding[46] recommendation in writing supported by reasons and approved by an affirmative vote of 2/3 of the voting members of the FSOC.[47] To date, no member agency has approached the FSOC to resolve a dispute under this authority.[48]

2.3. SUPERVISORY POWERS OF THE ESRB: WARNINGS, RECOMMENDATIONS AND OPINIONS

The ESRB was described as a "reputational body with a high level composition that should influence the actions of policymakers and supervisors by means of its moral authority".[49] To this end, article 16(1) of the ESRB Regulation empowers the ESRB to issue warnings when significant risks to the achievement of its objective, as set out in article 3(1), are identified and where appropriate, issue recommendations for a remedial action.[50] The warnings or recommendations

---

42 Section 120(d) Dodd-Frank Act.
43 Section 113 Dodd-Frank Act.
44 Section 119(a)(1) Dodd-Frank Act.
45 Section 119(a)(2)–(3) Dodd-Frank Act.
46 Section 119(d) Dodd-Frank Act.
47 Section 119(c) Dodd-Frank Act.
48 FSOC Annual Report 2017, available at <https://www.treasury.gov/initiatives/fsoc/studies-reports/Documents/FSOC_2017_Annual_Report.pdf>, 122.
49 Commission Proposal for a Regulation on Community Macro-prudential Oversight of the Financial System and Establishing a ESRB of 25 September 2009 COM (2009) 499 final, Explanatory Memorandum, 6.2.
50 There are no legal requirements in the ESRB Regulation to guide the ESRB in choosing whether to issue warnings or recommendations. It could be suggested that warnings are more suitable where a systemic risk emerges but as yet does not pose an immediate or concrete threat to the stability of the financial system. Furthermore, warnings can precede

do not apply in relation to individual financial institutions and the non-exhaustive list of addressees in article 16(2) of the ESRB Regulation, as amended, include, in particular, the Union or one or more Member States, one or more of the ESAs, or one or more of the national supervisory authorities, one or more national authorities designated for the application of measures aimed at addressing systemic or macro-prudential risk, the ECB in relation to supervisory tasks under the Single Supervisory Mechanism,[51] resolution authorities designated by Member States pursuant to Directive 2014/59/EU[52] or the Single Resolution Board (SRB).[53] Where the recommendations are with respect to relevant Union legislation, they can be addressed to the European Commission.[54]

---

a recommendation and highlight an emerging systemic risk, when a recommendation still requires time to formulate.

As part of the ESFS Review in accordance with article 20 of the ESRB Regulation, the European Commission Report to the European Parliament and the Council on the Mission and Organisation of the ESRB COM (2014) 508 final, 11 recommended extending its current toolbox to include other soft powers in the form of letters or statements that will precede warnings or recommendations. This could enhance the preventive role of the ESRB allowing for a more flexible tool to be applied at early stages of systemic risk build-up even before a formal warning or recommendation is initiated. Nonetheless, including other types of soft powers may weaken the ESRB primary tools, warnings and recommendations, and unless a clear framework is established to specify which tool is to be used in which circumstances, it is submitted that widening the net is not advisable.

[51] In accordance with Articles 4(1), 4(2) and 5(2) of Regulation (EU) No 1024/2013 conferring specific tasks on the European Central Bank Concerning Policies relating to the Prudential Supervision of Credit Institutions OJ L 287 p 63.

[52] Directive 2014/59/EU of 15 May 2014 Establishing a Framework for the Recovery and Resolution of Credit Institutions and Investment Firms OJ L 173 p 190.

[53] Article 16(2) ESRB Regulation, as amended. The SRB was established by Regulation (EU) No 806/2014 of 15 July 2014 Establishing Uniform Rules and a Uniform Procedure for the Resolution of Credit Institutions and certain Investment Firms in the Framework of a Single Resolution Mechanism and a Single Resolution Fund OJ L 225 p 1.

The Regulation amending the ESRB Regulation extended the list of addressees. In practice and to reflect the institutional changes since the drafting of the ESRB Regulation, for a while, the ESRB has been directing its recommendations to a broader range of addressees including the ECB (in relation to its supervisory tasks but not monetary) and to the Member States' macroprudential authorities. For instance, Decision of the ESRB of 16 September 2014 on the Extension of certain Deadlines set by Recommendation ESRB/2012/2 on Funding of Credit Institutions (ESRB/2014/4) addressed, inter alia, to national macroprudential authorities; ESRB Follow-up Report on US Dollar Denominated Funding of Credit Institutions (ESRB/2011/2), March 2015 specifically notes that the ECB, as a competent authority, should follow the recommendation.

The ESRB Regulation, Preamble 31 refers to the EU Court of Justice judgment of 2 May 2006 in Case C-217/04 *UK v European Parliament and Council of the EU* that held that "nothing in the wording of ... Article 114 ... TFEU implies that the addressees of the measures adopted by the Community legislature ... can only be the individual Member States ...".

[54] ESRB Regulation, article 16(2). In the Commission Staff Working Document Accompanying the Report on the ESRB Mission and Organisation SWD (2014) 260 final para 2.2.4 many stakeholders expressed a preference to advance the ESRB involvement to the earliest stages of the process.

The ESRB is required to inform the Council of warnings or recommendations prior to their publication sufficiently in advance so that the Council is able to react.[55] In practice, the notification requirement means that there is a delay of around three weeks from the approval of the recommendation by the ESRB General Board until its publication, negatively affecting the timeliness of the ESRB's outputs.[56] Once issued, warnings and recommendations are transmitted, subject to strict rules of confidentiality, to the European Parliament, the Council and the Commission and to the ESAs.[57]

As will be discussed in length below, article 17 of the ESRB Regulation sets out a "comply or explain" mechanism which applies to recommendations (but not warnings) and to the addressees that are listed in article 16(2) of the ESRB Regulation, as amended.[58]

In addition to the warnings and recommendations mandated in the ESRB Regulation, the Capital Requirements Directive (CRD IV)[59] and the Capital Requirements Regulation (CRR)[60] mandate the ESRB to issue opinions in response to the adoption of national macroprudential measures within the EU in defined areas.[61] Member States may also ask the ESRB to issue recommendations to the other Member States requiring reciprocation of their macroprudential policy measures.[62]

Finally, the ESRB also issues, on its own initiative as well as upon request, provides advice from a macroprudential perspective on issues with potential

---

[55]   ESRB Regulation, article 18(1).

[56]   High-Level Group on the ESRB Review (March 2013) <http://www.esrb.europa.eu/pub/pdf/other/130708_highlevelgroupreport.pdf>, 12. The ESRB informs the Council and then votes on its publication again. To address this shortcoming, the High-Level Group on the ESRB Review suggested (p 18) that the ESRB approve and decide on the publication at the same time whilst enabling the Council to react prior to publication within ten days.

[57]   ESRB Regulation, article 16(3), as amended. The Regulation amending the ESRB Regulation added to the list the European Parliament and amended the requirement to inform the ESAs in any case (and not solely when it is addressed to one or more national supervisory authorities).

[58]   ESRB Regulation, article 17(1), as amended.

[59]   Directive 2013/36/EU of the European Parliament and of the Council of 26 June 2013 on Access to the Activity of Credit Institutions and the Prudential Supervision of Credit Institutions and Investment Firms OJ L 176, 27 June 2013, 338–436, article 133.

[60]   Regulation (EU) No 575/2013 of the European Parliament and of the Council of 26 June 2013 on Prudential Requirements for Credit Institutions and Investment Firms and amending Regulation (EU) No 648/2012 (OJ L 176, 27 June 2013, 1), article 458. The opinion should cover the justification of effectiveness and proportionality of the measure, why other instruments in the CRD IV/CRR (alone or in combination) cannot adequately address the systemic risk and the likely impact on the internal market.

[61]   See also article 138 of CRD; Decision of the ESRB of 16 December 2015 on a Coordination Framework for the Notification of National Macroprudential Policy Measures by Relevant Authorities, the Issuing of Opinions and Recommendations by the ESRB, ESRB/2015/4 OJ C 97.

[62]   See Chapter 6, section 3.1.

---

implications for financial stability, including on various draft legislation and consultations, labelling them "responses and letters".[63]

3. THE LEGALISATION THEORY AND ITS APPLICATION IN THE MACROPRUDENTIAL SPHERE

3.1. A CONTINUUM APPROACH TO "SOFT" AND "HARD" LAW

There is a prolific literature on hard and soft law in the international governance field.[64] Many scholars in this field distinguish between two types of law according to a clear binary divide of binding and non-binding.[65] Others, however, completely depart from this dichotomy,[66] and view law as lying on a continuum from "soft" to "hard" with its character being determined across three dimensions:

1. Obligation, or the extent to which a state or other actors are bound by a rule or commitment in the sense that their behaviour thereunder is subject to scrutiny under the general rules, procedures and discourse of international

---

63   Available at <https://www.esrb.europa.eu/mppa/responses/html/index.en.html>.

64   C Chinkin, "The Challenge of Soft Law: Development and Change in International Law" (1989) 38(4) International and Comparative Law Quarterly 850; T Granchalla-Weiesierski, "A Framework for Understanding Soft Law" (1984) 30 McGill L Journal 37.

65   G Shaffer and M Pollack, "Hard vs. Soft Law: Alternatives, Complements and Antagonists in International Governance" (2009) University of Minnesota Legal Studies Research Paper Series 23; M Bothe, "Legal and Non-Legal Norms – A Meaningful Distinction in International Relations?" (1980) 11 Netherlands Yearbook of International Law 65; D Shelton, "Introduction: Law, Non-Law and the Problem of 'Soft Law'" in D Shelton (ed), *Commitment and Compliance: The Role of Non-Binding Norms in International Legal System* (Oxford University Press, 2003), 5; J Klabbers, "The Redundancy of Soft Law" (1996) 65(2) Nordisk Journal of International Law 167.
      A separate question would be whether soft law is law at all: P Weil, "Toward Relative Normatively in International Law" (1983) 77 American Journal of International Law 413; A D'Amato, "International Soft Law, Hard Law and Coherence" (2008) Northwestern Public Research Paper 1 <http://ssrn.com/ abstract= 1103915>.

66   KW Abbott and others, "The Concept of Legalisation" (2000) 54(3) International Organization 17; KW Abbott and D Snidal, "Hard and Soft Law in International Governance" (2000) 54 International Organisation 421.
      See also A Guzman and T Meyer, "International Soft Law" (2010) 2(1) Journal of Law Analysis 171, 173 view soft law on a continuum or spectrum though they are still using the binary divide as "nonbinding rules or instruments that interpret or inform our understanding of binding legal rules or represent promises that in turn create expectations about future conduct" or "nonbinding rules that have legal consequences because they shape states' expectations as to what constitutes compliant behaviour."; in the EU context see E Korkea-Aho, "EU Soft Law in Domestic Legal Systems: Flexibility and Diversity Guaranteed?" (2009) 16 Maastricht Journal of European and Comparative Law 271.

law and often of domestic law as well;[67] in other words, obligation is "the binding requirement of a certain conduct or omission, whatever the circumstances, is formulated by subjects who are vested with the necessary competence and according to pre-established procedures. The addressees of these rules of conduct are informed of their existence and are prepared to acknowledge their authority and they are able and willing to effectively comply with them."[68]

2. Precision, or the extent to which the rules specify clearly and unambiguously what is expected of a state in terms of both the intended objective and the means to achieve it; and

3. Delegation, or the extent to which legal authority has been granted to a third-party decision-maker for implementing broad principles, adjudicating or enforcing the rules and (possibly) making more rules.[69] (hereinafter together: "Abbott's continuum").

Hard law, accordingly, refers to "legally binding obligations that are precise (or can be made precise through adjudication or the issuance of detailed regulations) and that delegate authority for interpreting and implementing the law."[70] However, where one or more of these elements is weakened, soft law is formed.[71] Being on a continuum means that the differences between the various degrees of "hardness" and "softness" of the law can be very subtle.[72] Moreover, while these elements are said to be independent,[73] they are interlinked. For instance, where

---

67 Abbott and others (2000) (n 66), 17.

68 K Wellens and G Borchadt, "Soft law in European Community Law" (1989) European Law Review 267, 280.
    See also O Schachter, "The Twilight Existence of Nonbinding International Agreements" (1977) 71 American Journal of International Law 296.

69 "Delegation means that third parties have been granted authority to implement, interpret, and apply the rules; to resolve disputes; and (possibly) to make further rules". Abbott and others (2000) (n 66), 17.
    For criticism on this framework see L Bélanger and K Fontaine-Skronski, "'Legalization' in International Relations: A conceptual Analysis" (2012) 51 Social Science Information 238.

70 Abbott and Snidal (2000) (n 66), 422 observe that the "realm of 'soft law' begins once legal arrangements are weakened along one or more of the dimensions of obligation, precision, and delegation".

71 Ibid.

72 The difficulty in drawing clear boundaries between the two categories of law has resulted in criticism of this approach. M Finnemore and S Toope, "Alternatives to Legalisation: Richer Views of Law and Politics" (2001) 52 International Organisation 743 suggest that referring to legalisation as a collection of formalised and institutionalised features is misleading. Law, they argue, encompasses much more than largely technical and formal criteria of obligation, precision and delegation, such as features and effects of legitimacy and practices and traditions; P Weil, "Towards Relative Normatively in International Law" (1983) 77 American Journal of International Law 413.

73 Abbott and others (n 66), 404.

soft law rules are more precise and specific, the expectations accordingly are more clearly defined and tend to be more obliging for the addressee.[74]

The non-binary theory of legalisation has been commonly invoked to analyse international soft law principles. Similarly, EU soft law is generally referred to as rules of conduct that are laid down in instruments, which have not been given a legally binding force as such, but nevertheless may have certain (indirect) legal effects, and that are aimed at and may produce practical effects.[75] The scholarly definition, accordingly, outlines three core elements of soft law in the EU: it is concerned with rules of conduct or commitments; there is an agreement on the fact that these rules or commitments are laid down in instruments which have no legally binding force as such, but are nonetheless not devoid of all legal effect and finally, they aim at or may lead to some practical effect or impact on behaviour. Therefore, similarly to the non-binary approach in international governance, the view of soft law in the EU context sees it as an umbrella concept which encompasses a huge variety of different instruments with different characteristics and fulfilling different functions.[76]

The flexible characteristic of soft law is suitable to the nature of macroprudential policy. It allows for a policy area that may be politically sensitive to develop in a cooperative manner,[77] emphasising exchange of information between macroprudential authorities and other policy setters and utilising a wide range of expertise. Nonetheless, given the potential unpopularity of macroprudential measures, the inherent tension between financial stability and economic growth as well as the potential trade-offs with other policy areas, it is not surprising that macroprudential powers are often located somewhere along the Abbott's continuum, between soft and hard law. This can be achieved through a variety of reinforcing mechanisms that strengthen the three elements of legalisation.

---

[74] "International Soft Law and the Formation of Binding International Financial Regulation", Chapter 4 in A Kern, R Dhumale and J Eatwell (eds), *Global Governance of Financial Systems-The international Regulation of Systemic Risk* (Oxford University Press, 2005), 140.

[75] F Snyder, "Soft Law and Institutional Practice in the European Community" in S Martin (ed), *The Construction of Europe: Essays in Honour of Emile Noël* (Kluwer Academic Publishers, 1994), 198. This definition was referred to in the European Parliament Resolution of 4 September 2007 on Institutional and Legal Implication of the Use of "Soft Law" Instrument (2007/2028 (INI)), para K.

See also M Giovanoli, "Reflections on International Financial Standards as Soft Law" *Essays in International Financial and Economic Law* No 37 (London Institute of International Banking, Finance and Development, 2002); F Snyder, "The Effectiveness of European Community Law: Institutions, Processes, Tools and Techniques" (1993) 56(1) Modern Law Review 19.

[76] L Senden, "Soft Law, Self-Regulation and Co-Regulation in European Law: Where Do They Meet?" (2005) 9(1) Electronic Journal of Comparative Law 22, para 4.2.

[77] This may also be the case when analysing macroprudential policy from an international perspective. See Kern, Dhumble and Eatwell (2006) (n 74), 134 who examine international financial regulation along the Abbott's continuum. Note that the authors refer to sanctions as the fourth element, but it is to be noted that this element is explicitly excluded from the legalisation theory and should therefore be considered separately.

3.2. THE ROLE OF LEGITIMACY IN ENHANCING COMPLIANCE WITH SOFT LAW

The legalisation theory conceptualised hard and soft law in terms of the key characteristics of rules and procedures as opposed to their effects.[78] For instance, it includes delegation of legal authority as an element on the Abbott's continuum, but leaves out the degree to which rules are actually implemented domestically or whether states comply with them. Although the issue of compliance with soft law is distinct from its legal nature, it is, nevertheless, the soft law's Achilles Heel and is vital for the assessment of the effectiveness of soft-law powers in achieving the macroprudential mandate.

Theories in international law can be helpful, once again, in conceptualising compliance with the powers of macroprudential authorities. The high-level of compliance with international law has been explained, inter alia, by the legitimacy of rules.[79] According to the legitimacy theory, states obey rules because they see these rules and their institutional framework as possessing a high degree of legitimacy. Legitimacy is defined as "a property of a rule or rule-making institution that in itself exerts a pull towards compliance on those addressed normatively because those addressed believe that the rule or institution has come into being and operates in accordance with generally accepted principles of right process".[80] The "compliance pull" is powered by the quality of the rule

---

[78]   Abbott and others (2000) (n 66). Compliance is defined as a state of conformity or identity between an actor's behaviour and a specified rule. K Raustiala and A Slaughter, "International Law, International Relations and Compliance" in *Handbook of International Relations*, Chapter 28, 538. Compliance is distinct from but closely related to effectiveness and implementation (the process of putting international commitments into practice: the passage of legislation, creation of institutions and enforcement of rules). For the flow of the discussion, compliance thereafter will include implementation as well.

[79]   T Franck, *The Power of Legitimacy Among Nations* (Oxford University Press, 1990). Other scholars assess the qualities of soft and hard law according to effectiveness and legitimacy criteria (S Karlsson and A Vihama, "Comparing the Legitimacy and Effectiveness of Global Hard and Soft Law: An Analytical Framework" (2009) 3(4) Regulation and Governance. It is suggested here that legitimacy and effectiveness are intertwined: legitimacy enhances compliance and thus advances the effectiveness of the law. D Levi-Faur (ed), *Handbook on the Politics of Regulation* (Edward Edgar, 2011), 611.
For a comprehensive account of criticism of the legitimacy theory see HH Koh, "Why Do Nations Obey International Law?" (1997) Yale Faculty Scholarship Series 2101, available at <https://digitalcommons.law.yale.edu/fss_papers/2101>.

[80]   T Franck, *Fairness in International Law and Institutions* (Oxford University Press, 1995), 24. See also A Guzman, "A Compliance-Based Theory of International Law" (2002) 90 California Law Review 1823; I Hurd, "Legitimacy and Authority in International Politics" (1999) 53 International Organisation 379; Franck (1990) (n 79), 24–26.
In fact, legitimacy distinguishes soft law as law: C Kelly, "The Hardening of Soft Law in Securities Regulation" (2009) 34(3) Brooklyn Journal of International Law 883, 932;

or the rule-making institution and not by coercive authority.[81] For a rule to promote compliance, it needs to come into existence and to be accepted by the formal institutions or procedures required for its existence to be acknowledged. Legitimacy that originates from the procedural quality of the law-making process is, therefore, an important factor in achieving such an acceptance.

These concepts, though tailored to international law theories, are helpful in conceptualising compliance with macroprudential authorities' soft/semi-soft powers. Similar to other international institutions that use soft methods, the strength of the legitimacy of the macroprudential authority enhances the "compliance pull" of its outputs on the addressees.

What form of legitimacy should be at the centre of macroprudential regimes? Chapter 7 will suggest that in the macroprudential sphere, legitimacy should primarily derive from the decision-making process and understood as throughput legitimacy. This means a continuous legitimisation of the supervisory decision-making process across all its stages, beginning with data collection, analysis and ending with issuance of warnings and recommendations and their follow-up.

Overall, legitimacy, alongside mechanisms that reinforce the legalisation elements on the Abbott's continuum and harden the soft nature of powers, can enhance the willingness of the addressees to cooperate and comply with macroprudential authorities' outputs. This process, however, as will be discussed in Section 4, may be fraught with institutional turfs and other legal limitations.

4. THE NATURE OF MACROPRUDENTIAL SEMI-SOFT POWERS: THE CASE OF THE ESRB'S WARNINGS AND RECOMMENDATIONS

This section takes the ESRB's power to issue warning and recommendations as a case study and, based on its institutional setting, positions it on the Abbott's continuum of "soft" and "hard" law.

J Pauwelyn and others, "Informal International Lawmaking: An Assessment and Template to Keep It Both Effective and Accountable" in Pauwelyn and others (eds), *Informal International Lawmaking* (Oxford University Press, 2012), 509.

[81] Franck (1990) (n 79), 26. The four factors that determine whether a state complies with these international rules are determinacy (clarity of the rule or norm or transparency), symbolic validation (authority approval), coherence (consistency or general application) and adherence (falling within an organised hierarchy of rules). Where all of these are present, the theory predicts strong pressure towards compliance.

4.1. THE ESRB'S WARNINGS AND RECOMMENDATIONS ARE HARDENED ALONG THE "OBLIGATION ELEMENT"

The ESRB Rules of Procedure include an explicit negation of intent for the warnings and recommendations to be legally binding on the addressees.[82] Thus, on the face of it, the ESRB's outputs are positioned on the "soft" end of the spectrum.[83] Nevertheless, there are numerous considerations that suggest that they are not purely soft but rather have a hybrid or semi-soft nature. Not all the ESRB public recommendations to date use hortatory language and they cannot be said to be regarded solely as preferences changes.[84] Moreover, several mechanisms in the ESRB Regulation are designed to "harden" the "obligation element" of the warnings and recommendations.

To begin with, the ESRB General Board has the power to decide on a case-by-case basis, with a simple majority and a quorum of two-thirds, to make a warning or recommendation public thus creating a reputational incentive that strengthens the obligation element.[85]

Where the recommendation (but not warning) is addressed to the addressees listed in article 16(2) of the ESRB Regulation, the ESRB Regulation sets out a "comply or explain" mechanism to be followed.[86] The ESRB must set defined time limits for the required policy response.[87] The addressee of the recommendation

---

[82]   Decision of the ESRB of 20 January 2011 adopting the Rules of Procedure of the European Systemic Risk Board (ESRB/2011/1) OJ C 58/4, 27.

[83]   Abbott and others (2000) (n 66), 410. Being a soft law institution allows the ESRB to "work around" the strict limits on the powers that can be delegated to regulatory agencies in the EU legal system. See Commission, "European Governance: A White Paper", COM (2001) 428; Commission, "Communication: European Agencies – The Way Forward", COM (2008) 135 final, 5.

[84]   For instance, in the ESRB Recommendation of 21 March 2016 on Funding of Credit Institutions (ESRB/2016/2) authorities "are requested to deliver"; in contrast, Recommendation on Recognising and Setting Countercyclical Buffer Rates for Exposures to Third Countries (ESRB/2015/1) and Recommendation on the Assessment of Cross-border Effects of and Voluntary Reciprocity for Macroprudential Policy Measures (ESRB/2015/2) addressees or relevant authorities "should"; in Recommendation ESRB of 20 December 2012 on Funding of Credit Institutions (ESRB/2012/2) and Recommendation of the ESRB of 22 December 2011 on US Dollar Denominated Funding of Credit Institutions (ESRB/2011/2) authorities are "recommended to …". ESRB Recommendations of 21 March 2019 amending Recommendation ESRB/2016/14 on closing real estate data gaps (ESRB/2019/3) use national macroprudential authorities "are recommended" and "should".

[85]   ESRB Regulation, article 10 (3).

[86]   ESRB Regulation, article 17, as amended. There are two important points to reiterate: (1) The comply or explain mechanism does not apply to warning. (2) whilst the list of the addressees of warnings and recommendations is not exhaustive (article 16 includes "in particular"), the list of the subjects of the follow-up mechanism is exhaustive (ESRB Regulation, article 17). The Regulation amending the ESRB Regulation expands the list of addressees and brings them within the comply or explain mechanism in article 17 of the ESRB Regulation. See n 53 above.

[87]   ESRB Regulation, article 16(2), as amended though this requirement is not new.

is required to act on them and communicate to the European Parliament, the Council, the Commission and the ESRB the actions undertaken in response to the recommendation or substantiate any inaction.[88]

In addition, the ESRB is tasked with monitoring the follow-up on warnings and recommendations[89] and assessing the actions and justifications reported by the addressees.[90] The ESRB analyses the information provided by the addressee and verifies whether their actions duly achieve the objective of the recommendation.[91] The outcomes of the compliance assessment appear in a compliance report that includes a detailed description of the addressees' implementation of the recommendation, the grading and reasoning, and a colour-coded table with grades.[92] The ESRB then published a "summary compliance report" on its website.[93] Where the addressee has not complied with the recommendation, there is a separate set of criteria for assessing the justification provided for inaction (sufficiently or insufficiently explained).[94] This "name and shame" technique can be a powerful force to compliance. In international law, it is perceived to heighten the potential reputational consequences of non-observance resulting in additional costs for non-complying states, such as diminished influence in shaping standards in the future.[95] Additionally, public shaming can also sharpen

---

[88] ESRB Regulation, article 17(1), as amended. Where relevant, the ESRB is required, subject to strict rules of confidentiality, to inform the ESAs without delay of the answers received.

[89] ESRB Regulation, article 3. The Secretariat monitors the follow up of warnings and recommendations (ESRB Rules of Procedure, article 15(3)(e)) and the General Board assesses and decides whether the "recommendation has not been followed or that the addressees have failed to provide adequate justification for their inaction" (ESRB Rules of Procedure, article 20).

[90] ESRB Rules of Procedure, article 20.

[91] ESRB Secretariat, "Handbook on the Assessment of Compliance with the ESRB Recommendations", April 2016, available at <http://www.esrb.europa.eu/pub/pdf/other/160502_handbook.en.pdf> (Compliance Handbook).

[92] Compliance Handbook, section 4.1.4. The grades include fully compliant; largely compliant; partially compliant; materially non-compliant; and non-compliant.

[93] Compliance Handbook, section 5.2.

[94] Compliance Handbook, section 4.1.1. The previous version of the Compliance Handbook included a more detailed criteria for assessing justification based on the completeness and quality of the explanation provided and the reason for inaction.

[95] Especially in areas of public goods. See AT Guzman, *How International Law Works: A Rational Choice Theory* (New York: Oxford University Press, 2008), 69.
On the Financial Action Task Force and enforcing soft-law anti-money laundering standards, see D Kerwer and R Hülsse, "How International Organisation Rule the World: The Case of the Financial Action Task Force on Money Laundering" (2011) 2(1) Journal of International Organisations Studies 50; A Clunan, "The Fight against Terrorist Financing" (2006) 121(4) 569; C Brummer, "Why Soft Law Dominates International Finance-and not Trade" (2010) 13(3) Journal of International Economic L 623. C Brummer, *Soft Law and the Global Financial System Rule Making in the 21st Century* (Cambridge University Press, 2012), 304.
See also C Giannini, "Promoting Financial Stability in Emerging Market Countries: The Soft-Law Approach and Beyond" (2002) 44(2) Comparative Economic Studies 31 observed that "if the soft law strategy is to have real content 'Name and shame' is probably the best method for doing so."

the market consequences of non-compliance as market actors take cues from regulators' disapproval.[96] The ESRB Hearings before the European Parliament are another platform, where compliance can be advanced and Members States, which are lagging behind in implementing recommendations, can be publicly flagged up.[97]

Where the ESRB considers that its recommendation has not been followed or that the addressees have failed to provide adequate justification for inaction, it will inform the addressees, the European Parliament, the Council and the relevant ESA, subject to strict rules of confidentiality.[98] This means that there is no direct legal sanction for non-compliance or failure to provide adequate justification for non-compliance with the ESRB recommendations. Nevertheless, informing the relevant ESA regarding non-compliance may have a more concrete and stronger impact in strengthening the "obligation element" of the ESRB recommendations. The ESAs are under a specific duty to cooperate closely and on a regular basis with the ESRB.[99] Where a warning or recommendation is addressed to a Member State's competent authority, the ESA is required to use, where relevant, the powers conferred upon it by its founding regulation ensure a timely follow-up.[100] In case the competent authority does not intend to follow the recommendation, it is obliged to discuss the reasons for not acting with the relevant ESA Board of Supervisors.[101]

---

[96]   C Brummer, "Key Theoretical Parameters of the Soft Law Debate: A Basic Overview" in F Weis and A Kammel (eds), *The Changing Landscape of Global Financial Governance and the Role of Soft Law* (Brill, 2015), 151.

[97]   ESRB Regulation, article 19. For instance, during the November 2014 parliamentary hearing, the ESRB's chair took the occasion to flag up Member States that were lagging behind in implementing one of the ESRB public recommendations and publicly suggested that these Member States "step up their game". M Draghi, Introductory Statement Hearing before the ECON, Brussels, 17 November 2014.

[98]   ESRB Regulation, article 17(2), as amended. The results of the assessment may be further communicated to the ECOFIN Council and the Economic and Financial Committee. (Compliance Handbook, section 5.1).

[99]   EBA Regulation, article 36(1). Failure to do so can be considered violation of their EU obligations. E Ferran and K Alexander, "Can Soft Law Bodies be Effective? Systemic Risk Oversight Bodies and the Special Case of the of the European Systemic Risk Board" (2011) University of Cambridge Faculty of Law Research Paper No 36.
         The Regulation amending the ESAs Regulations deleted the requirement in article 36(6) for the ESA to take "utmost account" of warnings and recommendations.

[100]   For instance, EBA Regulation, article 36(5), as amended. See article 36(4) of the EBA Regulation, as amended for the procedure when the recommendation is addressed to the ESA.

[101]   Ibid. The Regulation amending the ESAs Regulations amended article 36(5) and added that: "... Where the competent authority, in accordance with Article 17(1) of Regulation (EU) No 1092/2010, informs the European Parliament, the Council, the Commission and the ESRB of the actions it has undertaken in response to a recommendation of the ESRB, it shall take due account of the views of the Board of Supervisors."

Finally, where a decision of the ESRB on inaction concerns a public recommendation, the European Parliament is entitled to invite the Chair of the ESRB to present that decision and the addressee is entitled to request to participate in the exchange of views.[102]

Overall, the ESRB recommendations (but to a lesser extent its warnings) are embedded in a detailed procedural framework that provides for an internal review of compliance or a qualitative assessment of justifications for non-compliance. The transparency of this process and its framing within a legal framework strengthens the obligation element of the ESRB's outputs.

4.2. THE ESRB WARNINGS AND RECOMMENDATIONS ARE HARDENED ALONG THE "DELEGATION ELEMENT"

Abbott and others explain that "As one moves up the delegation continuum, the actions of decision-makers are increasingly governed, and legitimated, by rules. (Willingness to delegate often depends on the extent to which these rules are thought capable of constraining the delegated authority)."[103]

The "hardening" of the delegation element on the Abbott's continuum of the ESRB warnings and recommendation is achieved through strengthening the institutional stand of the ESRB and ensuring that it is governed, and legitimated, in itself by a legal framework and internal procedures and criteria.[104] The adoption of a recommendation or the making of warnings and recommendations public is embedded within a formal procedure provided by the ESRB Regulation. It requires a qualified majority of the ESRB General Board, i.e. at least two-thirds of the voting members of the General Board.[105] Confidential warnings can be adopted by a simple majority of the General Board voting members present.[106] Warnings and recommendations are thus a product of an inclusive (and thus more legitimated) participation of potential addressees and where appropriate, seeking the views of relevant private sector stakeholders.[107] Moreover, as

---

[102] ESRB Regulation, article 17(3).
[103] Abbott and others (2000) (n 66), 416–417.
[104] Abbott and others (2000) (n 66), 418.
[105] ESRB Regulation, article 10(3); ESRB Rules of Procedure, article 19(2).
[106] ESRB Regulation, articles 10(2) and 18(1).
[107] ESRB Regulation, article 6, as amended. The participation of those affected by the rules of an institution reinforces its legitimacy (known as "representative legitimacy"). See, for instance, R Keohane and J Nye, "Between Centralisation and Fragmentation: The Club Model of Multilateral Cooperation and Problems of Democratic Legitimacy" (2001) Kennedy School of Government Harvard University Faculty Research Working Paper 4 on the importance of participation of interested parties in strengthening legitimacy of the World Trade Organisation.

discussed in the previous section, the ESRB follows a panoply of procedural rules to guide the issuance of its recommendations, support their follow-up and facilitate their compliance, inter alia, through disseminating information on compliance and non-compliance.[108] Last but not least, transparency of the decision-making process and publication of all public warnings and recommendations in the Official Journal of the EU enhance the legal validity of the warnings and recommendations.[109]

4.3. THE ESRB WARNINGS AND RECOMMENDATIONS ARE HARDENED ALONG THE "PRECISION ELEMENT"

In practice, the ESRB recommendations that have been published to date generally display a high degree of precision that, in turn, enhances their obligations element. They often clarify what is expected of the addressees, set out possible courses of actions to achieve the recommendation, for instance, through national legislation or creating ESA's guidance[110] and invariably lay out the reasons for issuing the recommendation.[111]

Any relative weakness of the precision element in the ESRB warnings and recommendations may be attributed to the absence of a one-size-fits-all policy framework and the need to accommodate macroprudential tools to domestic factors (Chapter 6). As a regional macroprudential authority the ESRB may, at times, drift away from precision for the benefit of a more accommodative

---

Before the adoption of a warning or of a recommendation, the ESRB can seek the views of potential addressees that are not represented on its board and from private stakeholders (ESRB Rules of Procedures, article 18(1)(b)).

See also article 14 of the ESRB Regulation on consultation with relevant private sector stakeholders in performing the ESRB tasks set out in article 3(2). The Regulation amending the ESRB Regulation also added the requirement that "Such consultations shall be conducted as widely as possible to ensure an inclusive approach towards all interested parties and relevant financial sectors and shall allow reasonable time for stakeholders to respond."

[108] ESRB Rules of Procedure, article 20; Compliance Handbook, section 2.2 on setting compliance criteria; section 3.2 on creating Assessment Teams and section 4.1 on the assessment principles. Similarly, for internal restrictions, such as internal decision-making and review procedures in international law (procedural guarantees) see S Duquet and others, "Upholding the Rule of Law in Informal International Lawmaking Processes" (2014) 6(1) Hague Journal on the Rule of Law 75.

[109] Article 19(5) ESRB Rules of Procedure.

[110] Compliance Handbook, sections 2.1–2.3.

[111] Public recommendations often include an annex that analyses the significant systemic risks to the financial stability in the Union that are posed by subject matter of the recommendation. See, for instance, Recommendation of the ESRB of 7 December 2017 on Liquidity and Leverage Risks in Investment Funds (ESRB/2017/6) OJ C 151/1, Annex II Economic Rationale and Assessment.

discretion. The ESRB public recommendations often refer to national specificities[112] and the need to allow room for interpretation at the national level.[113] For instance, the ESRB Recommendation on the Macro-prudential Mandate of National Authorities states that "It is necessary to provide guiding principles on core elements of national macro-prudential mandates, balancing the need for consistency among national approaches with the flexibility to accommodate national specificities."[114] More recently, Recommendation of 18 June 2014 on Guidance for Setting Countercyclical Buffer Rates requires national authorities to include in their decision of setting buffer information that reflects national specificities, taking into account "… the heterogeneity and dynamic nature of financial systems, the specificities of national economies and material differences in data availability in the European Union".[115] This natural accommodative discretion may diminish over time, as the process of "learning by experience" gains track, and more evidence is accumulated to guide policy decisions.[116]

---

[112] In accordance with the principle for proportionality as a guiding principle in drafting recommendations. ESRB Compliance Handbook, sections 2.2 and 4.1 ("actions to be taken by the addressees are country-specific, and relative to the intensity of risks targeted by the recommendation in the specific Member State").

[113] For instance, ESRB Recommendation of 31 October 2016 on Closing Real Estate Data Gaps ESRB/2016/14: "… does not prevent national macroprudential authorities from relying … on real estate indicators based on their own definitions and metrics, which may be better suited to accommodate national requirements"; ESRB Recommendation of 4 April 2013 on Intermediate Objectives and Instruments of Macro-prudential Policy ESRB/2013/1 C 170/1: "Member States may want to select instruments that best address specific risks to financial stability at the national level"; ESRB Recommendation of 20 December 2012 on Funding of Credit Institutions ESRB/2012/2 C 119/1 state that "It could be adapted according to the specificities of the different.
Member States and of different business models"; ESRB Recommendations of 20 December 2012 on MMF ESRB/2012/1 OJ C 146/01 national specificities are taken into account in Table 9; ESRB Recommendation of 22 December 2011 on US dollar Denominated Funding of Credit Institutions ESRB/2011/2 OJ C 72/0 "There are differences between national banking systems: using this method and these data, the US dollar shortage is relatively small in some countries and larger in others … this is a crude measure and other calculation methods are possible."

[114] ESRB Recommendation of 22 December 2011 on the Macro-prudential Mandate of National Authorities ESRB/2011/3 OJ C41/01, para 4 Preamble. Similarly, the ESRB Recommendation on Lending in Foreign Currencies states that "Due regard will be paid to the principle of proportionality in the implementation of recommendations B to F with reference to the different systemic relevance of foreign currency lending among the Member States and taking into account the objective and the content of each recommendation." ESRB Recommendation of 21 September 2011 on Lending in Foreign Currencies (ESRB/2011/1) OJ C 342/1.

[115] Recommendation of 18 June 2014 on Guidance for Setting Countercyclical Buffer Rates ESRB/2014/1 OJ C/1, paras 7, 14 and 18 of the Preamble. In fact, the term "National Specificities" is mentioned six times in this Recommendation.

[116] See Chapter 5 on supervisory approaches in macroprudential policymaking.

5. SEMI-SOFT POWERS AND THE "COMPLY OR EXPLAIN" AS A REINFORCING MECHANISM: HURDLES AND CHALLENGES

On paper, semi-soft powers seem to provide a balance between flexibility, on the one hand, and legalisation, legitimacy and compliance, on the other. Yet, the prospects of success of semi-soft powers largely depend on the legal framework and institutional setting. This section presents two key challenges in the use of the "comply or explain" procedure as a reinforcing mechanism to macroprudential authorities' soft powers. The first is the use of proportionality as a justification for non-compliance and the second, the emergence of sub-optimal regulatory turf wars.

5.1. PROPORTIONALITY AS A JUSTIFICATION FOR NON-COMPLIANCE

Even a cursory examination of the ESRB's compliance reports[117] reveals that a widespread justification for Member States' non-compliance is the proportionality principle.[118] In that case, the Member State shows that the practice or the subject of the recommendation is limited in material terms in their jurisdiction and therefore, compliance is not essential.[119] Interestingly (and perhaps anticipating the behaviour of Member States), the ESRB stated that certain recommendations may include a provision that limits, to a certain extent, the possibility for the addressees to explain their inaction by initiation of the proportionality argument.[120] The primary problem with invoking proportionality as a justification for non-compliance with the ESRB recommendations is timing. It may be that, at the time of the compliance review, the practice or the subject of the recommendation is not material in that Member State but this position may change quickly in the future. Hence, invoking proportionality as a reason for not complying with the ESRB recommendation may counter the pre-emptive nature

---

[117] ESRB Compliance Handbook, section 4.1.4.

[118] In accordance with article 5(4) of the TFEU. For instance, Follow-up Report on ESRB Recommendation on Lending in Foreign Currencies ESRB/2011/1 November 2013; Follow-up Report US Dollar Denominated Funding of Credit Institutions ESRB/2011/2 14 April 2014.

[119] To be accurate, Member States refer here to the materiality principle, which is considered one of the dimensions of proportionality. EBA Banking Stakeholders Group, "Proportionality in Bank Regulation" (December 2015), available at <http://www.eba.europa.eu/documents/10180/807776/European+Banking+Authority+Banking+Stakeholder+Group-+Position+paper+on+proportionality.pdf>.

[120] For instance, Recommendation ESRB/2011/1 on Lending in Foreign Currencies (n 113) clearly states that the principle of proportionality cannot be invoked by Member States to justify inaction with regard to some sub-recommendations.

of the ESRB toolkit. In addition, in the absence of a rule of thumb for materiality of the activity (e.g. a defined percentage), proportionality can become a general "ready-made" argument for non-compliance and result in a "box-ticking" rather than a meaningful engagement with the ESRB recommendations.

Providing justifications for noncompliance does not seem to be a thorny matter in the macroprudential framework in the UK. To date, past recommendations to the FCA and the PRA have been, overwhelmingly, accepted and followed.[121] Moreover, to date, all the petitions that the FPC made to the UK Government to expand its powers of directions have been successful.[122] The FPC received an unequivocal support, ensuring that it "has all the weapons it needs to guard against risks in the housing market".[123] It is therefore not surprising that the FPC is described as "the most muscular macroprudential regulator in the world".[124]

The speed of implementation of the FPC's recommendations should also be commended. It is to be recalled that the PRA and the FCA must, as soon as is reasonably practicable, comply with the FPC's recommendation or provide reasons for non-compliance.[125] While this timeframe leaves much room for discretion, there seems to be a quick turnaround for implementation. For instance, in June 2014, the FPC issued a recommendation to the PRA and FCA regarding mortgage loan-to-income ratio.[126] By October 2014, the PRA has issued a policy statement, including rules[127] and the FCA has issued an initial general guidance.[128] Other times, the timeframe for compliance was even

---

[121] 2018 Financial Stability Report points out that "currently, there are no Recommendations or Directions awaiting implementation".

[122] For instance, on 2 October 2014, the FPC recommended that it be granted powers of direction in relation to housing market tools (owner-occupied mortgages and buy-to-let residential mortgages). FPC Statement from its policy meeting, 26 September 2014, available at <https://www.bankofengland.co.uk/-/media/boe/files/statement/2014/fpc-statement-from-its-policy-meeting-26-september-2014>. In April 2015, the Government gave the FPC powers of direction over the PRA and the FCA in relation to LTV and DTI limits in respect of owner-occupied mortgage lending.

[123] The Chancellor of the Exchequer, Philip Hammond, said: "It is crucial that Britain's independent regulators have the tools they need to keep our financial system as safe as possible." C Binham, "UK Treasury Grant BoE New Powers Over Buy-to-Let Lending" *Financial Times* (London, 16 November 2016).
See also the Chancellor's speech at the Mansion House on 12 June 2014 stating: "I say today, very clearly: the Bank of England should not hesitate to use these new powers if they think it necessary to protect financial stability."

[124] D Aikman, J Bridges, A Kashyap and C Siegert, "Would Macroprudential Regulation Have Prevented the Last Crisis?" (August 2018) Bank of England Staff Working Paper No 747.

[125] Section 9Q(3) BEA 1998.

[126] This recommendation remains in place as of the FPC's meeting of 11 July 2019.

[127] PRA, "Implementing the Financial Policy Committee's Recommendation on Loan to Income Ratios in Mortgage Lending", October 2014 Policy Statement PS9/14.

[128] FCA, "Guidance on the Financial Policy Committee's Recommendation on Loan to Income Ratios in Mortgage Lending" (October 2014) FG14/8, available at <https://www.fca.org.uk/publication/finalised-guidance/fg1408.pdf>.

---

shorter. For instance, in its meeting on 20 September 2017, the FPC issued a recommendation to the PRA on its rules on leverage. The records of the meeting point out that "The FPC was informed after its meeting that the PRA would comply with this Recommendation. The PRA planned to publish its rules on how this change would be implemented alongside publication of the Record of the FPC's meeting."[129]

This rosy picture can be attributed to the coherent regulatory framework that aligns the mandates of the PRA and FCA with the Bank of England Financial Stability Objective. The PRA general objective is to be advanced primarily by

(a) seeking to ensure that the business of PRA-authorised persons is carried on in a way which avoids any adverse effect on the stability of the UK financial system, and (b) seeking to minimise the adverse effect that the failure of a PRA-authorised person could be expected to have on the stability of the UK financial system.[130]

Similarly, the FCA "integrity objective" includes its soundness, stability and resilience;[131] and the FCA is required to take such steps as it considers appropriate to cooperate with the Bank of England in connection with the pursuit by the Bank of its Financial Stability Objective.[132] In the same vein, the FPC is required, so far as is possible while complying with its objectives, to seek to avoid prejudicing the PRA's objectives and the FCA's operational objectives.[133] This alignment could help reduce the potential for a regulatory turf war and conflicts and increase compliance with the FPC's recommendations.[134] The alignment of the macroprudential mandate with the mandates of other prudential supervisors will be further discussed in Chapter 8.

5.2.   THE PROBLEM WITH RELYING ON OTHERS "TO DO THE JOB" OR THE OLD CASE OF A REGULATORY TURF WAR

Semi-soft law powers mean that the macroprudential authority "does not have the powers itself. It has the capacity to influence those who do have the

---

[129]   Record of the Financial Policy Committee Meeting on 20 September 2017, para 82.
[130]   Section 2B(3) Financial Services Act 2000 inserted by the Financial Services Act 2012 c 21. See also section 3I(4) Financial Services Act 2000 with regard to the power of PRA to require FCA to refrain from specified action, when certain conditions are met and where it is of the opinion that the exercise of the power in the manner proposed may: (a) threaten the stability of the UK financial system, or (b) result in the failure of a PRA-authorised person in a way that would adversely affect the UK financial system.
[131]   Section 1(D)(2)(a) of Financial Services Act 2000 inserted by the Financial Services Act 2012.
[132]   Section 3Q Financial Services Act 2000 inserted by the Financial Services Act 2012.
[133]   Section 9F(2) BEA 1998.
[134]   IMF UK: Financial Sector Assessment Program IMF Country Report 16/160, 10.

powers."[135] In other words, the effectiveness of semi-soft powers largely depends on the willingness of other agencies to assist.[136] This reliance brings about the risk of a turf war amongst agencies[137] and potential tensions, differing perspectives and risk-appetite of the macroprudential authority and the "implementing" prudential agencies. Arguably, where financial stability does not form part of the mandate of prudential agencies, their inaction bias (and thus their reluctance to follow recommendations) is even stronger than that of the macroprudential authority.

Indeed, "sharing regulatory space" or "a fragmented delegation"[138] is viewed as one of the greatest challenges of modern governance.[139] The benefits of a diffused structure are sizable and include harnessing "the unique expertise and competencies of different agencies" needed to deal with complex social and economic problems.[140] Nonetheless, sharing regulatory space and in particular, decoupling the macroprudential mandate from the activation of policy measures, can lead to inaction, unproductive conflicts and destructive turf battles between the macroprudential authority and the "implementing agencies.[141]

The proposed reform of money market mutual funds (MMFs) provides a constructive example for the manifestation of turf-building and the weakness of the FSOC's semi-soft powers. In August 2001, the SEC's Chairman at the time

---

[135]   Lord Myners, Treasury Committee, UK House of Commons, Opinion on the Proposals for European Financial Supervision, The ESRB (Part 3), Session 2008–2009, Sixteenth Report, para 51.

[136]   European Parliament, "Review of the New ESFS (Part 1): The Work of the ESAs" (2013), 44 (Table 5).

[137]   Though note that this may arise also in relation to the FSOC's hard power of designation See D Schwarcz and D Zaring, "Regulation by Treat: Understanding Dodd Frank' s Regulation of Systemically Important Non-Bank Financial Companies" (2017) 84(4) University of Chicago Law Review 1813.

[138]   J Freeman and J Rossi, "Agency Coordination in Shared Regulatory Space" (2012) 125(5) Harvard Law Review 1131 suggest that delegations create situations in which different agencies possess the authority necessary to tackle different aspects of a larger problem.

[139]   Ibid, 1134.
          See also DK Tarullo, Member Board of Governors of the Federal Reserve System, Remarks at the University of Pennsylvania Law School Distinguished Jurist Lecture, Financial Stability Regulation 25 (10 October 2012), available at <http://www.federalreserve.gov/newsevents/speech/tarullo20121010a.htm>, suggests that during the debates preceding the Dodd–Frank Act there were suggestions to empower the FSOC to override action or inaction within its sphere of authority. Instead, a more limited semi-soft powers were adopted.

[140]   Freeman and Rossi (2012) (n 138), 1142.

[141]   On the fragmented regime and information exchange and coordination challenges see US Government Accountability Office, Dodd-Frank Act Regulations: Implementation Could Benefit from Addition Analyses and Coordination GAO-12-151 (2011), 27.
          Turf-building in a regulatory state is the "tendency to substitute private, self-interested objectives for the public objectives that provided the impetus for their origination." JR Macey and GP Miller, "Reflections on Professional Responsibility in a Regulatory State" (1995) Faculty Scholarship Series Paper 1442, available at <http://digitalcommons.law.yale.edu/fss_papers/1442>.

announced that, due to lack of support from a majority of Commissioners, the SEC would not advance proposed money market fund reforms.[142] Soon after, in November 2012, the FSOC used, for the first time, its recommendation authority under section 120 of the Dodd-Frank Act. The FSOC's proposed recommendation to the SEC provided for three alternative options for reform to MMFs.[143] The proposed recommendation attracted criticism regarding the procedures leading to its adoption as well as its substance.[144] In June 2013, the SEC issued for public comment a proposal to amend the rules that govern MMFs to address potential systemic risks.[145] In its statement, the SEC, however, revealed, its building tensions with the FSOC:

> The staff's work is a testament as to why the SEC should take the helm of matters that are within its jurisdiction … The SEC's expertise brings a clear-eyed experience and practical knowledge that can target needed change, while being mindful of unintended consequences.[146]

In July 2014, the SEC adopted new MMFs rules,[147] but these have been observed to be falling far short of the FSOC's proposed recommendation. The rules were largely viewed as the lesser of two evils, "necessary to fend off the FSOC and the Fed from taking other action against SEC regulated entities."[148] It may be that the motivation behind adopting the rules was related to the threat of using the FSOC's designation authority under section 113 of the Dodd-Frank Act. However, given that this "threat" is now largely muted (Chapter 5), the FSOC may have substantially lost its key leverage for compliance with its recommendations.

"Relying on others to do the job" is particularly a concern where the objective and mandate of the implementing regulators do not have an explicit objective

---

[142] SEC Press Release Statement of SEC Chairman, ML Schapiro, on Money Market Fund Reform, Washington, DC, 22 August 2012 2012-166.

[143] FSOC, Proposed Recommendations Regarding Money Market Mutual Fund Reform (13 November 2012), available at <http://www.treasury.gov/initiatives/fsoc/Documents/ Proposed Recommendations Regarding Money Market Mutual Fund Reform – November 13, 2012.pdf>.

[144] PS Atkins and others, "Comment Letter on Proposed Recommendations Regarding Money Market Mutual Fund Reform" (20 February 2013), available at <http://perma.cc/ B3CR-NAPP>.

[145] Commissioner LA Aguilar, "Striving to Restructure Money Markets Funds to Address Potential Systemic Risk", 5 June 2013, available at <https://www.sec.gov/news/public-statement/2013-06-05-open-meeting-statement-laa>.

[146] Ibid.

[147] SEC Press Release, "SEC Adopts Money Market Fund Reform Rules" (23 July 2014), available at <https://perma.cc/LD53-TAXY>. The rules came into effect in October 2016.

[148] ML Crochran, DF Freeman and HM Clark, "Money Market Fund Reform: SEC Rulemaking in the FSOC Era" (2015) 3 Columbia Business Law Review 862, at 962.

of maintaining financial stability[149] and thus are not necessarily aligned with the macroprudential objective and may even cut across the macroprudential authority policy agenda. This is far from being a theoretical concern and has become a bitter one, as evident in the words of an SEC Commissioner:

> With the Council's steady march, led by its self-appointed "alpha dog" – the Fed – into areas that are solely within the SEC's jurisdiction [referring to capital markets and trading – author's addition], I am concerned that our mission to protect investors, maintain fair, orderly, and efficient markets, and promote capital formation is being compromised.[150]

Addressing this concern, one of the SEC's Commissioners urgently called for the FSOC and primary regulators to work together to ameliorate the tendency for a turf war:

> I'm disappointed, however, to see that the FSOC suffers from much more squabbling among regulators than it should. The point of the FSOC was for regulators with expertise in particular areas to identify potential risks, and then enlist the help of the entire council to address them. The intention was to get each regulator to become more resourceful and start thinking in new and different ways. While some of that may be happening, in other cases, members of the FSOC are merely trying to dictate to, or control, regulators with primary jurisdiction over certain areas. The FSOC needs to come together as a team to focus and provide mutual support. And, I fear that individual members defending their territorial jurisdiction detracts from the FSOC's critical mission to promote financial stability … The FSOC's mission is far too important to be bogged down in a regulatory turf war. We all share a common purpose: to make sure the foundation of our financial markets is strong so it can support a strong and thriving economy.[151]

There is also dissatisfaction with the disconnect between the role the SEC's chair plays in the FSOC and the other SEC Commissioners:

> Unfortunately, the Commission, as a body, does not have input or influence into what FSOC … says or does. Only the SEC's Chair or her designee participates in FSOC meetings … Thus, my fellow Commissioners and I have very little control

---

[149] Kohn (2014) (n 38).
[150] SEC Commissioner MS Piwowar Remarks at American Enterprise Institute Conference on Financial Stability Washington, DC, 15 July 2014, available at <https://www.sec.gov/news/speech/2014-spch071514msp>.
[151] SEC Commissioner KM Stein Remarks before the Peterson Institute of International Economics, Washington DC, 12 June 2014, available at <https://www.sec.gov/news/speech/remarks-peterson-institute-international-economics>.

or input over the content and output of projects undertaken by FSOC, as well as the behavior, inputs, and conclusions supplied by others from the SEC working with FSOC ...[152]

Turf wars across agencies might result in an ineffective implementation of macroprudential policy measures or an adjustment of perspectives with the aim of making them more aligned. Where the adjustment is coming from the macroprudential authority, it will effectively narrow the scope of its risk analysis, reflecting "the sectoral perspectives of individual agencies, rather than providing a system-wide view of interconnections and exposure to risk."[153] Thus, an adjustment of perspectives on behalf of the regulatory agencies is preferable, such that – "Although systemic risk has not traditionally been a focus of the SEC, it is now. And we need to embrace that mission and that responsibility."[154]

Nonetheless, aligning the regulatory objectives of the implementing regulatory agencies to reflect systemic risks concerns would not solve the problem of regulatory gaps or "falling-between-two stools".[155] In the US, there are areas and macroprudential tools, for instance, household debt limits (in the form of loan-to-value ratio and loan-to-income ratio), where no federal regulator has jurisdiction over. Therefore, as will be discussed in Section 6 below, it is important that the legal framework of the macroprudential authority enables, where necessary, expanding the regulatory perimeter to close these gaps.

Overall, decoupling the mandate from the authority to implement macroprudential policy or "relying on others to do the job" may open up an accountability gap[156] and result in destructive turf-wars. Nonetheless, in its recent interpretive guidance on nonbank financial company determinations,[157] the FSOC seems to be rather optimistic regarding the necessity and effectiveness of its cooperation with primary prudential regulators. The FSOC suggests that the first port of interaction between the FSOC and the primary authority in

---

[152] SEC Commissioner LA Aguilar, "Taking an Informed Approach to Issues Facing the Mutual Fund Industry" Washington, DC, 2 April 2014, available at <https://www.sec.gov/news/speech/2014-spch040214laa>.

[153] FSB, Peer Review of the United States, 27 August 2013, available at <https://www.fsb.org/wp-content/uploads/r_130827.pdf>, 7.

[154] Stein (2014) (n 152).

[155] FSA, *The Turner Review: A Regulatory Response to the Global Banking Crisis* (March 2009), para 2.6.

[156] AWS Duff, "Central Bank Independence and Macroprudential Policy: A Critical Look at the U.S. Financial Stability Framework" (2014) 11 Berkeley Business Law Journal 183, 214.

[157] FSOC, "Authority to Require Supervision and Regulation of Certain Nonbank Financial Companies", Final Interpretive Guidance 84 Fed. No 249 Reg. 71740 (30 December 2019), available at <https://www.govinfo.gov/content/pkg/FR-2019-12-30/pdf/2019-27108.pdf> (hereinafter: "The FSOC's Guidance").

making a recommendation under section 120 of the Dodd-Frank Act would be informal, explaining that:

> The Council intends to make recommendations under section 120 of the Dodd-Frank Act only to the extent that its recommendations are consistent with the statutory mandate of the relevant primary financial regulatory agency.

and that

> much of its initial identification and assessment of risks, and engagement with regulators, will be informal and nonpublic in nature. The staffs of Council members and member agencies will likely be responsible for much of the market monitoring, risk identification, information sharing, and analysis ... This engagement may yield a range of diverse outcomes, including the sharing of data, research, and analysis among the Council and regulators ...[158]

The limitations of semi-soft law and the "comply-or-explain" mechanism are not unique to the macroprudential framework in the US. In the EU, the implementation of the ESRB recommendations largely depends on the willingness of the national authorities to cooperate. The establishment of national authorities with a defined macroprudential mandate can clearly assist in fostering the implementation of ESRB warnings and recommendations.[159] However, coherent implementation may be inhibited since the scope of the mandate, governance and toolkit available to the national macroprudential authorities as well as the legal framework within which they operate differ from one Member State to another.

The ESAs are under an obligation to cooperate closely with the ESRB and ensure a timely follow-up on warnings and recommendations addressed to a competent national supervisory authority[160] and where they fail to use their powers to that end it can be considered a violation of their obligations under EU law.[161] However, the follow-up process on the ESAs' guidelines and

---

[158] Ibid, 71747 and 71749.

[159] All Member States but one (Italy) now have a macroprudential authority in place. ESRB, "A Review of Macroprudential Policy in the EU in 2018", April 2019, available at <https://www.esrb. europa.eu/pub/pdf/reports/esrb~32aae4bd95.report190430_reviewofmacroprudentialpolicy. pdf>.

[160] ESRB Regulation, article 15(2); ESAs Regulation, article 36, as amended. On the changes to this article in the Regulation amending the ESAs Regulation see n 100.
In addition, the ESAs Chairpersons are members of the ESRB Steering Committee, ESRB Regulation, article 11(1)(e)–(g).

[161] Ferran and Alexander (2011) (n 99), 30 refer to the duty to ensure a timely follow-up on the ESRB warnings and recommendations as an enforceable obligation under the Treaties.

recommendations is not legally binding upon national authorities and is based, similarly to the ESRB's framework, on the comply-or-explain mechanism.[162]

Where a national competent authority has not applied the acts referred to in article 1(2) of the ESAs Regulations[163] or applied them in a way that appears to be a breach of Union law, the ESAs are assigned with a stronger power to investigate alleged breach or non-application of Union law.[164]

Where necessary and within two months after initiating the investigation, the ESA can address a recommendation to the national competent authority setting out the action necessary to comply with Union law.[165] Where the competent authority has not complied with the Union law within one month from the receipt of the recommendation, the Commission may issue a formal opinion requiring the national competent authority to take action.[166] Following a formal opinion, the competent authority is required, within ten working days, to inform the Commission and the ESA of the steps taken to comply with the formal opinion.[167] As a last resort, the ESAs can issue a decision directly applicable to a financial institution requiring the necessary action to comply with its obligations under Union law.[168] In practice, however, these

---

[162] ESAs Regulations, article 16(3). On the uncertainties regarding the legal basis and status of the ESMA guidelines and recommendations see MV Rijsbergen, "On the Enforceability of EU Agencies Soft Law at the National Level: The Case of the European Securities and Markets Authority" (2014) 10(5) Utrecht Law Review 116.

[163] Including all directives, regulations, and decisions based on those acts, and of any further legally binding Union act which confers tasks on the ESA.

[164] ESAs Regulations, article 17(1).

[165] ESAs Regulations, article 17(3). The Regulation amending the ESAs Regulation inserted article 17(2a) with a requirement that prior to resorting to such a recommendation the ESA must, where it considers it appropriate, engage with the competent authority in an attempt to reach an agreement on actions necessary to comply with the Union law.

[166] On the operational challenges of this procedure, see A Millar, "EU Banking Union-Operational Issues and Design Considerations" City of London Report prepared for the International Regulatory Strategy Group, October 2012.

[167] ESAs Regulations, article 17(5).

[168] ESAs Regulations, article 17(6), as amended. The power is available only where the competent authority did not comply with a formal opinion of the Commission and where it is necessary to remedy it in a timely manner in order to maintain or restore neutral conditions of competition in the market or ensure the orderly functioning and integrity of the financial system and where the relevant requirements of the acts referred to in article 1(2) are directly applicable to financial institutions. The decision has to be in conformity with the Commission's formal opinion. Recital 27 to the EBA Regulation further specifies that this mechanism "should apply in areas where Union law defines clear and unconditional obligations." The Regulation amending the ESAs Regulation adds to the acts in article 2(1) other matters relating to the prevention and countering of money laundering and terrorist financing to financial sector operators.

See T Tridimas, "Financial Supervision and Agency Power: Reflections on ESMA" in N Shuibhne and L Gormley (eds), *From Single Market to Economic Union: Essays in Memory of John Usher* (Oxford University Press, 2012), 55–83 suggests that despite the awkward wording, the Opinion of the Commission is binding on the national authority.

powers will hardly assist the ESRB in ensuring compliance by the addressees with its warnings and recommendations. Where the ESRB warnings and recommendations do not relate to the legislative acts in article 1(2) of the ESAs Regulations, they cannot instigate the binding power of the ESAs and hence, may not be easily enforceable. In addition, the ESAs rarely take formal action under this procedure and seem to take a narrow approach to what is considered a breach of EU law that can trigger their binding powers. As such, to date, the ESAs have only resorted to this authority twice and in both cases, the investigation related to prudential supervision.[169] Nevertheless, Annex 2 of the EBA Decision of December 2016 adopting Rules of Procedure for Investigation of Breach of Union Law provides a non-exhaustive list of examples of factors that the EBA will take into account when considering potential investigation including "The alleged breach may have significant, direct impact on EBA's objectives concerning: contributing to the short, medium and long-term stability and effectiveness of the financial system ...".[170] This provision may open the door, under certain circumstances, to the use of the binding power of the EBA in ensuring addressees' compliance with the ESRB warnings and recommendations.

Despite these challenges, overall, the ESRB's compliance reports that have been published to date show an impressive record of follow-up with the ESRB's recommendations.[171] This is even the case when politically charged tools are concerned (Chapter 6). For instance, in November 2016, the ESRB published a set of eight country-specific warnings on medium-term vulnerabilities in the

---

[169] EBA issues recommendation to the Maltese Financial Intelligence Analysis Unit in Relation to its Supervision of Pilatus Bank 11 July 2018, available at <https://eba.europa.eu/eba-issues-recommendation-to-the-maltese-financial-intelligence-analysis-unit-in-relation-to-its-supervision-of-pilatus-bank>.
The European Commission requested the EBA to start an investigation into supervisory failure in the case of Danske Bank's breach of anti-money laundering regulation (Request to investigate a possible breach of Union law under Article 17 of Regulation (EU) No 1093/2010, 21 September 20187). The EBA commenced an investigation in February 2019 but following a preliminary inquiry the investigation was closed. See J Bardsen, "EBA Faces Calls to Reform After Dropping Danske Bank Probe", *Financial Times* (28 April 2019).
See also See also P Schammo, "Actions and Inactions in the Investigation of Breaches of Union law by the European Supervisory Authorities" (2018) 55(5) Common Market Law Review 1423.
[170] Annex 2 of the EBA Decision of December 2016 Adopting Rules of Procedure for Investigation of Breach of Union Law EBA/DC/2016/174.
[171] For instance, Summary Compliance Report on ESRB Recommendation on Guidance for Setting Countercyclical Buffer Rates, May 2019 (ESRB/2014/1) concludes that "Overall, the addressees were all graded as being either fully compliant (FC) or largely compliant (LC) with the Recommendation"; Similarly, see, for instance, Summary Compliance Report on ESRB Recommendation on Funding of Credit Institutions, March 2018 ESRB/2012/2.

Residential Real Estate Sector.[172] By and large, authorities have welcomed the warning and addressed the ESRB's concerns.[173]

6. A PROPOSED BENCHMARK FOR ASSESSING THE EFFECTIVENESS OF MACROPRUDENTIAL SOFT/SEMI-SOFT POWERS

To date, there is no specific international best practice for the conduct of macroprudential policy. It may be that given the specificities-dependency nature of macroprudential policy, no best practice can be identified. Alternatively, it may be that such principles would be developed in due course, as more evidence is gathered.

The Core Principles for Effective Banking Supervision (the Core Principles) were revised in 2012, inter alia, to reflect the need for macroprudential perspective of the financial system. However, the BCBS intentionally did not include a specific stand-alone Core Principle on macroprudential issues, suggesting that the 'broad financial system perspective is integral to many of the Core Principles'.[174]

The contention that macroprudential policy is entwined within general supervisory practices is rather peculiar. Given its myriad unique and distinct features, macroprudential policy demands a distinct framework to guide the design and assessment of its powers and outputs.

This section, therefore, offers, in broad lines, a set of non-exhaustive questions to guide a qualitative assessment of the effectiveness of a macroprudential

---

[172]   ESRB Warnings on Medium-term Vulnerabilities in the Residential Real Estate Sector: Austria (Warning ESRB/2016/05); Belgium (Warning ESRB/2016/06); Denmark (Warning ESRB/2016/07); Finland (Warning ESRB/2016/08); Luxembourg (Warning ESRB/2016/09); the Netherlands (Warning ESRB/2016/10); Sweden (Warning ESRB/2016/11); and the UK (Warning ESRB/2016/12).

[173]   For replies of the authorities Austria, Belgium, Denmark, Finland, Luxembourg, the Netherlands, Sweden and the UK see <https://www.esrb.europa.eu/mppa/warnings/html/index.en.html>.
The Austrian authorities, however, disputed the warning and concluded that "the ESRB has not based its assessment on a balanced view of the empirical evidence". Federal Ministry of Finance Letter addressed to the ECB, "Views of the Austrian Authorities on the Warning of the ESRB on Medium Term Vulnerabilities in the Residential Real Estate Sector of Austria" (2016), available at <https://www.esrb.europa.eu/pub/pdf/warnings/161128_ESRB_AT_response.en.pdf>.

[174]   BCBS, Core Principles for Banking Supervision, para 21. Other than listing a well-established framework for financial stability policy formulation and a clear framework for macroprudential surveillance as preconditions for effective banking supervision, Principles 47 and 49.

authority's powers. This is done based on two key benchmarks: (1) whether the macroprudential authority's soft or semi-soft powers are effective in achieving the macroprudential objective?; and (2) the quality of the decision-making process that leads to the use of these powers and review of their outputs.

The guiding questions can be adjusted in light of the specificities of the macroprudential framework (in particular, mandate, rules of procedure and transparency and accountability arrangements), and where applicable, other general principles of good administration and governance.[175]

The guiding questions are as follows:

1. Does the exercise of powers reflect the risks identified during the risk identification and analysis and their prioritisation?
2. Is the exercise of powers conducted in a timely manner to prevent and mitigate systemic risks before they materialise?
3. Are there too burdensome procedural requirements that can inhibit the timeliness of the macroprudential authority's outputs?
4. Are the reasons for the use of power and the manner it is being used transparent and clear?
5. Are the outputs appropriate in terms of taking into account, where necessary, the national/sectoral specificities? Do they leave room for interpretation by the national/authorities/implementing prudential agencies at a satisfactory level?
6. Are the potential spillover effects of macroprudential measures being considered? Are potential secondary effects on or from other policy areas being considered?
7. Are the addressees appropriate?
8. Are the outputs complied with and if not – is there a satisfactory justification?
9. Is implementation done in a timely manner?
10. Did implementation of the output achieve its purported intermediate objective?

In time, international institutions responsible for global systemic risk oversight must develop international principles or guidelines on the design and implementation of macroprudential frameworks and in particular, establish a tailored methodology to assessing the effectiveness of the macroprudential outputs.

---

[175] For instance, when issuing warnings and recommendations and conducting their follow-up, the ESRB should adhere to general principles of good governance such as the principle of "sincere cooperation". Preamble (para 14) and article 1(4) ESRB Regulation.

7. ADAPTABILITY: EXPANDING REGULATORY SCOPE AND EMERGENCY SITUATIONS

7.1. EXPANDING REGULATORY PERIMETER

In light of the complex and evolving nature of financial markets (Chapter 2), ensuring that the macroprudential authority has the power to recommend expanding the regulatory perimeter or initiate new legislation is vital in the macroprudential domain.

The FPC assesses and reviews the regulatory perimeter and if needed, can recommend to the Treasury changes in the perimeter, in particular via expanding the macroprudential toolkit[176] and adding unregulated entities who may be required by the PRA to provide information.[177] When issuing such recommendation, the FPC is required to provide evidence that the change is a necessary and proportionate response to the risks it had identified, that existing provisions cannot effectively mitigate those risks[178] and that "changes would not create unintended consequences or costs in excess of the benefits."[179]

There is evidence that the FPC's power to recommend changes in the regulatory perimeter allows the FPC to be proactive. For instance, in its meetings on 20 and 27 November 2018, the FPC considered the importance of the cyber resilience of third-party providers that were important for the UK financial system but were outside the regulatory perimeter and concluded that for the time being, it is not necessary to recommend a change.

Similarly, the FSOC can expand the regulatory perimeter by using its power of designation under section 113 of the Dodd-Frank Act and subjecting the financial institution to the supervision of the Federal Reserve and subject to prudential standards under Title 1 of the Dodd-Frank Act. In addition, where the FSOC issues a recommendation and no primary financial regulatory agency exists for the non-bank financial company conducting financial activities or practices that require additional standards for financial stability purposes, the

---

[176] Section 9P(1) and 9P(2)(a) BEA 1998. The FPC holds, at least annually, a regular dedicated discussion on the appropriate boundaries around, and within, the regulatory perimeter. FPC Response to HM Treasury Remit and Recommendations to the FPC, 26 March 2015.
See also Treasury Committee, Financial Regulation: a Preliminary Consideration of the Government's Proposals, Seventh Report of Session 2010–11, HC430-I, para 79.
This monitoring role is done with the FPC's statutory objective of protecting and enhancing financial stability in mind. See section 9S(2)(c) BEA 1998.

[177] Section 9P(2)(e) BEA 1998, but see Section 9P(5) BEA 1998.
See also House of Lords House of Commons Joint Committee on the Draft Financial Services Bill Session 2010/12 HL Paper 236, HC 144737.

[178] HM Treasury, Remit and Recommendations for the FPC, 29 October 2018, available at <https://www.gov.uk/government/collections/financial-policy-remit>.

[179] HM Treasury, Remit and Recommendations for the FPC, 18 March 2015, available at <https://www.gov.uk/government/collections/financial-policy-remit>.

FSOC must report to Congress on recommendations for legislation that would prevent such activities or practices from threatening the stability of the financial system of the US.[180]

The ESRB has the power to issue a recommendation to the Commission to issue draft legislation.[181] Furthermore, the ESRB issues, on its own initiative as well as upon a request, opinions on various draft legislation, labelled "reply" or "response",[182] thus bringing in systemic risk perspectives to legislation that its impact on financial stability may be indirect.

7.2. ALLOWING MODALITIES IN EMERGENCY SITUATIONS

The ESRB is tasked with issuing a confidential warning addressed to the Council where it determines that an emergency situation may arise and provide it with an assessment of the situation.[183] An emergency situation is defined as "adverse developments that could seriously jeopardise the orderly functioning and integrity of financial markets or the stability of the whole or part of the Union's financial system".[184] The Council, in consultation with the ESRB and the Commission, can adopt a decision addressed to the ESAs determining the existence of an emergency situation.[185] There is no indication of any factors that should be taken into account in determining whether an emergency situation exists and the Council's decision is subject to a sunset clause.[186] Moreover, the relation between the emergence of systemic risk and the existence of an emergency situation is not clearly defined in the ESRB Regulation though it is to be assumed that the degree of interruption to the financial markets is the key factor.[187]

---

[180]   Section 120(d)(3) Dodd-Frank Act.

[181]   ESRB Regulation, article 16(1)–(2).

[182]   For instance, the ESRB Reply to the Commission's Public Consultation on Shadow Banking commenting that it is responding to the consultation "as institutional stakeholder"; Letter to the ECOFIN on the Principles for the Development of a Macro-prudential Framework in the EU in the Context of the Capital Requirements Legislation, 29 March 2012. It should be ensured, though, that the opinion is given in the initial stages of consultation to avoid inefficiencies Commission Report on the High-level Group on the ESRB Review (2013) (n 50), 10.

[183]   ESRB Regulation, section 3(2)(e). This is inconsistent with article 18(2) of the ESAs Regulations that state that when the ESRB considers that an emergency situation may arise, it shall issue a confidential recommendation addressed to the Council.

[184]   ESAs Regulations, article 18(1).

[185]   ESAs Regulations, article 18(2). On its own initiative or following a request of the Commission, the ESRB or ESA.

[186]   The Council needs to reconsider it at least once a month and if the declaration is not renewed at the end of the month-period it lapses (ESAs Regulations, article 18(2)).

[187]   Systemic risk is defined as "a risk of disruption in the financial system with the potential to have serious negative consequences for the real economy of the Union or of one or more of its Member States and for the functioning of the internal market" (ESRB Regulation, article 2 (c), as amended).

The initiation of this power, if at all, will be very rare. To date, no emergency has been declared and the Council have not been called upon to declare such a situation. Even in the midst of the euro crisis in 2011, an emergency situation was not declared perhaps fearing that it would aggravate negative market sentiment. The ESRB Chair publicly highlighted the systemic nature of the euro crisis at the hearing before the ECON on 11 October 2011 but in its 2011 Annual Report, it clarified that "the reference to the crisis as systemic was not intended as a declaration of a general state of emergency, but was rather a call for prompt action by all the relevant authorities to take the measures needed to alleviate concerns".[188] It is not surprising that the EBA's Chair described the ESRB emergency powers as a more "nuclear deterrent than an actual power".[189]

Additionally, even if an emergency procedure is declared, the measures that it can activate are restricted. Following the determination of an emergency situation by the Council and "in exceptional circumstances where coordinated action by competent authorities is necessary to respond to adverse developments which may seriously jeopardise the orderly functioning and integrity of financial markets or the stability of the whole or part of the financial system in the Union", the ESAs can adopt individual decisions addressed directly to competent authorities requiring them to take the necessary action to comply with EU law.[190] These decisions are, however, subject to a safeguard clause that prohibits impinging upon the fiscal responsibilities of Member States.[191]

The content of the action is at the discretion of the ESA, but it has to be based on a requirement that is already provided for in EU law. Where a national competent authority has not complied with the decision, as a last resort, the ESAs are entitled to address a decision to financial institutions or market participants requiring them to take the necessary action[192] including the cessation of any practice.[193]

The FSOC's framework also allows for modalities in emergency situations. Procedural requirements of notice and hearing before designation under

---

[188] ESRB 2011 Annual Report, 19 (para 2.2.1).

[189] EU Committee of the House of Lords, "EU Financial Supervisory Framework (Ch 2): The ESAs Powers", para 20, available at <http://www.publications.parliament.uk/pa/ld201012/ldselect/ldeucom/181/18104.htm>.
See also High-Level Group on the ESRB Review (2013) (n 56), 9; S Macphilemy and J Roche, "Review of the New ESFS, Part 2: The Work of the ESRB-The ESFS'S Macro-Prudential Pillar" (2013) Study Commissioned by the ECON, 42 emphasise that there was a broad agreement amongst stakeholders that the emergency procedure in its current form is flawed and requires clarification.

[190] ESAs Regulations, article 18(3), as amended. The Regulation amending the ESAs Regulation add also "which may seriously jeopardise … or customer and consumer protection".

[191] ESAs Regulations, article 38. Member States are prohibited from abusing this safeguard clause.

[192] ESAs Regulations, article 18(4).

[193] ESAs Regulations, article 18(4).

section 113(e) can be waived or modified for emergency necessity by a majority of two-thirds and an affirmative vote of the FSOC chair.[194] Still, the discretion of the FSOC is not without limitations. The FSOC must provide notice of the waiver to the non-bank financial company,[195] allow it to request an opportunity for a written or oral hearing to contest the waiver[196] and consult the primary regulatory agency before it makes any determination.[197]

As discussed in Section 1, the FPC's framework also allows for certain modalities by reason of urgency. For instance, macroprudential measures that are within the FPC's power of direction can be adjusted, from time to time, by an order prescribed by Treasury after consulting with the FPC and approved by Parliament.[198] However, if the Treasury considers that the delay involved in consulting the FPC would be prejudicial to the stability of the UK financial system, it can consult the Governor of the Bank.[199] In addition, an order can be made without a draft being laid before and approved by Parliament if the Treasury is of the opinion that it is necessary to do so, by reason of urgency.[200]

8. CONCLUSION

The macroprudential regulatory and supervisory cycle can be grouped into three phases: "make", "operate" and "review".[201] The chapter critically analysed these phases through the lenses of international law theories and identified a host of challenges and hurdles that could impede the effectiveness of macroprudential policymaking.

In the "making" phase, the chapter outlined the scope of macroprudential powers and the prevalent current state of semi-soft powers. These powers can be strengthened, to varying degrees, along the Abbott's continuum through reinforcing mechanisms such as "comply or explain", the precision of the macroprudential authority's outputs and their formation within a legal framework and pre-defined decision-making procedures. The chapter presented a myriad of challenges posed by the "comply or explain mechanism" in the macroprudential setting. In particular, decoupling the macroprudential mandate from the activation of policy measures may result in a suboptimal regulatory

---

[194] Section 113(f)(1) Dodd-Frank Act.
[195] Section 113(f)(2) Dodd-Frank Act.
[196] Section 113(f)(4) Dodd-Frank Act.
[197] Section 113(g) Dodd-Frank Act.
[198] Sections 9L and 9N BEA 1998.
[199] Section 9L(2)(b) BEA 1998.
[200] Section 9N(2) BEA 1998.
[201] OECD, *Best Practice Principles for Regulatory Policy The Governance of Regulators*, 2014, available at <https://www.oecd.org/gov/regulatory-policy/governance-regulators.htm>, 25.

turf war between the macroprudential authority and the "implementing" prudential agencies. This becomes a salient concern if it results in inaction. The chapter suggests that the macroprudential legal framework should anticipate the inherent difficulties in "sharing regulatory space" and resolve them by aligning the mandate of the "implementing" regulators to reflect financial stability and putting coordination mechanisms in place. Greater coordination is "likely to improve the overall quality of decision making by introducing multiple perspectives and specialised knowledge and structuring opportunities for agencies to test their information and ideas. Coordination instruments can incentivise and equip agencies to monitor each other."[202] To maximise these benefits, the macroprudential authority should seek input from stakeholders and regulatory agencies with expertise at earlier stages of the policymaking. At the same time, it is important to be cognisant of the potential pay-off of procedural requirements in terms of impeding the timeliness of the macroprudential authority's outputs.

The assessment of the "operate" phase in the policy cycle focused on compliance as the Achilles Heel of semi-soft powers. The chapter underlined the procedural quality of the law-making process and the legitimacy that flows from it as key factors in ensuring compliance. Finally, in the review phase, the chapter signals out adaptability as a key component for the design of macroprudential powers and in particular, the ability to expand, where necessary the regulatory perimeter and the macroprudential toolkit.

---

[202] Administrative Conference of the United States, "Improving Coordination of Related Agency Responsibilities" (2012), available at <https://www.acus.gov/recommendation/improving-coordination-related-agency-responsibilities>.

CHAPTER 5

FORMULATING A TAXONOMY OF SUPERVISORY APPROACHES IN MACROPRUDENTIAL POLICYMAKING

Being a relatively new policy area, macroprudential policy has not yet developed a coherent and effective set of approaches to guide its decision-making process.[1] The aim of this chapter is to fill in this gap by formulating a taxonomy of approaches in macroprudential policymaking and critically evaluating their suitability and effectiveness in achieving the financial stability mandate.

Chapter 7 will suggest that in macroprudential policy, the causal link between the macroprudential authorities' performance and the outcome (prevention or mitigation of systemic risks) is difficult to establish. Moreover, what constitutes a "good" outcome can also be disputed. These challenges advocate evaluating the performance of macroprudential supervision at the process level and reiterate the importance of the quality of the decision-making process. To this end, a structured policy process and well-thought-through supervisory approaches can broaden the sources of information, strengthen legitimacy and provide a benchmark to hold, where appropriate, macroprudential authorities accountable.

---

[1] This is to be differentiated from the attention given to supervisory approaches in micro-prudential policy.

On the changes in supervisory approaches following the 2007–2009 financial crisis see J Palmer and C Cerruti, "Is There a Need to Rethink the Supervisory Process?" (The World Bank and Banco de Espana International Conference "Reforming Financial Regulation and Supervision: Going Back to Basics", Madrid, 15 June 2009). For instance, in the UK, the FSA was blamed for having a "light touch" approach to supervision rather than taking a proactive and more intrusive approach. FSA, *The Turner Review: A Regulatory Response to the Global Banking Crisis*, March 2009, 86–88.

In particular, financial supervisors moved away from a reactive and box-ticking approach to an adaptive and more intrusive one. See S Lautenschläger, "Ten Years After the Crisis – Risks, Rules and Supervision", the 13th Association of Supervisors of Banks of the Americas – BCBS – Financial Stability Institute High-Level Meeting on Global and Regional Supervisory Priorities in Nassau, Bahamas, 30 October 2018, available at <https://www.bankingsupervision.europa.eu/press/speeches/date/2018/html/ssm.sp181030.en.html>.

This chapter, accordingly, develops a taxonomy of the potential approaches to guide the decision-making process in the macroprudential sphere and explores the viability and desirability of these approaches. In addition, where information is available, it seeks to establish the current state of approaches adopted by national and regional macroprudential authorities and identify any legal, practical or other obstacles in their implementation.

The chapter suggests the taxonomy of macroprudential supervisory approaches to be categorised as follows: (1) a cost-benefit approach, which is currently embedded in both the FPC and the FSOC's legislative frameworks; (2) an entity-based approach or an activity-based approach (the former focuses on the designation of individual institutions as systemically important and subjecting them to enhanced regulation, whilst the latter focuses on regulating activities that could potentially result in the emergence of systemic risk); (3) a rule-based approach, a discretionary approach or a middle positioned approach that is based on "constrained discretion".

These approaches can be embedded in the legislative framework of the macroprudential authority or adopted as a procedure routinely pursued, without a legal basis, by a macroprudential authority to guide its policy analysis.[2]

1.   A COST-BENEFIT APPROACH

1.1.   A CRITICAL ASSESSMENT OF A COST-BENEFIT ANALYSIS IN MACROPRUDENTIAL POLICYMAKING

In a broad-brush view, a cost-benefit analysis is often described as a simple pragmatic tool; a decision procedure or an "analytical template" designed to promote a better appreciation of and close attention to the consequences of regulation.[3] In its pure quantified form it involves an effort "(1) to quantify the anticipated consequences of regulatory action and (2) to monetise those consequences in terms of benefits and costs, subject to (3) a feasibility constraint, which is meant to acknowledge that some consequences may be hard or

---

[2]   This was the encompassing approach adopted in JC Coates, "Cost-Benefit Analysis of Financial Regulation: Case Studies and Implications" (2015) 124(4) Yale Law Journal 882, 891.

[3]   C Sunstein, *Risk and Reason: Safety, Law and the Environment* (Cambridge University Press, 2002), 9; MD Adler and EA Posner, *New Foundations of Cost-Benefit Analysis* (Harvard University Press, 2006) refer to cost-benefit analysis as a decision procedure (p 167); H Manne, "Will the SEC's New Embrace of Cost-Benefit Analysis Be a Watershed Moment?" (2012) 35 Regulation 20, 23 refers to it as an analytical template for the consideration of new rules.

impossible to quantify or monetise".[4] Therefore, in its pure form, a cost-benefit approach entails quantification of all benefits and costs in a single bottom-line metric which represent the net welfare effects of a proposed regulation.[5]

A cost-benefit approach has long been employed in many areas of regulation, such as in environment and health and safety regulation.[6] Financial regulation was no exception.[7] The general trend in the US, EU and the UK seem to favour a robust costs-benefit analysis in the regulatory decision-making.[8] So much so that it was observed that "The American Regulatory state and indeed regulatory states all over the globe are becoming costs-benefit states" and suggested that there should be a presumption in favour of a cost-benefit analysis in a regulatory decision-making.[9]

More recently, a cost-benefit analysis has been introduced to the sphere of macroprudential policymaking. But does a cost-benefit analysis fit in with macroprudential policy, being quite different from other policy areas? If so, what are the challenges it will need to overcome, and can it be designed in a manner which reflects the uncertainties of costs and benefits associated with macroprudential policymaking?

---

4   C Sunstein, "Financial Regulation and Cost benefit Analysis A response to Cost-Benefit Analysis of Financial Regulation: Case Studies and Implications" (2015) 124 Yale Law Journal Forum 263.

5   Ibid.

6   For instance, AC Harberger, "Three Basic Postulates for Applied Welfare Economics: An Interpretive Essay" (1971) 9(3) Journal of Economic Literature 785.

7   E Posner and EG Weyl, "Benefit-Cost Analysis for Financial Regulation" (2013) 103(3) The American Economic Review Papers and Proceedings 393; Sunstein (2015) (n 4). Though it faces great resistance.
     For instance, JH Cochrane, "Cost-Benefit Analysis as a Framework for Financial Regulation" (16 February 2014), available at SSRN: <https://ssrn.com/abstract=2425885>; Coates (2015) (n 2); RL Revesz, "Cost-Benefit Analysis and the Structure of the Administrative State: The Case of Financial Services Regulation" (2016) Institute of Policy Integrity New York University School of Law, available at <https://policyintegrity.org/files/publications/CBA_and_the_Structure_of_the_Administrative_State.pdf>.

8   Sunstein (2002) (n 3), 4; In the UK, for instance, FCA duty in section 138I FSMA 2000; FCA, "How We Analyse the Costs and Benefits of Our Policies", July 2018, available at <https://www.fca.org.uk/publication/corporate/how-analyse-costs-benefits-policies.pdf>; PRA consultation duty before making rules in section 138J of FSMA 2000 and on the predecessor, the FSA see I Alfon and P Andrews, "Financial Services Authority, Cost-benefit Analysis in Financial Regulation: How to Do it and How it Adds Value" (1999) 7(4) Journal of Financial Regulation and Compliance 339.
     See also P Rose and C Walker, "The Importance of Costs Benefit Analysis", Center of Capital Markets Ohio State University, March 2013, available at <http://www.centerforcapitalmarkets.com/wp-content/uploads/2010/04/CBA-Report-3.10.13.pdf>.

9   CR Sunstein, "Is Cost-Benefit Analysis for Everyone?" (2001) 53 Administrative Law Review 299.

To begin with, the approach can be adopted at various conjunctures of the regulatory and supervisory decision-making process. At the regulatory realm, a cost-benefit analysis can be taken before introducing new macroprudential regulation and standards. At the supervisory realm, the approach can appear at multiple phases. First, at the introduction and implementation of a particular macroprudential instrument by the macroprudential authority. Second, when the macroprudential authority is considering adjusting the intensity (calibration) of a macroprudential instrument, for instance, through releasing the instrument or tightening it. Third, when considering designating a financial institution as systemically important and thus subjecting it to stricter regulation and supervision. Finally, a cost-benefit approach can be adopted to guide the assessment of the effectiveness of a macroprudential tool following its implementation.

The benefits of utilising a more formalistic approach in the various phases of macroprudential decision-making are apparent. A cost-benefit analysis promotes a more evidence-based and rational decision-making process.[10] It provides a structured method for macroprudential authorities to conduct informed deliberation, consider the effectiveness of alternative measures and select the most suitable and targeted tool to address the specific source of systemic risk. Furthermore, a cost-benefit analysis can assist a macroprudential authority in bringing to light unintended consequences of its policy decisions, identify potential trade-offs with other policy areas and accordingly, the need for coordination (Chapter 8). For instance, in taking a cost-benefit approach, prior to the implementation of mortgage lending-related provisions, a macroprudential authority will be forced to consider wider housing and socio-economic factors.[11] A cost-benefit approach can also strengthen compliance with policy measures. Where the implementation of macroprudential tools embodies the underlying justifications, it will be more difficult for market players to "game" and circumvent their effect. Furthermore, a cost-benefit analysis is often viewed as a corrective tool that can enhance the quality of the decision-making process through ameliorating cognitive biases.[12] For instance, a cost-benefit analysis

---

[10] On the importance of an evidence-based approach in macroprudential policymaking see A Keller, "Debiasing Macroprudential Policy: An Evidence-Based Approach and the Precautionary Principle" (2018) 34(1) JIBLR 5.

[11] See Inquiry into the Financial Policy Committee's Macroprudential Tools (June 2012) Submission by the Council of Mortgage Lenders to the Treasury Committee's Call for Evidence.

[12] CR Sunstein, "Cognition and Cost-Benefit Analysis" (1999) The Chicago Working Paper in Law and Economics No 85, 9–10; CR Sunstein, "Cost-Benefit Default Principles" (2001) 99 Michigan Law Review 1651, 1662. Sunstein discussed costs-benefit analysis as a mechanism to fight demand for regulation by the public but in the context of macroprudential policymaking it would be the opposite – demand to delay or tone down policy measures.

may be used as a way to overcome the availability heuristic, i.e. the tendency to judge frequency or probability of risks "by the ease with which instances or associations could be brought to mind".[13] The availability heuristic can limit the accuracy of predictions of macroprudential authorities and gradually result in a premature easing of policy measures.[14] The challenge of macroprudential authorities in making unpopular decisions and going against the natural perception that "this time is different"[15] will grow stronger with the lapse of time since the last crisis.[16] A well-informed policy decision based on a cost-benefit analysis can correct, at least in part, this "mental short-cut that produces errors".[17]

Finally, taking a cost-benefit approach could promote good governance and accountability in macroprudential policymaking. To begin with, a more fine-grained analysis promotes transparency of the decision-making process and the understanding of the public and relevant stakeholders of the considerations and reasons behind policy decisions. This, in turn, can alleviate concerns with regard to the legitimacy of macroprudential authorities as unelected technocrats, by shifting the emphasis to their expertise and the robustness of the decision-making process as a genuine deliberative and informed process (Chapter 7). The conduct of a cost-benefit analysis provides a structured framework and benchmark for challenging policy decisions and where appropriate, holding the macroprudential authority to account for its actions (or inactions). It also brings to the fore a more evidence-based decision-making process thus insulating, to some extent, macroprudential authorities from unwanted political and industry pressure.[18]

Conversely, there are particularly strong grounds for resistance to pursuing a cost-benefit approach in the macroprudential sphere. First, the static nature of the cost-benefit analysis is not compatible with the complex, adaptive and dynamic nature of financial systems and the macroprudential mandate (Chapter 2).

---

[13]   A Tversky and D Kahneman, "Availability: A Heuristic for Judging Frequency and Probability" (1973) 5(2) Cognitive Psychology 207, 208.

[14]   A Khan, "A Behavioral Approach to Financial Supervision, Regulation, and Central Banking" (2018) IMF Working Paper 178.

[15]   On this recurrent syndrome in the history of crises, see C Reinhart and K Rogoff, This Time is Different: Eight Centuries of Financial Folly (Princeton University Press, 2011).

[16]   See, for instance, M Taylor, External member of the FPC, "Questionnaire for Treasury Select Committee" (21 March 2018), available at <https://www.bankofengland.co.uk/-/media/boe/files/about/people/martin-taylor/martin-taylor-questionnaire-2018.pdf> confessing that "... perhaps most dangerous, the lapse of time since the crisis makes it harder to maintain the necessary vigilance".

[17]   Sunstein (1999) (n 12), 8.

[18]   E Posner, "Controlling Agencies with Cost-Benefit Analysis: A Positive Political Theory Perspective" (2001) 68 University Chicago Law Review 1137, at 1198 suggests that a cost-benefit analysis reduces the influence of interest groups on regulations.

Where a financial system continuously evolves through innovation and regulatory arbitrage, in effect, it challenges the assumptions on which any purported cost-benefit analysis relied upon.[19] In this environment, rule adoption becomes impossible to quantify in a meaningful way and the rigid exercise of a cost-benefit analysis is even viewed by some as fruitless.[20] This is a compelling argument but a contrary view would suggest that in fact, a cost-benefit analysis instigates dynamism. It does so by indicating where future research is most needed, creating an incentive to close data gaps and even stimulating the development of methods to analyse these factors.[21]

Nonetheless, it cannot be denied that in practical terms, it is hard (and some would argue impossible) to estimate the benefits of particular macroprudential measures, i.e. the expected gains from a reduction of systemic risk in the form of lower probabilities of crises and their associated costs.[22] This estimate depends on a variety of factors, such as the interpretation of past crises, the model used to infer from past crises to the occurrence of future crises,[23] and on behavioural elements and the irrational reaction of financial actions that are intrinsically hard to predict. A cost-benefit assessment is also affected by other

---

[19]   JN Gordon, '"The Empty Call for Benefit-Cost Analysis in Financial Regulation" (2014) Columbia Law and Economics 464, available at SSRN: <https://papers.ssrn.com/sol3/papers.cfm?abstract_id=2378562>, 19.

[20]   Ibid, 4; Coates (2015) (n 2) provides examples on the weakness of contestable assumptions made in a cost-benefit analysis.
On the difficulty to assess systemic risk see PP Hansen, "Challenges in Identifying and Measuring Systemic Risk" (2012) NBER Working Paper No 18505.

[21]   E Posner and EG Weyl, "Cost-Benefit Analysis of Financial Regulations: A Response to Criticisms" (2015) 124 Yale Law Journal Forum 246, 249.

[22]   On the difficulty in assessing the real costs of a financial crisis see Cochrane (2014) (n 7), 7.
In contrast, see E Posner and EG Weyl, "Speculation, Insurance, and Financial Regulation Benefit-Cost Analysis for Financial Regulation" (2013) 103(3) American Economic Review: Papers and Proceedings 393 suggest assigning a monetary value to the cost of a statistical crisis (CSC), i.e. the reduced chance of both individual bank failures and systemic, observe that estimating is "relatively easy" and advocate a figure in the $1–2 trillion range.
See also E Posner and EG Weyl, "Benefit-Cost Paradigms in Financial Regulation" (2013) Coase-Sandor Institute for Law and Economics Working Paper No 660.
But see Brief of Amici Curiae in Support of Appellant and Reversal, *MetLife Inc. v Financial Stability Oversight Council* No 16-5086 WL 4440274 (C.A.D.C. 22 August 2016), 24–25 suggesting that there are systemic risk measurement tools, such as Value-at-Risk and stress tests, that enable the FSOC to conduct the cost-benefit analysis. These mechanisms, however, have been criticised for relying on arbitrary assumptions. See, for instance, VV Acharya, R Engle and D Pierret, "Testing Macroprudential Stress Tests: The Risk of Regulatory Risk Weights" (2013) NBER Working Paper No 18968.

[23]   D Kohn and RS Kerr, "Macroprudential Policy: Implementation and Effectiveness", Speech at the Brookings European Central Bank, Frankfurt, 27 April 2016, available at <https://www.bankofengland.co.uk/-/media/boe/files/speech/2016/macroprudential-policy-implementation-and-effectiveness>.
See also Coates (2015) (n 2), 967.

(practically endless) exogenous factors, such as interaction with other policy areas, the real economy and other macroprudential tools (Chapter 6). Moreover, there are indirect or unintended costs that may become evident only after the implementation of a particular macroprudential tool consequently falling outside the scope of the initial analysis.[24]

It, therefore, comes as no surprise that these predictions or estimates are often referred to as mere guesswork.[25] To put it simply, if there is no single definition of financial stability and the variables used for assessing systemic risk are still evolving (Chapter 1), how can there be a meaningful cost-benefit analysis in macroprudential policymaking?

Another crucial limitation of a cost-benefit analysis is that, in its pure quantitative form, it fails to consider distributional effects of policy decisions and regards transfers as neutral:

> "… how should cost-benefit analysis handle large transfers? Are huge bailouts, from taxpayers to bank creditors and stockholders, from equity investors to creditors, from old homeowners to young home buyers, really neutral in cost-benefit analysis? … But of course most of the fights over government policy are exactly about enacting or limiting zero-sum transfers, and much of the public outrage during the financial crisis was about transfers … it seems foolish to ignore transfers. Yet it is inconsistent with economic principles to enshrine them as 'costs.'"[26]

A pure cost-benefit analysis may, therefore, ignore the distributional effects of an LTV cap (Chapter 6) or the imbalance of powers between developed and emerging and developing economies in the global financial architecture (Chapter 10). Moreover, the use of a cost-benefit analysis can act as camouflage and obscure the true process behind it, which involves subjective judgement and much uncertainty. It might reflect a "pretence to information that regulators

---

24 On unintended consequences of macroprudential tools see K Forbes, "Macroprudential Policy: What We've Learned, Don't Know and Need to Do" (2019) 109 American Economic Review Papers and Proceedings 470.
    The position on the financial cycle at the time of the implementation of the tools will also affect the costs and benefits in the short and medium term. See ESRB, "Features of Macroprudential Stance: Initial Considerations", April 2019, available at <https://www.esrb.europa.eu/pub/pdf/reports/esrb.report190408_features_macroprudential_stance_initial_considerations~f9cc4c05f4.en.pdf>, 27.

25 Posner and Weyl (2015) (n 22), 21 acknowledge that regulators "would need to fund additional studies before they can-do high-quality BCAs and so in the interim would need to rely largely on informed guesswork".

26 Cochrane (2014) (n 7), 7.
    There are ways to consider distributional effects within the cost-benefit framework. See, for instance, in the UK the FCA considers distributional effects in its cost-benefit analysis – FCA, "How We Analyse the Costs and Benefits of Our Policies", July 2018, available at <https://www.fca.org.uk/publication/corporate/how-analyse-costs-benefits-policies.pdf>, 35.

simply lack"[27] and potentially mislead the public[28] and stakeholders who are tasked with holding macroprudential authorities accountable.

Such arguments are indeed convincing if a cost-benefit analysis is used in its pure form. Introducing a qualitative assessment that complements the quantitative assessment,[29] however, may resolve the problems of pretence and blindness to distributional effects in the decision-making process of macroprudential authorities.

Finally, and perhaps most importantly, a cost-benefit balancing may exacerbate the tendency of macroprudential authorities to inaction bias. Macroprudential authorities may be incentivised to "sit and wait" until further data is collected, and deeper analysis can be performed resulting in "paralysis by analysis".[30] The risk of stagnation by analysis is a real concern for macroprudential authorities, as explained in a recent ESRB Working Paper:

> The assessment of short-term costs and the tolerance to bear those before reaping benefits may delay or even impede policy actions. While the objective of macroprudential policy is financial stability, there is a trade-off between growth and risk as reducing systemic risk may have short-run costs in terms of lower economic growth ... Since the benefits of macroprudential policy usually materialise later or are less obvious, while at the same time the costs have a more immediate visibility, short-term calculations of the net benefits can be difficult. A strong time preference for the present (as opposed to the future) may lead to the conclusion that macroprudential policy actions would create excessive costs when accounting for their overall discounted costs and benefits.[31]

The use of a cost-benefit analysis in the macroprudential decision-making process thus faces many practical impediments.[32] The scepticism about

---

[27] L Heinzerling, "Regulatory Costs of Mythic Proportions" (1985) 107 Yale Law Journal 1981 2068; Sunstein (2015) (n 4).

[28] Coates (2015) (n 2), 902.

[29] Sunstein (1999) (n 12), 37.

[30] C Sunstein, "Cost-Benefit Default Principles" (2001) 99 Michigan Law Review 1651; Cochrane (2014) (n 7), 5 also suggests that a cost-benefit analysis adds "more layers of process risk the danger that nothing gets done."

[31] Moreover, costs occurring in the short run can normally be allocated to existing stakeholders while medium benefits cannot be attributed to specific parts of the society. ESRB, "Features of Macroprudential Stance" (2019) (n 24), 26–27. More generally, on the status quo bias, i.e. the fact that the costs of a policy change are often far easier to quantify than its benefits see RH Frank, "Why is Costs-Benefit Analysis So Controversial?" in DM Hausman (ed), *The Philosophy of Economics an Anthology* (Cambridge University Press, 2008), 251, 266.

[32] In practice, it is largely feasible to conduct such an assessment. See, for instance, M Behn, M Gross and T Peltonen, "Assessing the Costs and Benefits of Capital-based Macroprudential Policy" (2016) ECB Working Paper Series No 1935, available at <https://www.ecb.europa.eu/pub/pdf/scpwps/ecbwp1935.en.pdf>.

quantification is somewhat justified given that measuring long-term benefits is particularly elusive. Nonetheless, the approach offers a structured framework within which policy decisions are supported by available evidence, rationalised and transparent. Following the implementation of macroprudential measures and after sufficient time has passed, a cost-benefit analysis can also enable macroprudential authorities to gauge the effectiveness of the measures.[33] The analytical limitations should not result in the rejection of a cost-benefit balancing to guide macroprudential policymaking. The adoption of a tailored version that considers distributional and qualitative aspects[34] and offers ranges with a full appreciation of the possibility of uncertainty[35] will address some of the concerns raised here.

But how will this rather amorphous approach work and look in practice in macroprudential policymaking? A recent ESRB working paper provides a useful insight and a more concrete description of an ex-ante cost-benefit analysis in the macroprudential decision-making process:

> Before specific policy decisions are taken, ex-ante evaluation provides information on their likely costs and benefits. Policy evaluation builds on the policy objectives and intermediate objectives of macroprudential policies as benchmarks. Such benchmarks can include qualitative objectives, such as improving the resilience of the financial system, but these should ideally be linked to the policy objectives through a measurable metric (indicator) such as the degree of capitalization of the financial system. Once such a metric has been identified and quantified, work needs to be done to examine how alternative policy choices affect the probability of reaching that target. Comparing alternative ways of reaching the same target allows cost-benefit analysis to be performed.[36]

Three important observations can be made here. First, a cost-benefit analysis has to be conducted against the macroprudential mandate (on its various components and intermediate objectives). Second, while a qualitative assessment is an integral part of the process (and accordingly, the conduct of a value judgment), it should still be linked to a quantitative measurement. Any other approach would render the exercise pointless. Third, a key component of

---

See also M Brooke and others, "Measuring the Macroeconomic Costs and Benefits of Higher UK Bank Capital Requirement" (2015) Bank of England Financial Stability Paper No 35, available at <https://www.bankofengland.co.uk/financial-stability-paper/2015/measuring-the-macroeconomic-costs-and-benefits-of-higher-uk-bank-capital-requirements>.

33   CM Buch, E Vogel and B Weigert, "Evaluating Macroprudential Policies" (2018) ESRB Working Paper Series No 76, 10.

34   Ibid, 18.

35   Sunstein, *Risk and Reason* (2002) (n 3), 292. Coates (2015) (n 2), 893 terms this approach "a conceptual cost-benefit analysis".

36   Buch and others (2018) (n 33), 10.

the cost-benefit analysis should be considering alternative approaches.[37] This form of a cost-benefit analysis has the best of both worlds: it acknowledges the analytical limitations (i.e. it is subject to feasibility) and incorporates qualitative assessment thus enabling it to be used as a good governance tool.

1.2. ARE MACROPRUDENTIAL AUTHORITIES ADOPTING A COST-BENEFIT ANALYSIS TO GUIDE THEIR POLICY DECISIONS?

In the UK, the FPC is required when exercising its functions under the Bank of England Act 1998 to "be sure that (a) the principle that a burden or restriction which is imposed on a person, or on the carrying on of an activity, should be proportionate to the benefits, considered in general terms, which are expected to result from the imposition of that burden or restriction".[38] In addition, an explanation of the reasons for the FPC's decision to exercise its powers and their compatibility with the FPC's duties must include an estimate of the costs and benefits that would arise from compliance with the direction or recommendation in question, unless in the opinion of the FPC, it is not reasonably practicable to include such an estimate.[39]

In its response to the Chancellor's remit and recommendations, the FPC explained how it views this duty:

> In deriving quantitative estimates of costs and benefits, it will be important to recognise that such estimates are inevitably highly uncertain, and that costs of compliance with regulatory actions are often tangible and immediate, while benefits can be material but more distant and uncertain. In some cases, therefore, the Committee [FPC – author's addition] may explore the practicality of publishing indicative ranges for the costs and benefits. The Committee may conclude, as it is able to under the legislation,

---

[37] This is not always taken for granted. In the context of consumer protection see for instance, FCA Consultation Paper Rules and Guidance on Payment Protection Insurance Complaints: Feedback on CP15/39 and Further Consultation, CP16/20 August 2016, 139: "The CBA [cost-benefit analysis – author's addition] was conducted against the counterfactual of the status quo, which we consider the relevant counterfactual in this situation. We are not required to assess a proposed intervention against other possible interventions or counterfactual scenarios".

[38] Section 9F(3)(a) BEA 1998.

[39] Sections 9S(3) and 9S(1) BEA 1998 in relation to specified powers as defined in section 9S(2) BEA 1998; Bank of England, "The Financial Policy Committee Framework for Systemic Risk Buffer", May 2016, available at <https://www.bankofengland.co.uk/-/media/boe/files/paper/2016/the-financial-policy-committees-framework-for-the-systemic-risk-buffer>, 23 provides an example of a cost-benefit analysis of the Systemic Risk Buffer calibration, referring to the exercise as "impact assessment".

that quantitative estimates are not reasonably practicable, though it will nevertheless set out qualitatively its reasoning for its policy actions.[40]

In the UK, a cost-benefit analysis is, therefore, the default position and is viewed as a vital accountability mechanism.[41] The FPC is expected to produce it unless there are *very strong reasons* to justify why, in that particular instance, it is not practicable to do so.[42]

In the US, the recent decision in the *MetLife* case, as will be discussed in length below, renewed the debate on the suitability of a cost-benefit analysis in macroprudential regulation and supervision. Section 113 of the Dodd-Frank Act assigns to the FSOC the authority to determine that a non-bank financial company's material financial distress – or the nature, scope, size, scale, concentration, interconnectedness, or mix of its activities – could pose a threat to US financial stability and subject it to consolidated supervision by the Federal Reserve and enhanced prudential standards.[43] In making a determination, the FSOC is required to consider specific factors such as the leverage of the company and the amount and nature of assets and liabilities of the company.[44] There is also a catch-all factor referring to – "any other risk-related factors that the Council deems appropriate".[45]

In 2014, the FSOC designated MetLife as a non-bank financial company under section 113 of the Dodd-Frank Act and in 2015, MetLife contested that determination in court proceedings, inter alia, on the ground that the FSOC failed to consider the costs to the designated company.[46] In 2016, the US District Court ruled in favour of MetLife, finding the determination to be

---

[40] A letter from Mark Carney as the Chairman of the FPC to George Osborne Chancellor of the Exchequer dated 31 March 2014, available at <https://www.bankofengland.co.uk/-/media/boe/files/letter/2014/governor-letter-010414>.

[41] HM Treasury, "Detail of Outcome for FPC's Leverage Ratio Consultation Framework", January 2015, available at <https://assets.publishing.service.gov.uk/government/uploads/system/uploads/attachment_data/file/400447/PU1749_Consultation_Leverage_Response.pdf>, para 2.67. For the challenges in conducting a cost-benefit approach see D Kohn and RS Kerr, "Macroprudential policy: Implementation and Effectiveness", Speech at the Brookings European Central Bank, Frankfurt, 27 April 2016, available at <https://www.bankofengland.co.uk/-/media/boe/files/speech/2016/macroprudential-policy-implementation-and-effectiveness>.

[42] HM Treasury, "Detail of Outcome for FPC's Housing Market Tools", January 2015, available at <https://assets.publishing.service.gov.uk/government/uploads/system/uploads/attachment_data/file/400448/PU1748_Consultation_Housing_Response.pdf>, para 2.6. Note that the words "very strong reasons" are not found in the BEA 1998.

[43] Section 113(a)(1) Dodd-Frank Act. Often referred to as Systemically Important Financial Institution (SIFI) designation.

[44] Section 113(a)(2)(A)–(J) Dodd-Frank Act.

[45] Section 113(a)(2)(K) Dodd-Frank Act.

[46] *MetLife Inc. v Financial Stability Oversight Council*, Civil Action No 15-0045, US District Court, District of Columbia (Washington, 30 March 2016).

arbitrary and capricious and therefore must be rescinded.[47] The FSOC appealed and later on, the appeal was held in abeyance until the issuance of a report made by the Treasury Department.[48] The US Treasury Report titled "Financial Stability Oversight Council Designations" was issued in November 2017.[49] It recommended that a cost-benefit analysis informs the determination of a non-bank financial company and that for a designation to proceed the FSOC will need to conclude that "the expected benefits from financial stability Federal Reserve supervision and enhanced prudential standard outweigh the costs that designation would impose".[50] The Treasury Report acknowledged the limitations of a cost-benefit analysis but suggested that these are side-stepped by the good governance benefits associated with it, observing that:

> Financial stability benefits may be difficult to quantify, and some of the costs may be difficult to forecast with precision. But the analytical discipline of weighing costs against benefits – and quantifying those impacts to the extent feasible – improve the quality of administrative decision-making and ensures that agencies take account of the relevant trade-offs and alternatives.[51]

Thereafter, the FSOC and MetLife jointly filed a motion to dismiss the case and MetLife was rescinded from its designation as SIFI under section 113 of the Dodd-Frank Act.[52]

---

[47] Ibid, citing *Michigan v Environmental Protection Agency*, U.S. 135 S. Ct. 2699, 192 L.Ed. 2d 67 (2015) where the court held that considering the cost of regulation is essential to reasoned rulemaking.
According to section 113(h) Dodd-Frank Act judicial review of determination will be limited to whether it was arbitrary and capricious.
On the challenges of judicial review of supervisory decisions see JC Laguna de Paz, "Administrative and Judicial Review of EU Supervisory Decisions in the Banking Sector" (2019) 20 Journal of Banking 159. See Chapter 7 on judicial review as an accountability mechanism and its limitations.

[48] Pursuant to the Presidential Memorandum for the Secretary of the Treasury issued by President Donald Trump on 21 April 2017, available at <https://www.whitehouse.gov/presidential-actions/presidential-memorandum-secretary-treasury/>.

[49] The Department of Treasury, Report to the President of the United States Financial Stability Oversight Council Designation, 17 November 2017, available at <https://www.treasury.gov/press-center/press-releases/documents/pm-fsoc-designations-memo-11-17.pdf> (Treasury Report).

[50] Ibid, 27.

[51] Ibid.

[52] Following this, in October 2018 the FSOC rescinded Prudential Financial Inc, the last designated non-bank financial company, from its designation. FSOC, Notice and Explanation of the Basis for the Financial Stability Oversight Council's Rescission of Its Determination Regarding Prudential Financial Inc. 2 (16 October 2018).
For criticism on de-designation of Prudential Financial Inc. suggesting that the FSOC relied on questionable reliable analyses and rejected more reliable evidence see JC Kress, "The Last SIFI: The Unwise and Illegal Deregulation of Prudential Financial" (2018) 71 Stanford Law Review Online 171.

Both the District Court's decision and the Treasury Report's recommendations were subject to heavy criticism in light of the analytical challenges of a cost-benefit analysis, suggesting that such an approach will result in holding the FSOC to an impossible standard.[53] Nonetheless, the move to a cost-benefit approach when using the designation authority is now final. Following the MetLife case, the FSOC issued a final interpretive guidance ("FSOC's Guidance") that includes a requirement to perform a cost-benefit analysis before making a designation.[54] Under the FSOC's Guidance, the FSOC will make a designation only if the expected benefits justify the expected costs that the determination would impose. The FSOC will quantify reasonable estimable benefits and costs (using ranges, as appropriate), and consider non-quantified benefits and costs, in assessing the net benefits of a designation.[55] When evaluating a company for potential designation, the FSOC will consider not only the impact of an identifiable risk but also the likelihood that the risk will be realised. Therefore, when evaluating the overall impact of a designation for any company under review, the FSOC will assess the likelihood of a company's material financial distress.[56]

As will be discussed in Section 3 below, the formal introduction of a cost-benefit analysis to the FSOC's designation process fits in well with the move to an activity-based rather than an entity-based approach but it can also mean raising the non-bank SIFI bar so high that few, if any, companies would be designated, thereby potentially foregoing the resulting benefits of additional US Federal Reserve oversight.[57]

To conclude, it is indisputable that macroprudential policymaking involves trade-offs, weighing normative considerations and distributional effects. Nonetheless, this difficulty only underscores the need for a cost-benefit analysis

---

[53]   JC Kress, PA McCoy and DB Schwarcz, "Regulating Entities and Activities: Complementary Approaches to Nonbank Systemic Risk" (2019) Southern California Law Review 1455, available at SSRN <https://ssrn.com/abstract=3238059>; PA McCoy, "Knightian Uncertainty, Systemic Risk Regulation, and the Limits of Judicial Review" (31 March 2017), available at SSRN: <https://ssrn.com/abstract=2944297>.

[54]   FSOC, "Authority to Require Supervision and Regulation of Certain Nonbank Financial Companies", Final Interpretive Guidance 84 Fed. No 249 Reg. 71740 (30 December 2019), available at <https://www.govinfo.gov/content/pkg/FR-2019-12-30/pdf/2019-27108.pdf>, 71754.

[55]   Ibid, at 71766.

[56]   Ibid, at 71767. In addition, the FSOC's Guidance (n 54), at 71763 defines "threat to financial stability of the United States" a threat of an impairment of financial intermediation or of financial market functioning that would be sufficient to inflict "severe damage" on the broader economy. This is to be differentiated from the previous 2012 Guidance that used a lower bar of "significant damage". FSOC Authority To Require Supervision and Regulation of Certain Nonbank Financial Companies Final Rule and Interpretive Guidance Federal Register 21637 Vol 77 No 70, 11 April 2012, at 21657.

[57]   Moody's Vice President Laura Bazer as reported by G Gonzalez, "FSOC Nonbank Designation Proposal Negative for Insurers: Moody's", BusinessInsurance.com (8 March 2019).

to form an integral part of the decision-making process of macroprudential authorities. A cost-benefit analysis would move policy decisions away from a subjective and intuitive judgment and unaccountable criteria to a more neutral and evidence-based framework. Having a well-defined framework that presents rationales behind decisions and considers alternative approaches will enhance the transparency of the decision-making process and provide a benchmark for holding macroprudential authorities accountable.[58]

2. A RULE-BASED APPROACH, A DISCRETIONARY APPROACH OR SOMEWHERE IN BETWEEN

2.1. THE PROMINENCE OF A "CONSTRAINED DISCRETION" APPROACH

Another suggested taxonomy differentiates between a discretionary approach, a rule-based approach or a "constrained discretion" approach as a basis for macroprudential policy decisions. In a discretionary framework, a macroprudential authority will use judgment in determining whether, when and at what intensity to implement macroprudential measures. Clearly, this approach provides flexibility, an important feature in a relatively new policy domain that is not yet fully tested. It makes it easier for macroprudential authorities to calibrate and adjust policy measures to target evolving risks and consider potential cross-policies and cross-tools effects. Additionally, where policy decisions are solely based on judgment, it becomes much more difficult for market players to "game the system" as they do not have a clear benchmark against which they can plan their actions.[59] Accordingly, regulatory arbitrage and avoidance of measures are minimised.[60] Moreover, in the absence of specific triggers and indicators that constrain judgment, a macroprudential authority is also able to make much greater use of all the available data and make a better assessment of the risks.[61] Nonetheless, a discretionary approach introduces a

---

[58] Either in the form of a judicial review as is the case with the FSOC power to designate SIFIs or as an information base and benchmark for other accountability mechanisms (for instance, hearing of the FPC before the Treasury Committee in the UK).

[59] As shall be seen below there is however a trade-off between flexibility and predictability of policy measures.

[60] L Laeven and X Freixas, *Systemic Risks Crises and Macroprudential Regulation* (MIT Press, 2015), 287.

[61] M Kowalik, "Countercyclical Capital Regulation: Should Bank Regulators Use Rules or Discretion?" (2011) Federal Reserve Bank of Kansas City Economic Review Second Quarter, available at <https://www.kansascityfed.org/publicat/econrev/pdf/11Q2Kowalik.pdf>, 67–68.

time-inconsistency problem.[62] A macroprudential authority may succumb to political and industry pressures and avoid taking a pre-emptive action necessary to meet its financial stability objective in favour of meeting a more immediate objective of not inhibiting economic growth.[63] The approach may also negatively affect the predictability of the policy resulting in market players accumulating precautionary liquidity and capital buffers thus unnecessarily increasing the overall cost of capital and credit in the economy.[64]

A rule-based macroprudential framework is based on pre-defined rules that will automatically trigger the implementation of certain instruments when a single indicator or a set of indicators breached a pre-defined threshold. The pros and cons arguments mirror the ones discussed with regard to the discretionary approach. In short, policy decisions that are guided by rules enhance the predictability and transparency of policy decisions[65] and can better shield macroprudential policymakers from political and industry resistance. Furthermore, by putting constraints on the discretion of the macroprudential authority, the approach can mitigate the risk of inaction bias. The rule-based approach faces, however, practical difficulties in designing reliable indicators that would automate the use of instruments.[66] Currently, it seems that it is simply not a feasible option and that we are "many years from having rules to guide macroprudential policy."[67]

A middle-ground approach, the "constrained discretion" or "guided discretion", places constraints on the exercise of discretion.[68] Its flexibility

---

[62]   BL Horvath and W Wagner, "Macroprudential Policies and the Lucas Critique" (2016) BIS Papers No 86, available at <https://www.bis.org/publ/bppdf/bispap86f.pdf>.

[63]   Kowalik (2011) (n 61), 68–69 demonstrates this shortcoming in the context of implementing countercyclical buffer. Moreover, this problem will be self-reinforcing since banks will anticipate it and adjust their behaviour accordingly. I Agur and S Sharma, "Rules, Discretion, and Macro-Prudential Policy" (2013) IMF Working Paper 13/65, available at <https://www.imf.org/external/pubs/ft/wp/2013/wp1365.pdf>.

[64]   Bank of England, "The Role of Macroprudential Policy" (November 2009) Discussion Paper, available at <https://www.bankofengland.co.uk/-/media/boe/files/paper/2009/the-role-of-macroprudential-policy>, 28.

[65]   CGFS, "Macroprudential Instruments and Frameworks: A Stocktaking of Issues and Experiences" (2010) CGFS Papers No 38, 6–7.

[66]   IMF-FSB-BIS, "Elements of Effective Macroprudential Policies Lessons from International Experience" (2016), available at <https://www.imf.org/external/np/g20/pdf/2016/083116.pdf>; Agur and Sharma (n 63), 50 suggest that it is like "Trying to define pre-emptive responses to a rare event using fuzzy measures to calibrate (infrequently used) tools …".

[67]   A Brazier, "How to: MACROPRU 5 Principles for Macroprudential Policy" speech at London School of Economics, Financial Regulation Seminar, 13 February 2017, available at <https://www.bankofengland.co.uk/-/media/boe/files/speech/2017/how-to-macropru-5-principles-for-macroprudential-policy.pdf>.

[68]   Bank of England (2009) (n 64), 28; The ESRB Handbook on Operationalising Macroprudential Policy in the Banking Sector, 22; D Aikman, AG Haldane, M Hinterschweiger and S Kapadia, "Rethinking Financial Stability" (2018) Bank of England Staff Working Paper No 712, available at <https://www.bankofengland.co.uk/-/media/boe/files/working-paper/2018/rethinking-financial-stability.pdf>, 24–25.

---

allows macroprudential policymakers to address unforeseen circumstances while at the same time, its constraints ensure a degree of consistency and can alleviate the time-inconsistency problem.[69] In practice, most countries follow such an approach that combines rules in the form of early warning indicators and discretion.[70] Expert judgment retains a particularly important role when assessing the influence of policy on market participants' behaviour and expectations or where there is uncertainty regarding the extent of an activity being migrated away from the policy measure's reach.[71]

2.2. WHAT IS THE FORM OF THE CONSTRAINTS IN A "CONSTRAINED DISCRETION" APPROACH?

A set of widely accepted early warning indicators which tend to precede financial crises can guide macroprudential policy decisions.[72] Where these indicators reach critical levels, the macroprudential authority will be expected to conduct a more in-depth analysis and take measures to prevent or mitigate emerging risks.[73] Alternatively, it will have to explain in public why a pre-emptive action is not necessary.[74] This approach is often used in practice by macroprudential authorities in the form of risk dashboards that include a set of quantitative and/or qualitative indicators of systemic risk[75] and/or colour-coded "heat maps" that visualise possible sources of systemic risks.[76]

---

[69]   Making it easier for macroprudential authorities to implement politically unpopular measures. Aikman and others (2018) (n 68), 26. This has some similarities with monetary policy frameworks in a number of countries that have proved to be effective. In monetary policy, BS Bernanke and SF Mishkin, "Inflation Targeting: A New Framework for Monetary Policy?" (1997) 11 Journal of Economic Perspectives 97; FE Kydland and EC Prescott, "Rules Rather than Discretion: The Inconsistency of Optimal Plans" (1977) 85(3) The Journal of Political Economy 473.

[70]   IMF-FSB-BIS (2016) (n 66), 13; IMF, "Key Aspects of Macroprudential Policy", 2013, available at <https://www.imf.org/external/np/pp/eng/2013/061013b.pdf>, 23.

[71]   CGFS, "Experiences with the Ex-Ante Appraisal of Macroprudential Instruments" (2016) CGFS Papers No 56. Another reason for expert judgment to retain an overseeing role is that data and analytical tools are not as developed.

[72]   C Goodhart, "The Macroprudential Authority: Powers, Scope and Accountability" (2011) 2 OECD Journal: Financial Market Trends, 24. These include the following when they are growing significantly faster and above their normal trend: a rate of growth of (bank) credit; a rate of growth of housing (and property) prices and a rate of growth of leverage.

[73]   CGFS (2016) (n 71). Supervisory information, including data gathered from market participants and stress tests, will provide a more targeted guidance to inform the setting of macroprudential instruments.

[74]   Goodhart (2011) (n 72), 24.

[75]   For instance, the ESRB publishes quarterly its risk dashboard, following its adoption by the General Board. The dashboard is accompanied by an explanation of the recent development of the indicators and the methodology and description of the indicators.

[76]   For instance, in the US the Office of Financial Research's Financial System Vulnerabilities Monitor is a heat map of 58 indicators of potential vulnerabilities in the US financial system.

International standards set by the BCBS to guide the introduction of a countercyclical capital buffer (CCyB) are a constructive example for the use of guided discretion. The standards combine a reference to the Credit-to-GDP gap to gauge the build-up of systemic risk as well as the use of more discretionary elements reflecting specific economic and financial conditions.[77] Macroprudential authorities are explicitly cautioned to avoid relying mechanistically on the credit/GDP guide and apply judgment.[78]

A guided discretion approach to setting CCyB is widely adopted. In the US, the Federal Reserve considers a number of quantitative indicators indicative of potential vulnerabilities including the Credit-to-GDP gap, with judgment playing an important role in the process.[79] In the UK, the FPC follows a similar approach in its high-level strategy for setting a CCyB.[80] The FPC's strategy includes key indicators as guidance while reiterating that decisions are not mechanically tied to any specific set of indicators and that judgment plays a material role.[81] In the

---

Indictors are colour-coded based on their positions within a long-term range, where scores closer to red signal higher potential vulnerability and scores closer to green signal lower potential vulnerability.

See J McLaughlin and others, "The OFR Financial System Vulnerabilities Monitor" (March 2018) OFR Working Paper.

[77] BCBS, "Guidance for National Authorities Operating the Countercyclical Capital Buffer" (December 2010), available at <https://www.bis.org/publ/bcbs187.pdf>. In the EU, See ESRB Recommendation of 18 June 2014 on Guidance for Setting Countercyclical Buffer Rates (ESRB/2014/1), Recommendation A.

[78] Ibid, 3. There may be cases where the guide may even convey misleading information and should not be followed. The Guidance takes account of local market conditions to reflect different stages of development across jurisdictions, on p 10.

[79] Federal Reserve System, "Regulatory Capital Rules: The Federal Reserve Board's Framework for Implementing the U.S. Basel III Countercyclical Capital Buffer" (Docket No R-1529 RIN 7100 AE-43) Final Policy Statement 14 October 2016. Based on a set of quantitative indicators of financial and economic conditions and a set of empirical models. But "no single indictor or fixed set of indicators can adequately capture all the vulnerabilities in the U.S. economy and financial system." And "in the event that the Board considered that a change in the CCyB were appropriate, it would, in proposing the change, include a discussion of the reasons for the proposed action as determined by the particular circumstances."

See also speech by Mr Randal K Quarles, Vice Chairman for Supervision of the Board of Governors of the Federal Reserve System, at the "Strategic Approaches to the Fed's Balance Sheet and Communications" Spring 2019 Meeting of the Manhattan Institute's Shadow Open Market Committee, New York City, 29 March 2019.

In Canada see DX Chen and I Christensen, "The Countercyclical Bank Capital Buffer: Insights for Canada" Financial Stability Review, December 2010, available at <https://www.bankofcanada.ca/wp-content/uploads/2011/12/fsr-1210-xiao.pdf> and in Switzerland see Swiss National Bank, "Implementing the Countercyclical Capital Buffer in Switzerland: Concretising the Swiss National Bank's Role" (2012) (Bern: Swiss National Bank).

[80] The Financial Policy Committee's Approach to Setting the Countercyclical Buffer, A Bank of England Policy Statement, April 2016, available at <https://www.bankofengland.co.uk/ / media/boe/files/statement/2016/the-financial-policy-committees-approach-to-setting-the-countercyclical-capital-buffer>

[81] Ibid.

EU, "guided discretion" may not be limited to setting a CCyB and may also serve as a model for the implementation of other macroprudential instruments.[82]

But theory and practice are not the same. Recent evidence suggests that in the EU, the BCBS credit-to-GDP gap has had a limited influence on the actual decision-making of macroprudential authorities.[83] Moreover, new challenges in the use of Credit-to-GDP guide are emerging:

> Due to the data lags, the latest available credit gap data are usually from two quarters before the decision ... This data lag could be challenging for communication if the argumentation for a particular decision is heavily built on the level of the Basel gap [Credit-To-GDP gap – author's addition], which might decrease or be revised afterwards. Such a policy error or a revoked build-up could potentially tarnish institutional reputation.[84]

Constraints to discretion should not, therefore, be limited to widely accepted indicators used as a common reference point to guide policy decisions but also include other constraining mechanisms such as explaining the rationales underpinning the decision and communicating them to the public. A cost-benefit based approach can also be viewed as a constraint mechanism to the discretion of the macroprudential authority.

3. ENTITY-BASED AND/OR ACTIVITY-BASED AND/ OR BEHAVIOUR-BASED APPROACH

3.1. LIMITATIONS OF AN ENTITY-BASED APPROACH AND AN ACTIVITY-BASED APPROACH

Designation and supervision of SIFIs took centre stage in the post-crisis regulatory reforms.[85] Because of their size, complexity and interconnectedness,

---

[82]   ESRB Handbook on Operationalising Macroprudential Policy in the Banking Sector (n 68), 11.

[83]   D Babić and S Fahr, "Shelter From the Storm: Recent Countercyclical Capital Buffer Decisions" (2019) ECB Macroprudential Bulletin, available at <https://www.ecb.europa.eu/pub/financial-stability/macroprudential-bulletin/html/ecb.mpbu201903_04~b8ad0c67e9.en.html#toc7>.

[84]   Ibid.

[85]   This is often referred to as Too-Big-To-Fail (TBTF), i.e. the disorderly failure of an institution would cause widespread disruptions in financial markets. M Labonte, "Systemically Important or Too Big To Fail Institutions" (2018) Congressional Research Service R42150, available at <https://fas.org/sgp/crs/misc/R42150.pdf> suggests, however, that TBTF is merely a "popular" term for SIFIs and has inherent limitations.
        G20 leaders called at the Pittsburgh Summit in 2009 on the FSB to propose measures to address the TBTF. The FSB has identified and published every year a list of global systemically

the disorderly failure of these institutions may cause significant disruption to the wider financial system and the economy.[86] An entity-based approach in macroprudential policymaking focuses on the risks of failure of individual institutions and their potential contagion effects (often referred to as the domino perspective).[87] In addition to enhanced regulation and supervision of financial institutions that are designated as SIFIs,[88] an entity-based approach can be used as an effective deterrent tool. As such, "The mere prospect of being designated as a SIFI creates uncertainty, which a firm will likely seek to avoid by reducing its size and complexity."[89]

A common criticism of an entity-based approach, however, is that a designation may result in a market expectation for a government bailout in the event of the SIFI's failure thus creating moral hazard.[90] It can be argued that an entity-based approach does not capture the full breadth and essence of systemic risks that may stem from common exposures of a few large or many small financial institutions that are not designated as SIFIs (known as the

---

important banks (G-SIB). The BCBS publishes the Methodology for Assessing and Identifying Global Systemically Important Banks: Revised Assessment Methodology and the Higher Loss Absorbency Requirement, July 2018 and the IAIS publishes the Methodology for Assessing and Identifying Global Systemically Important Insurers (G-SIIs). However, recently, the FSB, in consultation with the IAIS and national authorities has decided not to publish a new list of G-SIIs for 2017. The background for this decision is outlined below.

[86] FSB, "Reducing the Moral Hazard Posed by Systemically Important Financial Institutions FSB Recommendations and Timelines", 20 October 2010, available at <https://www.fsb.org/wp-content/uploads/r_101111a.pdf>; FSB, Progress and Next Steps towards Ending "Too-Big-To-Fail" Report to the G20, 2 September 2013, available at <http://www.fsb.org/wp-content/uploads/r_130902.pdf>.
These SIFIs are accordingly subject to enhanced prudential oversight, including additional capital buffers. See FSB Report on Intensity and Effectiveness of SIFI Supervision Recommendations for Enhanced Supervision, November 2010, available at <https://www.fsb.org/wp-content/uploads/r_101101.pdf>.

[87] V Acharya, "Are Insurance Firms Systemically Important?" Presentation at Stockholm Institute for Financial Research 2015; IMF, "Global Financial Stability Report Potent Policies for a Successful Normalization", April 2016, 90. The domino perspective considers six key characteristics that guide the assessment of systemic risk posed by individual financial institutions: size, Interconnectedness and integration in financial sector infrastructure, substitutability, leverage, funding liquidity risk and complexity.

[88] See, for instance, BCBS, "Methodology for Assessing and Identifying G-SIBs and Higher Loss-Absorbency Requirement", updated 5 February 2019.

[89] Treasury Report (n 49), 18; Testimony of Jeremy C Kress Before the US Senate Committee on Banking, Housing, and Urban Affairs Hearing on "Financial Stability Oversight Council Nonbank Designations", 14 March 2019.

[90] Treasury Report (n 49), 18. But evidence on these institutions having a funding advantage or an implicit subsidy is mixed.
See also M Labonte "Systemically Important or 'Too Big to Fail' Financial Institutions" 2018 Congressional Research Office, available at <https://fas.org/sgp/crs/misc/R42150.pdf>, 5; A Persaud, "'Too Big to Fail' is No Redemption Song" (February 2010) VoxEU.org argue that in crisis almost everyone is "too big to fail".

"tsunami view").[91] Furthermore, the consequential de-risking of SIFIs following their designation can result in selling off assets to institutions that are not subject to prudential regulation and supervision and in a migration of risks within the financial system instead of elimination of risks.[92]

In light of these concerns, another school of thought advocates targeting financial activities that could create systemic risk, irrespective of the type and characteristics of financial institutions that engage in those activities and independent of their failure or distress.[93] In contrast to the entity-based approach, which takes an impact given default approach, the activity-based approach focuses on common exposures and behaviours that could collectively result in the propagation of systemic risk.[94] It can thus capture systemic risk arising from potentially systemic activities or behaviours by a number of entities or within a particular sector in the financial system.[95]

How do macroprudential authorities identify SIFIs (entity-based approach) and systemic markets/activity (activity-based approach)? An IMF, BIS and FSB report submitted to the G20 Finance Ministers and Central Bank Governors in October 2009 sets out three key criteria for assessing the systemic importance of financial institutions and financial markets: size, interconnectedness and substitutability.[96] The size criterion refers to the volume of financial services provided by the individual component of the financial system;[97] substitutability

---

[91] Acharya (2015) (n 87); K Knot and HV Voorden, "Systemically Important Banks – Possible Options for Policymakers" in A Dombret and O Lucious (eds), *Stability of the Financial System Illusion or Feasible Concept* (Edward Elgar, 2013), 288, 292.
See also ST Omarova, "The 'Too Big To Fail' Problem" (2019) 103 Minnesota Law Review 2495; Cornell Legal Studies Research Paper No 6, available at SSRN <https://ssrn.com/abstract=3309305> discussing "the fundamental paradox at the heart of the TBTF idea: TBTF is an entity-centric, micro-level metaphor for a complex of interrelated systemic, macro-level problems".

[92] Treasury Report (n 49), 19.

[93] For an interesting view of an entity-based approach at the global level see M Kranke and D Yarrow, "The Global Governance of Systemic Risk: How Measurement Practices Tame Macroprudential Politics" 24(6) New Political Economy 1–17 who highlight the potential danger in the IMF taking an entity-based approach to systemic risk by singling out "systemically important" national financial sectors and subjecting them to mandatory FSAP assessment.

[94] International Association of Insurance Supervisors (IAIS), "Holistic Framework for Systemic Risk in the Insurance Sector" Public Consultation, 14 November 2018, 12; IAIS, "Activities Based Approach to Systemic Risk" Public Consultation, December 2017, both available at <www.IAISweb.org/home>.

[95] IMF, "The Insurance Sector – Trends and Systemic Risk Implications" (2016) Global Financial Stability Report, Chapter 3; IMF, "Macroprudential policy-an Organising Framework Background Paper" 2011, 4.

[96] IMF, BIS and FSB, "Guidance to Assess the Systemic Importance of Financial Institutions, Markets and Instruments: Initial Considerations" (October 2009) Report to the G-20 Finance Ministers and Central Bank Governors, available at <https://www.imf.org/external/np/g20/pdf/100109.pdf>, 2.

[97] Ibid, 15.

refers to the extent to which other components of the system can provide the same services in the event of a failure;[98] and interconnectedness refers to the linkages with other components of the system.[99] The activity-based approach essentially derives its criteria from the entity-based approach but according to the Report, "[f]or markets, assessing systemic importance presents more conceptual challenges."[100] While the systemic importance of a market derives to some extent from participating institutions, "the size of a market is a determinant of potential economic costs in case of malfunction" and that "if the function of a stressed market cannot be replicated by other mechanisms, the economic impact can be significant."[101] The Report suggests that an assessment based on the three criteria of size, interconnectedness and substitutability "should be complemented with reference to financial vulnerabilities and the capacity of the institutional framework to deal with financial failures."[102]

Moreover, macroprudential authorities will avoid labelling specific products or activities as intrinsically systemic and instead focus on their design, management,[103] distribution and propagation through the system that could increase their potential to pose systemic risk.[104] As such, activities may pose greater risks if they are "complex or opaque, are conducted without effective risk-management practices, are significantly correlated with other financial products, or are either highly concentrated or significant and widespread."[105]

3.2. THE FSOC SHIFT TO AN ACTIVITY-BASED APPROACH

It is to be recalled that the FSOC has two discretionary authorities to address systemic risk to financial stability. The first, discussed in Section 2, is the entity-based authority in section 113 of the Dodd-Frank Act, which empowers the FSOC to designate individual non-bank financial companies as SIFIs and thus subject them to an enhanced prudential regulatory regime in accordance with Title 1 of the Dodd-Frank Act. The second authority, found in section 120 of the Dodd-Frank Act, is an activity-based authority. It enables the FSOC to issue non-binding recommendations to the primary financial regulatory agencies to apply new or heightened standards and safeguards, for a financial activity

---

[98]   Ibid, 9.
[99]   Ibid.
[100]   Ibid, 3.
[101]   Ibid.
[102]   IMF, BIS and FSB (2009) (n 96), 3.
[103]   EIOPA, "Systemic Risk and Macroprudential Policy In Insurance" (2017), available at <https://eiopa.europa.eu/>, 27.
[104]   M Goldby and A Keller, "Product Intervention as a Macroprudential Tool: The Case of Catastrophe Bonds" (2019) 51(1) George Washington International Law Review 1.
[105]   FSOC's Guidance (n 54), 71761.

or practice conducted by bank holding companies or non-bank financial companies.

During the first few years of its establishment, the FSOC focused, to a large extent, on its entity-based authority, using only once its activity-based authority.[106] The MetLife case and the Treasury Report that followed, already discussed in Section 2, were a turning point in the FSOC's approach to non-bank systemic risk, signalling a shift away from an entity-based approach to an activity-based one.[107] The Treasury Report noted that the FSOC authority to designate non-bank financial companies is a blunt instrument for addressing potential risks to financial stability and recommended that the FSOC prioritises its efforts to address risks to financial stability through a process that emphasises an activity-based or industry-wide approach.[108] It suggested that focusing on activities and products will enable the FSOC to identify the underlying sources of risks to financial stability. The option to consider designation should be preserved and used "in the rare instance, such as the historical case of Fannie Mae and Freddie Mac, where it was clear that individual institutions could pose a threat to financial stability, but a primary regulator has not taken or cannot take adequate steps to address the risk."[109]

Aligned with the Treasury Report, the FSOC's Guidance suggests prioritising its efforts to identify, assess, and address potential risks and threats to US financial stability through a process that emphasises an activities-based approach.[110] Pursuing entity-specific determinations will only take place if a potential risk or threat cannot be addressed through an activities-based approach.[111]

The FSOC's Guidance establishes a two-step process for the FSOC's activities-based approach. In the first stage, the FSOC intends to monitor diverse financial markets and market developments, in consultation with relevant financial regulatory agencies, to identify products, activities, or practices that could pose risks to financial stability.[112] In this stage, the FSOC will focus and analyse in a collaborative discussion with relevant regulators the following four

---

[106]   FSOC Proposed Recommendations Regarding Money Market Mutual Fund Reform, 77 Fed. Reg. 69,455 (19 November 2012).

[107]   Robert Jackson, Panel 1 in the Office Financial Research (OFR) and University of Michigan Conference Using Activity and Entity based – Regulation to Strengthen the Financial System (Washington DC, 15–16 November 2018).

[108]   The Treasury Report (n 49), 10.

[109]   The Treasury Report (n 49), 19.

[110]   FSOC's Guidance (n 54), 71761.

[111]   Ibid.

[112]   Ibid. The FSOC will evaluate at this stage the extent to which certain characteristics could amplify potential risks to US financial stability arising from products, activities, or practices. These characteristics include asset valuation risk or credit risk, leverage and the transparency of financial markets.

framing questions: (1) triggers of potential risks; (2) how adverse effects of the potential risk may be transmitted to financial markets or market participants; (3) the effects the potential risk could have on the financial system; and (4) whether the adverse effects of the potential risk could impair the financial system in a manner that could harm the nonfinancial sector of the US economy (for example, through curtailed or interrupted provision of credit to nonfinancial companies).

If the FSOC identifies in the first stage of the activities-based approach a potential risk to US financial stability, then in the second step, it will work with the relevant financial regulatory agencies at the federal and state levels to address the identified risks. The FSOC will assume here a coordinating role amongst its members and member agencies and ensure that existing regulators take appropriate action to mitigate potential risks to US financial stability.[113]

If after engaging with relevant financial regulatory agencies, the FSOC finds that those regulators' actions are insufficient to address the identified risks to financial stability, it will turn to its authority to issue a nonbinding recommendation to primary financial regulatory agencies under section 120 of the Dodd-Frank Act. Finally, if a potential risk or threat cannot be addressed through an activities-based approach, only then will the FSOC pursue entity-specific determinations under section 113 of the Dodd-Frank Act.[114]

Overall, requiring activity-based regulatory manoeuvers prior to reaching the "last resort" designation authority and adding other procedural[115] and analytical[116] barriers to the designation process would mean that designation would become much more cumbersome and difficult to survive judicial review.[117]

The expected transformation in the FSOC supervisory approach to identifying and addressing potential risks to US financial stability is not idiosyncratic. Rather, it seems to be part of a wider evolution away from

---

[113]   Ibid, 71762.

[114]   Ibid.

[115]   Such as a requirement for the FSOC to vote to commence any review of a non-bank financial company in Stage 1 (FSOC's Guidance, 71767) and additional procedural steps for annual re-evaluations (FSOC's Guidance, 71769).

[116]   The Treasury Report (n 49), 27 (para 2.3.2); The FSOC's Guidance (n 54), 71766. The FSOC's Guidance is "intended to ensure that the Council's work is clear, transparent and analytically rigorous, and to enhance the Council's engagement with companies, regulators, and other stakeholders" (71750). For instance, on p 71767, there is a requirement for staff on the analytical team to provide, upon request, the company under review with a list of the primary public sources of information being considered during its analysis.

[117]   Testimony of JC Kress Before the US Senate (2019) (n 89).

entity-based nonbank systemic risk regulation among international financial regulators.[118] Recently, the FPC has also acknowledged the importance of an activity-based approach to the regulation and supervision of payment systems explaining that:

> The application of current regulatory and supervisory frameworks for payments differed primarily by type of entity. Given the increasingly diverse nature of companies becoming involved in payments, it was important to focus on the functions they undertook, and the risks that those functions posed to the stability of payment systems, rather than the nature of the company itself.[119]

A complete departure from an entity-based approach in macroprudential policymaking can be challenged on several grounds. A well-executed activities-based approach may mitigate some sources of systemic risks particularly those arising from correlations across investment activities, risk-management practices, or product features of numerous non-bank financial institutions.[120] Nonetheless, it can be argued that an activity-based approach cannot prevent systemic insolvencies since it fails to consider the cumulative effect and interrelation of activities in a firm.[121] Moreover, it may fall short of preventing runs at nonbank financial firms. While individually each activity may not create excessive short-term liabilities, the aggregate reliance on all activities may result in the risk of run materialising.[122]

The cumulative aspect of interconnectedness is also of essence here. An activity-based approach ignores the interconnectedness of individual firms with the broader financial system and in particular, it is blind to the identity of the firm's major counterparties and the size of their corresponding exposures.[123]

---

[118]   Kress, McCoy and Schwarcz (2018) (n 53), 17; International Association of Insurance Supervisors, "Activities Based Approach to Systemic Risk Public Consultation Document" (2018), available at <https://www.iaisweb.org/page/consultations/closed-consultations/2018/activities-based-approach-to-systemic-risk>; FSB, "Statement on Identification of Global Systemically Important Insurers" (21 November 2017).
See also Panel 3 in the OFR and University of Michigan Functions and Firms: Using Activity- and Entity-Based Regulation to Strengthen the Financial System (US Department of Treasury, 15–16 November 2018).

[119]   Summary and Record of the Financial Policy Committee Meeting on 2 and 9 October 2019, 25.

[120]   Kress, McCoy and Schwarcz (2018) (n 53), 32.

[121]   Ibid.

[122]   Ibid, 36.

[123]   Ibid. Also suggesting that an effective activity-based approach is impossible in the current regulatory regime in the US, in particular due to jurisdictional fragmentation in the regulatory structure. With certain regulatory changes, Kress, McCoy and Schwarcz support an activity-based approach as a complement to an entity-based approach.

Finally and similarly to the entity-based approach, it can be argued that an activity-based approach may incentivise regulatory arbitrage as financial institutions will seek to engage in activities that have not been identified by macroprudential authorities as "risky" or activities that are not appropriately regulated.[124] Consequently, macroprudential measures to tackle non-bank systemic risk may come too late to be effective.

3.3. ADVOCATING A COMPLEMENTARY AND MUTUALLY REINFORCING APPROACH

Considering these arguments, there is a growing support for the view that entity- and activity-based approaches are mutually reinforcing and are both essential to prevent or mitigate non-bank systemic risk.[125] This complementary approach has been adopted in the EU. The ESRB employs in its shadow banking monitoring a combination of an entity-based approach and an activity-based approach.[126] EIOPA went even further and suggested to use alongside these two approaches a behaviour-based approach.[127] Under the behaviour-based approach, macroprudential authorities will consider collective behaviour by insurers that may exacerbate market price movements such as fire-sales or herding behaviour, excessive risk-taking such as "search for yield" and excessive concentrations.[128]

At the global setting, the IAIS has recently issued a Public Consultation Document proposing to move away from using the binary entity/activity

---

[124] On the risk of recharacterising or restructuring transaction to escape regulation potentially undermining an activities-based approach, see Professor Anat Admati, Panel 1 in the OFR and University of Michigan Functions and Firms: Using Activity- and Entity-Based Regulation to Strengthen the Financial System (US Treasury, 15 November 2018).

[125] Highlighted in the Panel 2 Functions and Firms: Using Activity- and Entity-Based Regulation to Strengthen the Financial System Office of Financial Research-University of Michigan Center on Finance, Law, and Policy Fourth Annual Financial Stability Conference (US Department of Treasury, 15–16 November 2018). Professor K Judge (Colombia University) suggested that by taking an activities-based approach, regulators may be better positioned to identify firms where risk is concentrated. In contrast, Professor D Schwarcz (University of Minnesota Law School) suggested that a firm-based supervision provides regulators with a unique vantage point through which to identify potentially risky activities.
See also IMF, "The Insurance Sector – Trends and Systemic Risk Implications" (2016) Global Financial Stability Report, Chapter 3 suggests supplementing an entity-based approach with an activity-based approach.

[126] ESRB, EU Shadow Banking Monitor No 3, September 2018, available at <https://www.esrb.europa.eu/pub/pdf/reports/esrb.report180910_shadow_banking.en.pdf>.

[127] EIOPA, "Systemic Risk and Macroprudential Policy in Insurance", 2017, available at <https://www.eiopa.europa.eu/sites/default/files/publications/pdfs/003systemic_risk_and_macroprudential_policy_in_insurance pdff>, 50.

[128] Ibid.

based approach terminology and follow a "holistic perspective".[129] This holistic framework, to be implemented by 2020, will enable "a proportionate application of an enhanced set of policy measures to address activities and exposures that can lead to systemic risk targeted to a broader portion of the insurance sector."[130] Therefore, rather than applying policy measures to a particular group of insurers (Identified Global Systemically Important Insurers G-SIIs), the new framework proposes applying various policy measures, including those that currently only apply to G-SIIs, to a broader portion of the insurance sector, where the nature, scale and complexity of the activities indicate increased systemic risk exposures.[131]

In practical terms, a prioritised key component of the holistic framework is the activity-based approach[132] and its implementation would remove the need for the identification of G-SIIs by the FSB and national authorities.[133] This is not to say that an entity-based approach is completely to be dispensed with. The IAIS reiterates that the holistic framework to systemic risks will be "Taking into account both relevant sources of systemic risk: the first stemming from the potential knock-on effects from the failure or distress of individual insurers, the second stemming from the propagation or amplification of shocks from even solvent firms, through their collective risk exposures or responses to shocks", as well as "Addressing cross-sectoral aspects of systemic risk, by comparing the potential systemic risk of insurers with other parts of the financial system, notably the banking sector".[134]

The discussion in this section yields a number of observations and suggestions. First, systemic risk, in its nature, is dynamic and multifaceted. The approach to regulation should cast, accordingly, the net wide and employ an entity-based approach alongside an activity-based approach. An activity-based approach is suited to address system-wide risks that originate, for instance, from correlations amongst individual institutions ("too many to fail"). Complementary approaches will also limit the potential for regulatory arbitrage to entities that are outside the regulatory perimeter or are lightly regulated. Similarly, it will mitigate the risks of movement from activities defined as "systemic" to activities that their

---

[129] IAIS (2018) (n 94).
[130] Ibid, 5.
[131] Ibid, 23–24.
[132] This is also the understanding of the FSB. FSB, "Release of IAIS Proposed Holistic Framework for the Assessment and Mitigation of Systemic Risk in the Insurance Sector and Implications for the Identification of G-SIIs and for G-SII Policy Measures" (November 2018), available at <https://www.fsb.org/wp-content/uploads/P141118-2.pdf>.
[133] Ibid, 6.
[134] Ibid.

risks are not yet fully appreciated by regulators.[135] A full departure from the entity-based approach, however, risks exacerbating the "Too Big To Fail" problem or more accurately, the Too Systemically Important To Fail and the moral hazard that may flow from it. The absence of an effective SIFI designation can potentially remove the disincentive for banks and non-banks to get even bigger or more systemically important.[136] Second, when discussing an activity-based approach, it is important to emphasise that it refers to monitoring more broadly financial markets and market developments, i.e. not only activities but also products and practices that could pose risks to financial stability.[137] It may be, for instance, that specific trading practices of particular financial instruments increase volatility in markets.[138] Moreover, activities or products themselves may not inherently create systemic risk but rather the way they are designed, distributed and propagated through the system may be a concern.[139] Relying on market intelligence and exchange of information between macroprudential authorities and other supervisors (such as conduct of business) can provide useful insights into the manner in which activities are carried.

4. SUMMARY

This chapter constructs a coherent taxonomy for supervisory approaches in macroprudential policymaking. As a starting point, it identifies three types

---

[135]   This was the case in AIG that issued credit default swaps through AIG Financial Products division. See Testimony of Joel Ario Insurance Commissioner Pennsylvania Insurance Department Before the Subcommittee on Capital Markets, Insurance, and Government Sponsored Enterprises Committee on Financial Services United States House of Representatives regarding "American International Group's Impact on the Global Economy: Before, During and After Federal Intervention", 18 March 2009.

[136]   As evident in the case of JP Morgan. L Noonan and P Jenkins, "JP Morgan Defying Attempts to End the Too Big To Fail", *Financial Times* (12 September 2018).
         The case of General Electric is perhaps an instructive example of the effectiveness of an entity-based approach of the FSOC. The FSOC "designated GE Capital in 2013 after identifying a number of key concerns, including the company's reliance on short-term wholesale funding and its leading position in a number of funding markets. Since then, GE Capital has made fundamental strategic changes that have resulted in a company that is significantly smaller and safer, with more stable funding. After a rigorous review and engagement with the company over the last year, the Council determined that based on these changes, the designation is no longer warranted." FSOC Announces Rescission of Nonbank Financial Company Designation, 29 June 2016, available at <https://www.treasury.gov/press-center/press-releases/Pages/jl0503.aspx>.
         See also Maxine Waters Statement at Hearing with Treasury Secretary Jacob J Lew on the FSOC's Annual Report to Congress, on 22 September 2016.

[137]   FSCO's Guidance (n 54), 71744.

[138]   Ibid, 71761.

[139]   Goldby and Keller (2019) (n 104).

of potential supervisory approaches: the first is based on the analytical basis for policy decisions and the suitability of a cost-benefit analysis to guide macroprudential decisions. The second refers to the nature of the mandate of macroprudential authorities and the framework within which the decision-making process is taking place – whether it is solely based on supervisory discretion or constrained by certain indicators. Finally, the chapter made a distinction as to the perspective of regulation and supervision, which could be conducted based on a legal form, activities or a complementary approach that combines the two. The chapter provided evidence and rationale for the growing support for a complementary and mutually reinforcing entity-based and activity-based approach in macroprudential policymaking. It suggested, however, that the drifting away from an entity-based approach, as is the case with the FSOC, could be a dangerous move, impinging on the scope and strength of macroprudential policy.

CHAPTER 6

ACTIVATING AND CALIBRATING MACROPRUDENTIAL INSTRUMENTS

This chapter considers the challenges that macroprudential authorities face in activating, calibrating and deactivating macroprudential tools and seeks to bring greater clarity on the legal and practical ways to address these challenges. It, accordingly, addresses the following questions: which macroprudential tools are currently available? Should combined tools be used? Should a cautious and gradual or more activist approach be taken when calibrating tools? How targeted should the tools be?

Section 1 begins with outlining the prevalent taxonomies of macroprudential tools and the state of use of these tools around the globe. Section 2 presents the potential approaches in selecting and calibrating macroprudential tools, including a multi-pronged approach; a gradual or active and bold approach; targeted or broad-based action and flexible policy at the national level or policy that focuses on creating a level playing field. The section then critically analyses the strengths and weaknesses of these approaches. Section 3 delves deeper into the challenges of activating and calibrating macroprudential tools. These range from difficulties in assessing the effectiveness of the tools, in timely activation and deactivation, in controlling leakages domestically and across borders, in coordinating between macroprudential tools and other policy areas and utilising complementarities. Section 3 also addresses the potential distributional effects of the macroprudential sectoral housing tools. Section 4 provides a brief summary of the evidence available to date on the effectiveness of macroprudential tools and explores the legal and practical ways to address the identified challenges and enhance the effectiveness of the tools.

1.   PREVALENT TAXONOMIES OF MACROPRUDENTIAL TOOLS

There is a broad array of macroprudential tools that could be used to prevent or at least, mitigate systemic risks. Many of the tools are in effect micro-prudential tools, which are adapted and deployed with a systemic perspective in mind,[1] but there are also taxes and levies as well as newly designed macroprudential tools.[2] Experience with implementing macroprudential instruments can be dated back as far as the 1930s.[3] Nevertheless, in the years following the 2007–2009 financial crisis, macroprudential measures have been deployed far more actively compared to the pre-crisis,[4] particularly in Asia-Pacific and Central and Eastern Europe.[5]

Naturally, the activation and use of macroprudential tools are subject to their availability in the macroprudential authority's toolkit and this feature may differ across jurisdictions. As discussed in Chapter 4, macroprudential authorities may have a direct authority to activate specific instruments or have the power to recommend other authorities to implement suitable macroprudential tools, where needed. It may be that the activation of macroprudential tools does not reside with one authority and spreads across the macroprudential authority and other designated authorities for the purpose of activating particular tools.[6]

---

[1] CGFS, "Macroprudential Instruments and Frameworks: A Stocktaking of Issues and Experiences" (2010) CGFS Papers No 38; L Ellis, "Macroprudential Policy: A Suite of Tools or a State of Mind?" Paul Woolley Centre for the Study of Capital Market Dysfunctionality Annual Conference (Sydney, 11 October 2012).

[2] S Claessens, "An Overview of Macroprudential Policy Tools" (December 2014) IMF Working Paper No 214. For other classifications see CGFS (2010) (n 1); IMF, "Macroprudential Policy: An Organising Framework Background Paper" (2011); Bank of England, "Instruments of Macroprudential Policy" (2011) Bank of England Discussion Paper, available at <https://www.bankofengland.co.uk/-/media/boe/files/paper/2011/instruments-of-macroprudentia l-policy>; ESRB, "The ESRB Handbook on Operationalising Macroprudential Policy in the Banking Sector" (2014), available at <https://www.esrb.europa.eu/pub/pdf/other/140303_ esrb_handbook_mp.en.pdf>; IMF, "Staff Guidance Note on Macroprudential Policy-Detailed Guidance on Instruments" (November 2014), available at <https://www.imf.org/en/ Publications/Policy-Papers/Issues/2016/12/31/Staff-Guidance-Note-on-Macroprudential-Policy-Detailed-Guidance-on-Instruments-PP4928>.

[3] For a summary of selected studies on experience with macroprudential tools see G Galati and R Moessner, "What Do We Know About the Effects of Macroprudential Policy?" (2018) 85(340) Economica 735, 738–739 and Table A2 at 760; AG Haldane, "Risk off" Bank of England, speech delivered on 18 August 2011, available at <https://www.bankofengland. co.uk/news/2011/august/risk-off-paper-by-andy-haldane>.

[4] O Akinci and J Olmstead-Rumsey, "How Effective Are Macroprudential Policies: An Empirical Investigation" (2015) International Finance Discussion Papers 1136, 9; E Cerutti and others, "The Use and Effectiveness of Macroprudential Policies: New Evidence" (2017) 28 Journal of Financial Stability 203 also show that macroprudential policies are increasingly used and that emerging economies use them most.

[5] BIS, "Moving Forward with Macroprudential Frameworks" BIS Annual Economic Report (June 2018), available at <https://www.bis.org/publ/arpdf/ar2018e4.htm>; United Nations, World Economic Situation and Prospects Report 2019, available at <https://www.un.org/ development/desa/dpad/wp-content/uploads/sites/45/WESP2019_BOOK-web.pdf>, 140.
See also L Zhang and E Zoli, "Leaning Against the Wind: Macroprudential Policy in Asia" (2014) IMF Working Paper No 22 on Asia as a region that have made greater use of macroprudential measures, compared to other regions, especially housing-related measures.

[6] For instance, in the EU, macroprudential authorities are the ones established in accordance with ESRB Recommendation on the Macro-prudential Mandate of National Authorities ESRB/2011/3 while designated authorities are established in accordance with article 136 of

Legal restrictions on the power to activate tools or recommend activation may also apply. For instance, there may be a requirement in legislation to cooperate with the government or other authorities or there may be a requirement for a pecking order of instruments assigning specific mandatory sequencing for their activation.

The taxonomy of macroprudential tools often reflects the two dimensions of systemic risks – the time dimension and the structural dimension (Chapter 1). Tools used to address the time-dimension of systemic risk increase resilience of the financial system to shocks and contain the pro-cyclical build-up of vulnerabilities.[7] They are often used in a dynamic fashion and change according to the evolving risks: tightening when risks build-up and relaxing as risks abate or crystallise.

There are three core sets of macroprudential tools aimed at addressing the build-up of systemic risks through time:[8]

1. *Capital-based tools (both broad-based and sectoral)* address risks from a credit boom. These tools include, for instance, a countercyclical capital buffer (CCyB) which is designed to accumulate capital, when systemic risk builds up during the expansion phase of the financial cycle so that it can be released and used in the contraction phase when risks materialise.[9] The aim of the CCyB is, therefore, to limit the amplitude of financial cycles.[10] The deviation of Credit-to-GDP gap[11] is used as an indicator for the activation

---

Directive 2013/36/EU (CRD IV) and are responsible for setting the CCyB rates. In fact, in slightly more than half of the Member States, the designated authority coincides with the macroprudential authority. In Member States where the two authorities are different, the macroprudential authority often takes the form of a committee and the designated authority is either the central bank, the financial supervisory authority or more rarely, a government agency such as the Ministry of Finance. See ESRB, "A Review of Macroprudential Policy in the EU in 2017" (April 2018), figure 1, 6. In the US, the FSOC is the macroprudential authority but the Federal Reserve is the authority responsible, for instance, for setting a CCyB.

[7] IMF, FSB and BIS, "Elements of Effective Macroprudential Policies Lessons from International Experience" (2016), available at <https://www.bis.org/publ/othp26.pdf>.
 See also CGFS, "Operationalising the Selection and Application of Macroprudential Tools" (December 2012) CGFS Paper No 48; ESRB (2014) (n 2); IMF Guidance Note on Instruments (2014) (n 2).

[8] Lim and others, "Macroprudential Policy: What Instruments and How to Use Them? Lessons from Country Experiences" (2011) IMF Working Paper No 238, 8.

[9] Broad-based tools apply to all exposures and sectoral tools apply to particular types of exposures, or loan segments. The boundaries are not always clear. For instance, a CCyB can be broad-based but it can also be applied to particular exposures (and thus considered sectoral). IMF, FSB and BIS (2916) (n 7), 10.
 Other capital-based tools include restrictions on profit distribution and time varying/ dynamic provisioning.

[10] C Borio, "Rediscovering the Macroeconomic Roots of Financial Stability Policy: Journey, Challenges and a Way forward" (2011) BIS Working Paper No 354, 13.

[11] The difference between the ratio of indebtedness of household and corporate sectors to GDP (credit to GDP ratio) and its long-term trend. See BIS, "The credit-to-GDP Gap and Countercyclical Capital Buffers: Questions and Answers" (March 2014) BIS Quarterly Review.

of the countercyclical buffer though the judgment of macroprudential authorities remains a critical element in the process (Chapter 5).[12] According to the 2018 IMF Macroprudential Annual Survey, among the broad-based tools, CCyB is the most frequently used measure and is currently in place in 76 countries.[13]

2. *Credit-related tools* address vulnerabilities that arise from credit growth or asset price inflation. These include sectoral capital tools, such as sectoral capital requirements and risk-weight floors that help maintain the resilience of lenders as well as loan restrictions, such as caps on loan-to-value (LTV),[14] debt-service-to-income (DSTI)[15] or loan-to-income (LTI)[16] ratios.

3. *Liquidity-related tools* address systemic liquidity risks. These tools include, for instance, an extended Liquidity Coverage Ratio (LCR) which incorporate countercyclical elements[17] and caps on Loan-to-Deposit (LTD) ratios.[18]

---

[12] BCBS, "Guidance for National Authorities Operating the Countercyclical Capital Buffer" (December 2010), available at <https://www.bis.org/publ/bcbs187.htm>, 2–3.

[13] Out of the 141 countries that responded to the survey. IMF, "Annual Macroprudential Policy Survey – Objectives, Design, and Country Responses" (April 2018), available at <https://www.imf.org/en/Publications/Policy-Papers/Issues/2018/04/30/pp043018-imf-annual-macroprudential-policy-survey>, 6. Furthermore, given that the CCyB has been required since early 2016 under the CRRIV and CRDIV framework of the EU, it is most frequently used in Europe compared to most other regions.

[14] See n 11.

[15] The ratio between the annual costs of debt servicing and a borrower's annual income.

[16] The ratio between the loan amount and the annual income of the borrower. Limits on LTV ratio have been in use since the early 1990s. IMF, "Macroprudential Policy: An Organising Framework" (2011) (n 2), 26. LTV is the ratio of the loan value to the underlying collateral (property) value and a cap on it ensures that if the borrower defaults, the collateral value is sufficient to cover the loan.

[17] ECB Task Force on Systemic Liquidity, "Systemic Liquidity Concept, Measurement and Macroprudential Instruments" (October 2018) ECB Occasional Paper Series No 21, 16.
LCR, for instance, promotes "the short-term resilience of the liquidity risk profile of banks. It does this by ensuring that banks have an adequate stock of unencumbered high-quality liquid assets (HQLA) that can be converted easily and immediately in private markets into cash to meet their liquidity needs for a 30-calendar day liquidity stress scenario". BCBS, "Basel III: The Liquidity Coverage Ratio and Liquidity Risk Monitoring Tools" (January 2013), available at <https://www.bis.org/publ/bcbs238.pdf>. However, it is important to note that Basel III LCR as well as the Net Stable Funding Ratio (NSFR) are considered micro-prudential standards. While they strengthen the resilience of individual institutions, they do not allow for cyclically adjusted constraints or requirements; it is not their objective to prevent the build-up of excessive maturity transformation across the system or provide an effective protection against aggregate liquidity shocks, affecting a large set of financial intermediaries. J-P Landau, "A Liquidity Based Approach to Macroprudential Policy" BIS Paper No 86 147, 149.
On how to design a macroprudential instrument based on the NSFR see ECB, "Financial Stability Review" (November 2014), 118.

[18] The ratio between a bank's total outstanding loans for a period to its total deposit balance over the same period. CGFS (2012) (n 7), 10.

In addition, there is a range of tools that aim to contain structural risks from interconnectedness and contagion within the financial system.[19] Structural tools can be calibrated, for instance, to enhance the resilience of SIFIs to shocks via imposing appropriate capital surcharges.[20] They can also reduce interlinkages within the financial system, for instance, through large exposures limits.[21]

Macroprudential instruments can also be classified according to the externalities they can address, including externalities related to strategic complementarities, fire sales and interconnectedness.[22] However, the connection between the tools and externalities is far from being linear since each externality can be addressed by different tools that are often complementary.[23]

Related to that, another distinction, frequently used in literature, is between borrower-based measures, such as LTVs and DTIs and lender or financial-institutions targeted measures, such as a CCyB and a leverage ratio.[24]

The taxonomy of the macroprudential tools presented in the 2018 IMF Annual Macroprudential Survey is more detailed and includes six broad categories that are associated with the different sources of systemic risk being addressed by the tools: (1) tools applied to all (aggregate) exposures of the banking system ("broad-based tools"); (2) tools to address risks from banks' exposure to households ("household sector tools"); (3) tools to address risks from banks' exposure to non-financial firms ("corporate sector tools"); (4) tools to address liquidity risks and foreign exchange mismatches in the banking sector ("liquidity and foreign exchange tools"); (5) tools to address systemic liquidity risk and fire-sale risk in the non-bank financial sector ("non-bank tools"); and (6) tools to address risks from systemically important institutions and interconnectedness within the financial system ("structural tools").[25]

---

19 IMF-FSB-BIS (2016) (n 7), 10. Some tools can be used to address both the cyclical and the structural dimensions of systemic risks. T Grace, N Hallissey and M Woods, "The Instruments of Macroprudential Policy" (January 2015) Central Bank of Ireland Quarterly Bulletin 90, 93. See also E Nier and Others, "Key Aspects of Macroprudential Policy" IMF (2013), 21; IMF Guidance Note on Instruments (2014) (n 2), 94.

20 See, for instance, BCBS, "Global Systemically Important Banks: Assessment Methodology and the Additional Loss Absorbency Requirement" (February 2019); FSB, "Higher Loss Absorbency Requirement for Global Systemically Important Insurers" (G-SIIs) 5 October 2015.

21 IMF-FSB-BIS (2016) (n 7), 11.

22 De Nicolo and others, "Externalities and Macroprudential Policy" (2012) IMF Staff Discussion Note 5.

23 Ibid, 3.

24 S Claessens, S Ghosh and R Mihet, "Macroprudential Policies to Mitigate Financial System Vulnerabilities" (2013) 39 Journal of International Money and Finance 153; E Cerutti, S Claessens and L Laeven, "The Use and Effectiveness of Macroprudential Tools: New Evidence" (2015) IMF Working Paper 61.

25 The IMF 2018 Annual Macroprudential Policy Survey (n 13); IMF Guidance Note on Instruments (2014) (n 2). The scope of what is considered a macroprudential tool (as almost every other aspect in this policy sphere) is subject to debate. For instance, some scholars also

Moving away from "on paper" taxonomy, which are the most commonly used macroprudential tools to date? In recent years, macroprudential measures have focused on the size and composition of banks' balance sheets[26] but this could quickly change with the growing importance of capital markets and the potential corresponding financial stability implications.[27] The most frequently used macroprudential tools are tools to manage liquidity and foreign exchange mismatches in the banking sector, followed by tools to manage risks from exposures to the household sector, and broad-based tools applying to all exposures.[28] More specifically, in advanced economies the most commonly used tools are LTV limits and these tools are also very common in emerging and developing economies.[29]

The package of reforms developed by the BCBS commonly known as "Basel III" introduced a macroprudential overlay aimed at promoting financial stability and limiting systemic risks.[30] In addition, Basel III enhances capital adequacy requirements and introduces liquidity requirements.

The macroprudential overlay includes both time-dimensional tools and cross-sectional tools. Very briefly, these tools include:[31]

---

include ex-post crisis management resolution measures as macroprudential tools. See, for instance, K Alexander, *Principles of Banking Regulation* (Cambridge University Press, 2019), 402; SL Schwarcz, "Beyond Bankruptcy: Resolution as a Macroprudential Regulatory Tool" (2018) 94(2) Notre Dame Law Review 709.

[26]   Galati and Moesnner (2018) (n 3), 741 in particular LTD caps, institution-specific capital add-ons or time-varying capital charge.

[27]   The IMF Guidance Note on Instruments (2014) (n 2), 56.

[28]   The 2018 IMF's Macroprudential Policy Survey (n 13), 6.

[29]   Alter and others, "Unveiling the Effects of Macroprudential Policies: The IMF's New iMaPP Database", April 2019, available at Vox <https://voxeu.org/article/imf-s-new-macroprudentia l-database>; O Akinci Ozge and J Olmstead-Rumsey, "How Effective Are Macroprudential Policies? An Empirical Investigation" (2018) 33(c) Journal of Financial Intermediation 33.

[30]   BCBS, "Basel III: A Global Regulatory Framework for More Resilient Banks and Banking Systems" Revised version June 2011; BCBS, "Basel III: Finalising Post-crisis Reforms", December 2017.

[31]   In addition, Basel III's Pillar 2 Supervisory Review Enhancement Process (SREP) provides bank supervisors with a broad set of supervisory tools to improve corporate governance structures and risk management practices. It can be used for macroprudential purposes and there is evidence that some countries are already utilising it to that end. While the measures are firm-specific, they allow prudential authorities to address the sources of systemic risks that require rapid intervention. BCBS, "Overview of Pillar 2 Supervisory Review Practices and Approaches" (June 2019), available at <https://www.bis.org/bcbs/publ/d465.pdf>, 19. And in the EU, see M Bevilacqua and others, "The Evolution of the Pillar 2 Framework for Banks: Some Thoughts After the Financial Crisis" (April 2019) Banca D'Italia Occasional Papers No 494, available at <https://www.bancaditalia.it/pubblicazioni/qef/2019-0494/ QEF_494_19.pdf>; The ESRB Handbook on Operationalising Macro-prudential Policy in the Banking (2014), available at <https://www.esrb.europa.eu/pub/pdf/other/140303_ esrb_handbook_mp.en.pdf>, Chapter 6, 134; On the pros and cons of the use of Pillar 2 for macroprudential purposes also see ESRB, "A Review of Macroprudential Policy in the EU in 2017" (April 2018), 9.

First, a leverage ratio is defined as the capital measure (the numerator) divided by the exposure measure (the denominator) expressed as a percentage and is intended to restrict the build-up of leverage in the banking sector during the boom phase and reduce the destabilising deleveraging dynamic during the bust.[32] It is a simple, non-risk-based measure that serves as a "backstop" against the potential gaming of risks by banks and measurement errors of the risk-based approach.[33]

Second, a capital conservation buffer and a countercyclical buffer to address the procyclicality of the financial system:

The capital conservation buffer is designed to ensure that banks build up capital buffers outside periods of stress which can be drawn down as losses are incurred. It means that a constraint on a bank's discretionary distributions will be imposed when banks fall into the buffer range.[34]

With regard to the countercyclical buffer, the BCBS explains that – "Losses incurred in the banking sector can be extremely large when a downturn is preceded by a period of excess credit growth. These losses can destabilise the banking sector and spark a vicious circle, whereby problems in the financial system can contribute to a downturn in the real economy that then feeds back on to the banking sector. These interactions highlight the particular importance of the banking sector building up additional capital defences in periods where the risks of system-wide stress are growing markedly."[35] The countercyclical buffer is, accordingly, deployed by national jurisdictions when excess aggregate credit growth is judged to be associated with a build-up of system-wide risk to ensure that the banking system has a buffer of capital to protect it against future potential losses.[36]

Third, in the cross-sectional dimension, the BCBS developed a capital surcharge for global systemically important banks (G-SIBs) that reduces the probability

---

[32]   BCBS Basel III (2017), 139. The capital measure for the leverage ratio at a particular point in time is the applicable Tier 1 capital measure at that time under the risk-based framework and the exposure measure includes both on-balance sheet exposures and off-balance sheet items. See BIS, 'Basel III Leverage Ratio Framework – Executive Summary' (October 2017), available at <https://www.bis.org/fsi/fsisummaries/b3_lrf.htm>.

[33]   Ibid. The minimum leverage requirement is set at 3 per cent. In addition, the 2017 reforms of Basel III also added a requirement that banks identified as global systemically important banks (G-SIBs) are subject to higher leverage ratio requirements; BCBS, "The Regulatory Framework: Balancing Risk Sensitivity, Simplicity and Comparability" (July 2013) BCBS Discussion Paper, 18.

[34]   BCBS, Basel III (2011), 54–55. Comprising a common equity Tier 1 of 2.5 per cent of risk-weighted assets for all banks.

[35]   BCBS, Basel III (2011), 57–58.

[36]   Ibid. The countercyclical buffer ranges from 0 to 2.5 per cent of risk-weighted assets. However, national authorities can implement a buffer in excess of 2.5 per cent where it is deemed appropriate in their national context.

of failure of these large, complex organisations.[37] The EU introduced an additional capital buffer in the form of the systemic risk buffer (SRyB) designed to prevent and mitigate systemic risks of a long-term, non-cyclical nature, such as interconnectedness, which are not sufficiently addressed by other measures in the CRR.[38]

While these measures are a big step to promoting financial stability and addressing the regulatory deficiencies identified during the 2007–2009 financial crisis, they only apply to the banking sector, and therefore do not directly prevent systemic risk from building up in other parts of the financial system (i.e. non-bank intermediaries). As discussed in Chapter 1, macroprudential policy's overreach must go beyond the banking sector, expanding to any sector, financial institution or financial market infrastructures, practices and products, whatever their source or legal form may be.

2. APPROACHES TO ACTIVATING AND CALIBRATING MACROPRUDENTIAL TOOLS

2.1. A MULTI-PRONGED APPROACH

The multifaceted nature of systemic risk may require employing not just one instrument but a set of instruments.[39] A single macroprudential tool may not be able to address all dimensions of systemic risk (cyclical and/or structural) and/or all potential sources of systemic risk (for instance, banks, borrowers or particular activities).[40] Casting the net wide through a multi-pronged

---

[37] BCBS, "Global Systemically Important Banks: Revised Assessment Methodology and the Higher Loss Absorbency Requirement", July 2018, available at <https://www.bis.org/bcbs/publ/d445.htm>. Systemic importance reflects the size of banks, their interconnectedness, the lack of readily available substitutes or financial institution infrastructure for the services they provide, their global (cross-jurisdictional) activity and their complexity.
See also BCBS, "A Framework for Dealing with Domestic Systemically Important Banks", October 2012, available at <http://www.bis.org/publ/bcbs233.pdf>; FSB TLAC Term Sheet (November 2015), available at <https://www.fsb.org/2015/11/total-loss-absorbing-capacity-tlac-principles-and-term-sheet/> setting out a total loss-absorbing capacity (TLAC) requirement, which ensures that these banks also have sufficient loss absorption capacity on a gone-concern basis and thus reduce the probability of their failure.
[38] It is not specifically referenced in the Basel Framework; it is implemented in the EU under article 133 CRD and is within a range of 1.0–3.0 per cent of risk-weighted assets.
[39] The ESRB Handbook on Operationalising Macroprudential Policy (n 2), 17; Nier and others (2013) (n 19), 19; CGFS (2012) (n 7), 39.
[40] D Aikman and others, "Rethinking Financial Stability" (2018) Bank of England Staff Working Paper No 712 apply the Tinbergen Rule to financial regulation and contend that macroprudential policy needs at least "one instrument for each market failure" or for each operational objective.
J Tinbergen, *On the Theory of Economic Policy* (Amsterdam: North Holland, 2nd edition, 1952). See also Lim and others (2011) (n 8), 27.

approach can address risks from several angles and act as insurance against the uncertainties surrounding the assessment of risks, how they are propagated and the effectiveness of the tools.[41] As such, implementing macroprudential tools that address the build-up of systemic risk during upswing ("speed limit") as well as tools that enhance resilience during the downswing and reduce the probability and impact of shocks ("airbags") is considered to be more effective.[42] Similarly, macroprudential authorities can implement borrower-based limits such as caps on LTV and LTI that can reduce the demand for credit and promote the resilience of borrowers alongside capital tools that act on the supply side and promote the resilience of banks.[43] In addition, evidence suggests that the use of a single tool is likely to create incentives for circumvention and distortions.[44] A comprehensive multi-pronged approach could guard against the risk of arbitrage and is considered more precise and thus less distortionary.[45]

Despite these weighty factors, macroprudential authorities should be cognisant of the drawbacks of a multi-pronged approach. Utilising a suite of macroprudential tools makes coordination more difficult since the tools could overlap[46] and even be distortive.[47] Furthermore, the use of a multi-pronged approach can complicate the calibration of individual instruments, making it harder to assess the interaction and overall effect of individual instruments.[48]

---

[41]   Aikman and others (2018) (n 40) apply the famous Brainard rule that under uncertainty, pursuing a given objective with a range of different instruments is likely to lead to better outcomes. WC Brainard, "Uncertainty and the Effectiveness of Policy" (1967) 57(2) The American Economic Review 411–425 "with one target and two instruments it will generally be optimal to use some combination of both instruments".
        See also P Turner, "Macroprudential Policies in EMEs: Theory and Practice" in Financial Sector Regulation for Growth, Equity and Stability (2012) BIS Papers No 62 (Proceedings of a conference organised by the BIS and CAFRAL, Mumbai, 15–16 November 2011), 125, 130.

[42]   A Brazier, "How To: Macropru 5 Principles for Macroprudential Policy" speech at London School of Economics, Financial Regulation Seminar Monday 13 February 2017.

[43]   IMF-FSB-BIS (2016) (n 7), 12.

[44]   Ibid; IMF, "The Interaction of Monetary and Macroprudential Policies" (2013), available at <https://www.imf.org/external/np/pp/eng/2013/012913.pdf>, 3; Lim and others (2011) (n 8), 4.

[45]   Turner (2012) (n 41), 130.

[46]   For instance, S Cecchetti and A Kashyap, "What Binds? Interactions between Bank Capital and Liquidity Regulations Part II – Financial Stability and Regulatory Policy" in P Hartmann, H Huang and D Schoenmaker, The Changing Fortune of Central Banking (Cambridge University Press, 2016), 192, available at <https://faculty.chicagobooth.edu/anil. kashyap/research/papers/What_Binds_Interactions-between-bank-capital-and-liquidity-regulations_2016.pdf>.

[47]   For instance, R Greenwood, S Hanson, J Stein and A Sunderam, "Strengthening and Streamlining Bank Capital Regulation" (2017) Brookings Papers on Economic Activity 479, 482 suggest that multiple independent constraints on bank levels of equity capital can be distortive.

[48]   BIS Annual Economic Report (2018) (n 5).

Finally, deploying a large suite of instruments may be more expensive to implement[49] and harder to communicate.[50]

2.2. A CAUTIOUS AND GRADUAL APPROACH OR BOLD AND DECISIVE?

So far, macroprudential policy has been implemented largely without an overarching theoretical structure or pre-eminent modelling approach that would help macroprudential authorities understand its full effect.[51] The absence of a comprehensive and integrated analytical framework means that some macroprudential authorities have taken a more gradual approach to the implementation of tools. Such an approach involves setting measures cautiously and then, increasing their intensity, scope and frequency.[52] Following this approach, macroprudential authorities adjust the instruments early and in small thus retaining the ability to observe the impact of the tools and where necessary, calibrate them.[53]

A cautious approach to activating macroprudential tools is consistently advocated in policy papers. For instance, a recent IMF research paper emphasised that: "much remains to be studied, including tools' costs – by adversely affecting resource allocations; how to best adapt tools to country circumstances; and preferred institutional designs, including how to address political economy risks. As such, policymakers should move carefully in adopting tools."[54] More specifically, the IMF recommended a gradual phase-in of capital buffers and liquidity requirements[55] as well as a gradual tightening of LTV and DSTI.[56] By the same token, the IMF suggested that a gradual release of buffers may be warranted.[57]

---

[49] A Dombret and O Lucius, "Stability of the Financial System Illusion or Feasible Concept" (Edward Elgar, 2013), 36.

[50] FSB, IMF and BIS, "Macroprudential Tools and Frameworks Progress Report to the G-20" (October 2011), available at <https://www.imf.org/external/np/g20/pdf/102711.pdf>, 11.

[51] P Mizen, M Rubio and P Turner, *Macroprudential Policy and Practice* (Cambridge University Press, 2018).

[52] BIS Annual Economic Report (2018) (n 5), 70.

[53] CGFS (2012) (n 7), 17.

[54] Claessens (2014) (n 2), 1.

[55] IMF Guidance Note on Macroprudential Policy (2014), available at <https://www.imf.org/external/np/pp/eng/2014/110614.pdf>, 16; IMF Guidance Note on Instruments (2014) (n 2), 16. On p 84 also observing that "In light of limited experiences with liquidity tools, there can be merit in a gradual tightening of policy measures".

[56] IMF Guidance Note on Macroprudential Policy (n 55), 17.

[57] Ibid, 19.

Another interesting concept, which has found its way to the literature on macroprudential policy, is the "Bayesian" updating approach.[58] According to this approach, macroprudential authorities use tools for which impact is well known while other tools are only used as one learns more.[59] The Bayesian approach can, however, lead to narrow macroprudential policymaking that could miss new sources of risks and the opportunity to address them in a timely manner. Another limitation of such a cautious approach is immediately visible: how can macroprudential authorities learn more if they do not use these tools? This limitation perhaps explains why, in some cases, macroprudential authorities may choose to proceed in full force in implementing tools with only a partial analytical support. On the face of it, a pre-emptive, active approach that is not fully supported by evidence is far from being ideal but is it a necessity in light of the great social costs of a systemic crisis?

In contrast, a prevalent view, based on Brainard's seminal work, is that where uncertainty over the impact of policy instruments exists, policymakers are more cautious and less active in implementing policy measures.[60] A recent paper, however, challenges this view and contends that Brainard's model does not have a general application and in particular, may not apply in the complex reality of macroprudential policymaking.[61] Bahaj and Foulis, accordingly, suggest that macroprudential authorities are more likely to follow an active stance in implementing tools. To begin with, macroprudential authorities have a strong desire to learn more about policy tools and their effectiveness. Since evidence on macroprudential tools is scarce, macroprudential authorities can primarily learn about the impact of these tools by observing what happens when they use them. Being active enables macroprudential authorities to accumulate first-hand new evidence, which is relevant to their particular country, and thus reduce the uncertainty as to the effectiveness of the tools in future. Moreover, while Brainard's model assumes symmetric objectives, the authors suggest that this assumption may not apply in the macroprudential sphere. In contrast to other policy objectives, financial stability is asymmetric, i.e. the losses associated with a financial crisis may be significantly greater than the costs of having excessive stability. In other words, "the costs of missed downside risks may be much larger than benefits of erring towards looser policy."[62] Finally, Brainard's model is based on the assumption that policymakers are able to assign probabilities to

---

58   Claessens (2014) (n 2), 22.
59   C Calomiris, "Managing the Risks of the New Macro-prudential Policy Regime" (2013) 13(4) Borsa Istanbul Review 65.
60   Brainard (1967) (n 41).
61   S Bahaj and A Foulis, "Macroprudential Under Uncertainty" (2017) 13(3) International Journal of Central Banking 119.
62   Ibid, 127.

potential future scenarios. The authors suggest that this assumption, however, may be unrealistic when describing the uncertainty faced by macroprudential policymakers[63] given that

> … complexity obscures the past and the present and makes the future harder to predict. Particularly where evolution is accelerating, and new complexities are emerging, it gets easier and easier to make mistakes. In many ways, the breakdown in the securitization process [during the 2007–2009 financial crisis – author's addition] was due to the fact that it was rapidly evolving – becoming more complex, etiolated and very opaque. Few market practitioners and fewer regulators understood it from stem to stem soon enough to do anything about it.[64]

The paper goes on to conclude that macroprudential policymaking is, therefore, largely calibrated to prepare for severe outcomes and avoid large losses regardless of how likely any given scenario is.[65] Consequently, rather than being hesitant and cautious in activating tools, as would be expected in an uncertain environment under Brainard's rule, the authors argue that macroprudential authorities are more likely to be active.[66]

While Bahaj and Foulis's theory is compelling, their reasoning can result in viewing a cost-benefit analysis as an exercise that should be dispensed with, going against the discussion in Chapter 5 and the added benefits of such an analysis in enhancing the accountability of macroprudential authorities. Moreover, the danger in resorting to a decisive and bold approach in macroprudential policymaking without a solid analytical grounding and rigorous analysis should not be underestimated. An active approach is effectively a pre-emptive cautious approach in disguise[67] which may result in potential real-economy costs and unnecessarily inhibit economic growth. This may be considered the lesser of two

---

63 Sometimes referred to as "Knightian uncertainty" as an unmeasurable probability to be differentiated from "risk" where the distribution of future outcomes is known and therefore measurable. FH Knight, *Risk, Uncertainty and Profit* (Boston: Houghton Mifflin, 1921).
    For a discussion of the feasibility of a cost-benefit analysis in macroprudential policymaking see Chapter 5.
    See also I Agur and S Sharma, "Rules, Discretion and Macro-prudential Policy" (2013) IMF Working Paper 65.
64 C Taylor, *Evolution and Macro-prudential Policy* (2011) Centre for the Study of Financial Innovation No 102, 15.
    On the complexity and evolving nature of financial markets see A Haldane, "Rethinking the financial Network" speech at the Financial Student Association, Amsterdam 28 April 2009.
65 Bahaj and Foulis (2017) (n 61), 128.
66 Ibid, 132.
67 I Webb, D Baumslag and R Read, "How Should Regulators Deal with Uncertainty Insights from the Precautionary Principle", BankUnderground, available at <https://bankunderground.co.uk/2017/01/27/how-should-regulators-deal-with-uncertainty-insights-from-the-precautionary-principle/>.

evils but there are also added costs of losing the credibility of macroprudential authorities. Understanding the difference between Type I errors (failing to predict a financial crisis that later occurs) and Type II errors (false alarms) is of essence here. Ideally, policymaking should minimise both types of errors but clearly there is a trade-off between them. In decisive macroprudential policymaking, the focus is overall on reducing Type I errors but at the same time, it creates more frequent false activation.[68] If macroprudential authorities persistently produce false alarms, their credibility could be severely undermined and, consequently, the effectiveness of their future policy decisions weakened. This is a particularly acute concern in the macroprudential sphere since the powers of macroprudential authorities are often based on soft law and the effectiveness of their policy decisions heavily relies on their reputation and credibility.

In light of these considerations, which approach is chosen, in practice, by macroprudential authorities? In the UK, Donald Kahn, an external member of the FPC, observed that "… we have made many judgments and taken quite a few actions based on a variety of indicators and techniques. Although identifying risks and gauging resilience poses significant challenges, we have found sufficient empirical regularities tied to financial instability in historical experience to justify taking action."[69] Another FPC member observed that the FPC "learn by doing".[70] Nonetheless, the considerations laid out in the FPC minutes as to the activation of a CCyB uncover a "waiting to see" and more gradual approach:

> On the one hand, there were arguments for setting the UK CCyB rate a little above 1%. Risks had increased since the Committee first judged that a 1% UK CCyB rate was appropriate … waiting for a more marked evolution in domestic risks before acting could result in a need to consider sharper adjustments to the UK CCyB rate, which would likely carry larger economic costs. A measured increase this quarter could be accommodated by banks without a need to tighten credit conditions and would not be unexpected for banks and market participants, relative to the case in November, given the Committee previous communications … On the other hand, there were

---

[68]   N Albacete, P Fessler and P Lindner, "One Policy to Rule Them All? On the Effectiveness of LTV, DTI and DSTI Ratio Limits as Macroprudential policy Tools" (2018) Australian Central Bank Financial Stability Report, 67, at 79 suggest that "Risks to financial stability can be reduced most effectively by policies putting more effort into preventing the error of not identifying vulnerable households (type II error). However, at the same time, these policies will increase the occurrence of the error of denying credit to nonvulnerable households (type I error), which harms economic welfare."

[69]   D Kohn, "How Can the Objective of Macroprudential Policy be Operationalised Given the High Uncertainty about the State of the Financial System?", speech at the Joint Bundesbank-ECB Spring Conference 15 May 2019, Frankfurt, available at <https://www.bankofengland.co.uk/-/media/boe/files/speech/2019/how-can-the-objective-of-macroprudential-policy-be-operationalised-speech-by-donald-kohn>.

[70]   Sir Jon Cunliffe, "Housing Tools Revisited" speech delivered at the Bank of Portugal, Lisbon, 3 July 2019, available at <https://www.bankofengland.co.uk/-/media/boe/files/speech/2019/housing-tools-revisited-speech-by-jon-cunliffe.pdf>.

also arguments for maintaining a 1% UK CCyB rate at this meeting. First, given the relatively modest growth that had been observed in aggregate credit quantities, it might be appropriate to put less weight on signs of intensifying risk appetite in some sectors at this stage; some members thought that these signs would need to persist in order to consider acting. Second, if risks grew in particular areas, the Committee might judge that further, more targeted, policy responses could be appropriate. There were likely to be benefits therefore *to waiting to see* [author's emphasis] whether risk-taking continued to grow over the coming months. Third, the Committee re-emphasised its preference to vary the UK CCyB rate *in a gradual manner* [author's emphasis], in part to allow banks to factor it into their capital planning appropriately. At this stage, it might be beneficial to note the probable direction for the UK CCyB rate, given how risk-taking had developed, and to observe the evolution of risks over the coming months in considering whether a rise was warranted.[71]

The gradual approach to activation of macroprudential tools is widely adopted. In France, for instance, authorities followed a gradual implementation of CCyB "so as to reduce any adjustment costs and to avoid potential spurious sentiment of a looming crisis".[72]

The ECB follows what is termed "cautious experimentation", somewhere in between an active and cautious approach: "For the decisions we have to take in the near term, we will have to rely more on incompletely tested theories and sometimes precarious econometric evidence. This means that we have to accept uncertainty and cautious experimentation when we decide what is necessary to stabilise the financial system."[73]

In the US, there seems to be more hesitation, particularly with regards to activation of time-varying tools. In 2013, the Federal Reserve Governor emphasised uncertainty as a rationale for a more cautious approach in activating cyclical tools explaining that "… questions of economic knowledge and institutional capacities should be grounds for proceeding cautiously".[74] This meant that "a set of structural, or through-the-cycle, regulatory and supervisory policies" are the primary macroprudential tools.[75] More recently, however, there

---

[71]   Bank of England, Record of the Financial Policy Committee Meeting 12 March 2018.

[72]   ESRB, A Review of Macroprudential Policy in the EU in 2018, April 2019, 23, available at <https://www.esrb.europa.eu/pub/pdf/reports/esrb~32aae4bd95.report190430_reviewofmacroprudentialpolicy.pdf>.

[73]   V Constâncio, "The ECB and Macro-prudential Policy: From Research to Implementation" speech at the Third Conference of the Macro-prudential Research Network, Frankfurt-am-Main, 23 June 2014.

[74]   Governor DK Tarullo, "Macroprudential Regulation", speech at the Yale Law School Conference on Challenges in Global Financial Services, New Haven, Connecticut, 20 September 2013, available at <https://www.federalreserve.gov/newsevents/speech/tarullo20130920a.htm>.

[75]   RK Quarles, "Monetary Policy and Financial Stability" ("Developments in Empirical Macroeconomics" Conference sponsored by the Federal Reserve Board and the Federal Reserve Bank of New York, Washington, DC, 30 May 2019), available at <https://www.federalreserve.gov/newsevents/speech/quarles20190530a.htm>.

is an indication that the wind might be changing and more open to activation of anti-cyclical tools.[76]

It is important to note that the UK approach to setting the CCyB rate to be in the region of 2 per cent in "normal times" (risks are judged to be neither subdued not elevated) is unique.[77] This means effectively activating the buffer before risks become elevated and enabling the FPC to vary it more gradually as risks build.[78] Should a stress materialise and where appropriate, the FPC will cut the CCyB rate (possibly to 0 per cent) and thus reduce banks' perceived need to hoard capital and restrict lending, with consequent negative impacts for the real economy.[79]

2.3. TARGETED V BROAD-BASED ACTION

Activation and tightening of broad-based tools affect all exposures and accordingly, widen the impact of the tools and reduce the scope for their circumvention. Yet, a broad-based approach may also be more costly, result in larger distortions and overall, can be quite blunt in addressing specific sources of risk.[80]

In contrast, targeted tools enable macroprudential authorities to control more effectively specific activities and exposures of financial institutions to risks.[81] A key drawback of a targeted action is that it tends to have more immediate and visible distributional consequences, which could result in

---

[76] Vice Chair for Supervision RK Quarles, "Refining the Stress Capital Buffer" (Program on International Financial Systems Conference, Frankfurt, Germany, 5 September 2019).

[77] This was increased from 1 per cent in December 2019 and will take effect in one year. Summary and Record of the FPC Meeting on 13 December 2019, available at <https://www.bankofengland.co.uk/financial-stabilityreport/2019/december-2019>. In contrast, the framework adopted in many other countries the CCyB is raised to positive values only at times when vulnerabilities are above normal. RK Quarles, "Frameworks for the Countercyclical Capital Buffer", speech at the "Strategic Approaches to the Fed's Balance Sheet and Communications" (Spring 2019 Meeting of the Manhattan Institute's Shadow Open Market Committee, New York City, 29 March 2019).

[78] Donald Kohn, Member of the Financial Policy Committee, "Stress Tests and the Countercyclical Capital Buffer: The U.K. Experience" (London School of Economics, Money Macro and Finance 50th Anniversary Conference, 4 September 2019).

[79] Bank of England, "The Financial Policy Committee's Approach to Setting the Countercyclical Capital Buffer" (2016).

[80] See, for instance, Tarullo (2013) (n 74) with regard to the CCyB.

[81] Lim and others (2011) (n 8), 4; C Crowe, G Dell'Ariccia, D Igan and P Rabanal, "How to Deal with Real Estate Booms: Lessons from Country Experiences" (2013) 9(3) Journal of Financial Stability 300; M Costa de Moura and FM Bandeira, "Macroprudential Policy in Brazil" in *Macroprudential Frameworks, Implementation and Relationship with Other Policies* (2017) BIS Papers No 94, 77.
    See also Akinci and Olmstead-Rumsey (2015) (n 4), 3 suggesting that targeted policies tend to be more effective.

greater political pressure. This concern is evident in the statement of the FSOC Chairperson:

> if a regulator is too specific or clear in how to use tools then there will be those stating that such usage would be deeply unfair and improper. So, the tools are rarely well targeted because such targeting would be the subject of deep controversy and if the likely targeting of the tools is readily discernible from the tools itself then it is also subject to withering attack.[82]

Furthermore, targeted action can be more susceptible to circumvention[83] via migration of activity outside the scope of the tool's application; migration of activity to other (less regulated) parts of the financial system or migration to riskier forms of activity.

Overall, there is no silver bullet but experience to date suggests that "although macroprudential tools could, in principle, be targeted very precisely, circumvention by lenders and borrowers require more broad-based approaches."[84]

2.4. FLEXIBLE V LEVEL PLAYING FIELD

When setting macroprudential tools at the global and regional levels, certain flexibility at the national level has to be maintained to adjust them to the country's specificities and heterogeneities. This means considering factors such as the size, structure and complexity of the financial system, economic structure, the strength of the legal framework and the availability of data for macroprudential purposes, the degree of alignment of the financial and economic cycles[85]

---

[82] K Alexander and SL Schwarcs, "The Macroprudential Quandary: Unsystematic Efforts to Reform Financial Regulation" in R Buckley, E Avgouleas and D Arner (eds), *Reconceptualising Global Finance and Its Regulation* (Cambridge University Press, 2016), 127, 138, email from Charles Klingman (US Treasury; FSOC0) to the author on 12 May 2014.

[83] For instance, in Korea, tighter LTV limits for interest-only bullet loans with less than three years of maturity resulted in a boom in the same type of loans originated with maturity of three years and one day. G Dell'Ariccia and D Igan, "Dealing with Real Estate Booms" presented at Bank of Korea – IMF Workshop Managing Real Estate Booms and Busts (South Korea, 11–12 April 2011), 15, 21.
LTV caps can lead to credit expansion from non-banks or foreign banks. C Kim, "Macroprudential Policies in Korea: Key Measures and Experiences" (2014) Banque de France Financial Stability Review 18, 126; C Crowe, G Dell'Ariccia, D Igan and P Rabanal, "How to Deal with Real Estate Booms: Lessons from Country Experiences" (2011) IMF Working Paper No 91.

[84] C Upper, "Macroprudential Frameworks, Implementation and Relationship with Other Policies" (2017) BIS Paper No 94, 3.

[85] IMF Guidance Note on Macroprudential Policy (2014) (n 55), 28.

and the nature and measures of macroeconomic, structural and social policies in place. This dimension of macroprudential policy is most evident in the multi-layered setting in the EU. As discussed in Chapter 4, the ESRB recommendations often reiterate the importance of national specificities and the principle of proportionality is enshrined in assessing compliance with the recommendations.[86] Additionally, article 458 of the CRR enables the authority in charge of the application of the article, when identifying changes in the intensity of systemic risk in the financial system with the potential to have serious negative consequences to the financial system and the real economy, to draft national measures for domestically authorised institutions, or a subset of those institutions and notify the European Parliament, the Council, the Commission, the ESRB and EBA of the need for stricter national measures.[87] Implementation of national measures, however, should strike the balance between ensuring flexibility and a tailored approach to activation and calibration of macroprudential tools, on the one hand, and maintaining the level playing field in the single market, on the other hand.[88]

---

[86] I.e. actions to be taken by the addressees are country-specific, and relative to the intensity of risks targeted by the recommendation in the specific Member State. ESRB Secretariat, "Handbook on the Assessment of Compliance with ESRB Recommendations" (April 2016), 15.

In practice, even where extensive international and European guidance exist for the use of CCyB, there are large differences as regards key features of the national frameworks of Member States, including the objective of the instrument, the neutral rate and the indicators used to inform the activation of the buffer. ESRB (2018) (n 31), 3.

[87] Within one month of receiving the notification referred to in para 2, the ESRB and EBA shall provide their opinions on the points in article 458(2) of the CRR to the Council, the Commission and the Member State concerned. Then, taking utmost account of the opinions and if there is robust, strong and detailed evidence that the measure will have a negative impact on the internal market that outweighs the financial stability benefits resulting in a reduction of the macroprudential or systemic risk identified, the Commission may, within one month, propose to the Council an implementing act to reject the draft national measures. In the absence of a Commission proposal within that period, the Member State concerned may immediately adopt the draft national measures for a period of up to two years or until the macroprudential or systemic risk ceases to exist if that occurs sooner.

[88] Indeed, according to article 458 of the CRR after receiving the opinions of the EBA and the ESRB if there is robust, strong and detailed evidence that the measure *will have a negative impact on the internal market that outweighs the financial stability* [author's emphasis] benefits resulting in a reduction of the macroprudential or systemic risk identified, the Commission may, within one month, propose to the Council an implementing act to reject the draft national measures. In the absence of a Commission proposal within that period, the Member State concerned may immediately adopt the draft national measures for a period of up to two years or until the macroprudential or systemic risk ceases to exist if that occurs sooner. The Council must then decide on the proposal by the Commission within one month after receipt of the proposal and state its reasons for rejecting or not rejecting the draft national measures. See also A Dombret, "How to Manage Financial Crisis from a Systemic Viewpoint", Speech at 40th Economics Conference of the Central Bank of the Republic of Austria European Monetary Union: Lessons from the Debt Crisis (Vienna, 10 May 2012); ESRB, "A Review of Macroprudential Policies in the EU in 2018", April 2019, 72–79.

3. CHALLENGES OF ACTIVATING AND CALIBRATING MACROPRUDENTIAL TOOLS

3.1. LEAKAGES: DOMESTIC AND CROSS-BORDER

When activating tools, macroprudential authorities must consider their potential leakages. For instance, capital tools may increase the cost of loans and can potentially lead to arbitrage and provision of credit by institutions not covered by the tool.[89] This can be achieved through lending by domestic non-banks, off-balance-sheet provision of credit as well as lending by foreign financial institutions.[90] Where the leakages are domestic,[91] they can be addressed by expanding the regulatory perimeter to include nonbanks or by consolidating activity when it is conducted as part of a banking group.

Activating macroprudential tools domestically may also have positive and/or negative effects on other jurisdictions. Given the international nature of financial markets, increasing resilience domestically should also reduce contagion of vulnerabilities across countries. However, differences in macroprudential requirements across jurisdictions could potentially create incentives for regulatory arbitrage and undermine the effectiveness of the domestic macroprudential measures.[92] For instance, where a macroprudential authority raises capital requirement to limit excessive credit growth domestically, banks with cross-border lending activities may cut back their lending in other countries as well. If those countries are in a different phase of the financial cycle, this could inhibit their economic growth with a negative impact on their real economy.[93]

Cross-border leakages of capital tools can be addressed, inter alia, by reciprocity arrangements.[94] Reciprocation ensures that the application of a

---

[89] For instance, S Aijar, CW Calomiris and T Wieladek, "Does Macro-pru Leak? Evidence from a UK Policy Experiment" (2012) NBER Working Paper No 17822 show that in response to tighter national capital requirements, UK-owned banks resident foreign subsidiaries were offset by an increase in capital by resident foreign banks that were not regulated.

[90] Staff Guidance Note on Macroprudential Instruments (2014) (n 2), 8.
This is a real concern for macroprudential authorities: "If the measures are designed to be targeted, questions of efficacy may be raised by those who believe that suppression of excess credit or asset price increases in one sector will likely result only in the redirection of credit and speculation to other sectors until underlying macroeconomic and financial conditions have ceased enabling such activities". Tarullo (2013) (n 74).

[91] For instance, J Cizel, J Frost, A Houben and P Wierts, "Effective Macroprudential Policy: Cross-Sector Substitution from Price and Quantity Measures" (2016) IMF Working Paper 94.

[92] These spillovers are more likely when the financial cycles of the respective jurisdictions are out of sync. ESRB Handbook on Operationalising Macroprudential Policy in the Banking Sector (n 2), 18.

[93] Ibid, 56.

[94] Another way to mitigate cross-border leakages is by imposing a greater host control over foreign branches. IMF Guidance Note on Macroprudential Instruments (2014) (n 2), 21.

macroprudential tool in a given jurisdiction is recognised in another jurisdiction or an equivalent measure is applied. As such, under Basel III, there is a mandatory reciprocity requirement for CCyB capped at 2.5 per cent of risk-weighted assets applying to all international active banks in member jurisdictions of the BCBS.[95] The jurisdictional reciprocity principle is designed to ensure a level playing field between domestic banks and foreign banks.[96] BCBS member jurisdictions differ widely in their reciprocity practices.[97] While Australia, Brazil, Hong Kong SAR, Korea and Russia require reciprocation of all jurisdictions, Japan, Switzerland and Turkey reciprocate only the CCyBs of BCBS member jurisdictions.[98]

In the EU, reciprocity is automatic and mandatory up to a buffer rate of 2.5 per cent of risk-weighted assets for all banks incorporated in the European Economic Area (whether a BCBS or non-BCBS member).[99] In addition, the ESRB also put in place a framework of voluntary reciprocity for macroprudential policy measures.[100] Nevertheless, evidence suggests that, at least in the EU, voluntary reciprocation is used only occasionally.[101]

3.2. INTERACTION WITH OTHER POLICY AREAS AND OTHER INSTRUMENTS

Chapter 8 explores the interaction of macroprudential policy with other policy areas notably monetary policy, micro-prudential policy and fiscal policy.

---

[95] BCBS, "Basel III: A Global Regulatory Framework for More Resilient Banks and Banking Systems" (Revised June 2011); BCBS, "Guidance for National Authorities Operating the Countercyclical Buffer" (2010). Jurisdictions can implement larger countercyclical buffer requirements, and, in that case, the reciprocity provisions of the regime will not apply to the additional amounts or earlier timeframes.

[96] Guidance for National Authorities Operating the Countercyclical Buffer (n 95), 5.

[97] BCBS, "Range of Practices In Implementing the Countercyclical Capital Buffer Policy", 2017, available at <https://www.bis.org/bcbs/publ/d407.htm>, 9.

[98] Ibid.

[99] Rates in excess of 2.5 per cent are subject to voluntary reciprocity. For a detailed guidance on the CCB in the EU see Chapter 2 in The ESRB Handbook on Operationalising Macro-prudential Policy in the Banking Sector (n 2).

[100] The framework is set out in ESRB Recommendation of 15 December 2015 on the Assessment of Cross-border Effects of and Voluntary Reciprocity for Macroprudential Policy Measures ESRB/2015/2 OJ C 97/9; ESRB/2017/4 amending Recommendation ESRB/2015/2 OJ C 431/1 on the Assessment of Cross-border Effects of and Voluntary Reciprocity for Macroprudential Policy Measures (ESRB/2017/4); Decision ESRB/2015/4 on a Coordination Framework regarding the Notification of National Macroprudential Policy Measures by Relevant Authorities (ESRB/2015/4) OJ C 97/28.
See also Chapter 11 "Cross-border Effects of Macroprudential Policy and Reciprocity" in the ESRB Handbook on Operationalising Macroprudential Policy (n 2), 226.
There is also a voluntary arrangement of reciprocity for a systemic risk buffer in article 134 of the CRD.

[101] EBA, "The Range of Practices Regarding Macroprudential Policy Measures", July 2015.

It reiterates inter alia that macroprudential policy cannot be conducted in silos and should inform and be informed by these policies.[102] Macroprudential authorities should, therefore, take advantage of any complementarities with other policy areas that may, in turn, reinforce the effectiveness of macroprudential tools.[103] For instance, prior to activating sectoral housing tools, macroprudential authorities should consider the implications of macroeconomic policies (monetary and fiscal), prudential supervision policies, building (zoning) regulations and other structural policies which can affect the construction industry.[104] These policies can have an impact on the demand and supply of housing markets and accordingly, the cost and ease of financing house purchases.[105] As such, fiscal measures (such as stamp duty and capital gains taxes) can cool down rising house prices and contribute to reducing risks but will require coordination with macroprudential authorities on the timing of their implementation.[106]

Macroprudential authorities should also be cognisant of any potential tensions between the activation of macroprudential tools and other policy measures. Such tension may arise, for instance, between macroprudential capital measures and micro-prudential capital measures, particularly during the downswing of the financial cycle. Then, the micro-prudential policy setter tends to tighten the capital requirements for individual institutions while the macroprudential authority tends to relax them. From a system-wide view, tightening of capital could lead to deleveraging, asset fire sales and eventually, an adverse effect on the real economy. There may also be a more direct interaction between macroprudential tools and other policy areas. For instance, a CCyB may have an effect on the price of credit, influence the transmission of interest rate changes and thus, interact with monetary policy.[107]

Finally, as discussed in Section 1, in addition to the interaction between macroprudential policy and other policy areas, there are potential interactions between different macroprudential tools. For instance, imposing limits on LTV ratio could result in banks changing their assets holding and thus have an impact

---

[102] The Group of 30, Enhancing Financial Stability and Resilience: Macroprudential Policy, Tools and Systems for the Future (2010), 76.
       See also M Lee, R Gaspar and MLC Villaruel, "Macroprudential Policy Frameworks in Developing Asian Economies" (2017) Asian Development Bank Economics Working Paper Series No 510, available at <http://dx.doi.org/10.22617/WPS178676-2>; V Bruno and others, "Comparative Assessment of Macroprudential Policies" (2017) 28(c) Journal of Financial Stability 183.
[103] Lim and others (2011) (n 8), 15 suggest that combined use of macroprudential tools with other policy tools "typically occurs when the credit cycle coincides with the business cycle and there is a generalized risk of excessive credit growth and economic overheating".
[104] P Hilbers and others, "House Price Development in Europe: A Comparison" (2008) IMF Working Paper 211, 9–10; Lim and others (2011) (n 8).
[105] Hibers (2008) (n 104), 9.
[106] IMF Guidance Note on Macroprudential Instruments (2014) (n 2), 45.
[107] ESRB Handbook on Operationalising Macroprudential Policy (2014) (n 2), 33.

on capital requirements.[108] Similarly, imposing capital requirements could, amongst other things, reduce house prices and consequently, affect the tightness of LTV policies.[109]

3.3. UNPOPULARITY AND A DISTRIBUTIONAL EFFECT

To be contrasted with monetary policy, which is often viewed as "blindfolded to its distributional consequences",[110] the macroprudential authority's toolkit may include measures that have clear distributional effects. Adjustments to caps on LTV ratio and other household sectoral tools can be used to limit unsustainable credit expansion in the real estate market during boom times thereby assisting in containing the build-up of systemic risk throughout the financial cycle.[111] These tools, however, are often viewed as cutting across lenders' judgments on the creditworthiness of individual borrowers[112] and limiting lending to individuals and/or businesses that otherwise could afford a high LTV mortgage.[113] These tools may exclude potential first-time home-buyers from the property market and reduce access to finance for often younger and less wealthy groups.[114] Politicians are particularly keen to support these segments of the electorate and promote the democratisation of homeownership.[115] The pressure on the

---

[108] Chapter 9 in X Freixas, L Laeven and JL Peydró (eds), *Systemic Risk, Crises and Macroprudential Regulation*, (MIT Press, 2015), 279.

[109] Ibid.

[110] A Haldane, "Macroprudential Policies: When and How to Use Them?" ("Rethinking Macro-prudential Policy 2: First Steps and Early Lessons", IMF, Washington DC, 16–17 April 2013). But there are voices who suggest that the ECB's monetary policy does have distributional consequences. See, for instance, F Scharpf, "Political Legitimacy in a Non-Optimal Currency Area" (2013) Max Planck Institute for the Study of Societies Working Paper 15.

[111] C Crowe and others, "Policies for Macro-financial Stability: Options to Deal with Real Estate Boom" (2011) IMF Staff Discussion Note, 19; D Igan and H Kang, "Do Loan-to-Value and Debt-to-Income Limits Work? Evidence from Korea" (2011) IMF Working Paper 297.

[112] Records of the Interim FPC Meeting, 16 March 2012, available at <http://bankofengland. co.uk/publications/Documents/records/fpc/pdf/2012/record1203.pdf>.

[113] Ibid, para 31 concluding that more public discussion and understanding is needed for the FPC to have such a power. In April 2015, UK Parliament passed legislation granting the FPC powers of Direction over LTV and DTI ratio limits for owner-occupied mortgages.
See also, "The Financial Services Bill: the FPC's Macro-prudential Tools, a Consultation on its Proposals for the FPC Direction-making Tools" (September 2012); Bank of England, "Instruments of Macro-prudential Policy" (n 2); Bank of England, "The FPC's Powers over Housing Tools" (February 2015) Draft Policy Statement.

[114] Turner Review, 110; C Goodhart, "The Macro-prudential Authority: Powers, Scope and Accountability" (2011) 2 OECD Journal: Financial Market Trends 17.

[115] FSA, "The Turner Review: A Regulatory Response to the Global Financial Crisis" (March 2009), 110; Lord Turner's evidence at the House of Commons, "Banking Crisis: Regulation and Supervision" (2009), para 128.

macroprudential authority to delay, avoid or tune down the implementation of these tools may accordingly increase.[116] This is particularly the case given that a restriction on LTV ratios (similarly to other anti-cyclical macroprudential tools) is likely to take place when the danger to financial stability is least apparent, thereby rendering the decision to implement the tool very unpopular.[117] In that environment, going against the stream and not succumbing to the claims that "this time is different" could be very challenging for a macroprudential authority.[118] These pressures are likely to be exacerbated in light of the difficulty in identifying a real estate bubble, let alone a "costly" bubble that will destabilise the financial system.[119] Moreover, rationalising the policy decision to implement these tools to the public is challenging since the tool's adverse effects are

---

    On the historical roots of pursuing home-ownership as a social policy in the US and the part it played in attributing to the global financial crisis: P Wallison, "Dissent from the Majority Report of the Financial Crisis Inquiry Commission" (American Enterprise Institute Press, 15 May 2011); V Acharya and others, *Guaranteed to Fail: Fannie Mae, Freddie Mac and the Debacle of Mortgage Finance* (Princeton University Press, 2011); A Shlay, "Low-Income Homeownership: American Dream or Delusion" (2006) 43(3) Urban Studies 511.

    See also M Watson, "Constituting Monetary Conservatives via the 'Savings Habit': New Labour and the British Housing Market Bubble" (2008) 6 Comparative European Politics 28; H Schwartz and L Seabroke, "Varieties of Residential Capitalism in the International Political Economy: Old Welfare State and the New Politics of Housing" (2008) 6 Comparative European Politics 237.

[116]   This is far from being a theoretical concern. In the UK, for instance, the Financial Services Authority was under pressure from politicians to avoid its plan to reign in the mortgage lending market, suggesting that it would hinder the extension of mortgage credit and the democratisation of home ownership. Lord Turner's Evidence (2009) (n 115), para 128.

[117]   Often described as "taking the punch bowl just as the party gets going". Drawing on W McChesney Martin Jr, Chairman Board of Governors of the Federal Reserve System address before the New York Group of the Investment Bankers Association of America, New York City, 19 October 1955; C Goodhart, *The Regulatory Response to the Financial Crisis* (Edward Elgar, 2009), 98; L Seabrooke and E Tsingou, "Responding to the Financial Global Credit Crisis: the Politics of Financial Reform" (2010) 12(2) British Journal of Politics and International Relations 313.

[118]   The phrase draws on Reinhart and Rogoff, *This Time Is Different: Eight Centuries of Financial Folly* (Princeton University Press, 2009).

    See also Evidence of the Institute of Economic Affairs to the HL EU Committee during discussion on "The Future of Economic Governance in the EU" (December 2010) HL Paper 124-II, 149.

[119]   C Bean, "Asset Prices, Financial Imbalances and Monetary Policy: Are Inflation Targets Enough?" (2003) BIS Working Paper 140; V Burgy, L Clerc and J Renne, "Asset-price Boom-bust Cycles and Credit: What is the Scope of Macro-prudential Regulation?" (2009) Banque de France Working Paper 263; P Praet, "Housing Cycles and Financial Stability-The Role of the Policymaker" (European Mortgage Federation Annual Conference, Brussels, 24 November 2011). But not all booms are followed by busts: IMF, "When Bubbles Burst", Chapter 2 in World Economic Outlook April 2003, 61 observing that booms have been followed by busts about 40 per cent of the time; L Agnello and L Schuknecht, "Booms and Busts in the Housing Markets, Detriments and Implications" (2009) ECB Working Paper 71. Particularly so since macroprudential authorities still lack comprehensive and comparable data on the real estate market (Chapter 9).

immediate and visible while the wider benefits to the society as a whole will not be easily quantified let alone felt at the implementation stage.

Macroprudential authorities may thus need to face political and industry pressures, particularly when activating macroprudential tools with potential distributional effects. For instance, the decision of the Central Bank of Israel to use LTV ratio as a macroprudential tool[120] led to a great deal of media and public debate, criticising the policy for discriminating against young couples and favouring foreign investors over first-time buyers.[121] Limiting access to credit by implementing caps on LTV raised not only the issue of creditworthiness of individuals and businesses but deeper issues of social inequalities.[122] The pressures may indeed have resulted in more stringent limits on investors than on first-time homebuyers in the measures that were eventually adopted.[123]

3.4. DIFFICULTIES IN ASSESSING THE EFFECTIVENESS OF MACROPRUDENTIAL TOOLS

Given the relatively short experience in using macroprudential tools particularly in advanced economies,[124] empirical evidence on the effectiveness of the tools is still limited and tentative.[125]

---

[120] OECD Economic Surveys Israel, December 2011, 8, available at <https://www.oecd-ilibrary. org/economics/oecd-economic-surveys-israel-2011_eco_surveys-isr-2011-en>; IMF Country Report September 2015 No 261, available at <http://www.imf.org/external/pubs/ft/scr/2015/ cr15261.pdf>.

[121] A Keller, "The Possible Distributional Effects of the Loan-To-Value Ratio and Its Use As a Macro-prudential Tool by the European Systemic Risk Board" (2013) 28(7) JIBLR 266 and the references there, including "Fisher is Trying to Punish Netanyahu by Punishing Young Couples", *Globes* (1 July 2012); A Meirovsky, "Fisher will Become the Enemy of Young Couples", *The Marker* (15 August 2012); A Lahav, "Fischer Deflects Criticism: I Care About Young Couples", *YNET* (17 June 2012).
On the protests in Israel in 2011 that followed the rise in house prices see A Odenheimer and G Ackerman, "Fischer Battling Israel's Housing Bubble: Mortgages", *Bloomberg* (31 October 2012).

[122] J Greenberg, "Housing Protests Galvanize Young Israelis", *The Washington Post* (26 July 2011).

[123] In Israel, the Supervisor of Banks published in 2012 a Draft Directive that limits LTV ratios in housing loans differentiating between loans granted to investors, those upgrading their home and first-time buyers; Bank of Israel, "The Supervisor of Banks publishes a Draft Directive to Limit the Loan-to-value Ratio in Housing Loans" (Press Release, 29 October 2012). This came into force in November 2012.

[124] Galati and Moessner (2018) (n 3). To be contrasted with emerging market economies, see R McCauley, "Macroprudential Policy in Emerging Markets" (Central Bank of Nigeria's 50th Anniversary International Conference on Central Banking, Financial System Stability and Growth, Abuja, 4–9 May 2009).

[125] T Poghosyan, "How Effective is Macroprudential Policy: Evidence from Lending Restrictions Measures in EU Countries" (2019) IMF Working Paper No 45; Galati and Moessner (2018) (n 3), 1; although there is an increase in body of empirical research IMF-FSB-BIS (2016) (n 7); OECD Economic Outlook Issue 1, May 2019, 39.

The difficulty in conducting an empirical analysis on macroprudential instruments is largely attributed to "the lack of established models of the interaction between the financial system and the macroeconomy, as well as the scarcity of data needed to conduct empirical tests."[126]

To begin with, despite a booming use of macroprudential tools in recent years,[127] the set of instruments that have been implemented to date is relatively narrow[128] and most of these measures have not been tested over a full financial cycle.[129] Studies often include a large number of heterogeneous countries and the selection is subject to a bias that favours high-risk countries where measures were implemented in response to adverse financial developments.[130] In addition, studies often focus on the short-term effect of tools and thus ignore the full effect that may take time to materialise.[131]

Probably the most acute difficulty in assessing the effectiveness of macroprudential tools relates to its endogeneity, i.e. identifying the impact of macroprudential tools on macroeconomic and financial variables. In addition, there is a difficulty to find correlation and causation across and between macroprudential tools. This means that it is highly difficult to isolate or disentangle the effect of a single macroprudential tool from the effect of other macroprudential tools or other policy tools that are often used in conjunction.[132] In rapidly changing financial markets and economies, quantifying the effects of specific macroprudential instruments and attributing the relative strength of their effect is challenging.[133] Furthermore, the common use of a dummy (a binary approach) to assess the effectiveness of macroprudential tools does not account for the magnitude of the tools and/or fine-tuning of the tools that may follow the implementation stage and, therefore, may not accurately assess the effectiveness of the tools.[134]

---

[126] Galati and Moessner (2018) (n 3), 747 also providing a comprehensive review of the available methods to assessing the effectiveness of macroprudential tools.

[127] Both in advanced and emerging and developing economies. Alter and others (2019) (n 29).

[128] Thus, limiting the number of observations for empirical analysis. Poghosyan (2019) (n 125); R Barwell, "Macroprudential Policy" in P Mizen, M Rubio and P Turner, *Macroprudential Policy and Practice* (Cambridge University Press, 2018), 294.
In the EU, for instance, macroprudential policy measures targeting the non-bank financial sector are rare. ESRB (2018) (n 31), 3.

[129] Ibid.

[130] Lim and others (2011) (n 8), 15.

[131] Poghosyan (2019) (n 125), 10. In addition, they often fail to consider how the effectiveness of the tools varies according to the type of measures (for instance, legally binding or soft recommendations).

[132] Galati and Moessner (2018) (n 3), 747.

[133] IMF (2013) (n 19), 23; Barwell (2018) (n 128), 291 observed that "so much is changing that it is hard to pin down the impact of one particular intervention."

[134] But there are increasing efforts to fill in these analytical gaps. See, for instance, Z Alam and others, "Digging Deeper-Evidence on the Effects of Macroprudential Policies from a New Database" (2019) IMF Working Paper with a new feature "numerical information on the calibration of LTV limits – to quantify more precisely the impact of changes in these limits".

Most importantly, while cross-country data is helpful in expanding the number of observations. it should be exercised with cautious when used to draw inferences for individual countries.[135] Evidence that emerges on the effectiveness of macroprudential tools is often contextual and subject to particularities of the setting and policy mix and may not provide a good indication of the suitability of the tools and their effectiveness across countries. As such, evidence on a successful implementation in an emerging economy may not be transferable to a developed economy.

Time lags are another factor that can have a bearing on the assessment of the effectiveness of macroprudential tools.[136] Three types of policy lags have been identified in the literature. The first is the recognition lag, i.e. the lag between a need for action and the recognition of this need. The second is the action lag, i.e. the lag between recognition of the need for action and the taking of action and the third is the impact lag between the action and its effects.[137] The recognition lag poses a serious challenge for macroprudential authorities in light of the analytical impediments in identifying systemic risks and ascertaining the relevant tools to address them (Chapter 5). The action lag will depend on the institutional setting of the macroprudential authority, the nature of its powers and the level of coordination with implementing regulators. Finally, given the relatively short history of macroprudential policy, evidence on the impact lag is still scarce.[138] In addition, the impact lag may differ across macroprudential tools.[139] For instance, LTV and DTI caps can be implemented rather rapidly whilst the time needed for banks to adjust to higher capital or liquidity requirements, without being forced into fire sales or deleveraging, is much longer.[140]

---

[135] Poghosyan (2019) (n 125), 5.
[136] ESRB, "Features of a Macroprudential Stance: Initial Considerations" (April 2019), 30; H Kawata, Y Kurachi, K Nakamura and Y Teranishi, "Impact of Macroprudential Policy Measures on Economic Dynamics: Simulation Using a Financial Macro-Econometric Model" (2013) Bank of Japan Working Paper Series No 13E-3.
[137] M Friedman, "A Monetary and Fiscal Framework for Economic Stability" (1948) 38 American Economic Review 245.
[138] Based on evidence to date macroprudential policy has a relatively short impact lag and transmits relatively rapidly to the economy. ESRB (2019) (n 136), 40; Transmission can range between one quarter – see Akinci and Olmstead-Rumsey (2018) (n 29) and one year – see Cerutti and others (2017) (n 4).
       See also G Runstler and K Budnik, "The Dynamic Effects of Macroprudential Effects in the Euro Area: Evidence from the Bayesian Narrative Panel VAR" (Annual International Conference on Macroeconomic Analysis and International Finance, 1 June 2019) show that reaction to capital-based macroprudential policies is relatively quick but that the maximum effect on credit is only observed after two to three years.
[139] ESRB (2019) (n 136), 30.
[140] CGFS (2012) (n 7), 17.

3.5. TIMELY ACTIVATION AND RELEASE

The precise timing of activating and deactivating macroprudential tools is critical. Delayed activation of a macroprudential tool may render it less effective or ineffective considering the time it takes for it to gain traction.[141] In extreme cases, it can even trigger a crisis.[142] For instance, activation or tightening of CCyB that comes too late might lead banks to curtail lending and thus create unintended additional pro-cyclicality of credit.[143] Premature activation, on the other hand, can result in unnecessary regulatory costs and allow sufficient time for market participants to find ways to circumvent the tool.[144] Generally, it can be observed that delayed action is more costly than premature intervention.[145] However, as discussed in Section 1 above, the implication of this asymmetry on the approach taken by macroprudential authorities is still under debate and can range from an active, pre-emptive and decisive approach to a more cautious and gradual one.

A timely deactivation is also of essence. Done too early – it may give market participants the wrong signal, create moral hazard and prolong the crisis; when done too late – it may demand banks to hold buffers more than is necessary and amplify pro-cyclical effects.[146] For instance, where a CCyB is released too early, it may continue fuelling a boom phase and where it is released too late, markets may question its effectiveness in withstanding shocks.[147] Overall, given that the costs of mistimed policy action (or inaction) can be significant, it is critical to get the timing of activation and withdrawals of measures right.

---

[141] B Gadanecz and J Kaushik, "Macroprudential Policy Frameworks, Instruments and Indicators: A Review" in Irving Fisher Committee on Central Bank Statistics Bulletin No 41 (Proceedings of the IFC Workshop on "Combining Micro and Macro Statistical Data for Financial Stability Analysis: Experiences, Opportunities and challenges" Warsaw, Poland, 14–15 December 2015).
See also CGFS (2012) (n 7), 3, which outlined three high-level criteria to guide the selection and application of macroprudential tools: (1) the ability to determine the appropriate timing for the activation or deactivation of the tool; (2) the effectiveness of the tool in achieving the stated policy objective (will be discussed in Section 4 below); and (3) the efficiency of the instruments in terms of a cost-benefit analysis, taking into account the impact of other regulatory measures (discussed in Chapter 5).

[142] Freixas and others (2015) (n 108), 277.

[143] IMF Guidance Note on Instruments (2014) (n 2), 15.

[144] Freixas and others (2015) (n 108), 277–278.

[145] CGFS (2012) (n 7), 5.

[146] Freixas and others (2015) (n 108), 278.

[147] The ESRB Handbook on Operationalising Macroprudential Policy (2014) (n 2), 32 and 43–44. Also suggesting that the release stage will require more discretion from macroprudential authorities since indicators are less robust at that stage.

4. THE EFFECTIVENESS OF MACROPRUDENTIAL TOOLS AND HOW TO ENHANCE IT

There is a growing body of literature aimed at assessing the effectiveness of macroprudential tools[148] but, overall, to date, evidence is mixed.[149] A recent study of macroprudential policies in 57 advanced and emerging economies, covering the period from 2000 to 2013, show that macroprudential tightening is associated with lower bank credit growth, housing credit growth, and house price appreciation.[150] Similarly, a more comprehensive study of 119 countries, over the same period, demonstrated that deploying macroprudential tools is generally associated with lower growth in credit, notably in household credit.[151] Interestingly, however, the latter study also shows that these effects are found to a lesser extent in advanced and open economies. It suggested that advanced and open economies tend to have a more developed financial system with various alternative sources of finance and a greater cross-border borrowing, resulting in increased scope for avoidance, possibly making it harder for macroprudential policies to be effective.[152]

---

[148]   Claessens (2014) (n 2); Galati and Moessner (2018) (n 3); Nier and others (2013) (n 19), 23 reiterate that while progress is being made in empirical research and assessing effects of tools on resilience and growth in credit and asset prices "the benefits of macroprudential action for the ultimate objective of reducing the probability and depth of future crises, remains difficult to quantify".

[149]   Y Arslan and C Upper, "Macroprudential Frameworks: Implementation and Effectiveness" in Macroprudential Frameworks, Implementation and Relationship with Other Policies (2017) BIS Papers No 94, 34. Also pointing out that the impact of many macroprudential instruments may not be symmetrical (for instance, the tool can be more effective in the boom than in the bust phase).
On the effectiveness of a single macroprudential tool see, for instance, MF Castro, "A Quantitative Analysis of Countercyclical Capital Buffers" (2019) Federal Reserve Bank of St Louis Working Paper 8C, available at <https://research.stlouisfed.org/wp/more/2019-008>.

[150]   Akinci and Olmstead-Rumsey (2018) (n 29). The authors also suggest that targeted policies, which are specifically intended to limit the growth of credit in a certain sector, seem to be more effective.

[151]   Cerutti and others (2017) (n 4), 217.
See also K Budnik and J Kleibl, "Macroprudential regulation in the European Union in 1995–2014: Introducing a New Data Set on Policy Actions of a Macroprudential Nature" (2018) ECB No 2123 show that in the EU, targeted instruments such as limits on LTV ratios and broader instruments such as macroprudential capital requirements may have an impact on credit growth. Interestingly, the authors show that "in most cases where credit growth was on average lower after a policy change, it started to decline already a year prior to the entering into force of a measure, which could be due to possible announcement effects"; Assessing Macroprudential Tools in OECD Countries Within a Cointegration Framework (2018) 37 Journal of Financial Stability 102.

[152]   Cerutti and others (2017) (n 4), 217.

Effectiveness of macroprudential tools is country-dependent and will vary according to the country's structure of its banking and non-banking sector, homeownership, monetary policy, the phase of the financial cycle or the business cycle and other political economy considerations.[153] In addition, macroprudential policy measures may also have asymmetric effects across the financial cycle with evidence showing that macroprudential policies may have increased effectiveness during the boom phase compared to the bust phase.[154]

How can macroprudential authorities enhance the effectiveness of macroprudential tools? The book has already discussed reciprocity as a way to address the problem of arbitrage and leakages. Another way to minimise the risk of arbitrage is by the expediency of the implementation period thus leaving less time for market players to adjust and find ways to "game" the system (front-running or front-loading).[155] A combined approach which targets activities, as well as systemically important entities, can also reduce the probability that activities will migrate from regulated entities to other less-regulated entities.

As will be discussed in the following chapter, clear communication of activation and calibration of macroprudential tools can facilitate accountability and foster the achievement of the macroprudential objective. In addition, it can enhance the effectiveness of the tools through the expectation channel.[156] Once market participants anticipate that macroprudential tools will step in to stabilise imbalances, these imbalances may not build up in the first place.[157] Yet, the timing of the communication of the planned measures to authorities and market participants should be considered carefully. When done too early it can result in strong lobbying and front running as market participants rush to take action before the measure takes effect.[158] In contrast, late communication can reduce the effectiveness of the tools.[159]

---

[153]   IMF, "Macro-prudential Policy; What Instruments and How to Use them? Lessons from Country Experiences" (2011) IMF Working Papers 238.

[154]   Ibid. B Richter, M Schularick and I Shim, "The Macroeconomic Effects of Macroprudential Policy" (2018) BIS Working Paper No 740 also find that tightening LTV limits has larger economic effects than loosening them.

[155]   IMF Guidance Note on Macroprudential Policy (n 55), 16; CGFS, "Experiences with the Ex ante Appraisal of Macroprudential Instruments Report" submitted by a Study Group established by the CGFS chaired by A Le Lorier (July 2016) CGFS Papers No 56, 25.

[156]   IMF Guidance Notes on Macroprudential Instruments (n 2), 47.

[157]   D Schoenmaker and P Wierts, "Macroprudential Policy: The Need for a Coherent Policy Framework" (1 July 2011) Duisenburg School of Finance Policy Paper No 13, available at SSRN <https://ssrn.com/abstract=1876595> or <http://dx.doi.org/10.2139/ssrn.1876595>, 6.

[158]   IMF Guidance Note on Macroprudential Policy Instruments (n 2), 47 particularly when measures will have an impact on the flow of new credit.

[159]   IMF Guidance Note on Macroprudential Policy (n 55), 27. The latter is a particular concern when activating sectoral capital requirements that target lenders' exposures. In that case, an announcement should be done well in advance since lenders will ned to make significant adjustment.

CHAPTER 7

INDEPENDENCE, ACCOUNTABILITY AND TRANSPARENCY OF MACROPRUDENTIAL POLICY

An independent macroprudential authority can make "tough" policy decisions that can have distributional effects and reduce economic growth in the short term (Chapter 6), without succumbing to political pressures and industry capture. Nonetheless, the discretion of the macroprudential authority cannot be without constraints and must be complemented by strong accountability and transparency arrangements. The effectiveness of accountability and transparency as a countervailing force to independence in macroprudential regimes is likely to be dependent on the legal and institutional context in which the macroprudential authority operates.[1] Therefore, the form of these arrangements and their strength will naturally differ widely across jurisdictions. Still, independence, accountability and transparency mechanisms may share a common ground that can be traced back to the concept of legitimacy on its various dimensions. Understanding legitimacy and particularly throughput legitimacy as a theoretical underpinning of good governance in macroprudential regimes and its balance with expertise and discretion will be the focus of this chapter.

The aim of this chapter is, accordingly, threefold. The first is to provide a theoretical framework for the independence, accountability and transparency of macroprudential authorities, by synthesising diverse concepts and ideas developed in the literature on bureaucratic discretion and delegation to independent regulatory agencies. In particular, the chapter draws parallels (alongside fundamental differences) with the burgeoning academic discussion of central banks' independence. Second, after establishing the need (and the associated risks) for macroprudential authorities to be independent, the chapter sets out to make its complementary concepts, transparency and accountability, operational. It does so by identifying their key dimensions and the unique demands they present in the macroprudential sphere and drawing upon procedural mechanisms that are firmly anchored in administrative law traditions.

---

[1]   In financial supervision see M Quintyn and M Taylor, "Regulatory and Supervisory Independence and Financial Stability" (2002) IMF Working Paper 46, available at <https://www.imf.org/external/pubs/ft/wp/2002/wp0246.pdf>, 26.

Third, the chapter assesses how accountability and transparency arrangements can be designed and implemented to improve the macroprudential authority's various forms of legitimacy. The transparency and accountability frameworks of the FPC, FSOC and ESRB are used as case studies for that purpose.

It is suggested that in the macroprudential sphere, the focus of accountability mechanisms, at least in the early stages of the policy development, should be on the decision-making process (to be differentiated from policy results). The conception of accountability at the process-level will provide a solid and clear benchmark against which the macroprudential authority can be assessed and held accountable. Governance structure and decision-making procedures that enhance pluralism and inclusiveness of the public through transparency and awareness of the rationales behind policy decision can also assist in legitimising the macroprudential authority.

The chapter proceeds as follows. Section 1 presents the rationales for delegating a macroprudential mandate to an independent agency. It then assesses the suitability and strength of the various forms of independence in the macroprudential setting. Section 2 moves on to explore the concept of accountability, as a necessary complement to independence. It begins with analysing the unique challenges of accountability in the macroprudential sphere and positions them within a theoretical framework of legitimacy. In the course of uncovering these problems, Section 2 seeks to dissect how these unique features and theoretical foundations translate into an operational framework of accountability. In light of the preceding theoretical framework of legitimacy, it assesses the accountability arrangement adopted in the legal frameworks of the FPC, the FSOC and the ESRB. Section 3 explores transparency as a key mechanism to fostering accountability of macroprudential authorities. The section focuses on prevalent channels of communications: Financial Stability Reports and minutes of the macroprudential authority's meetings. It follows with suggestions on how to enhance the effectiveness of transparency arrangements adopted in the legal frameworks of the FPC, FSOC and ESRB. Section 4 then concludes.

1. DELEGATING A MACROPRUDENTIAL AUTHORITY TO AN INDEPENDENT AGENCY

1.1. THE RATIONALE FOR DELEGATING A MACROPRUDENTIAL MANDATE TO AN INDEPENDENT AGENCY

There is abundant literature on the emergence of regulatory state and the concomitant trend of delegating authority to independent regulatory agencies that are neither elected nor managed by elected officials.[2] Technical expertise is often cited as a prominent factor in the decision to delegate authority to an independent agency.[3] In highly complex and technical matters, political principals delegate regulatory powers to an independent regulatory agency and utilise their superior expertise so as to increase the level of efficiency and effectiveness in carrying out policy decisions.[4] Alesina and Tabellini, accordingly, observed that "The bureaucrat is preferable [to politicians – author's addition] for technical tasks for which ability is more important than effort …".[5] In addition, an independent agency is insulated from day-to-day politics and therefore, not subject to the problems of time-inconsistency and short-termism that often distort political incentives[6] and move decisions away from optimal social welfare. Alesina and Tabellini's following quote is rather telling: "Bureaucrats are likely to be better than politicians if the criteria for good performance can be

---

[2]   G Majone, "The Rise of the Regulatory State in Europe" (1994) 17(3) West European Politics 77, 94; often referred to as non-majoritarian institutions, G Majone "Temporal Consistency and Policy Credibility: Why Democracies Need Non-Majoritarian Institutions" (1996) European University Institute Working Paper No 96/57. The regulatory state is to be contrasted with the traditional form of governance provided by the "positive state". G Majone, "From the Positive to the Regulatory State: Causes and Consequences of Changes in the Mode of Governance" (1997) 17(2) Journal of Public Policy 139.
    See also A Sweet and M Thatcher, "Theory and Practice of Delegation to Non-Majoritarian Institutions" (2002) 25(1) West European Politics 1; F Gilardi, "Policy Credibility and Delegation to Independent Regulatory Agencies: A Comparative Empirical Analysis" (2002) 9(6) Journal of European Public Policy 873; D Levi-Faur, "The Global Diffusion of Regulatory Capitalism" (2005) 598(1) The Annals of the American Academy of Political and Social Science 12; F Vibert, *The Rise of the Unelected Democracy and the New Separation of Powers* (Cambridge University Press, 2007) views these institutions as a new branch of the government.
    In financial supervision context see F Amtenbrink and R Lastra, "Securing Democratic Accountability of Financial Regulatory Agencies – A Theoretical Framework" in RV De Mulder, *Mitigating Risk in the Context of Safety and Security – How Relevant is a Rational Approach?* 115–132 (Rotterdam: OMV, 2008), available at SSRN <https://ssrn.com/abstract=1330309>.

[3]   Majone (1996) (n 2); Vibert (2007) (n 2); More generally on the role of expertise in policymaking see S Callander, "A Theory of Policy Expertise" 3(2) (2008) Quarterly Journal of Political Science 139.

[4]   G Majone, "The Transformations of the Regulatory State" in L Leisering (ed), *The New Regulatory State Regulating Private Pensions in Germany and the UK* (Palgrave, 2011).

[5]   A Alesina and G Tabellini, "Bureaucrats or Politicians? Part I: A Single Policy Task" (2007) 97 American Economic Review 169; A Alesina and G Tabellini, "Bureaucrats or Politicians? Part 2: A Single Policy Task" (2008) 92 Journal of Public Economics 426.

[6]   Majone (1996) (n 2), 3. Time inconsistency essentially occurs when the principal's present preference may conflict with its future preferences. On the time inconsistency (or credibility) problem of the government that can result in inflation bias when setting monetary policy see F Kydland and E Prescott, "Rules Rather Than Discretion: The Inconsistency of Optimal Plans" (1977) 85(3) Journal of political Economy 473; R Barro and D Gordon, "Rules, Discretion and Reputation in a Model of Monetary Policy" (1983) NBER Working Paper No 1079; B Levy and P Spiller, "The Institutional Foundations of Regulatory Commitment: A Comparative Analysis of Telecommunications Regulation" (1994) 10(2) Journal of Law, Economics, and Organization 201–246.

easily described *ex-ante* and are stable over time, and if political incentives are distorted by time-inconsistency or short-termism".[7]

There are, of course, additional explanations for delegating authority to an independent agency.[8] For instance, it can be done in order to shift the blame of unpopular decisions with clear winners and losers away from the government[9] or alleviate problems of incomplete information thus reducing the amount of uncertainty.[10]

The considerations of enhanced expertise and insulation from politics and industry pressures become even more pertinent in the macroprudential domain. Macroprudential policymaking requires a great deal of analytical skills, capacity to process large and complex amount of information and expertise.[11] Moreover, the achievement of the ultimate objective of financial stability often does not coincide with short-term political interests, such as the continuance of lending, asset price increases and housing democratisation (Chapter 6). Imposing macroprudential tools, especially countercyclical measures, will often require the macroprudential authority to "go against the stream" with immediate and visible costs (and at times, with distributional effects) while the benefits are far from view and not easily measurable. The risk of industry lobbying and the resulting regulatory capture[12] is therefore significant in macroprudential policymaking, particularly where policy measures are targeted to particular sectors.[13]

---

[7]   Alesina and Tabellini (2008) (n 5), 444. This was indeed the basis for granting independence to central banks, who, in contrast to elected politicians, are not subject to political incentives and ex-post democratic control. See K Rogoff, "The Optimal Degree of Commitment to an Intermediate Target" (1985) 100(4) Quarterly Journal of Economics 1169.

[8]   D Lombardi and M Moschella, "The Symbolic Politics of Delegation: Macroprudential Policy and Independent Regulatory Authorities" (2016) 22(1) New Political Economy 92 suggest that the delegation a macroprudential authority to systemic regulatory authorities was driven by the need to provide "a quick institutional 'fix' following the 2007–2009 financial crisis".

[9]   M Fiorina, "Legislative Choice of Regulatory Forms: Legal Process or Administrative Process?" (1982) 39(1) Public Choice 33, 46–47; RK Weaver, "The Politics of Blame Avoidance" (1986) 6(4) Journal of Public Po 371, 386.
      In the macroprudential context, D Lombardi and M Moschella, "Why Are Central Banks Delegated Macroprudential Responsibilities?" (ECPR Joint Sessions, Salamanca, 10–15 April 2014), 22 suggest that delegation is aimed at deflecting accountability for the distributional implications of macroprudential policy.

[10] "The Decision to Delegate", Chapter 4 in D Epstein and S O'Halloran (eds), *Delegating Powers: A Transaction Cost Politics Approach to Policy Making Under Separate Powers* (New York: Cambridge University Press, 1999), 79–80.

[11] For instance, BS Bernanke, "Implementing a Macroprudential Approach to Supervision and Regulation" (The 47th Annual Conference on Bank Structure and Competition, Chicago, Illinois, 5 May 2011).

[12] G Stigler, "The Theory of Economic Regulation" (1971) 2(1) Bell Journal of Economics and Management Science 3 though not using the term "regulatory capture".

[13] This is far from being a theoretical concern, as discussed in Chapter 6.
      See also concerns on the impact of the FPC's measures on first-time buyers in Bob Pannell, "Has Macro-prudential Policy Served the Market Well?" (Mortgage Strategy, 28 June 2019), available at <https://www.mortgagestrategy.co.uk/analysis-has-macro-prudential-policy-served-the-market-well/>.

Delegation to an independent agency can remove the concern of short-term temptation to buckle under electorates' pressure for political gain, ensuring that timely action is taken to prevent or mitigate the build-up of systemic risks.[14] Insularity from political pressure will also allow the macroprudential authority to further develop expertise[15] and form, in time, a solid evidence-based approach to its policy decisions.[16]

Nonetheless, delegation of macroprudential policymaking to an independent agency is not without risks and limitations.[17] The regulatory state, in general and the delegation to an independent regulatory agency, in particular, bring about the conventional concerns of legitimacy and democratic deficit.[18] The independent agency, it is argued, falls outside the traditional *trias politica* and the system of checks and balances that supports it and thus lacks democratic legitimacy.[19]

---

[14] I Agur and S Sharma, "Rules, Discretion, and Macro-Prudential Policy" (2013) IMF Working Paper 65.

[15] I.e. reduction of technical uncertainty. K Bawn, "Political Control Versus Expertise: Congressional Choices About Administrative Procedures" (1995) 89(1) The American Political Science Review 62. Though pointing out that there is a trade-off between expertise and the level of political control over policy decisions. This point will be discussed in Section 9.

[16] On the benefits of an evidence-based approach in macroprudential policymaking see A Keller, "Debiasing Macroprudential Policy: Part 1: An Evidence-Based Approach and the Precautionary Principle" (2018) 34(1) JIBLR 5.

[17] The need to balance between the benefits and the transactions costs of delegation was acknowledged in D Epstein and S O'Halloran, *Delegating Powers: A Transaction Cost Politics Approach to Policy Making Under Separate Powers* (New York: Cambridge University Press, 1999), contending that the decision to delegate is similar to a firm's "make or buy decision", at 7–8.

[18] G Majone, "Nonmajoritarian Institutions and the Limits of Democratic Governance: A Political Transaction-Cost Approach" (2001) 157(1) Journal of Institutional and Theoretical Economics 57; G Majone, "The Regulatory State and its Legitimacy Problems" (1999) 22 (1) West European Politics 1; M Maggetti, "Legitimacy and Accountability of Independent Regulatory Agencies: A Critical Review" (2010) 2 Living Reviews in Democracy 1–9.
See also M Lodge, "Accountability and Transparency in Regulation: Critiques, Doctrines and Instruments" in J Jordana and D Levi-Faur (eds), *The Politics of Regulation* (Cheltenham: Edward Elgar, 2004).
In monetary policy, see A Cukierman, "Central Bank Independence and Monetary Control" (1994) 104 (427) Economic Journal 1437, 1443.
Criticism of unconstrained discretion and legitimacy is frequent in the real world. The FSOC, for instance, was viewed as an institution that has "almost unlimited, unreviewable and sometimes secret bureaucratic discretion". B Gray, "Dodd-Frank, The Real Threat to the Constitution", *Washington Post* (31 December 2010); Similarly, PA Wallack, *To the Edge: Legality, Legitimacy and the Responses to the 2008 Financial Crisis* (Brookings Institution Press, 2015), 203 "Its procedures are minimally defined, and it is given enormous discretion to fashion policies regulating systemically important financial institutions and to deal with their failures. Although FSOC might use its discretionary power productively, it is unfortunate that the law did not help it achieve legitimacy by providing a better-defined process, clear accountability mechanisms, and a clear statement of the outer limits of its authorities."

[19] G Majone, "Independence versus Accountability? Non Majoritarian Institutions and Democratic Government in Europe" (1994) 94(3) European University Institute Working Paper No 94.
See also Amtenbrink and Lastra (2008) (n 2), 121.

More generally, expertise is never neutral, and technocrats are not apolitical. Thus, politics is not eliminated from the decision-making process but rather replaced by the "politics of expertise".[20] In fact, scholars even suggested that to be "apolitical" is in itself a political strategy with political results.[21] The problems in the macroprudential sphere are similar in kind. Accountability as a mechanism to address democratic deficit may, in practice, open the door to new opportunities for public debates on societal choices, distributional effects and the delicate balance between financial stability and economic growth. In fact, the very effort to insulate macroprudential policymaking from politics can bring it back to the scene in full force. In other words, "depoliticisation begets politicisation."[22] Mark Carney, in his role as the chair of the FPC, was subject to strong criticism when highlighting risks to financial stability from Brexit prior to the referendum and following the referendum, on risks emanating from a

---

[20] F Fischer, *Technocracy and the Politics of Expertise* (Sage Publications, 1990); F Fischer, *Citizens, Experts and the Environment The Politics of Local Knowledge* (Durham: Duke University Press, 2000), 8 suggests that "expertise itself turns out not to be the neutral, objective phenomenon that it has purported to be. Indeed, it has all too often served the ideological function of legitimizing decisions made elsewhere by political rather than scientific means".

See also LS Schrefler, *Economic Knowledge in Regulation the Use of Expertise by Independent Agencies* (CEPR, 2013), inter alia, on p 186 suggests that "the traditional dichotomy between neutral/bureaucratic and political decision making cannot be upheld. Regulatory policy making is better depicted as a continuum ranging from 'government by experts' and 'government by politicians'. In this context, there is no such thing as neutral policy appraisal. Nor is it realistic to conceive that a purely technical use of power exists".

U Beck, "Politics of Risk Society", Chapter 1 in J Franklin (ed), *The Politics of Risk Society* (Cambridge Polity Press, 1988), 9, 13–14 argues that in the "risk society" where risks are manufactured and produced by mankind, reliance on traditional securities of scientific knowledge is mistaken and can no longer persist.

[21] Such that "claims to disinterestedness are strategies for eliminating the suspicion of partisanship or self-interest". S Turner, "Filling the Gap: The Rise of Knowledge Associations and 'Expertization'", Chapter 4 in St Turner, *Liberal Democracy 3.0: Civil Society in an Age of Experts* (Sage Publications, 2003), 83.

This still resonates even more than ever in criticism of central banks. For instance, L Elliott, "Central Banks Were Always Political – So Their 'Independence' Doesn't Mean Much", *The Guardian* (12 September 2019); "How Central Bankers Can Survive Populist Attacks", *Financial Times* (30 August 2019); C Giles, "How Star Central Bank Governor Turned into Brexit Target", *Financial Times* (30 October 2016).

[22] A Baker, "'The Bankers' Paradox: The Political Economy of Macroprudential Regulation" (2015) 120 LSE Systemic Risk Centre Discussion Paper No 37, 26–27 observing that "efforts to depoliticise macroprudential policy by allocating power and responsibility to unelected central banks, whose claims to authority are based on technical expertise, actually runs the risk of not only politicising macroprudential policy, but also politicising central banks themselves."

See also W Buiter, "Dysfunctional Central Banking. The End of Independent Central Banks or a Return to 'Narrow Central Banking' – or Both?'" (December 2016) Citi Research, Multi-Asset, Global, Global Economics View.

disorderly Brexit.[23] These assessments attracted much of the media attention suggesting that the Bank of England was "dragged into the political sphere".[24] From there, it is a short way to the suggestion that macroprudential authorities have excessive powers and are unaccountable[25] ultimately leading to a general distrust in their policymaking.[26]

Concerns of erosion of public trust in macroprudential authorities can be attributed, at least in part, to two factors. The first is the general decline in trust in central banks following the 2007–2009 financial crisis[27] and the

---

[23] MP Jacob Rees-Mogg suggested during the Treasury Committee hearing on 4 December 2018 that Mark Carney's observation that it is beneficial in economic terms to stay within the EU was in fact giving a political opinion; Mark Carney's response was that the FPC is aware of its statutory responsibilities and that assessments are done in a professional and objective manner. Similarly, see comments by a former Bank of England Governor M King, "May's Brexit Deal is a Betrayal of Britain", *Bloomberg* (4 December 2018), available at <https://www.bloomberg.com/opinion/articles/2018-12-04/mervyn-king-says-may-s-brexit-deal-is-a-betrayal>.

[24] This phrase was used in a question presented to the Governor of the Bank of England, Mark Carney during "The Economist Ask: Mark Carney How Do Central Bank Deal with a Riskier World?" with regard to its involvement in areas such as low-carbon investments and Brexit. The interview is available at <https://www.economist.com/podcasts/2019/07/05/how-do-central-banks-deal-with-a-riskier-world>; W De Haan, and others, "Is the Era of Central Bank Independence Drawing to a Close?", Blog Entry in *LSE Business Review* (10 January 2017). Similarly, with regard to monetary policy see A Blinder, M Ehrmann, J de Haan and David-Jan Jansen, "Necessity as the Mother of Invention: Monetary Policy after the Crisis" (2017) 32(92) Economic Policy 707.

[25] E Balls, J Howat and A Stansbury, "Central Bank Independence Revisited: After the Financial Crisis, What Should a Model Central Bank Look Like?" (2018) Harvard Kennedy School Working Paper 87. Though most of the examples in the paper relate to expansionary monetary policy rather than to their role in maintaining "financial stability"; CAE Goodhart, "The Changing Role of Central Banks" (2010) LSE Financial Markets Group Paper Series No 197, 30 observed that the "combination of operational independence to set interest rates and liquidity management together with prospective macroprudential regulation just vests too much power in a non-elected body". Therefore, WH Buiter, "Central Banks: Powerful, Political and Unaccountable?" (2014) 2 Journal of the British Academy 269, 272 concludes that "in performing other roles – including their legitimate financial stability role – central banks must be subject to material substantive accountability".

[26] A Posen, "In the Fray Not Above It" (Bank of England Conference "20 years on", London, 28 September 2017). This is already happening with regards to central banks' role as monetary policy setter, even more so in the macroprudential domain. C Giles and S Fleming, "Global Political Backlash Spreads Against Central Banks", *Financial Times* (9 December 2018); and the inevitable "push back" B Dudley, "The Fed Shouldn't Enable Donald Trump", *Bloomberg* (27 August 2019), available at <https://www.bloomberg.com/opinion/articles/2019-08-27/the-fed-shouldn-t-enable-donald-trump>.
See also Mario Marcel, Governor of the Central Bank of Chile ("Public Trust and Central Banking" XXIII Annual Conference of the Central Bank of Chile, 15 July 2019, Santiago, Chile) suggesting that the "trust" is better than the term credibility, available at <https://www.bis.org/review/r190816a.htm>.

[27] F Roth, "The Effect of the Financial Crisis on Systemic Trust" (2009) 44(4) Intereconomics 203–208;
See also "The independence of Central Banks is Under Threat from Politics", *The Economist* (13 April 2019).

expansion of their mandate to more distributive policy measures[28] and often, to macroprudential policymaking. The second is the "understanding deficit" of the public of economic policy matters (let alone macroprudential policies) that, in turn, has a negative effect on trust in technocrats who make policy decisions.[29]

Another concern that can emerge from the insularity of macroprudential authorities is that they can become over-confident, set in their own ways and largely "divorced from popular sentiments".[30] Clearly, being in their ivory tower may impede their ability to "think outside the box" and avoid the danger of groupthink.[31]

It, therefore, comes as no surprise that scholars advocated the delegation to independent agencies to be contained in particular areas and suggested that certain decisions may not be suitable at all for delegation. As such, "… significant redistributions of resources from one social group to another cannot be taken by independent experts but only by elected officials or those that report directly".[32] Similarly,

> Politicians … are better if the policy has far-reaching redistributive implications so that compensation of losers is important, if criteria of aggregate efficiency do not easily pin down the optimal policy, and if there are interactions across different policy domains (so that a single measure of performance is affected by several policy instruments and policy packaging or evaluating controversial trade-offs is required to build consensus or achieve efficiency).[33]

Arguably, macroprudential policymaking fulfils many of these conditions, with a rather vague target, trade-offs and potential distributional effects of policy measures. Accordingly, the suitability of macroprudential policymaking to delegation, without strong legitimacy reinforcing mechanisms, is vulnerable to

---

[28]   Balls and others (2018) (n 25). But see empirical evidence in J De Haan, R Hicks, C Bodea and S Eijffinger, "Central Bank Independence Before and After the Crisis" (2018) 60(2) Comparative Economic Studies 183.

[29]   For instance, AG Haldane, "Everyday Economic" (Nishkam High School, Birmingham, 27 November 2017), available at <https://www.bankofengland.co.uk/-/media/boe/files/speech/2017/everyday-economics.pdf>;
M Hannah, "Engaging with Our Stakeholders to Promote Understanding, Accountability, and Dialogue" (The Institute of Directors, Christchurch, 27 June 2017).

[30]   A Baker and W Widmaier, "The Institutionalist Roots of Macroprudential Ideas: Veblen and Galbraith on Regulation, Policy Success and Overconfidence" (2014) 19(4) New Political Economy 487–506, 502–503.

[31]   See Chapters 2 and 9. On the problem of groupthink and other biases in macroprudential policymaking see Keller (2018) (n 16) and the references there.
See also A Riles, "The Secret Life of Central Bankers", New York Times (20 October 2018), available at <https://www.nytimes.com/2018/10/20/opinion/sunday/fed-central-banks.html>.

[32]   G Majone, "Regulatory Legitimacy" in G Majone (ed), Regulating Europe (London: Routledge, 1996), 284, 295.

[33]   Alesina and Tabellini (2008) (n 5), 444.

challenge and the independence of macroprudential authorities is not yet settled as a best practice.[34] The resulting cautious approach to delegation is perhaps reflected in the prevalent institutional structure of macroprudential authorities that maintains a role, to varying degrees, to the treasury or fiscal authority (Chapter 3). Some scholars go even further and suggest that the institutional structure of macroprudential authorities even "reveals a renewed primacy of politics over expertise".[35]

Either way, where a delegation of macroprudential powers to an independent agency/central bank occurs, there is a strong case for defined (and pluralistic) restrictions on its discretion.[36] These restrictions have to be contained so as to allow for a warranted degree of latitude to react to unforeseen contingencies. The trade-off between expertise and discretion and legitimacy,[37] as we shall see below, lies at the core of designing accountability and transparency mechanisms in macroprudential regimes. The strong technical nature of this policy, on the one hand, and the contesting values at play, on the other, means that the equilibria will probably lean towards a great deal of discretion to macroprudential authorities.

1.2. INDEPENDENCE: POLITICAL AND/OR OPERATIONAL?

Independence relates to the ability of a macroprudential authority to formulate and implement the policies under its mandate without undue influence (or the perception of undue influence) from both executive and legislative interference and from the industry or other external stakeholders.[38]

---

[34]   R Sharp, "Central Bank Independence as a Prerequisite for Financial Stability" (Cass Business School, London, 19 March 2019), available at <https://www.bankofengland.co.uk/-/media/boe/files/speech/2019/central-bank-independence-as-a-prerequisite-for-financial-stabil ity-speech-by-richard-sharp>; R Edge and N Liang, "New Financial Stability Governance Structure and Central Banks" (2019) Hutchins Centre Working Paper 50, available at <https://www.brookings.edu/wp-content/uploads/2019/02/WP50-updated.1.pdf>.

[35]   Lombardi and Moschella (2014) (n 8), 22.

[36]   D Epstein and S O'Halloran, "Administrative Procedures, Information, and Agency Discretion" (1994) 38(3) American Journal of Political Science 697; Epstein and O'Halloran (1999) (n 17).
       The scope and nature of this discretion will depend on many factors, such as the structure of the legal system and legislative professionalism. JD Huber and CR Shipman, *Deliberate Discretion: The Institutional Foundations of Bureaucratic Autonomy* (Cambridge University Press, 2002), 212.

[37]   To be accurate K Bawn, "Political Control Versus Expertise: Congressional Choices about Administrative Procedures" (1995) 89(1) The American Political Science Review 62 refers to the trade-off between expertise (reduction of technical uncertainty) and control (reduction of procedural uncertainty).

[38]   OECD, *Being an Independent Regulator*, The Governance of Regulators, 2016.
       See also Quintyn and Taylor (2002) (n 1); but see P Tucker, *Unelected Power: The Quest for Legitimacy in Central Banking* (Princeton University Press, 2016), 11 referring only to insulation from executive branch and legislature.

The literature on central banks' independence distinguishes between political independence and operational (instrument) independence.[39] The former is defined as the absence of the possibility of political influence over policy decisions, including selecting goals (goal independence).[40] The latter refers to the ability to select and use instruments of monetary policy with autonomy.[41]

In monetary policy frameworks, advanced economies have largely converged on a model of high operational independence and low political independence.[42] Similarly, practitioners seem to put more weight on operational independence of central banks with some even suggesting that goal independence of central banks is not appropriate in a democracy.[43] But how do these concepts apply in the macroprudential domain?

On the differences between independence and autonomy see G Shabsigh and A Khan, IMF Staff Proposal to Update the Monetary and Financial Policies Transparency Code, May 2019.

[39] S Fischer, "Modern Central Banking" in F Capie, C Goodhart, S Fischer and N Schnadt (eds), *The Future of Central Banking* (Cambridge University Press, 1994). The literature on independent regulatory agencies also distinguishes between formal and de facto independence. See, for instance, M Maggetti, "De Facto Independence after Delegation: A Fuzzy-set Analysis" (2007) 1(4) Regulation and Governance 271.

[40] A Alesina and LH Summers, "Central Bank Independence and Macroeconomic Performance: Some Comparative Evidence" (1993) 25(2) Journal of Money, Credit and Banking 151 based on definition in R Bade and M Parkin, *Central Bank Laws and Monetary Policy* (1982) (unpublished) who construct a scale of central bank "political independence". Political independence is based on various factors such as whether the governor and the board are appointed by the government, the length of their appointments, whether government representatives sit on the board of the bank and whether government approval for monetary policy decisions is required.
Taxonomy differs across the literature on central banks, G Debelle and S Fischer, "How Independent Should a Central Bank Be?" (2005) Working Papers in Applied Economic Theory Federal Reserve Bank of San Francisco No 94 differentiate between goal and instrument independence; V Grilli, D Masciandaro and G Tabellini, "Political and Monetary Institutions and Public Financial Policies in the Industrial Countries" (1991) 6(13) Economic Policy 342 refer to political independence (capacity to choose the final goal of monetary policy) and economic independence (capacity to choose the instruments with which to pursue these goals) of central banks.

[41] Alesina and Summers (1993) (n 40), 153.

[42] In monetary policy, central banks typically possess "instrument independence" but some also possess goal independence. T Bayoumi and others, "Monetary Policy in the New Normal" (2014) IMF Staff Discussion Note 3. Balls and others (2018) (n 25) show that today, all central banks in advanced economies have converged on a model of full operational independence but mostly low political independence while in emerging and developing economies, both operational and political central bank independence are important.

[43] S Fischer, "The Independent Bank of England – 20 Years On" ("20 Years On" Conference sponsored by the Bank of England London, 28 September 2017); FS Mishkin, "Monetary Policy Strategy: Lessons from the Crisis" (ECB Central Banking Conference, Monetary Policy Revisited: Lessons from the Crisis, Frankfurt, 18–19 November 2010); C Briault, A Haldane and M King, "Independence and Accountability", Chapter 10 in I Kuroda (ed), *Towards More Effective Monetary Policy* (Palgrave Macmillan, 1997), 299, 307 observe that "If the central bank has goal as well as instrument independence, then accountability makes no sense: the institution is judged against targets it sets itself, so an accountability constraint on behaviour never binds."

Operational independence is a crucial component of effective governance of macroprudential policymaking.[44] The implementation of macroprudential tools is far from being a technocratic task that can be pre-defined in legislation. As already discussed in the previous chapter, macroprudential tools are not, as yet, linked to clearly defined "red alarms" of financial instability that can simply trigger the implementation of suitable macroprudential tools. The deployment of tools depends on many specificities and requires judgment and further research on their interaction with other macroprudential tools, other policies and the real economy (Chapter 6).

As for goal independence, the issue is not as clear-cut. The macroprudential mandate is set in relatively vague terms and is often translated, prior to the implementation of tools, to more measurable and concrete operational (intermediate) objectives by the macroprudential authority (Chapter 2). In some cases, the macroprudential mandate also entails a balancing act between a financial stability objective and other objectives such as sustainable economic growth (with or without a clear priority of the former). These characteristics clearly leave much discretion to the macroprudential authority in interpreting and implementing the mandate and may arguably, imply a certain degree of goal independence. Yet, macroprudential frameworks are far from being monolithic and exemplify a variety of goal-setting frameworks that limit the discretion within the mandate. For instance, while the FPC is a committee of the Bank of England,[45] its subordinate objective of "supporting the economic policy of Her Majesty's Government" is specified by the Treasury in an annual remit letter (Chapter 2).[46] Accordingly, the FPC was guided, for instance, to pay particular attention to "encouraging long term investment in economic capital, including

---

[44] For instance, ESRB Recommendations of 22 December 2011 on the Macro-prudential Mandate of National Authorities (ESRB/2011/3), Recommendation E(1) "in the pursuit of its objective, the macroprudential authority is as a minimum operationally independent, in particular from political bodies and from the financial industry".
See also P Tucker, "The Political Economy of Macroprudential Regimes" in D Schoenmaker, VoxEU.org, *Macroprudentialism*, 61, 70 suggesting that macroprudential policy should be a regime of instrument independence but not goal independence "Expert officials can help (and have helped) to frame public debate on how much resilience is warranted, but the degree of protection society wants is not for unelected officials to determine on their own."

[45] Section 9B(1) BEA 1998 as amended by section 6 of the Bank of England and Financial Services Act 2016.

[46] Sections 9C(1)(b) and 9D(1) BEA 1988 as amended by the Financial Services Act 2012.
In addition to making recommendations to the FPC about matters that the FPC should regard as relevant to the its understanding of the Bank's Financial Stability Objective and its responsibility in relation to the achievement of that objective and recommendations about the FPC's responsibilities in relation to support for the government's economic policy, as well as matters to which the FPC should have regard in exercising its functions. Section 9E(1) BEA 1998. The FPC must respond to these recommendations with action it took or intend to take or reasons for not intending to act (section 9E(3) BEA 1998).

infrastructure, skills and knowledge; and promoting a dynamic economy that encourages innovation and helps resources flow to their most productive use".[47] The remit, therefore, can be said to restrict, to some extent, the political independence of the FPC and in turn, strengthens its democratic legitimacy, as will be discussed in the following section.

2. ACCOUNTABILITY IN MACROPRUDENTIAL SETTING

2.1. ACCOUNTABILITY AS A *QUID PRO QUO* FOR WIDE DISCRETION AND INDEPENDENCE OF MACROPRUDENTIAL AUTHORITIES.

From the preceding discussion, it can be concluded that delegation to an independent macroprudential authority is compelling only when it comes alongside an accountability framework. Essentially, accountability can be viewed as a *quid pro quo* for granting wide discretion and independence to macroprudential authorities.[48] The central issue is how to preserve the advantages of political independence without abandoning the fundamental democratic principle of public accountability.[49] In other words, the question is how to ensure that the macroprudential authority is under control (but still that no one controls it)?[50]

The need to balance these considerations has been widely acknowledged from the early days of the formation of macroprudential regimes and borrowing from the rich literature on the role of central banks in monetary

---

[47] HM Treasury, Remit and Recommendations for the FPC, 29 October 2019. Unlike the Treasury's remit for the MPC, where the role of the Treasury is to complete the objective by defining a specific inflation target, the Treasury's remit for the FPC will take the form of recommendations around how the FPC should in general interpret and pursue its objective. HM Treasury, "A New Approach to Financial Regulation: The Blueprint for Reform", Cm 8083, June 2011, para 2.11.

[48] Briault, Haldane and King (1997) (n 43), 300 suggest that, in practice, the mapping between accountability and independence is far from being straightforward; D Masciandaro, M Quintyn and M Taylor, "Financial Supervisory Independence and Accountability – Exploring the Determinants" (2008) IMF Working Paper 187 show that in financial supervision decisions on the degrees of independence and accountability are not connected and that at best, independence and accountability are seen as weakly complementary to each other; R Lastra, "The Independence of the European System of Central Banks" (1992) 33(2) Harvard International Law Journal 475 argues that accountability is not simply an add-on to justify accountability and accordingly, refers to the term "accountable independence".

[49] Majone (1994) (n 19), 26.

[50] T Moe, "Interests, Institutions, and Positive Theory: The Politics of NLRN" (1987) 2 Studies in American Political Development 136, 291.

policymaking, it often relies on the concept of democratic legitimacy.[51] Yet, in the macroprudential setting, the need for accountability is more forceful and the design and implementation of accountability arrangements present three unique challenges.

To begin with, it can be more difficult to maintain accountability in a macroprudential setting given that there is no clear benchmark against which the "success" of the macroprudential authority in achieving its mandate can be judged.[52] It is indisputable that the ultimate macroprudential policy objective is a fuzzy[53] yardstick and lacks clear pre-defined indicators that can guide and govern the operation of macroprudential authorities (Chapter 2). To be differentiated from monetary policy, macroprudential policy lacks a symmetric and precise target that can be defined in terms of "no less than X and no more than Y failures".[54] Simply put, a full-blown financial crisis clearly equals financial instability and signifies the failure of the macroprudential authority in achieving its mission. The absence of a crisis, however, does not necessarily equate to effective macroprudential policymaking. The crisis may be waiting around the corner or it may simply take time to approach the tipping point.[55]

Second, in the macroprudential sphere, it can be difficult to identify causal effects between specific policy measures and the outcome in terms of financial stability and thus difficult to link and attribute accountability to policy decisions. There is a proliferation of potential macroprudential tools and many plausible policy decisions and additionally, the stability of the financial system depends on the culmination of multiple contingencies and policy measures.[56]

Third, the timing of the observation of the macroprudential authority's actions introduces another layer of complexity into its accountability framework. The benefits of macroprudential decisions (and accordingly the success of the macroprudential authority) must be judged in the long term and cannot always

---

[51]   Accountability and independence are often viewed as complementary. Majone (1994) (n 19), 6. Similarly, in the literature on financial regulatory agencies, see M Quintyn, M Ramirez and S Taylor, "The Fear of Freedom: Politicians and the Independence and Accountability of Financial Sector Supervisors" (2007) IMF Working Papers No 25.

[52]   Baker (2015) (n 22), 22.

[53]   C Goodhart, Oral Evidence before the Treasury Committee, 23 May 2011 in House of Commons and Treasury Committee, "Accountability of the Bank of England": Twenty-First Report of Session 2010–12 HC 874, Question 172.

[54]   L Garicano and R Lastra, "Towards a New Architecture for Financial Stability: Seven Principles" (2010) LSE Centre for Economic Performance Discussion Paper 990.

[55]   C Borio, "Towards a Macroprudential Framework for Financial Supervision and Regulation" (2003) BIS Working Paper 128 states that "Indicators of risk perceptions tend to decline during the upswing and, in some cases, to be lowest close to the peak of the financial cycle. But this is precisely the point where, with hindsight at least, we can tell that risk was greatest …".

[56]   On the multi-dimensional nature of systemic risks and its interaction with other policy areas see Chapter 2.

be put in quantifiable terms (Chapter 5). In contrast, the inadequacy of policy decisions and the failure of the macroprudential authority can only be tested when bad shocks happen, and these are rare.[57]

While the macroprudential authority independence is analogous, to some extent, to central banks' independence, its accountability arrangements should be richer and more complex to reflect these inherent limitations and unique challenges.[58] An automatic "theory transformation" of accountability arrangements which was designed for the monetary policy sphere to the macroprudential sphere should, therefore, be avoided. Rather, it should be shaped according to the level of independence within the domestic structural, political and legal environment of the macroprudential authority.

2.2. LEGITIMACY AS A CONCEPTUAL FRAMEWORK OF ACCOUNTABILITY IN MACROPRUDENTIAL POLICY

Democratic legitimacy is traditionally conceptualised according to three dimensions of input legitimacy, output legitimacy and throughput legitimacy.[59] Input legitimacy means that public policy decisions are legitimate if they are, directly or indirectly, the expression of the will of the people. Input legitimacy, therefore, stems from the way tasks have been delegated to the independent institution and from the political participation in it (for instance, through the appointment procedure). In contrast, output legitimacy relies on the result of the policy decisions: how well does the policy setter perform its delegated tasks and how successful is it in the pursuit of its mandate?

Output legitimacy exists where policy decisions meet the justified expectations and the needs of the people. Without it, democracy, it is argued, will become

---

[57]   A Brazier, "Citizens in Service, Not People in Power" (Allen and Overy, London, 17 May 2019). This does not happen very often. See, for instance, Pascal Paul, "Modelling Financial Crises", Federal Reserve Bank of San Francisco Economic Letters, 4 March 2009 suggests that "On average, crises occur about every 25 years or even less frequently".
On the difficulty of measuring regulatory quality in a decentred or networked system and the difficulty in ascribing responsibility see R Baldwin, M Cave and M Lodge, *Understanding Regulation Theory Strategy and Practice* (Oxford University Press, 2012), 36 and 74–75.

[58]   Similar to the changes in accountability following the shift to regulatory state and the corresponding fragmentation of responsibility. This necessitated extending "… accountability (of various forms) to actors previously immune, extending the range of values accounted for, and introducing new and more formal bodies for calling to account". C Scott, "Accountability in the Regulatory State" (2000) 27(1) Journal of Law and Society 38.

[59]   F Scharpf, *Governing in Europe: Effective and Democratic?* (Oxford University Press, 1999); V Schmidt, "Democracy and Legitimacy in the European Union Revisited: Input, Output and 'Throughput'" (2013) 61(1) Political Science 2. The three aspects signify Abraham Lincoln's famous dictum about democracy: "government by the people", "government for the people" and "government with the people" (19 November 1863, Gettysburg, Pennsylvania).

"an empty ritual".[60] Later, a third dimension of legitimacy has emerged termed "throughput legitimacy". It focuses on the quality of the governance processes and is judged in terms of efficacy, accountability and transparency of those processes along with their inclusiveness and openness to pluralistic consultation with the people.[61] To be differentiated from input legitimacy that exists at the initial policy setting process (delegation) and output legitimacy that exists at the end of it (policy outcomes), throughput legitimacy provides for a continuous legitimisation and is process-oriented.

Since, in the short term, macroprudential policy results are not easily observable or measurable, output legitimacy is practically absent or at least very fragile.[62] The legitimacy of macroprudential authorities, therefore, hinges on input legitimacy and/or throughput legitimacy. Input legitimacy largely depends on the specific institutional and governance structure of the macroprudential authority. Where the fiscal authority has the power to specify components of the mandate of the macroprudential authority (as is the case in the UK) or has a key role to play in its governance (as is the case in the US)[63] input legitimacy is, accordingly, enhanced.

Throughput legitimacy, whether as a complement to input and output legitimacy or in its own right, is an essential element in the design and implementation of a macroprudential framework. Bringing the decision-making process into prominence in macroprudential frameworks can provide a solid and clear benchmark against which the macroprudential authority can be assessed and held accountable.[64] This means that, instead of focusing solely on

---

60   FW Scharpf, "Economic Integration, Democracy and the Welfare State" (1997) 4(1) Journal of European Public Policy 18, 19.

61   FW Scharpf, *Governing in Europe: Effective and Democratic?* (Oxford University Press, 1999), 79; Schmidt (2013) (n 59), 6; V Schmidt, "Democracy in Europe", Chapter 16 in J Magone (ed), *Routledge Handbook of European Politics* (Routledge, 2015), 280; T Risse and M Kleine, "Assessing the Legitimacy of EU Treaty Revision Methods" (2007) 45(3) Journal of Common Market Studies 69 suggest that throughput legitimacy has three components: the legality of the process, the transparency of the decision-making process and the quality of the process. In particular, the authors emphasise the deliberative quality that involves arguing, reason-giving and mutual learning.
      On the pros and cons of civil society engagement as a form of legitimacy see also J Greenwood, "Organised Civil Society and Democratic Legitimacy in the European Union" (2007) 37(2) British Journal of Political Science 333.

62   A Keller, "Independence, Accountability and Transparency: Are the Conventional Accountability Mechanisms Suitable for the European Systemic Risk Board?" (2017) 5 International Company and Commercial Law Review 176.

63   With the Secretary of the Treasury as a voting member of the FSOC who serves as the Chairperson of the Council (Chapter 3).

64   BIS, Central Bank Governance and Financial Stability A report by a Study Group chaired by S Ingves, May 2011, 52 suggests that "accountability mechanisms for the latter [financial stability – author's addition] that are focused on decision processes may be more effective than mechanisms focused on outcomes".
      For the theoretical foundations see A Keller (2017) (n 62).

the ex-post control of policy outputs, the focus shifts to *ex-ante* monitoring tools, including adherence to administrative procedures.[65] These regulatory processes originate in modern administrative law and perform a legitimising function for regulatory bodies.[66] Weber aptly explains that: "They channel delegated discretionary power, narrowing the agency's decision space, so that it exercises power in non-arbitrary ways. Furthermore, procedures force agencies to move deliberately and openly, giving politicians and their constituents time to react before decisions become final."[67] Meaningful use of administrative procedures and process-oriented accountability can, therefore, assist the macroprudential authority in learning the boundaries of its mandate and instilling rigour in the analyses and policy decisions.[68]

The effectiveness of these procedures can be enhanced by traditional forms of accountability of judicial review and parliamentary scrutiny.[69] Otherwise, there is a real risk that procedures will become a mere box-ticking exercise.[70] Backed by other "checks and balances", procedural requirements will not result in paralysis[71] or weaken the importance of stimulating debate but rather facilitate it. As will be discussed below, these accountability mechanisms should be strengthened by the inclusiveness of the public and external experts in the decision-making process.

The chapter, therefore, advocates adopting in macroprudential regimes a complex web of checks and balances with a diversity of channels of accountability and transparency arrangements. This suggestion largely follows

---

65   M McCubbins, R Noll and B Weingast, "Administrative Procedures as Instruments of Political Control" (1987) 3(2) The Journal of Law, Economics, and Organization 243; L Schrefler, *Economic Knowledge in Regulation the Use of Expertise by Independent Agencies* (ECPR, 2013), 22.

66   Known as "deck-stacking" in the institutional design literature that revolves around steering regulators' behaviour through procedural means. See M McCubbins, R Noll and B Weingast, "Structure, Process, Politics and Policy: Administrative Arrangements and Political Control" (1989) 75 Virginia Law Review 431; M McCubbins, R Nolls and B Weingast, "Administrative Procedures as Instruments of Political Control" (1987) 3(2) Journal of Law, Economics and Organisation 243.

67   RF Weber, "The FSOC's Designation Program as a Case Study of the New Administrative Law of Financial Supervision" (2019) 36(1) Yale Journal on Regulation 359, 385–386.
      See also R Baldwin, M Cave and M Lodge, *Understanding Regulation Theory Strategy and Practice* (Oxford University Press, 2012), 70.

68   Ibid, 181–182.

69   The perverse effects of judicial review, however, should not be overlooked. As will be discussed below, the *MetLife* case in the US provides an instructive example of procedural rules that potentially could have long-term negative effects on the scope and formulation of macroprudential policy (see also Chapter 5).

70   Schrefler (2013) (n 65), 180.

71   JL Mashaw and DL Harfst, "Inside the National Highway Traffic Safety Administration: Legal Determinants of Bureaucratic Organization and Performance" (1990) 57 The University of Chicago Law Review 443.

192   Intersentia

the well-established redundancy model that views "overlapping (and ostensibly superfluous) accountability mechanisms …" as a way of reducing the centrality of any one of them[72] and mitigating their weaknesses. How does this theory translate into practice in the real world of macroprudential policymaking? How can throughput legitimacy be achieved in macroprudential regimes?

Several concurrent and complementary accountability mechanisms can be designed to enhance throughput legitimacy of macroprudential authorities:

First, establishing transparent legal rules that specify the procedures to be followed by the macroprudential authority, such as a requirement for a cost-benefit analysis, an evidence-based approach or constrained discretion based on indicators (Chapter 5), can provide a benchmark for assessing the achievement of the macroprudential mandate. These procedures can limit the range options and discretion[73] available to the macroprudential authority and thus ensure accountability in an environment where an outcome-judgement is hard to achieve.

Second, to ensure substantive accountability has taken place, these procedural legal requirements should be complemented by governance structure and decision-making process that promote open-mindeness and diversity of the deliberation process.[74] This can include, for instance, heterogenous composition

---

[72] Scott (2000) (n 58), 52. Also suggesting that in such a system conflicts and tensions exist but that "the objective should not be to iron our conflict, but to exploit it to hold regimes in appropriate tension." Ibid, 57.

But see J Black, "Constructing and contesting Legitimacy and Accountability in Polycentric Regulatory Regimes" (2008) 2(2) Regulation and Governance 137, 157–158 who concludes that "although regulators can often participate in a number of different legitimacy discourses simultaneously, and thus attempt to satisfy a range of different legitimacy communities, not only can this have a deleterious effect on the organization but the differences between communities may be such that organizations can face a legitimacy dilemma. Actions that organizations may need to take to render them legitimate for one legitimacy community can be in direct opposition to those they need to adopt to satisfy another."

[73] McCubbins and others (1987) (n 65); T Gilligan and K Krehbiel, "Collective Decision-Making and Standing Committees: An Informational Rationale for Restrictive Amendment Procedures" (1987) 3(2) Journal of Law, Economics and Organization 287.

K Bawn, "Political Control Versus Expertise" (1995) 89(1) American Political Science Review 62 suggesting that administrative procedures and the level of agency independence are not monolithic and vary according to the technical and political features of the policy area.

[74] This will also improve the quality of the decision-making. LR Hoffman, E Harburg and N Maier, "Differences and Disagreement as Factors in Creative Group Problem Solving" (1962) 64 Journal of Abnormal and Social Psychology 206; HC Triandis, ER Hall and RB Ewen, "Member Homogeneity and Dyadic Creativity" (1965) 18 Human Relations 33; C Nemeth, "Differential Contributions of Majority and Minority Influence" (1986) 93 Psychological Review 23. J Barabas "How Deliberation Affects Policy Opinions" (2004) 98(4) American Political Science Review 687, 699 explains that "Deliberation is an enlightened and open-minded search for consensus amid diverse participants."

of macroprudential authorities and seeking the views of external stakeholders and experts (Chapter 3).[75]

Third, inclusiveness of the public in the form of transparency and awareness of the "reasons" behind policy decisions[76] or via public consultation can strengthen the macroprudential authority throughput legitimacy.[77]

Finally, the inclusion of external forms of monitoring including ongoing legislative (or parliamentary) oversight and/or executive or government guidance (for instance, in the form of remit) as well as judicial review that introduces a meaningful and prodding oversight of the decision-making of the macroprudential authority.[78]

Still, there are trenchant limitations that could inhibit the effectiveness of these accountability mechanisms. There is an information asymmetry between the macroprudential authority and its political principals to which it is accountable.[79] In fact, literature in political science suggests that delegation occurs if policy issues are complex and if an agency's expertise is sufficiently difficult to invert.[80] In a highly technical domain, it is to be questioned whether

---

This resembles the suggestion for "extended peer community" made in JR Ravetz, "What is Post-Normal Science" (1999) Futures 647, 651 where traditional mechanisms of quality assurance are inadequate.
See discussion in Baldwin, Cave and Lodge (2012) (n 67), 97–98.

[76] A Keller, "Debiasing Macroprudential Policy: Part 2: Designing a New Diversity Criterion for Macroprudential Policy" (2019) 34(2) JIBLR 37. This, in many respects, also resembles the concept of participatory bureaucracy, L Moffitt, *Making Policy Public: Participatory Bureaucracy in American Democracy* (Cambridge University Press, 2014) as a way to resolve the tension between the need for expertise and democratic oversight.

[77] On throughput legitimacy see Schmidt (2013) (n 59), 3.
See also MF Cuellar, "Rethinking Regulatory Democracy" (2005) 57 Administrative Law Review 411 offering various participatory devices such as the majoritarian deliberation approach that involves getting a stratified random sample of the population as a whole. This, as shall be seen below, was recently adopted by the Bank of England through the Citizens Panel.

[78] M Everson, G Majone, L Metcalfe and A Schou, "The Role of Specialised Agencies in Decentralising EU Governance", Report Presented to the Commission, September 1999. Note that the suggestion in this report is for substantive and procedural judicial review but this may not be applicable to the macroprudential domain, as will be discussed below.

[79] DB Spence, "Agency Policy Making and Political Control: Modelling Away the Delegation Problem" (1997) 7(2) Journal of Public Administration Research and Theory 199, 214: "The problem is that unless and until politicians actually acquire the agency's expertise, their ability to understand and act upon agency policy choices is far more limited ..." However, the problem of asymmetry does not always lie with the amount of information available. A Lupia and MD McCubbins, *The Democratic Dilemma: Can Citizens Learn What They Need to Know?* (Cambridge University Press, 1998), 6 observe that "Ironically, for many political issues, information is not scarce; rather, it is the cognitive resources that a person can use to process information that are scarce".

[80] S Callander, "A Theory of Policy Expertise" (2008) 3 Quarterly Journal of Political Science 123, 125.
See also Epstein and O'Halloran (1999) (n 17), 10 suggesting that "informationally intense policy areas will be good candidates for delegation".

the general public or even arguably, its elected representatives have the necessary expertise and information to monitor the macroprudential authority's decisions in a rigorous and meaningful manner.[81] Additionally, there is a risk that openness and inclusiveness would also open the door to undue special interests and lobbying for an overly accommodative macroprudential policy.[82] Perhaps, a closer examination of the accountability mechanisms that were adopted in the legal frameworks of the FPC, the FSOC and the ESRB will assist in understanding these limitations in context and surface potential ways to address them.

2.3. ACCOUNTABILITY MECHANISMS OF MACROPRUDENTIAL AUTHORITIES: THE FPC, THE FSOC AND THE ESRB

2.3.1. Accountability Frameworks of the FPC

The legal framework of the FPC is designed with a view to enhancing throughput legitimacy, in particular via pluralistic governance and inclusive decision-making process. It is to be recalled that the FPC has five external members who are selected from outside the Bank of England[83] bringing a diverse set of skills and viewpoints and making room for a "creative tension" during its policy deliberations (Chapter 3).[84] The Communications Guidance

---

[81] N Jabko, "Democracy in the Age of the euro" (2003) 10(5) Journal of European Public Policy 710, 728.
The manner in which information is communicated to the public is thus of essence. D Bholat and others, "Enhancing Central Bank Communications with Behavioural Insights" (2018) Bank of England Staff Working Paper No 750 show in relation to inflation reports that visual presentation and making information more relatable can substantially increase general public comprehension.

[82] E Nier and others, "Towards Effective Macroprudential Policy Frameworks: An Assessment of Stylized Institutional Models" (2011) IMF Working Paper 250, 38.

[83] Section 9B(1)(e) BEA 1998. According to section 9B(3) before appointing an external member, the Chancellor of the Exchequer must be satisfied that the person has knowledge or experience which is likely to be relevant to the FPC's functions and consider whether the person has any financial or other interests that could substantially affect the functions as member that it would be proper for the person to discharge.
See also FPC Conflicts of Interest Code of Practice, 12 February 2019, available at <https://www.bankofengland.co.uk/-/media/boe/files/about/fpc/fpcconflictsinterestcodepractice>, section 3.

[84] HM Treasury, "A New Approach to Financial Regulation: Securing Stability, Protecting Consumers", January 2012 CM 8268, paras B.16–B.17; HM Treasury, "A New Approach to Financial Regulation: Judgment, Focus and Stability", July 2010, para 3.19; "A New Approach to Financial Regulation: Building a Stronger System" (February 2011) Cm 8012, paras 2.78–2.79; R Sharp, "The Financial Policy Committee of the Bank of England: An Experiment in Macroprudential Management – The View of an External Member" (London School of Economics, London, 4 June 2014).

for FPC members encourages members to make contact, subject to certain limitations, with financial market participants[85] and the 2016 Treasury remit to the FPC recommends it to seek the views of industry participants, academics, other regulators and the public, as appropriate to supplement its own expertise.[86] Furthermore, the Bank of England has recently set up Citizens Panels to facilitate a two-way dialogue and collaboration of the public at large with the Bank of England on the economy, financial system and policy.[87]

The FPC is accountable to Parliament through regular public testimonies before the Treasury Select Committee of the House of Commons (Treasury Committee).[88] These include hearings twice a year on the Financial Stability Reports (accompanied by a press conference with a Q&A session); appointment hearings with persons appointed or re-appointed to the FPC[89] and inquiries on

---

[85] Communications Guidance for FPC members, 28 April 2018, available at <https://www.bankofengland.co.uk/-/media/boe/files/about/fpc/fpccoc>.

[86] HM Treasury, "Recommendations as to Engagement with Financial Sector Participants and Other External Experts, Remit and Recommendations to the FPC", 8 July 2015; this was repeated in the Remit for the FPC from 16 March 2016, 8 March 2017 and 5 December 2018. The recommendation of HM Treasury to the FPC is in accordance with section 9E(1) BEA 1998. This is regularly conducted as a way for the members to inform themselves of the concerns and questions of financial market participants, to getting their reactions on the FPC actions and their views on what should be doing. Written Evidence submitted by Donald Kohn in Response to questionnaire from Treasury Committee, 21 March 2018, available at <http://data.parliament.uk/writtenevidence/committeeevidence.svc/evidencedocument/treasury-committee/reappointment-of-donald-kohn-to-the-financial-policy-committee/written/81464.pdf>, para 13.

[87] Implementing the recommendation in R Patel, K Gibbon and T Greenham, "Building a Public Culture of Economics" (March 2018) Report of the Royal Society for the Encouragement of Arts, Manufactures and Commerce (RSA) Citizens' Economic Council, available at <https://www.thersa.org/discover/publications-and-articles/reports/Building-a-public-culture-of-economics>, in particular pp 83–84; AG Haldane, "Climbing the Public Engagement Ladder" (RSA, 6 March 2018), available at <https://www.bankofengland.co.uk/-/media/boe/files/speech/2018/climbing-the-public-engagement-ladder.pdf>.
     But see MF Cuellar, "Rethinking Regulatory Democracy" (2005) 57 Administrative Law Review 411 who criticises the administrative pluralism that emphasises the value of expert and organised interest-group in shaping regulatory policy. The administrative pluralism is to be differentiated from participatory democracy which focuses on the importance of involving the public at large – whether they are individuals, unofficial associations, organised interest groups, or powerful interested parties.

[88] As a practice, the Treasury Committee takes, from time to time, views from the FPC external members without the presence of the FPC internal members and is particularly "keen to take individual views notwithstanding the desire to, as far as possible, to speak in consensus". See, for instance, FPC External Members Hearing in the Treasury Select Committee, Tuesday 24 May 2016, attending Richard Sharp, Donald Kohen and Martin Taylor.

[89] Analogous to the hearings held with MPC members. The assessment of selection is based on the criteria of personal independence and professional competence. The Treasury Committee does not have a veto power over the appointments.

---

specific topics.[90] The hearings are viewed as "intrusive and broad in scope"[91] and are used to conduct rigorous and meaningful "checks and balances" on the FPC decision-making process. A recurrent theme in those hearings, often advanced in a pertinent manner and at times, even adversarial, is whether FPC members feel that they have to conform with the majority so as to achieve a consensus; are guided or are under pressure to succumb to the governor of the Bank of England or subject to political or other pressure.[92] Though recommendations and conclusions of the Treasury Committee are not binding, they are influential and often capture the media attention.[93]

Another constraint on the FPC's discretion, already mentioned in Section 2, designed to enhance input legitimacy, is the power of the Treasury to set a remit and make recommendations to the FPC at least annually on: matters that it should regard as relevant to its understanding of the financial stability objective; its responsibility in relation to the achievement of that objective. In addition, it can make at any time a recommendation on the FPC responsibility in relation to the support for the economic policy of the government; and matters to which it should have regard in exercising its functions.[94] The power of the Treasury to set a remit and issue recommendations provides "continuing input from the Treasury into the framework for the FPC's work ... At the same time, the remit

---

[90]   For instance, Commons Select Committee, "Inquiry on Macroprudential Tools" (2012), available at <https://www.parliament.uk/business/committees/committees-a-z/commons-select/treasury-committee/inquiries1/parliament-2010/macroprudential-tools/>.

[91]   IMF, "Financial Sector Assessment Program of the United Kingdom – Macroprudential Institutional Framework" (June 2016) Technical Note No 160, 19.
        For an interesting study on the developing role and importance of the Treasury Committee, see SM Rombach, "The Development of the Treasury Select Committee 1995–2015" (2018) 71(2) Parliamentary Affairs 324.

[92]   See, for instance, the hearing on 24 May 2016, where the members of the Treasury Committee persistently ask the opinion of the external members on whether their view on Brexit being a risk to financial stability conforms with the Governor of the Bank of England. See, in particular, the question posed 14:35 minutes into the hearing. Similarly, on 12 July 2016 the Governor of the Bank of England was queried, in a rather adversarial manner, what his response was to the allegation that, following a discussion with the Chancellor of the Exchequer, he guided the decision of the FPC in relation to the assessment that Brexit poses risks to financial stability. The Governor replied that: "this is not how the committee works, the Chair does not guide conclusions, the committee is presented with a series of analysis and has robust discussion ...".
        See also George Kerevan, Bank of England and Financial Services Bill Session 2015–16, 9 February 2016, Hansard 39 column 19.

[93]   M Russell and M Benton, Selective Influence: The Policy Impact of House of Commons Select Committees (June 2011) Constitution Unit UCL, 39.

[94]   Sections 9D–9E BEA 1998. The FPC must respond to the recommendation indicating what action it has taken or intends to take to comply with it and if it does not intend to act in accordance with the recommendation, the FPC is required to state its reasons. Section 9F.(3) BEA 1998.

is designed to safeguard the FPC's independence from political influence by building in the ability for the FPC to reject any recommendations with which it does not agree".[95]

Input legitimacy is also ensured via a membership and appointment procedures as the FPC external members are appointed by the Chancellor of the Exchequer;[96] one member is appointed by the Governor of the Bank of England after consultation with the Chancellor of Exchequer[97] and a representative of the HM Treasury is a non-voting member of the FPC.[98]

Previously, the FPC was subject to an additional accountability mechanism and its performance and procedures were under the purview of an Oversight Committee, a sub-committee of the court of the Bank of England consisting of its non-executive members. The oversight committee played an important role as "an internal cross-check and as a disciplining device."[99] However, the Bank of England and Financial Services Act 2016 abolished the Oversight Committee and the oversight functions are now the responsibility of the Court of Directors of the Bank of England as a whole (both executives and non-executives).[100] To safeguard the prominence and the ability of the non-executive directors to scrutinise the executives' performance, the amendment retained their right to arrange for reviews (including performance reviews) if they consider that this would assist the Court of Directors in the exercise of its oversight functions.[101]

Finally, but most importantly, the FPC is required to submit in each calendar year two Financial Stability Reports (FSRs).[102] The aims of the FPC's FSR are to set out its "view of the outlook for UK financial stability, including its assessment of risks to the stability of the UK financial system, and the action it is taking to remove or reduce those risks."[103] It also reports on the activities of the FPC over the reporting period and on the extent to which the FPC's previous policy actions have succeeded in meeting its objectives.[104] The latter function enables

---

[95]   M Treasury, "A New Approach to Financial Regulation: The Blueprint for Reform", Cm 8083, June 2011, para 2.12.
[96]   Section 9B(1)(e) BEA 1998. See also section 1A BEA 1998. The Governor of the Bank of England and Deputy Governors of the Bank of England are appointed by Her Majesty the Queen on advice from the Prime Minister. The Chancellor of the Exchequer advises the Prime Minister and oversees the appointment process.
[97]   Section 9B(1)(d) BEA 1998.
[98]   Section 9B(1)(f) BEA 1998.
[99]   UK Financial Sector Assessment Program: Macroprudential Institutional Framework – Technical Note (June 2016) IMF Country Report No 160, 21.
[100] Section 3 Bank of England and Financial Services Act 2016.
[101] Section 3C(1A) BEA 1998 (inserted by section 3(5) Bank of England and Financial Services Act 2016).
[102] Section 9W(1)–(2) BEA 1998.
[103] Section 9W(3) BEA 1998.
[104] Section 9W(4) BEA 1998. See also section 9(W)(5)–(7) BEA 1998.

a certain degree of output legitimacy on the effectiveness of the FPC policy decisions in meeting its mandate.

2.3.2. Accountability Mechanisms of the FSOC

The governance of the FSOC chaired by the Treasury Secretary provides for a solid input legitimacy.[105] Its primary accountability is to the US Congress through the publication of an annual report. The annual report addresses the activities of the FSOC, including determination and recommendations;[106] significant financial market and regulatory developments, along with an assessment of those developments on the stability of the financial system and potential emerging threats to the financial stability of the US.[107] Each one of the voting members of the FSOC has to submit a signed statement to Congress certifying that the FSOC, the government and the private sector are taking 'all reasonable steps to ensure financial stability and to mitigate systemic risk that would negatively affect the economy' and if not what actions should be taken.[108] In addition, the Treasury Secretary as the Chairperson of the FSOC is required to appear regularly before the Committee on Financial Services of the House of Representatives and the Committee on Banking, Housing, and Urban Affairs of the Senate to discuss efforts, activities, objectives, and plans of the FSOC.[109] The FSOC's designation decision is subject to a judicial review and this warrants a separate discussion in Section 2.4 below.

With regard to inclusiveness, the FSOC actively seeks public comments on key issues under its consideration, including its proposed recommendations for money market mutual fund reform, and its rule and interpretive guidance related to the designation of nonbank financial companies.[110]

---

[105]   In addition, certain decisions cannot be made without the Treasury Secretary (FSOC's Chairperson)'s assent (see Chapter 3).

[106]   Section 112(a)(2)(N) Dodd-Frank Act. Referring to all determinations made under section 113 or Title VIII, and the basis for such determinations; all recommendations made under section 119 and the result of such recommendations; and recommendations: I. to enhance the integrity, efficiency, competitiveness, and stability of United States financial markets; II. to promote market discipline; and III. to maintain investor confidence.

[107]   Ibid. In 2016, the US Government Accountability Office, however, observed that "FSOC annual report recommendations can be broad and do not necessarily identify specific systemic risk mitigation actions for member agencies on specific timelines, and identified agencies are not required to respond to them". US Government Accountability Office, Complex and Fragmented Structure Could Be Streamlined to Improve Effectiveness, Report to Congressional Requesters, February 2016, available at <https://www.gao.gov/assets/680/675400.pdf>, 83.

[108]   Section 112(b) Dodd-Frank Act.

[109]   Section 112 (c) Dodd-Frank Act.

[110]   Testimony of Deputy Assistant Secretary for the FSOC, Amias Gerety on 15 March 2013, available at <https://www.treasury.gov/press-center/press-releases/Pages/jl1878.aspx>. On seeking the public comments as part of an inclusive institutional structure of macroprudential authorities see Chapter 5.

2.3.3. Accountability Mechanisms of the ESRB

The ESRB is accountable to the European Parliament and the Council.[111] The Chair of the ESRB is invited, at least annually and more frequently in the event of widespread financial distress, to a hearing in the European Parliament.[112] In practice, the frequency of the hearings before the Committee on Economic and Monetary Affairs (ECON) extends well beyond the statutory requirements.[113] In the hearing, the ESRB's annual report is made public to the European Parliament and the Council.[114] In addition, the ESRB Chair is required to hold a confidential discussion on the work of the ESRB at least twice a year and more often if deemed appropriate, with the Chair and Vice-Chairs of the ECON on the ESRB ongoing activity.[115] The Regulation amending the ESRB Regulation adds a duty for the ESRB to reply, without undue delay, orally or in writing to questions put to it by the European Parliament or the Council, subject to confidentiality requirements (added article 19(6)). Moreover, to enhance democratic control, the Regulation amending the ESRB Regulation also adds a requirement for the ESRB warnings and recommendations to transmitted to the European Parliament and to the ESAs (amended article 16(3)) and permits the President of the European Parliament or a representative of the European Parliament to be invited to attend General Board meetings on topics related to Union law in the field of macroprudential policy (replaced article 9(4)).

Elsewhere several limitations of these parliamentary hearings have been discussed.[116] Even though there should be a separation of the monetary dialogue and the macroprudential dialogue,[117] the discussion during the latter diverts too

---

[111]   Article 19(1) ESRB Regulation, as amended.
[112]   By the competent committee. Ibid. The Chair and the Vice-Chair of the ESRB are required to present to the European Parliament, during a public hearing, how they intend to discharge their function under the ESRB Regulation (article 5(4) ESRB Regulation).
    According to section 19(4) ESRB Regulation the European Parliament may request the Chair of the ESRB to attend a hearing of the competent Committees of the European Parliament.
    In addition, according to article 19(3) ESRB Regulation, the European Parliament, the Council or the Commission can invite the ESRB to examine specific issues.
    The hearings are public and available via a webcast on the ESRB's website.
[113]   High-level Group on the ESRB Review, March 2013, 11. On various occasions the ATC and the ASC Chair/Vice Chair have presented an update on their work separately to ECON.
[114]   Article 19(1) ESRB Regulation. The report is made available to the public and includes an account of the resources made available to the ESRB in accordance with article 3(1) of the ESRB Regulation. The report contains information that the ESRB General Board decides to make public in accordance with article 18 ESRB Regulation. Article 19(2) ESRB Regulation, as amended.
[115]   Article 19(5) ESRB Regulation.
[116]   Keller (2017) (n 62).
[117]   Article 19(1) ESRB Regulation.

often to monetary policy actions.[118] Furthermore, questions asked during these hearings are often of an "informational nature", asking the ESRB chair to explain or express its opinion on a specific issue that is of interest to the MEPs.[119] This is to be contrasted with questions that have the potential to challenge the ESRB's performance towards achieving its statutory mandate.

The parliamentary accountability of the ESRB is complemented by ministerial accountability. The ESRB is required to transmit warnings and recommendations, subject to strict rules of confidentiality to the Council and the Commission.[120] In order to prepare the Council's discussions and provide it with timely policy advice, the ESRB should inform the Economic and Financial Committee (EFC) regularly and send the texts of any warnings and recommendations as soon as they have been adopted.[121]

Throughput legitimacy and openness[122] is ensured through the ASC that is comprised of the Chair of the ATC and 15 independent persons who provide the ESRB with external expertise.[123] Where appropriate, the ASC is required to organise consultations at an early stage with stakeholders such as market participants, consumer bodies and academic experts, in an open and transparent manner, while taking into account the requirement of confidentiality.[124] The Regulation amending the ESRB Regulation inserted a similar duty for the ATC.[125]

---

[118] Ibid.
 See also the Commission Staff Working Document Accompanying the Report To The European Parliament and the Council on the Mission and Organisation of the European Systemic Risk Board (ESRB) SWD/2014/0260 final, para 4.2: "according to some stakeholders, the creation of a new function of a permanent Managing Director of the ESRB would be easier to hold to account for the output and progress of the ESRB as distinct from the ECB." According to the Regulation amending the ESRB Regulation (Preamble 8 "to strengthen the visibility of the ESRB as a body that is separate from its individual members, the Chair of the ESRB should be able to delegate tasks, such as tasks related to the external representation of the ESRB to the First Vice-Cahir or, if the first Vice-Chair is unavailable and where appropriate, to the second Vice-Chair or to the head of the ESRB Secretariat. Such delegation should not extend to the participation in public hearing and in discussions behind closed doors at the European Parliament" thus, replacing Article 5(8) of the ESRB Regulation.

[119] Keller (2017) (n 62).

[120] Article 16(3) ESRB Regulation, as amended. See Chapter 3 on the Regulation amending the ESRB Regulation and in particular, the amendment to section 16 of the ESRB Regulation.

[121] ESRB Regulation, Recital 19; The High-Level Group on Financial Supervision in the EU chaired by J De Larosière, 25 February 2009, 46. The President of the EFC is a member of the ESRB without voting right, article 6(2)(b) ESRB Regulation.

[122] Preamble 24 ESRB Regulation refers to "In a spirit of openness".

[123] Article 12 ESRB Regulation.

[124] Article 12(5) ESRB Regulation, as amended. The Regulation amending the ESRB Regulation added the requirement for such consultations to be conducted as widely as possible to ensure an inclusive approach towards all interested parties and relevant financial sectors and allow reasonable time for stakeholders to respond.

[125] Regulation amending ESRB Regulation, amendment to section 13 and inserting subsection 4a.

The ESRB is also required, in performing its tasks and where appropriate, to consult relevant private sector stakeholders.[126]

At this stage, it is worth making several observations. All three case studies (FPC, FSOC and ESRB) are firmly grounded in an elaborate administrative decision-making framework "designed to cabin, structure, and guide" the exercise of their discretion.[127] The list of procedures and rules in their legal frameworks is overwhelming, beginning with the imposition of certain methodologies such as cost-benefit analysis (Chapter 5), supervisory guidance; rules of procedures and codes of practice, to name a few.[128] In the absence of a clear and readily available benchmark for assessing policy outcomes, these accountability arrangements enable an assessment of macroprudential authorities decision-making process.

Conventional policy-making accountability arrangements typically include substantive accountability, i.e. the possibility to reward or punish the policymakers should the performance prove to be inadequate.[129] Such mechanisms do exist, for instance, in several legal systems regarding monetary policy through a performance-based dismissal of the governor.[130] With regard to macroprudential policy, the Chairperson of the FSOC, for instance, is the Secretary of the Treasury and as a member of the Cabinet, can be removed by the US President at will. In the UK, members of the FPC appointed under

---

[126]   Regulation amending ESRB Regulation, replacing article 14 ESRB Regulation.

[127]   Weber (2019) (n 67), 363 suggests that these procedural rules and processes can only perform a legitimising function if applied in a consistent and transparent manner.

[128]   Even in the absence of a legal requirement. For instance, with regard to the FSOC's Authority to Require Supervision and Regulation of Certain Nonbank Financial Companies Federal Register Vol 77, No 70, 11 April 2012 and Authority to Designate Financial Market Utilities as Systemically Important Federal Register Vol 76, No 144, 27 July 2011.

[129]   W Buiter, "How Robust is the New Conventional Wisdom in Monetary Policy? The Surprising Fragility of the Theoretical Foundations of Inflation Targeting and Central Bank Independence" (Bank of England's Chief Economists' Workshop, part 3, "The Useful but Dangerous Myth of Central Bank Independence", 16–18 April 2007, 41–101), 84.
See also A Sibert, "Accountability and the ECB" (2009) Note prepared for the European Parliament's Committee on Economic and Monetary Affairs, available at <http://www.europarl.europa.eu/document/activities/cont/200909/20090924ATT61145/20090924ATT61145EN.pdf>.

[130]   As is the case in the US. The US President can remove for cause Members of the Federal Reserve Board (section 10 Federal Reserve Act 1913). See *Humphrey's Executor v US* 295 US 602 (1935), 627 on removal for cause ("inefficiency, neglect of duty, or malfeasance") of Federal Trade Commission officers.
See also, H Hogue, M Labonte and B Webel, "Independence of Federal Financial Regulators: Structure, Funding, and Other Issues" (2017) Congressional Research Service 7–5700.
In the EU, on application by the Governing Council or the Executive Board, the Court of Justice of the EU may compulsorily dismiss a member of the ECB Executive Board if he no longer fulfils the conditions required for the performance of his duties or if he has been guilty of serious misconduct (Protocol of the Statute of the ESCB and of the ECB of 26 October 2012 OJ C 326/230, article 11.4).

section 9B(1)(d) or (e) can be removed by the court of directors of the Bank of England, with the consent of the Chancellor of the Exchequer, under limited conditions.[131]

Finally, much of the effectiveness of accountability in macroprudential policymaking relates to the question to what extent the legal requirements and formal mechanisms (de jure accountability) are employed in practice (de facto accountability).[132] Regrettably, and to be contrasted with monetary policy, de facto accountability of macroprudential authorities remains, to date, largely unexamined.

2.4. JUDICIAL REVIEW AS AN ACCOUNTABILITY MECHANISM: WHAT DEGREE OF DEFERENCE IS JUSTIFIED?

A review of a final determination of the FSOC to designate a non-bank financial company under section 113 Dodd-Frank Act is limited to whether it was "arbitrary and capricious",[133] a highly deferential standard of review.[134] Indeed, in the *MetLife* case (Chapter 5), the District Court held that the FSOC's

---

[131]   If it is satisfied: (a) that that member has been absent from three or more meetings of the FPC without the Committee's consent, (b) that the member has become bankrupt, subject to a debt relief order (under Part 7A of the Insolvency Act 1986), his/her estate has been sequestrated or that M has made an arrangement with or granted a trust deed for his or her creditors, or (c) that the member is unable or unfit to discharge his/her functions as a member (Schedule 2A BEA 1998, section 9). See also Schedule 2A BEA 1998, sections 7–8.

[132]   On an implementation gap between de-jure versus de-facto accountability see, for instance, V Mechkova, A Lührmann and S Lindberg, "From De-jure to De-facto: Mapping Dimensions and Sequences of Accountability" (2017) Background Paper for the World Development Report, available at <http://pubdocs.worldbank.org/en/585311486396458329/WDR17-BP-Accountability-paper.pdf>.
       See also T Besley, *Principled Agents?: The Political Economy of Good Government* (Oxford University Press, 2008), 101.

[133]   Section 113(h) Dodd-Frank Act. It is to be recalled that in the *MetLife* case, the District Court held that the decision was arbitrary and capricious; that the process was "fatally flawed given that the FSOC deviated from its own guidance without acknowledgement or explanation" and it also failed to consider the regulatory cost that the designation would impose on MetLife. Accordingly, the District Court ordered on 30 March 2016 the rescission of MetLife's designation. The FSOC initially had appealed but then voluntarily filed a motion to dismiss it in January 2018. For more details see Chapter 5.

[134]   On the standard arbitrary and capricious *Motor Vehicle Manufacturers Association v State Farm Mutual Auto. Insurance Co*, 463 U.S. 29 (1983) at 43–44: "While the scope of review under the 'arbitrary and capricious' standard is narrow, and a court is not to substitute its judgment for that of the agency, the agency nevertheless must examine the relevant data and articulate a satisfactory explanation for its action. In reviewing that explanation, a court must consider whether the decision was based on a consideration of the relevant factors and whether there was a clear error of judgment".

designation decision was arbitrary and capricious, but scholars warned of the broader implications of that decision:

> ... the court undermined the entire framework for systemic risk regulation that Congress specifically created. With its decision, the court brought FSOC's ability to designate nonbank firms as systemically risky in the future to a halt because the Council cannot forecast the likelihood of material financial distress or the magnitude of potential third-party losses. Even under a more charitable interpretation of the District Court's order, the economic analysis in FSOC nonbank SIFI designations going forward would remain subject to second-guessing and reversal by a single federal judge with no real expertise in systemic risk.[135]

These concerns reflect a broader debate on the warranted intensity of judicial review of decisions that require technical knowledge and exercise of discretion, such as the formation of economic and monetary policy.[136] It is largely agreed that the aim of the court is not to venture "into a highly technical terrain in which it is necessary to have an expertise and experience" and supplant or replace the decision taken by policymakers.[137] For instance, where the ECB was required to "make choices of a technical nature and to undertake forecasts and complex assessments",[138] judicial review of its decisions had a soft standard[139] characterised by a considerable degree of caution and maintained a "broad discretion" of the ECB.[140] Therefore, judicial review of the ECB policy decisions did not extend to their content but rather to the parameters and legal frameworks that surrounded the decisions "in order to determine whether or not the central

---

[135]   PA McCoy, "Knightian Uncertainty, Systemic Risk Regulation, and the Limits of Judicial Review" (2017), available at SSRN <https://papers.ssrn.com/sol3/papers.cfm?abstract_id=2944297>.

[136]   In the EU, see Case C-370/12 *Pringle v Government of Ireland* [2012] ECLI:EU:C:2012:756, concerning the compatibility of the European Stability Mechanism Treaty with the Union law; Case C-62/14 *Peter Gauweiler and Others v Deutscher Bundestag* [2015] ECLI:EU:C:2015:400 on the Outright Monetary Transactions (OMT) programme that was announced by the ECB in 6 September 2012 during the financial and sovereign debt crisis in the eurozone.
The danger is that a court might get entangled in economic debates and compromise its legitimacy when its views are contested by those with more expertise on the issue. M Goldmann, "Adjudicating Economics? Central Bank Independence and the Appropriate Standard of Judicial Review" (2014) 15 German Law Journal 265 argues that in the *Gauweiler* decision, the German Federal Constitutional Court replaced the ECB's policy choices with its own.

[137]   C Goodhart and R Lastra, "Central Bank Accountability and Judicial Review" (2018) SUERF Policy Note 2585, available at <https://www.suerf.org/policynotes/2585/central-bank-accountability-and-judicial-review/html#f1>.

[138]   In the course of preparing and implementing the OMT programme, see Case C-62/14 *Gauweiler*, para 68.

[139]   T Tridimas, and N Xanthoulis, "A Legal Analysis of the *Gauweiler* Case: Between Monetary Policy and Constitutional Conflict" (2016) 23(1) Maastricht Journal of European and Comparative Law 17, 26.

[140]   Case C-62/14 *Gauweiler* (n 136), para 68.

bank mandate has been exceeded."[141] As such, in the *Gauweiler* case, the ECB was required to follow, in its OMT programme, process safeguards including the obligation to examine carefully and impartially all the relevant elements of the situation in question and give adequate reasons for its decision.[142] The focus of the ECJ, in that case, was whether the required procedural requirements have been met, signifying a trend to "proceduralisation of review criteria".[143]

Similarly, in the US, the courts must not substitute their policy choices for those of the agency to which Congress has entrusted implementation of its laws.[144]

---

[141]   Opinion of Advocate General (AG) Cruz Villalón in Case C-62/14 *Peter Gauweiler and Others v Deutscher Bundestag*, delivered on 14 January 2015, available at <http://eur-lex.europa.eu/legal-content/EN/TXT/?uri=CELEX%3A62014CC0062>, para 111.

[142]   Case C-62/14 *Gauweiler* (n 136), para 69.

[143]   HC Hofmann, "Gauweiler and OMT: Lessons for Public Law and the European Economic Monetary Union" (2015), available at SSRN <http://papers.ssrn.com/sol3/papers.cfm?abstract_id=2621933>, 16.

[144]   For instance, *Phelps Dodge Corp v NLRB*, 313 U.S. 177 (1941) on 194 that courts must "guard against the danger of sliding unconsciously from the narrow confines of law into the more spacious domain of policy"; *Vermont Yankee Nuclear Power Corp v Natural Resources Defense Council*, 435 U.S. 519 (1978) on 549 that courts should "not stray beyond the judicial province to explore the procedural format or to impose upon the agency its own notion of which procedures are 'best' or more likely to further some vague, undefined public good").
See also PM Wald, "Judicial Review of Economic Analyses" (1983) 1 (Article 3) Yale Journal on Regulation 43 who highlights the challenges of juridical review of economic matters and suggests that a cost-benefit analysis can improve judicial review "Because the analyses, along with the comments they generate, will be part of the record, the courts will get not only more information but also an additional expression of agency balancing and reasoning" (61).
On the judicial deference and its various forms see JC Reitz, "Judicial Deference to the Administration in the United States" in *Deference to the Administration in Judicial Review* (Ius Comparatum Global Studies in Comparative Law Book Series Vol 39, Springer, 2019), 417; E Fisher, P Pascual and W Wagner, "Rethinking Judicial Review of Expert Agencies" (2015) 93(7) Texas Law Review 1681.
For instance, US courts follow judicial deference to agency rule interpretations. According to *Bowles v Seminole Rock and Sand Co*, 325 U.S. 410 (1945) courts should defer to the agency's interpretation of its rule unless it is "plainly erroneous or inconsistent with the regulation" (414).
According to the *Chevron v Natural Resource Defense Council* 467 US 837 when analysing an agency's interpretation of a statute that it administers, the court will ask whether the statute is ambiguous and, if so, whether the agency's interpretation is reasonable (at 842–843); R Baldwin, M Cave and M Lodge, *Understating Regulation Theory Safety and Practice* (Oxford University Press, 2012), 346 suggest that the *Chevron* decision restored "an emphasis on professional expertise of regulators, as it requires a court to defer to the agency's interpretation of its legislative mandate …". But see the recent decision *Kisor v Wilkie* 588 US 26 June 2019 that narrowed the deference doctrine.
On critique of the judicial deference doctrine see CJ Walker, "Attacking Auer and Chevron Deference: A Literature Review" (2018) 16 Georgetown Journal of Law and Public Policy 103. See also C Raso, "The Supreme Court Curtails but retains agency rule Deference – How Much Will It Matter?" (September 2019) Brookings, available at <https://www.brookings.edu/research/the-supreme-court-curtails-but-retains-agency-rule-deference-how-much-will-it-matter/>.

In cases of competition law enforcement, the courts of the EU do not substitute their own discretion for that of the European Commission.[145] The decisions often involve the need to make complex economic or technical appraisal[146] and thus, judicial review will be limited to checking "whether the relevant rules on procedure and on stating reasons have been complied with, whether the facts have been accurately stated and whether there has been any manifest error of assessment or a misuse of powers."[147]

In the UK, a judicial review of the provision of Lender of Last Resort (LOLR) in the field of macro-economic policy was also subject to limitations:

> ... The provision of LOLR was a measure which the Tripartite Authorities considered was objectively required to protect the banking system and thus the national economy. Their concerns were strategic and the outcomes of what was done likely to be profound ... In these circumstances the margin of appreciation must be in my judgment a wide one ... the court would only interfere if it were to conclude that the State's judgment as to what is in the public interest is manifestly without reasonable foundation.[148]

It can be anticipated that in the macroprudential sphere, where there are hardly clear right or wrong policy choices, macroprudential authorities are likely to enjoy a broad margin of discretion. The level of judiciary scrutiny is thus likely to be soft.[149] This may entail assessing whether the macroprudential authority has followed processes that were set in legislation or by the authority itself. It may alternatively follow a more flexible approach of "rationality check" i.e. whether the act in question is rationally justifiable in a deliberative sense, bearing in mind the possibility of rational disagreement."[150] When examining the court's decision in the *MetLife* case, the reasoning largely relied on procedural matters. The outcome, nevertheless, is highly substantive and the impact of a shift away

---

[145] JC Laguna de Paz, "Understanding the Limits of Judicial Review in European Competition Law" (2014) 2(1) Journal of Antitrust Enforcement 203, available at <https://doi.org/10.1093/jaenfo/jnt014>.

[146] Case T-201/04 *Microsoft Corp v Commission of the European Communities* [2007] European Court Reports 2007 II-03601, para 87.

[147] Ibid.

[148] *SRM Global Master Fund LP v The Commissioners of HM Treasury* [2009] EWCA Civ 788, para 75.

[149] But its strength will also depend on the strength of other available mechanisms to hold the macroprudential authority accountable.

[150] Goldmann (2014) (n 136), 274. Therefore, C Goodhart, "Populism and Central Bank Independence" (2018) 29(1) Open Economies Review 49 suggests that given the specificity and complexity of monetary policy and other central banking functions, the need for competence and expertise in the exercise of judicial review could be served by the establishment of a specialised chamber within the CJEU to deal with these issues.
On expertise in the macroprudential realm see Chapter 9.

from institution-based supervision could be highly dangerous and impede the effectiveness of macroprudential policy, as discussed in Chapter 5.

3. TRANSPARENCY IN MACROPRUDENTIAL POLICYMAKING

3.1. GOING TOO FAR IS DANGEROUS

Generally, transparency in the macroprudential sphere should include: (i) an ex-ante communication of the policymakers' overall strategy; (ii) a detailed communication of the deliberations that led to particular policy decisions; and (iii) an ex-post assessment of the effectiveness of action taken.

To achieve these macroprudential authorities utilise a myriad of channels, reflecting the diverse target groups and the purpose of policy communication, including Financial Stability Reports, press conferences, statements, testimonies, speeches, standalone papers and records of meetings.[151] Through these channels, macroprudential authorities communicate about the financial stability outlook, policy objectives, strategy, decisions and their likely path and the process by which policy is conducted.[152]

Transparency of macroprudential policy decisions and their rationales serves several purposes.

First and foremost, transparency enhances the democratic accountability of macroprudential authorities by ensuring that they explain both their policy actions and the thinking that underlies those actions.[153] Transparency can also

---

[151]   Committee on the Global Financial System (CGFS), "Objective-Setting and Communication of Macroprudential Policies" (2016) CGFS Papers No 57, available at <https://www.bis.org/publ/cgfs57.pdf>, 52 (Table 4).
   The forms of transparency mechanisms underlying monetary policy are also relevant in macroprudential policymaking: *political transparency* about the policy objectives and institutional arrangements; *economic transparency* about the data and models, *procedural transparency* about the internal decision-making process, *policy transparency* about "prompt announcement and explanation of policy decisions, and an indication of likely future policy actions in the form of a policy inclination and *operational* about instrument setting and control errors". P Geraats, "Central Bank Transparency" (2002) 112(483) The Economic Journal F532. As shall be seen below, some forms of transparency are and should be tuned down in macroprudential policy.

[152]   CGFS 2016 (n 151), 10–12.

[153]   In monetary policy, see Briault, Haldane and King (1997) (n 43), 7; AS Blinder, "Talking about Monetary Policy: The Virtues (and Vices?) of Central Bank Communication" (2009) BIS Working Papers 274, available at <https://www.bis.org/events/conf080626/blinder.pdf>, 1–2.
   See also RM Lastra and H Shams, "Public Accountability in the Financial Sector" in E Ferran and CAE Goodhart (eds), *Regulating Financial Services and Markets in the 21st Century* (Hart Publishing, 2001).

help establish and maintain a commitment of the macroprudential authority to take action and thus act as a counterbalance to its inherent inaction bias.[154]

Communication can improve public understanding and learning[155] of the macroprudential authority's preference and in particular, the extent of the financial stability continuum beyond which policy intervention is warranted. This, in turn, can discourage political pressure being introduced into the macroprudential regulatory and supervisory process and reduce the likelihood of attempts to derail policy decisions.[156]

Transparency can also have ex-ante benefits and enhance the effectiveness of macroprudential policymaking.[157] Communication can assist in shaping and anchoring the public and relevant stakeholders' expectations[158] and even alter risk assessment and moderate risk-taking behaviour of financial actors.[159]

---

[154]   C Baba, "Key Aspects of Macroprudential Policies: IMF Frameworks and Experience" (Joint IMF-FED-WB seminar for EM Senior Bank Supervisors, 2 November 2017, available at <http://pubdocs.worldbank.org/en/398361511190559091/9-Macroprudential-policies.pdf>.

[155]   J Dewey, *The Public and its Problems* (New York: Holt, 1927) advocated communication as a vital foundation of democracy that improves generation of knowledge and empowers the public.

[156]   In financial supervision, see Quintyn and Taylor (2002) (n 1), 21.
See also ESRB, "Features of a Macroprudential Stance: Initial Considerations" (April 2019), available at <https://www.esrb.europa.eu/pub/pdf/reports/esrb.report190408_features_macroprudential_stance_initial_considerations~f9cc4c05f4.en.pdf>.

[157]   Similar to the signalling channel in the literature on foreign exchange interventions, G Kaminsky and K Lewis, "Does Foreign Exchange Intervention Signal Future Monetary Policy?" (1996) 37(2) Journal of Monetary Economics 285. On the signalling channel in macroprudential policy see S Bahaj and A Foulis, "Macroprudential Policy under Uncertainty" (2017) 13(3) International Journal of Central Banking 119, 142–143 highlighting "the importance of a policymaker ensuring that private agents understand why a policy action is taken, in order to maximize the signaling value of a policy decision" and showing that private sector uncertainty over the financial stability objectives, may diminish the potency of the signalling impact of macroprudential policy; ESRB (2019) (n 155), 47. Accordingly, transparency has been framed as a macroprudential tool in its own right, designed to achieve the macroprudential objective. CGFS (2016) (n 150), 27. Nevertheless, the usefulness may be disregarded if policymakers are speaking with too many conflicting voices. See, in monetary policy, Blinder (2009) (n 153), 6.

[158]   Where policy decisions are made by reference to pre-established set of indicators, stakeholders can predict future policy actions based on the macroprudential authority's communication CGFS (2016) (n 151), 10–11.
See also HM Treasury, "Remit and Recommendations to the FPC", 8 March 2017 recommending that the FPC makes sure that "its policy actions are as predictable as possible" by "providing clear, focussed and consistent messages about the planned regulatory response to identified financial stability risks".

[159]   B Born, M Ehrmann and M Fratzscher, "Macroprudential Policy and Central Bank Communication" (2010) BIS Papers No 60 147.
See also, on the effect of disclosure of stress tests, WH Gick and T Pausch, "Optimal Disclosure of Supervisory Information in the Banking Sector" (15 February 2012), available at SSRN <https://ssrn.com/abstract=2006852> or <http://dx.doi.org/10.2139/ssrn.2006852> finding that disclosing result of stress tests affects investors' beliefs about the probability of a vulnerable banking sector (risk). But, more recently, a research on Financial Stability

Finally, transparency is an important source of data for researchers and can substantially assist in closing the "knowledge gap" of macroprudential policy (Chapter 9) as well as strengthening coordination with macroprudential authorities in other jurisdictions (Chapter 8).

Nonetheless, transparency in macroprudential policymaking is far from being an unmitigated good and is best described as a double-edged instrument.[160] When transparency goes too far,[161] it can potentially become counterproductive.[162] Macroprudential authorities must, therefore, be mindful of and guard against the potential damage it can bring.

To begin with, information about financial stability (or instability) is harder to summarise in compact and cogent ways.[163] Where a macroprudential mandate is entrusted with several agencies, there is an additional risk of contrasting messages from multiple agencies.[164]

The timing of the communication of macroprudential policy measures is also of essence. Often, macroprudential policy measures are deployed when the risks are not yet elevated and clear signs of incipient financial stress are absent. At that stage, the challenge of the macroprudential authority in communicating the need for policy intervention is greater. Costs are often immediate and visible while the benefits of policy measures can only be identified in the long-term

---

Reports RD F Harris, V Karadotchev, R Sowerbutts and E Stoja, "Have FSRs got News For You? Evidence from the Impact of Financial Stability Reports on Market Activity" (April 2019) Bank of England Staff Working Paper No 792 suggest that FSRs do not result in neither participant adjusting their portfolios nor levelling the information playing field. The authors find some evidence that this is because the content of the FSR is largely predictable and therefore anticipated by the market.

[160] S Morris and H Shin, "Social Value of Public Information" (2002) 92(5) The American Economic Review 1521.
In any case, transparency may have a long way to go before reaching the "too far" stage. According to the IMF Staff Proposal to Update the Monetary and Financial Policies Transparency Code, May 2019, 37 central banks are lacking transparency in macroprudential/ financial stability policy.

[161] FS Mishkin, "Can Central Bank Transparency Go Too Far?" (2004) NEBR Working Paper 10829.

[162] For empirical evidence of optimal level of transparency regarding policy framework to safeguard financial stability, see R Hovarth and D Vaško, "Central Bank Transparency and Financial Stability" (2015) Journal of Financial Stability 22 showing that if transparency is too high, it is not beneficial for financial stability.

[163] N Dincer, B Eichengree and P Geraats, "Transparency of Monetary Policy in the Postcrisis World" in DG Mayes, P Siklos and JE Strum (eds), The Oxford Handbook of The Economics of Central Banking (Oxford University Press, 2019), 291. It is particularly difficult to communicate information on financial stability where macroprudential responsibilities are shared amongst institutions and policy makers. This observation coincides with recent evidence on increased complexity in Financial Stability Reports in emerging market economies. N Patel, "Macroprudential Frameworks: Communication" (2017) in BIS Papers Macroprudential Frameworks, Implementation and Relationship with Other Policies No 94, 49–56.

[164] Patel (2017) (n 163), 52.

and not always with certainty (Chapter 6). Thus, getting the timing right is challenging:

> Early in the credit cycle, warnings on risk-taking may have limited effect as risky strategies still appear profitable. By contrast, at later stages, risk warnings may have a large impact on behaviour but, as economic agents tend to adjust their behaviour abruptly, it is possible that the warning may have unintended, destabilising results.[165]

One way to resolve this asymmetry would be to be open about the limitations of data and knowledge.[166] Openness about the inherent limitation of macroprudential policymaking and its indicators can also mitigate the danger of a false sense of confidence in the precision of those decisions.[167] Nonetheless, being too transparent about the limitations could undermine the credibility of the macroprudential authority and reduce its effectiveness.

Excessive transparency can be particularly dangerous in the macroprudential sphere given the self-fulfilling nature of public information.[168] Advance warning of risks to financial stability may have destabilising effects on financial markets[169] and in extreme cases, even cause panic and trigger a crisis.[170] In the UK, for instance, this danger is particularly acute as the concentrated nature of its banking sector means that the "FPC policy discussions are replete with bank-specific, confidential supervisory information."[171] Moreover, where macroprudential authorities engage in forward guidance about the likely path of their policy,[172] it may lead to front-running and undesired effects on risk-taking.[173] As an illustration, if the macroprudential authority advises households that LTV limits are likely to be tightened in the future, they might rush to take out high-LTV mortgages, thus increasing vulnerabilities. There is also a clear trade-off between being "fully transparent ex ante about how policy will be conducted and being able to react efficiently to events that could not

---

[165] GCFS (2016) (n 151), 2.
[166] Or in other words, being open about its ignorance. In monetary policy, see, for instance, A Cukierman, "The Limits of Transparency" (2009) 38(2) Economic Notes 1, 29–30.
[167] Ibid.
[168] S Morris and HS Shin, "Social Value of Public Information" (2002) 92(5) The American Economic Review 1521, 1522. It should not, however, be interpreted as an anti-transparency result. L Svensson, "Social Value of Public Information: Comment: Morris and Shin (2002) Is Actually Pro-Transparency, Not Con" (2006) 96(1) American Economic Review 448.
[169] Dincer and others (2019) (n 163), 291; B Born, M Ehrmann, M Fratzscher, "Communicating About Macro-prudential Supervision – A New Challenge for Central Banks" (2012) 15(2) International Finance 179.
[170] Cukierman (2009) (n 166).
[171] Kevin Warsh, "Transparency and the Bank of England's Monetary Policy Committee" December 2015, 11.
[172] For instance, *Australia Mortgage Lending Surges on Relaxation of the Rules* (FT, 9 September 2019).
[173] CGFS (2016) (n 151), 12.

have been formulated sufficiently precisely in advance."[174] In the same vein, withholding information when the risks are elevated, may be interpreted by markets as bad news and prolong uncertainty about how bad things really are.[175] Finally, excessive transparency may also facilitate the exertion of political pressures on macroprudential authorities.[176]

Another notable challenge of transparency in the macroprudential sphere relates to the difference between internal and external communication. Where the macroprudential authority is a committee, statements should be in the form of collegial communication strategy that displays a high degree of consistency among the statements of individual committee member and speaking in one voice.[177] A diversified communication might undermine clarity and common understanding of the public and the financial market thus creating a cacophony.[178] At the same time, it is also important to demonstrate that the decision-making process has a deliberative nature and takes into account a diversity of views.[179]

The balance between these considerations, as always, is delicate and therefore, a consistent, predictable and tailor-made communication strategy is imperative.[180] To maximise the benefits of transparency, much wider and deeper engagement with society is needed, in a form and manner that will increase their understanding and trust.[181] In that respect, the FPC takes a rather innovative approach and complements its approximately 100-page FSR with visual summaries and short tweets in order to make it more digestible and reach a wider audience.[182] Other macroprudential authorities are likely to follow suit.

---

[174] Ibid.

[175] CGFS (2016) (n 151), 28–29.

[176] Cukierman (2009) (n 166).

[177] M Ehrmann and M Fratzscher, "Communication by Central Bank Committee Members: Different Strategies, Same Effectiveness?" (2007) 39 (2–3) Journal of Money, Credit, and Banking 509. AS Blinder, M Ehrman and M Fratzcher, J de Haan and J Jansen, "Central Bank Communication and Monetary Policy: A Survey of Theory and Evidence" (2009) 46(4) Journal of Economic Literature 910.

[178] AS Blinder, "Monetary Policy by Committee: Why and How?" (2007) 23(1) European Journal of Political Economy 106, 114 notes that "A central bank that speaks with a cacophony of voices may, in effect, have no voice at all." This is still a problem in monetary policy – AS Blinder, "Through a Crystal Ball Darkly: The Future of Monetary Policy Communication" (2018) 108 American Economic Association Papers and Proceedings 567.

[179] BS Bernanke (at the time, Governor of the Federal Reserve) remarks at the Meetings of the American Economic Association, San Diego, California, 3 January 2004.

[180] M Ehrmann and M Fratzscher, "Communication and Decision-making by Central Bank Committees: Different Strategies, Same Effectiveness?" (2015) ECB Working Paper No 488.

[181] A Haldane, "A Little more Conversation. A little Less Action" (Macroeconomics and Monetary Policy Conference, San Francisco, 31 March 2017), 2.
A Blinder, M Ehrmann, J de Haan and D-J Jansen, "Necessity as the Mother of Invention Monetary Policy After the Crisis" (2017) NBER Working Paper 22735, 29 refer, amongst other things, to the expanded mandate of central banks that may include macroprudential policy and highlight a trend towards more transparency of central banks.

[182] A Brazier, "Citizens in Service, not People in Power" (Allen and Overy, London, 17 May 2019), available at <https://www.bis.org/review/r190517j.pdf>, 10.

3.2. PUBLICATION OF RECORDS OF MEETINGS

In contrast to monetary policy committees, to date, only a small number of macroprudential authorities publish records of their meetings.[183] This could be attributed, at least in part, to the lack of research on the effects of transparency in the macroprudential sphere and/or concerns as to the potential adverse impact on financial stability from excessive disclosure or disclosure of market-sensitive information. In addition, the publication of opinions of individual members in macroprudential committees is problematic since it may "inject short-term political and personal career factors into their deliberations and voting behaviour".[184]

In the UK, the Warsh Review recommended a package of reforms to the MPC transparency, including full transcripts of its meetings but emphasised that, for the time being, proposed MPC reforms are not applicable to the FPC, explaining that:

> At present, making sound policy decisions could be impaired if FPC discussions were made public through transcript release. The FPC benefits from an unconstrained space for open discussion and deliberation as its members seek to advance the new discipline … As the FPC's understanding of its new discipline advances, there may be scope for the adoption of greater transparency reforms.[185]

The records of the FPC quarterly meetings must specify any decision taken at the meeting (including decisions not to take action) and a summary of the deliberations that were considered in reaching any decision.[186] However, records of the meetings do not identify particular members[187] and the publication is subject to several statutory exceptions, most importantly, the public interest.[188] In the case of using public interest as a basis for non-publication, the FPC must consider whether to fix a date as the earliest date on which the information may be published, or otherwise, keep under consideration the question whether publication of the information would still be against the public interest.[189]

---

[183] CGFS (2016) (n 151), 12.

[184] Cukierman (2009) (n 166).

[185] Warsh Review (2014) (n 171), 11–12.

[186] Section 9U(1)–(6) BEA 1998. Records are published two weeks after the policy meeting. The records of the meetings include the range of views expressed in the FPC's regular briefing and issues meetings ahead of its policy meetings, in the event that these played a role in the forming of a consensus. See Record of the FPC meeting March 2015.

[187] Section 9U(7) BEA 1998.

[188] Section 9U(8)(b) BEA 1998.

[189] Section 9V(1) BEA 1998.

Where a vote is taken, the balance of arguments advanced for each position should be reflected in the record of the meeting and members are free to explain their differences and will be publicly accountable accordingly.[190] This recommendation is with the view to strengthening the importance of individual and idiosyncratic positions during deliberation and minimising the potential cohesiveness that could result from a 'striving for consensus' decision rule.[191]

The FPC's transparency model is in many respects attractive as it balances transparency and the need to ensure genuine and free deliberations during the FPC meetings. There is however room for improvement. Regrettably, on the rare occasion where the record revealed differing views that were voiced by FPC members before a consensus was reached, the reasons behind the change are not disclosed. For instance, the record of the FPC meeting on 23 March 2016 suggests that there was initially a disagreement amongst members regarding the level of the countercyclical buffer rate but that "… the Governor asked whether it was possible for the Committee to reach a consensus around 0.5%. Those members who had initially favoured moving to 0.75% were content to join a consensus".[192] Unfortunately, no explanation was provided in the records for this change of minds.

As for the FSOC, its meetings are open to the public whenever possible through live webstream.[193] The Transparency policy of the FSOC enumerates the reasons that the FSOC Chairperson may close a meeting, in whole or in part, including if disclosure would "lead to significant financial speculation, significantly endanger the stability of any financial market or financial institution, or significantly frustrate implementation of a proposed agency action".[194] Given

---

[190] See, for instance, HM Treasury, Remit and Recommendations to the FPC 2016 and 2017, available at <https://www.bankofengland.co.uk/financial-stability>.

[191] S Hansen, M McMahon and A Prat, "Transparency and Deliberation within the FOMC: A Computational Linguistics Approach" (2017) 133(2) Quarterly Journal of Economics 801.

[192] Record of the FPC Meeting, 23 March 2016, available at <http://www.bankofengland.co.uk/publications/Documents/records/fpc/pdf/2016/record160 4.pdf>.

[193] Transparency Policy for the FSOC, available at <https://www.treasury.gov/initiatives/Documents/FSOCtransparencypolicy.pdf>.
        The Transparency Policy was revised in May 2014 following GAO's criticism – see GAO, "New Council and Research Office Should Strengthen the Accountability and Transparency of Their Decisions" (September 2012) Report to Congressional Requesters, available at <https://www.gao.gov/assets/650/648064.pdf>.
        The FSOC is required to convene no less than quarterly (section 111(e)(1) Dodd-Frank Act), but historically the FSOC has convened on a more frequent basis.

[194] But it is committed to holding at least two open meetings each year.
        According to the FSOC Transparency Policy (n 193) other triggers for closed meetings are information generated by regulatory or supervisory operations, information that may lead to financial speculation, information that includes trade secrets or commercial and financial information considered privileged or confidential, or the discussion of agency memoranda or letters not otherwise available publicly.

market sensitivity of information, the FSOC is reluctant to provide transcripts of its meetings[195] and only releases records that are subject to redactions, as determined by its Chairperson.[196] The votes of the FSOC members are recorded and reflected in these minutes.[197] However, the account of the deliberations is often limited and does not go beyond "Members of the Council then asked questions and had a discussion".[198] Legislators should consider including a provision, similar to the provision in the BEA 1998, that allows the FSOC to reconsider the sensitivity of the data and publish it at an opportune time when disclosure no longer poses risk.[199]

The proceedings of the ESRB General Board are confidential.[200] Following their conclusion, the ESRB publishes on its website a press release with the key issues discussed, an assessment of the current key risks and the ESRB activities. The press release document is a brief one-page summary as opposed to a detailed record of the meeting.[201] The Regulation amending the ESRB Regulation now clarifies that "The General Board may decide to make an account of its deliberations public, subject to applicable confidentiality requirement and in a manner that does not allow for the identification of individual members of the General Board or individual institutions" and that the "General Board may also decide to hold press conference after its meetings."[202] The comparable restricted transparency of deliberation is understandable in light of the size of the ESRB General Board and the need to ensure free-flow of discussion and exchange of views without the fear of damaging national interests.

---

[195] See also GAO, "Who Is Too Big To Fail?' GAO's Assessment of the FSOC and the OFR", Hearing before the Subcommittee on Oversight and Investigations of the Committee on Financial Services, 14 March 2013, available at <https://www.govinfo.gov/content/pkg/CHRG-113hhrg80873/html/CHRG-113hhrg80873.htm>.
See also GAO, "FSOC Status of Efforts to Improve Transparency, Accountability, and Collaboration", 17 September 2014, available at <https://www.gao.gov/assets/670/665851.pdf> pointing out that FSOC staff said that they did not intend to keep detailed minutes because of the confidential information discussed.

[196] FSOC Transparency Policy (n 193).

[197] FSOC Transparency Policy (n 193).

[198] For instance, Minutes of the FSOC, 30 May 2019.

[199] GAO, "Financial Stability: New Council and Research Office Should Strengthen the Accountability and Transparency of Their Decisions", GAO-12-866, 11 September 2012.
See also Americans for Financial Reform, "Background on the Financial Stability Oversight Council" June 2014.

[200] Article 9(6) ESRB Regulation, as amended; Article 5(5) of the Decision of the ESRB of 20 January 2011 adopting the Rules of Procedure of the European Systemic Risk Board (ESRB/2011/1) OJ 58/4.

[201] Though it is referred to as minutes of the meeting in the ESRB Rules of Procedures (n 200), article 5(3)–(4).

[202] Article 9(6) ESRB Regulation, as amended.

4. CONCLUSION

The elusive nature of the macroprudential mandate makes the identification and in time, measurement of independence, accountability and transparency highly important. Moreover, when monetary policy and macroprudential policy are institutionally closely aligned, it is imperative to ensure the design of separate and tailored accountability arrangements for monetary and macroprudential policy.[203]

Yet, while accountability is clearly a pressing issue in the design and implementation of macroprudential regimes, the topic has been kept out of the limelight. In practice, accountability mechanisms, specifically designed to address these challenges, are very few. Recent evidence shows that "In most countries, accountability mechanisms exist for central banks and supervisory institutions, but formal accountability requirements for macroprudential policies *per se* are rare …"[204]

The picture is different when examining transparency arrangements in macroprudential policy. Over the recent decade, the degree of transparency of central banks in their financial stability frameworks has increased but variation across countries is still great.[205]

The chapter contextualised the literature on the delegation to independent regulatory agencies in the macroprudential sphere. Undoubtedly, an ideal structure for independence, accountability and transparency frameworks does not exist since these are heavily dependent on the legal and institutional context within which macroprudential authorities operate. Yet, by dissecting the unique features of macroprudential policymaking and the accompanying theoretical foundations, several observations emerged.

The first is that policy processes (such as a cost-benefit analysis) and adherence to transparent procedural rules, supported by limited judicial review, should take a centre stage in the accountability frameworks of macroprudential regimes. In the absence of a clear benchmark for assessing policy outcomes, at least in the short term, this approach is a good solution. In the real world, there are signs to the adoption of this approach. The legal frameworks of the FPC,

---

[203] IMF, "Macroprudential Policy: An Organizing Framework" 2011, 38.

[204] W Nier, J Osiński, LI Jácome and P Madri, "Towards Effective Macroprudential Policy Frameworks: An Assessment of Stylized Institutional Models" (2011) IMF Working Paper No 250. In some cases, such accountability mechanisms are being developed or have recently been introduced and they often involve accountability to the public and Parliament.

[205] R Horváth and D Vaško, "Central Bank Transparency and Financial Stability" (2016) 22 Journal of Financial Stability 45 show that transparency is greater in more developed countries. The authors also show that central banks with more transparent monetary policies tend to exhibit greater financial stability transparency.

FSOC and the ESRB have embraced the need to enhance throughput legitimacy and attempted (not always successfully) to assess policy processes. This is evident in the hearings of the FPC before the Treasury Committee that often focused on the deliberative process of the FPC as well as in the judicial review of the FSOC's designation power and the ESRB's myriad of procedural requirements to support its decision-making process.

Second, inclusiveness of experts and to a certain degree, non-experts and overall openness regarding the rationales for policy decisions should form a vital part in macroprudential legal frameworks. They play a crucial role in bolstering the much-needed legitimacy of macroprudential authorities. This should be done in a manner that acknowledges not only the growing trend of distrust in central banks but also the "understanding-gap" in such a complex and technical policy area. After all, legitimacy can only come from meaningful transparency, i.e. one that is comprehensible by the stakeholders that are supposed to hold macroprudential authorities accountable, may it be the public, parliamentary representatives or the judiciary.

Third and related to that, excessive transparency presents many risks in the macroprudential sphere, from front-running of financial markets to destabilising effects and increased politicisation of the process. The delicate balance between these considerations and the need to ensure accountability is evident in the divergence of practices of the FPC, FSOC and the ESRB in publishing the minutes of their meetings.

Overall, arrangements of independence, accountability and transparency should not be considered in isolation from each other as the strength (or lack thereof) of one component will have an impact on the others and even more so, reinforce them. Therefore, a system of checks and balances with multi-layered accountability mechanisms is a crucial element in macroprudential regimes.

CHAPTER 8

A NON-DICHOTOMOUS VIEW
OF MACROPRUDENTIAL POLICY
AND OTHER POLICY AREAS

"No one would dream of designing the human anatomy by disconnecting the controls of the left and right sides of the body"

William Naurdhaus, Yale University, 1994

The need for a clear framework for policy coordination has strong roots in theories of economic policy. It is even more salient in macroprudential policymaking given that, as shall be seen in the following chapter, the regulation of uncertainty cannot be "solved" by isolated knowledge.

This chapter analyses the potential tension between policy boundaries and coordination. Boundaries that define macroprudential policy as a distinct and specialised policy area are essential to ensure a high insulation of macroprudential authorities from political and industry pressures. Boundaries are also key to forming a defined accountability framework of macroprudential authorities. After all, accountability means the capacity to identify who did what and this may be slightly lost during a coordination process.[1] Yet, systemic problems, in their nature, necessitate a holistic solution[2] and coordination with other policy areas.[3] This is, of course, not a new contention. It has been

---

[1]   G Peters, "Managing Horizontal Government: The Politics of Co-Ordination" (1998) 76 Public Administration 295, 308.
      See also J Black, "Decentring Regulation: The Role of Regulation and Self-regulation in a 'Post-Regulatory World'" (2001) Current Legal Problems 103 suggesting that identifying regulatory failure becomes more complex in a decentred regulatory regime.

[2]   This is far from being the only policy area that requires more integration. See E Bardach, *Getting Agencies to Work Together: The Practice and Theory of Managerial Craftsmanship* (Brookings Institution Press, 1998), 14.

[3]   Coordination has many meanings. For instance, negative coordination occurs when decisions made in one program or organisation consider those made in others and attempt to avoid conflict while positive coordination would require "the organizations to go beyond simply avoiding conflicts and to seek to find ways to cooperate on solutions that can benefit all the organizations involved, and their clients". See G Peters, "The Challenge of Coordination" (2018) 1(1) Policy Design and Practice 1.

long acknowledged in the scholarly discourse in public policy that "Issues are becoming increasingly 'cross-cutting', and do not fit the ministerial boxes into which governments, and policy analysts, tend to place policies."[4] Boundaries can inhibit this coherence and form barriers to creative and multi-disciplinary thinking (Chapter 9).

The chapter is structured as follows. Section 1 lays out the theoretical foundations for policy coordination as developed by Tinbergen, Theil and others. It provides an insight into the progressing evolution from the classical theory of economic policy to a new theory that operates in a more complicated environment of interactions and strategic games. The section also draws on concepts developed in inter-organisational politics, particularly in relation to public policy organisations. Section 2 explores the interlinkages between macroprudential policy and other traditional policy areas and the possible frictions between their respective objectives, transmission mechanisms and instruments. Understanding these interlinkages is essential in order to choose the appropriate coordination mechanisms of macroprudential policy with other policy areas. It, accordingly, asserts that macroprudential policymaking cannot be conducted in silos. Its intersection with other policy areas should be acknowledged and legal (procedural and institutional) mechanisms to regulate them should be put in place. But saying "what we need is more coordination"[5] is not a panacea. The mode and degree of coordination are of significant importance. As such, should coordination be hierarchical with macroprudential policy at the top? At what level does coordination becomes unwanted cooperation that may subject the macroprudential authority to political or industry pressures? Section 3 moves from theory to practice. It critically analyses current coordination mechanisms that are adopted in macroprudential regimes in the UK, the US and the EU and assesses their effectiveness in ensuring that the policies are working in tandem to promote financial stability.

---

4 Peters (1998) (n 1), 296.
  See also G Bouckaert, BG Peters and K Verhoest, "The Main Argument: Specialization Without Coordination is Centrifugal", Chapter 1 in G Bouckaert, BG Peters and K Verhoest (eds), The Coordination of Public Sector Organizations: Shifting Patterns of Public Management (Palgrave Macmillan, 2010), 3, 12 who discuss the hypothesis that the specialisation trend in public policy results in fragmentation of public organisation and thus triggers solutions in the form of re-emerged coordination mechanisms.

5 JL Pressman and A Wildavsky, Implementation: How Great Expectations in Washington Are Dashed in Oakland; Or, Why It's Amazing that Federal Programs Work at All, This Being a Saga of the Economic Development Administration as Told by Two Sympathetic Observers Who Seek to Build Morals on a Foundation (University of California Press, 1984), 133 observe that the most common claim about federal bureaucracy is that there is lack of coordination.

1. THE THEORETICAL BACKGROUND OF POLICY COORDINATION AND ITS MECHANISMS

Jan Tinbergen was the first to present a golden rule to the existence and uniqueness of a policy that can control the economic system.[6] He classified some economic quantities as targets and others as instruments. Targets are those macroeconomic variables that a policymaker wishes to influence while instruments are the variables that the policymaker can directly control and which in turn influence the values taken by the target variables. Tinbergen demonstrated that a policymaker can reach (fixed) targets if the number of independent instruments equals or exceeds the number of independent targets.[7] Very soon, however, it became clear that allocation of policy instruments to targets does not necessarily eliminate interaction between policies and hence the need for coordination.[8] Tinbergen himself acknowledged that policymakers are often trying to offset the behaviour of the other policymakers, with spillovers that may lead to inferior performance.[9] Coordination between policies, it was argued, takes into account the possibility that helping other policy areas may put each policymaker in a stronger position to benefit from better outcomes himself.[10]

Robert Pindyck further addressed the possible decentralised structure of macroeconomic policies.[11] Pindyck's principal proposition was that a

---

[6] J Tinbergen, *On the Theory of Economic Policy* (North-Holland, 1952); A Hallet, G Di Bartolomeo and N Acocella, "The Old and the New Theory of Economic Policy" (2010) 6(1) International Journal of Public Policy 154; L Dymond, *A Recent History of Recognised Economic Thought: Contributions of the Nobel Laureates to Economic Science* (Dymond Associates Inc, 2015), 55.

[7] N Acocella, G Di Bartolomeo and AH Hallett, "An Overview: The Realm of Economic Policy", Chapter 1 in N Acocella, G Di Bartolomeo and AH Hallett, *The Theory of Economic Policy in a Strategic Context* (Cambridge University Press, 2008), 2.
These targets can be flexible, where they are not set in a numerically fixed way. See Tinbergen, *Centralization and Decentralization in Economic Policy* (North-Holland, 1954), 1.

[8] H Theil, "On the Theory of Economic Policy" (1956) 46(2) American Economic Review 360 acknowledged that the variables controlled by other policymakers bring uncertainty to the Tinbergen theory.

[9] Tinbergen (1954) (n 7) recognises the existence of multiple policymakers (domestically and internationally) and observe on p 18 that "in modern times economic policy often is a 'game' or a play between these various policy-makers, each of them pursuing different ends, which only partly coincide"; J Tinbergen, *Economic Policy: Principles and Design* (North-Holland, 1956), 220; R Cooper, "Macroeconomic Policy Adjustment in Interdependent Economies" (1969) 83(1) Quarterly Journal of Economics 1, 22 show, among other things, that lack of coordination among policymakers delays achievement of national objectives such as full employment and a targeted rate of growth.

[10] A Hallett, "Coordination Without Explicit Cooperation: Monetary-Fiscal Interactions in an Era of Demographic Change" (2008) European Commission Economic Papers 305.

[11] Where monetary and fiscal policies are exercised by independent authorities. R Pindyck, "The Cost of Conflicting Objectives in Policy Formulation" in *Annals of Economic and Social Measurement* (NEBR, 1976), Vol 5(2), 239–248.

decentralised structure might give rise to conflicting objectives and result in economic performance that is far from either objective.[12] The existence of spillovers from each policy onto the targets to which they are not principally assigned implied the need for policy coordination.[13] As such, it was suggested that coordination may prevent, for instance, monetary and fiscal policies from engaging in a tug-of-war by trying to offset each other's actions.[14] Conversely, lack of coordination may result in increased instability and inferior performance of the macroeconomic policy setters.

Various mechanisms can be adopted to formalise the interaction between policies and facilitate their coordination. These mechanisms lie on a wide spectrum and vary according to the desired level of policy coordination to be structured.[15] In the simplest form, coordination consists of cross-membership and includes legal frameworks that facilitate exchange of information. This means that policymakers will ensure an open dialogue about their objectives and priorities but will take their decisions autonomously while maintaining their independence. Other forms of coordination include a requirement to notify, "have regard to" or consult the other policymaker before taking decisions. "Best efforts" coordination governed by memoranda of understanding is another possibility.[16] On the other end of the spectrum, strong coordination mechanisms may entail veto rights for policymakers from other policy areas or a hierarchy between the policies where one authority has the power to override another authority. Naturally, movement on the spectrum towards "strong" coordination

---

[12]   Ibid, 239.

[13]   T Sargent and N Wallace, "Some Unpleasant Monetarist Arithmetic" (1981) 5 Minneapolis Fed Quarterly Review 1 characterised the coordination problem between monetary and fiscal policies as a game of chicken; E Leeper, "Equilibria under 'Active' and 'Passive' Monetary and Fiscal Policies" (1991) 27(1) Journal of Monetary Economics 129; M Canzoneri, R Cumby and B Diba, "The Interaction between Monetary and Fiscal Policy" in M Friedman and M Woodford (eds), *Handbook of Monetary Economics* (North-Holland, 2011), Vol 3B, 935.

[14]   A Hallett, J Libich and P Stehlík, "Welfare Improving Coordination of Monetary and Fiscal Policy" (2011) 5 AUCO Czech Economic Review 7; J Libich, D Nguyen and P Stehlík, "Monetary Exit Strategy and Fiscal Spillovers" [2011] Centre for Applied Macroeconomic Analysis Working Paper Series 4. In normal times, central banks want to achieve low inflation while the government prefers to spend excessively and would like the central bank to "inflate" away the resulting debt.

[15]   In analogy to the literature on international policy coordination (joint control of economic policies by several countries), D Currie, G Holtham and AH Hallett, "The Theory and Practice of International Policy Coordination: Does Coordination Pay?", Chapter 1 in RC Bryant, DA Currie, PR Masson, JA Frenkel, DP Currie and R Portes (eds), *Macroeconomic Policies in an Interdependent World* (Brookings/CEPR/International Monetary Fund, 1989), 36.

[16]   J Caruana, "Monetary Policy in a World with Macroprudential Policy" (SAARCFINANCE Governors' Symposium, Kerala, 11 June 2011); IMF, "Macroprudential Policy: An Organising Framework" (2011), available at <http://www.imf.org/external/np/pp/eng/2011/031411.pdf>, 12.

---

mechanisms may blur the boundaries between the policies and their respective objectives and even dilute accountability and transparency.[17]

It is important to note that these forms of coordination are to be distinguished from direct or face-to-face negotiations between policymakers over the details of each other's policy choices and the precise measures to be taken in any particular case. This type of explicit cooperation or full coordination is likely to compromise the independence of the respective policymakers from external influences and short-term political pressure and eventually, may lead to diversion from their respective objectives.[18]

2. INTERACTION OF MACROPRUDENTIAL POLICY WITH OTHER POLICY AREAS

Policies differ in their perspectives, objectives and tools as well as in the institutional structure and regulatory constraints in which their decisions are taking place. Hence, for the convenience of the discussion, the interaction of macroprudential policy with various policy areas is considered separately against each policy. This format, however, should not impair the need for consistency across all policy areas that have an impact, directly or indirectly, on financial stability.

With this in mind, the discussion begins with confronting the objectives and tools of macroprudential policy with those of micro-prudential supervision. This is a good starting point since, as discussed in Chapter 1, it was the contrast with micro-prudential supervision that brought macroprudential policy to the fore in the aftermath of the 2007–2009 global financial crisis. Then, the section proceeds with examining the close interactions between macroprudential policy and monetary policy as opposed to the arm's-length nature of the interaction between macroprudential and fiscal policies. Other policy areas, such as competition and conduct-of-business will reinforce the assertion that macroprudential policymaking cannot be conducted in silos. Its intersection with other policy areas should be acknowledged and legal mechanisms to regulate them should be put in place.

---

[17] A Clark and A Large, "Macroprudential Policy: Addressing the Things We Don't Know" (2011) Group of 30 Occasional Papers 83, 20 suggest that requiring macroprudential authorities to "have regard" to the other policy objectives is likely to dilute transparency and accountability and therefore, a hierarchy of objectives is more suitable as a coordination form.

[18] Macroprudential supervisors are particularly sensitive to the lobbying of dedicated interest groups, BIS Study Group chaired by S Ingves, "Central Bank Governance and Financial Stability" (May 2011); D Igan, M Prachi and T Thierry, "A Fistful of Dollars: Lobbying and the Financial Crisis" (2009) IMF Working Paper 287.

2.1. INTERACTION OF MACROPRUDENTIAL POLICY WITH MICRO-PRUDENTIAL POLICY

2.1.1. Different Objectives and Perspectives

The objective of micro-prudential policy is to limit the risk of episodes of financial distress at individual institutions.[19] Its prevailing rationale is protecting the interests of consumers – depositors, investors and insurance and pensions policyholders.[20] In contrast, the rationale of macroprudential policy, as has been seen in Chapter 1, is rooted in systemic risk externalities and the associated expectations of public support.[21] Accordingly, the primary objective of macroprudential policy is to limit the risk of episodes of financial distress with significant losses in terms of the real output for the economy as a whole.[22] Yet, it would be inaccurate to state that micro-prudential supervisors ignore in their policy decisions the health of the financial system as a whole. For instance, in the UK, the Financial Services Authority's "non-zero failure" approach, in the early 2000s, meant that individual financial institutions were allowed to fail where this did not cause disruption to the rest of the financial system.[23] Now, the PRA is following this approach and assesses the potential impact of firms, i.e. the significance of a firm to the stability of the UK financial system in order to determine the intensity of its supervisory activity.[24]

Micro-macro prudential policies differ not only in their objectives but also in their conception of the functioning of the economy. The macroprudential policy setter views system outcomes as critically determined by the collective

---

[19]   C Borio, "Towards A Macroprudential Framework for Financial Supervision and Regulation" (2003) BIS Working Paper No 128, 2.

[20]   M Dewatripont and J Tirole, *The Prudential Regulation of Banks* (MIT Press, 1994), 31–32 on the representation hypothesis. Inability or unwillingness of depositors to properly monitor their banks' risk taking, inter alia, due to asymmetric information, results in agency problems; S Hanson, A Kashyap and J Stein, "A Macroprudential Approach to Financial Regulation" (2011) 25(1) Journal of Economic Perspectives 3, 4–5.
       See also M Dewatripont, J Rochet and J Tirole, "Introduction" in M Dewatripont, J Rochet and J Tirole (eds), *Balancing the Banks Global Lessons from the Financial Crisis* (Princeton University Press, 2015), 3–5.

[21]   On the forms of negative externalities see Chapter 1.
       See also J Giese and others, "How Could Macro-prudential Policy Affect Financial System Resilience and Credit? Lessons from the Literature" [2013] Bank of England Financial Stability Paper 21, 5.

[22]   Borio (2003) (n 19), 2; FSB, IMF, BIS, "Elements of Effective Macroprudential Policies Lessons from International Experience" (2016) Report to G20, 4; IMF (2011) (n 16), 7.

[23]   UK Parliament House of Commons Treasury Select Committee, "Financial Regulation: A Preliminary Consideration of the Government's Proposals", Seventh Report of Session 2010–11, para 87 on p 33.

[24]   The Prudential Regulation Authority's Approach to Banking Supervision (October 2018), 6 emphasising that "Prudential regulation is necessary to address the risks that firms can pose more widely to the stability of the system."

behaviour of individual institutions ("endogenous") while the micro-prudential policy setter regards those outcomes as given to the individual institutions ("exogenous").[25] These differing conceptions may result in a logical contradiction between micro and macroprudential policies. The micro-prudential dimension views systemic failures as a consequence of domino effects triggered by the failure of individual institutions for idiosyncratic reasons. According to this view, by monitoring banks' performance, the micro-prudential supervisor can prevent banks from engaging in excessive risk-taking in the best interest of depositors who are unable or unwilling to monitor these risks.[26] The old dictum that followed from this conception was that "the whole financial system is sound if and only if each institution is sound".[27]

Following the 2007–2009 financial crisis, this dictum has been called into question. It is acknowledged that actions that may seem desirable from the perspective of individual institutions can result in dysfunctional outcomes at the system-wide level.[28] For example, in stress situations, when asset prices begin falling, prudent financial institutions will sell their assets, causing spirals of sale and further price drop. From a system-wide view, this behaviour, though individually prudent, jeopardises the stability of the financial system.[29]

2.1.2. Potential Conflict between Micro- and Macroprudential Instruments

As discussed in Chapter 6, micro and macroprudential policies often use the same instruments albeit with different objectives and in a different way.[30] This may result in misalignment and conflict between their respective instruments.

---

[25] Borio (2003) (n 19), 15.

[26] J Carmassi and S Micossi, *Time to Set Banking Regulation Right* (Centre for European Policy Studies, 2012), 2.

[27] A Crockett, "Marrying the Micro and Macro-prudential Dimension of Financial Stability" (Eleventh International Conference of Banking Supervisors, Basel, 20–21 September 2000) opposed this truism; S Morris and H Shin, "Financial Regulation in a System Context" [2008] Brookings Papers on Economic Activity No 2, 229.

[28] This was not a new recognition but rather a rediscovery (Chapter 1).
See also Borio (2003) (n 19); Borio, Furfine and Lowe, "Procyclicality of the Financial System and Financial Stability: Issues and Policy Options" (2001) BIS Paper No 1, 10; S Cecchetti, "The Future of Financial Intermediation and Regulation" (1999) 5(8) Federal Reserve Bank of New York Current Issues in Economics and Finance 1.

[29] Margin calls are clearly rationale from a micro-prudential perspective but could be hazardous from a macroprudential perspective when resulting in fire sales. During crisis, a micro-prudential supervisor would want to increase margins and collateral whilst macroprudential authority would want to decrease them to avoid fire sales. J Danielsson, M Fouché and R Macrae, "The Macro-Micro Conflict" (20 October 2015) VOX, CEPR's Policy Portal, available at <http://www.voxeu.org/article/macro-micro-conflict>.

[30] Though it is to be noted that the macroprudential policy toolkit extends beyond the traditional micro-prudential tools and encompasses tools borrowed from other areas of economic policies. See J Osinski, K Seal and L Hoogduin, "Macroprudential and Microprudential Policies: Toward Cohabitation" (2013) IMF Staff Discussion Note 5, 23

First, the policies' respective instruments differ in the contingents for their application. Macroprudential instruments aim to correct externalities arising from the actions of financial institutions. Consequently, these instruments do not depend on the institutions' characteristics taken in isolation (as in micro-prudential supervision), but rather on the aggregate behaviour of all institutions (financial cycle) and/or the position of an individual institution within the financial system (i.e. its systemic importance).[31]

Second, the policies' respective instruments may differ in the timings of their application resulting in their possible misalignment.[32] Capital requirement is an intuitive illustration of this potential conflict. As discussed in Chapter 6, as part of the macroprudential policy toolkit, capital requirements are designed to be higher during periods of booms (so as to limit the accumulation of financial imbalances) and lower during busts (to avoid fire sales). In contrast, the micro-prudential capital requirement is designed to be lower in booms and higher in busts in order to preserve the soundness of individual financial institutions.[33] The tension between the respective policies is most stark during the bust period. Then, a macroprudential authority would want to release capital buffers to prevent excessive deleveraging but this may have a negative effect for weaker financial institutions and can be problematic from a micro-perspective.[34]

Highlighting the possible conflicts between the respective objectives and instruments of micro- and macroprudential policies should not mask the principle that macroprudential supervision is a complementary policy to micro-prudential supervision. Those policies coexist in the current supervisory

---

(Annex 1); FSB, IMF, BIS, "Macroprudential Policy Tools and Frameworks" (February and October 2011) Report to the G20; Bank of England, "Instruments of Macro prudential Policy" (December 2011) Discussion Paper; E Nier and others, "Key Aspect of Macroprudential Policy" (IMF, 2013), 8.

[31]   De Nicolò and others, "Externalities and Macroprudential Policy" (2012) IMF Staff Discussion Note 5, 11.

[32]   ECB Financial Stability Review May 2014, 136.

[33]   Ibid, 139 suggest that the potential for conflict is likely to materialise mainly (or exclusively) during downturns. Such a conflict may materialise following the UK's exit from the EU. Capital buffers have been building up since financial crisis (Governor of the Bank of England's Statement following the EU Referendum result, 24 June 2016, available at <http://www.bankofengland.co.uk/publications/Pages/news/2016/056.aspx>) but while the FPC may want to lower these buffers to stimulate lending in the economy, the PRA may want to raise them.

[34]   Osinski and others (2013) (n 30), 15. The tension between micro- and macroprudential policies on the implementation of prudential tools is not an abstract one. For instance, the prudential supervisory authority in Switzerland (Swiss Financial Market Supervisory Authority or FINMA) has openly opposed the proposal of the central bank (Swiss National Bank or SNB) to activate CCyB as a macroprudential tool. SNB, "Implementing the Countercyclical Capital Buffer in Switzerland: Concretising the Swiss National Bank's Role" (Berne, February 2014); FINMA Press Release "FINMA to Oversee Sector-specific Countercyclical Capital Buffer" (13 February 2013). Similar opposition was found in Sweden. See also C Borio, "Macroprudential Frameworks: (Too) Great Expectations" in D Schoenmaker, *Macroprudentialism* (VOxEU.org, CEPR Press, 2014), 39.

framework (at times, even under the same agency) and there is a manifest need to strengthen both policies in a way that promotes their synergies.

2.1.3. Should there be a Hierarchy of Micro- and Macroprudential Objectives?

The view of micro and macroprudential policies as coexisting policies rather than hierarchical can be found in several policy documents of international standard-setting bodies.[35] However, where a conflict emerges and cannot be easily alleviated,[36] this approach may face practical impediments and is far from being a universal one. A contesting view, therefore, advocates a hierarchy of objectives. Schoenmaker and Weirts, for instance, suggest that the stability of the system (and equally, monetary policy) is more important than the soundness of its individual components and thus, that macroprudential policy should take precedence over micro-prudential policy.[37] As such, when a large unexpected stock market drop occurs, capital adequacy rules may be temporarily lifted to avoid fire sales that can be devastating from a system-wide perspective.[38] Osinski and others, however, warn that a macroprudential override should only be considered in exceptional circumstances otherwise it would risk gradually breaking down the international consensus on minimum micro-prudential

---

[35] PO Mulbert, "Managing Risk in the Financial System", Chapter 14 in N Moloney, E Ferran and J Payne (eds), *The Oxford Handbook of Financial Regulation* (Oxford University Press, 2015), 392 referring to support this contention, inter alia, to IOSCO, "Objectives and Principles of Securities Regulation" (2010), 3 outlining the three objectives of securities regulation: protecting investors; ensuring that markets are fair, efficient and transparent and reducing systemic risk; BCBS, "Core Principles for Effective Banking Supervision" (2012), 2 emphasising "the importance of applying a system-wide, macro perspective to the microprudential supervision of banks to assist in identifying, analysing and taking pre-emptive action to address systemic risk".

See also Osinski and others (2013) (n 30), 5; K Alexander, "The Role of Capital in Supporting Banking Stability", Chapter 12 in N Moloney, E Ferran and J Payne (eds), *The Oxford Handbook of Financial Regulation* (Oxford University Press, 2015) suggesting on p 348 that "Despite the enthusiasm for macro-prudential regulation … The micro-prudential approach will continue therefore to be important- if not primary- and serve as foundation for prudential financial regulation".

[36] For instance, via micro-prudential supervisors choosing to activate alternative micro measures which are less damaging at the macro level. D Schoenmaker, D Gros, S Langfield and M Pagano, "Allocating Macro-prudential Powers" (2014) Reports of the ESRB Advisory Scientific Committee No 5, 10. These conflicts are likely to become more prominent in coming years. See Danielsson, Fouché and Macrae (2015) (n 29).

[37] In their view, monetary policy is on an equivalent level to macroprudential policy. D Schoenmaker and P Wierts, "Macroprudential Policy: The Need for a Coherent Policy Framework" (July 2011) Duisenberg School of Finance Policy Paper No 13; J Kremers and D Schoenmaker, "Twin Peaks: Experiences in the Netherlands" (2010) LSE Financial Markets Group Special Paper No 196. But see J Danielsson and R Macrae, "The Hierarchy of Financial Policies", 12 September 2018, available at <voxeu.org> who argue that in the battle between micro- and macro "the micro authority has more power than the macro authority."

[38] ESRB ASC (2014) (n 36), 10.

requirements.[39] In addition, a macroprudential override could impinge on the discretion and potentially the independence of the micro-prudential authorities.[40]

Until a more solid body of evidence on the interaction between policies is gathered, it is perhaps wiser to resort to a softer mode of coordination that does not risk negating the importance of other policy areas. If, however, there is an override mechanism in place, it should be guided by a clear strategy and be reversible.[41]

2.2. INTERACTIONS BETWEEN MACROPRUDENTIAL AND MONETARY POLICIES

The interaction between macroprudential policy and monetary policy is probably the most wide-ranging and intense. It encompasses interaction through the dominant institutional model of macroprudential authorities that often gives a central role to central banks (Chapter 3) and extends to interaction via their respective objectives and transmission channels.

This close and unavoidable interaction is primarily a result of the link between financial stability and monetary policy. There is a consensus that in the long-run price stability and financial stability tend to mutually reinforce each other.[42] By eliminating inflation-related distortions in financial markets, price stability contributes to financial stability.[43] At the same time, financial stability ensures an orderly functioning of the transmission mechanism of monetary policy and enables the central bank to accomplish its mandate of price stability.[44] Moreover, the link between monetary policy and financial stability is inherent to the tasks of central banks, given their typical key role in overseeing the payments and settlement systems, analysing macroeconomic and financial vulnerabilities and acting as a lender-of-last-resort.

---

[39] Osinski and others (2013) (n 30), 20. There is, however, a case to allow an override where national micro-prudential supervisors apply requirement above the international agreed minimum standards.

[40] Ibid, 20–21. Though one way to resolve this tension is to allow for exceptions to the override.

[41] ESRB ASC (2014) (n 36), 10.

[42] The ultimate goal of both policies is to increase welfare, providing the foundations for maximum sustainable and stable real growth. S Cecchetti and M Kohler, "When Capital Adequacy and Interest Rate Policy are Substitutes (and When they Are Not)" (May 2012) BIS Working Paper 379; IMF, "The Interaction of Monetary and Macroprudential Policies" (January 2013), available at <http://www.imf.org/external/np/pp/eng/2013/012913.pdf>, para 27.

[43] A Schwartz, "Why Financial Stability Depends on Price Stability" (1995) 15(4) Economic Affairs 21, 24; C Borio and P Lowe, "Asset Prices, Financial and Monetary Stability: Exploring the Nexus" (2002) BIS Working Paper 114.

[44] J Stark, "Financial Stability-The Role of Central Banks A New Task? A New Strategy? New Tools?" BIS Review 146; L Papademos, "Price Stability, Financial Stability and Efficiency, and Monetary policy" BIS Review 64.

The 2007–2009 financial crisis exposed, however, an even more dynamic and complex interrelation between financial stability and monetary policy. The idea that trade-offs between macroprudential and monetary policies may occur is presented openly and frequently in academic and policy discussions and does not seem to contradict the axiom that these policies enjoy full autonomy.[45] Thus, it is argued that the division between macroprudential and monetary policies can no longer be said to be static and sharp but rather fluid and at times, adjustable. The following section seeks to validate this proposition and to explore interlinks between macroprudential and monetary policies through their respective objectives and transmission mechanisms.

2.2.1. Interaction via Respective Objectives: Complementarities or Rivals?

The primary objective of a monetary policy setter is typically set in terms of price stability.[46] Inflation targeting, with a two-year horizon, has become the dominant framework within which central banks formulate their monetary policy decisions and maintain price stability.[47] By the late 1990s, the firm commitment of central banks to price stability and inflation targeting was

---

[45]   P Grauwe and D Gros, "A New Two-Pillar Strategy for the ECB" (October 2009) CESifo Working Paper 2818; D Beau, L Clerc and B Mojon, "Macro-prudential Policy and the Conduct of Monetary Policy" Banque the France Paper (January 2012); IMF, "The Interaction of Monetary and Macroprudential Policies" (January 2013), available at <http://www.imf.org/external/np/pp/eng/2013/012913.pdf>, 12 (Box 3); O Issing, "Monetary Policy and Financial Stability-Is There a Trade-Off?" (BIS Conference, "Monetary Stability, Financial Stability and Business Cycle", Basel, 28–29 March 2003).

[46]   BIS, "The Evolution of Central Banking" (BIS 67th Annual Report, Basel, 9 June 1997), 140; C Cottarelli and C Giannini, "Credibility without Rules? Monetary Frameworks in the Post-Bretton Woods Era" (1997) IMF Occasional Paper 154; W White, "Changing Views on How Best to Conduct Monetary Policy" BIS Speeches, 18 October 2002. More recently, however, C Goodhart, *The Regulatory Response to the Financial Crisis* (Edward Elgar, 2009), 34 views "price stability" as the first core purpose (CP1) of monetary policy while maintaining financial stability as CP2. Also, according to the IMF, "Monetary Policy and Financial Stability" (September 2015), available at <http://www.imf.org/external/np/pp/eng/2015/082815a.pdf>, 44 "almost all advanced country monetary policy regimes focus on price stability as the primary mandate with financial stability often defined as a secondary objective … An exception is the U.K., where financial stability is defined as an explicit legal objective of the Bank of England. In practice, many of these central banks do already incorporate financial stability considerations in their monetary policy frameworks."

[47]   BIS, "Perspectives on Inflation Targeting, Financial Stability and the Global Crisis" (March 2010) BIS Paper 51; G Hammond, "State of the Art of Inflation" (2012) Bank of England Centre for Central Banking Studies Handbook 29; O Blanchard, G Dell'Ariccia and P Mauro, "Rethinking Macroeconomic Policy" (2010) 42 Journal of Money, Credit and Banking 199; B Bernanke and others, *Inflation Targeting: Lessons from the International Experience* (Princeton University Press, 1999), 10–25. But see Transcript of Federal Reserve Chairman Bernanke's Press Conference, 25 January 2012, available at <http://www.federalreserve.gov/mediacenter/files/FOMCpresconf20120125.pdf>, 23 and O Issing, "In search of Monetary Stability: The Evolution of Monetary Policy Some Reflections" (7th BIS Annual Conference, 26–27 June 2008).

backed by a strong consensus and deeply rooted credibility.[48] It became broadly acknowledged that an inflationary environment can undermine economic growth, may lead to financial instability and even bring other psychological costs associated with its arbitrary redistribution character.[49] Not surprisingly, the long period of the Great Moderation that followed the global inflationary stage was partly attributed to the successful anchoring of inflation around the globe.[50]

The consensus on the need to ensure price stability and tame inflation was complemented by the view that central banks safeguard financial stability best by maintaining price stability.[51] This approach maintained a clear dichotomy between monetary policy and financial stability and came to be known as the Jackson Hole consensus.[52] According to this view, asset markets are efficient at distributing and pricing risks and even though they might be subject to bouts of "exuberance" on the part of investors (bubbles) there is little monetary policy could do about them. Central banks should, therefore, only respond to asset prices and financial imbalances to the extent that they affect the shorter-term inflation forecast.[53] After the bubble bursts, central banks can "mop up" and inject liquidity to avoid a macroeconomic meltdown.

---

[48]   C Borio and W White, "Whither Monetary and Financial Stability? The Implications of Evolving Policy Regime" in *Monetary Policy and Uncertainty: Adapting to a Changing Economy*, 131–211 ("Monetary Policy and Uncertainty-Adapting to a Changing Economy", Jackson Hole, 28–30 August 2003).

It originated from the recognition of the absence of a long-run trade-off between inflation and unemployment during the global inflationary phase. M Friedman, "The Role of Monetary Policy" (1968) 57(1) American Economic Review 1; M Friedman, "Nobel Lecture: Inflation and Unemployment" (1977) 85(3) Journal of Political Economy 451.

[49]   M Bordo, "Sound Money and Sound Financial Policy" (2000) 18(2) Journal of Financial Services Research 129; M Bordo, M Dueker and D Wheelock, "Aggregate Price Shocks and Financial Instability: An Historical Analysis" (2000) NBER Working Paper No 7652; R Shiller, "Why Do People Dislike Inflation?" (1996) NBER Working Paper 5539.

[50]   The period from the mid-1980s to 2007. B Bernanke, "The Great Moderation" (2004) BIS Review 12; C Bean, "The Great Moderation, the Great Panic and the Great Contraction" (2010) 8(2–3) European Economic Association Journal 289.

[51]   A Schwartz, "Why Financial Stability Depends on Price Stability" (1995) 15(4) Economic Affairs 21.

[52]   Known as the "benign neglect". Bank of Kansas City Symposium, "New Challenges for Monetary Policy" (Jackson Hole, 26–28 August, 1999); Bean and others, "Monetary Policy after the Fall" (Bank of Kansas City Annual Conference, Jackson Hole, 28 August 2010); F Mishkin, "Monetary Policy Strategy: Lessons from the Crisis" ("Monetary Policy Revisited: Lessons from the Crisis", Frankfurt, 18–19 November 2010).

[53]   BS Bernanke and M Gertler, "Monetary Policy and Asset Volatility" (1999) 84(4) FRBKC Economic Review Quarter 4, 17–51; B Bernanke and M Gertler, "Should Central Banks Respond to Movements in Asset Prices?" 91(2) American Economic Review (113th Annual Meeting, American Economic Association, May 2001), 253; D Kohn, "Monetary Policy and Asset Prices" (Monetary Policy: A Journey from Theory to Practice, Frankfurt, 16 March 2006); J Yellen, "Monetary Policy and Financial Stability" (Michel Camdessus Central Banking Lecture, IMF, Washington DC, 2 July 2014).

The 2007–2009 financial crisis turned black and white into grey and brought to the fore the idea that a dichotomous view of monetary policy and financial stability may be flawed. Nonetheless, to draw an accurate portrait, the recognition of an implicit financial stability ingredient in the monetary policy objective was not completely new. It previously emerged in the form of "leaning against the wind" principle[54] entailing the idea that central banks should lean against the build-up of imbalances and raise interest rates even if near-term inflation pressures remain subdued.[55] Academics and policy setters have long been divided on the necessity and effectiveness of this principle and the debate is continuing vigorously.[56]

In the years that followed the financial crisis, the voice of those calling for monetary policy to explicitly take into account, to varying degrees, financial stability considerations was growing louder.[57] A moderate view suggests that

---

[54]   W White, "Is Price Stability Enough?" (2006) BIS Working Paper 205; P Angelini, S Neri and F Panneta, "Monetary and Macro-prudential Policies" (2010) Bank of Italy Discussion Paper 801; S Cecchetti, H Genberg and S Wadhwani, "Asset Prices in a Flexible Inflation Targeting Framework" in W Hunter, W Kaufman and M Pomerleano (eds), *Asset Price Bubbles: Implications for Monetary, Regulatory and International Policies* (MIT Press, 2002), 427; Borio and Lowe (2002) (n 43); A Filardo, "Monetary Policy and Asset Price Bubbles: Calibrating the Monetary Policy Trade-offs" (June 2004) BIS Working Paper 155; S Cecchetti and others, "Asset Prices and Central Bank Policy" (July 2000) Geneva Reports on the World Economy 2.

[55]   By lengthening the inflation targeting horizon and paying more attention to risks to the outlook. C Borio, "Monetary and Prudential Policies at a Crossroads: New Challenges in the New Century" (2006) BIS Working Paper 216.

[56]   Blanchard and others (2010) (n 47); P Catte and others, "The Role of Macroeconomic Policies in the Global Crisis" (2011) 33 Journal of Policy Modelling 787 provide evidence that if, prior to the global financial crisis, monetary and macroprudential instruments operated in tandem (tighter monetary policy and countercyclical tools) the US housing boom could have been dampened; L Gambacorta and F Signoretti, "Should Monetary Policy Lean Against the Wind? An Analysis Based on A DSGE Model with Banking" (2012) BIS Working Paper 418; Ø Olsen, "Integrating Financial Stability and Monetary Policy Analysis" (Systemic Risk Centre, London School of Economics, London, 27 April 2015). But more recently see T Kockerols and C Kok, "Leaning Against the Wind: Macroprudential Policy and the Financial Cycle" (2019) ECB Working Paper Series No 2223; I Agur, "Monetary and Macroprudential Policy Coordination Among Multiple Equilibria" (2018) IMF Working Paper 235 show that, under certain conditions, leaning could in fact worsen outcome of both monetary and macroprudential policies; L Svensson, "Cost-benefit Analysis of 'Leaning Against the Wind': Are costs Larger also with Less Effective Macroprudential Policy?", 12 January 2016, available at <voxeu.org> CEPR Policy Portal.

[57]   M Shirakawa, "Some Thoughts on Incentives at Micro- and Macro-level for Crisis Prevention" (8th BIS Annual Conference, Basel, 26 June, 2009); J Trichet, "Credible Alertness Revisited"; M Carney, "Some Considerations on Using Monetary Policy to Stabilize Economic Activity" both presented at (Financial Stability and Macroeconomic Policy, Jackson Hole, 22 August 2009); W White, "Should Monetary Policy 'Lean or Clean'" (August 2009) Dallas Fed Working Paper 34; B Bernanke, "Monetary Policy and the Housing Bubble" (American Economic Association, Atlanta, 3 January 2009); P Bloxham, C Kent and M Robson, "Asset Prices, Credit Growth, Monetary and Other Policies: An Australian Case Study" (2010) RBA Discussion Paper 6; A Cagliarini, C Kent and G Stevens, "Fifty Years of Monetary

monetary policy decision-makers should monitor a broad range of financial conditions and variables (such as lending, asset prices or leverage) in order to ensure price stability.[58] A more radical view suggests that since monetary policy is intrinsically linked to financial stability, under certain circumstances, it should be responsive to the build-up of financial imbalances and increase interest rates when asset prices are surging.[59]

Either pursuing the "leaning against the wind" principle, the moderate adjusted Jackson Hole view or the more radical approach which blurs the boundaries between monetary and macroprudential policies, it can be concluded that financial stability considerations are an essential ingredient in monetary policy and should be taken into account to ensure price stability in the long run.[60]

The resulting interrelation between monetary policy and macroprudential policy is, however, far from being settled and is still open for debate.[61] Often scholars emphasise the complementary (and equal) nature of macroprudential policy and monetary policy with financial stability as a common ground,[62] but

---

Policy: What Have We Learned?" (RBA's 50th Anniversary Symposium, Sydney, 9 February 2010); C Borio and P Disyatat, "Global Imbalances and Financial Crises: Link or No Link?" (2011) BIS Working Paper 346; C Borio, "Rediscovering the Macroeconomic Roots of Financial Stability Policy: Journey, Challenges and a Way Forward" (2011) BIS Working Paper 354; P Praet, "The (Changing) Role of Central Banks in Financial Stability Policy" (14th Annual Intl Banking Conference, Chicago Fed, 10 November 2011); O Issing, "Lessons for Monetary Policy: What Should the Consensus Be?" (2011) Centre for Financial Studies Working Paper 13; F Smets, "Financial Stability and Monetary Policy: How Closely Interlinked?" (2014) 10(2) International Journal of Central Banking 263.
But see L Svensson, "Monetary Policy Tradeoffs in CESEE" (Vienna, 24 November 2014); Sveriges Riksbank, "The Effects of Monetary Policy on Household Debt" Monetary Policy Report, February 2014; J Galí, "Monetary policy and Rational Asset Price Bubbles" (2014) 104(3) American Economic Review 751.

[58]   Smets (2014) (n 57) refers to this approach as "a modified Jackson Hole Consensus", 269.
       See also F Munoz and K Schmidt-Hebbe, "Do the World's Central Banks React to Financial Markets?" ("Financial Deepening, Macro-Stability and Growth in Developing Countries", September 2012); Y Merch, "Financial-Stability Policies in a Post-crisis World" (Czech National Bank, 4 March 2013); L Christiano and others, "Two Reasons Why Money and Credit May Be Useful in Monetary Policy" (4th ECB Central Banking Conference, Frankfurt, 9–10 November 2006); M Woodford, "Financial Intermediation and Macroeconomic Analysis" (2010) 24(4) Journal of Economic Perspectives 21; D Gray and others, "Incorporating Financial Sector Risk into Monetary Policy Models: Application to Chile" (2011) IMF Working Paper 228.
[59]   Borio (2011) (n 57); Trichet (2009) (n 57).
[60]   This does not imply a dual mandate of price stability and financial stability that could bring about other challenges and inefficiencies. See, for instance, U Kenichi and F Valencia, "Central Bank Independence and Macro-prudential Regulation" (2012) IMF Working Paper 101.
[61]   I Agur and M Demertzis, "Will Macroprudential Policy Counteract Monetary Policy's Effects on Financial Stability?" (2018) Bruegel Working Paper 1, 20.
[62]   Schoenmaker and Wierts (2011) (n 37); Caruana (2011) (n 16); O Canuto and M Cavallari, "Integrating Monetary Policy and Macroprudential Regulation", 21 May 2013, available at <voxeu.org>.

other scholars attribute a hierarchy with macroprudential, surprisingly, located at the bottom.[63]

2.2.2. Interaction via Transmission Mechanisms

Macroprudential and monetary policies operate through closely related variables, such as interest rates and credit supply.[64] These variables play a key role in the transmission mechanisms of monetary policy and consequently, macroprudential policy choices may have a direct impact on the transmission mechanisms of monetary policy.[65] For instance, prior to the 2007–2009 financial crisis, a large proportion of borrowers had high LTV mortgages.[66] Following a sharp fall in house prices, these borrowers were not able to refinance their loans and could not take advantage of an accommodative monetary policy and lower mortgage rates that followed. In other words, the transmission of lower monetary policy rates on conditions in mortgage markets was clogged-up during the downturn. Implementing macroprudential measures that limit the quantity of lending, such as LTV ratio limitation, during the upswing could have had a positive impact on the transmission of monetary policy during the downturn.[67]

Similarly, monetary policy choices may have implications for the stability of the financial system. A prolonged period of low interest rates can stimulate

---

63   Danielsson and Macrae (2018) (n 37) suggest that "when the objectives of ex-ante macropru are different than those of monetary policy, perhaps on interest rates or liquidity creation, the direct and immediate benefits from monetary policy are likely to trump the more distant advantage of reducing systemic risk, and particularly so when a macropru authority wishes to take a politically unattractive preventative stance." The authors contend that the hierarchy between monetary and macroprudential policy reflects, amongst other things, the democratic legitimacy of the policy, but it can be debated whether legitimacy should be the benchmark to determining the hierarchy of objectives and whether this is a statement of existing priorities or a normative contention.

64   MPC, "Transmission Mechanism of Monetary Policy", Bank of England Quarterly Bulletin, May 1999; "The Role of Banks in Monetary Policy Transmission Mechanism" (August 2008) ECB Monthly Bulletin; BCBS, "The Policy Implication of Transmission Channels between the Financial System and the Real Economy" (2012) Working Paper 20; H Shin, "Macroprudential Tools, Their Limits and their Connection with Monetary Policy" ("Rethinking Macro Policy III: Progress or Confusion?", IMF Conference, 15 April 2015).

65   For a schematic illustration of monetary policy transmission channels, see <http://www.ecb.europa.eu/mopo/intro/transmission/html/index.en.html>.
S Kim and A Mehrotra, "Effects of Monetary and Macroprudential Policies – Evidence from Four Inflation Targeting Economies" (2018) 50(5) Journal of Money, Credit and Banking 967 show that macroprudential policies used to contain credit growth also have a significant negative impact on macroeconomic aggregates such as real GDP and the price level; B Richter, M Schularick and I Shim, "The Macroeconomic Effects of Macroprudential Policy" (2018) BIS Working Paper No 740.

66   LTV is the ratio of the loan value to the underlying collateral (property) value and a cap on it ensures that if the borrower defaults, the collateral value is sufficient to cover the loan. See Chapter 6.

67   IMF, "The Interaction of Monetary and Macroprudential Policies" (January 2013), para 33.

excessive risk-taking by banks (the so-called "risk-taking channel"),[68] contribute
to the build-up of financial imbalances and increase systemic fragility.[69] There
is ample evidence to suggest that keeping nominal interest rates at historically
low levels in the period leading up to the 20072009 financial crisis contributed
to excessive credit growth and resulted in asset price bubbles.[70] The more
unconventional monetary policy measures, such as large-scale asset-purchase
programs (quantitative easing) and relaxation of collateral rules,[71] could also
negatively affect financial stability through exacerbating shortages of safe assets
and increased assets encumbrance.[72]

---

[68]   C Borio and H Zhu, "Capital Regulation, Risk-taking and Monetary Policy: A Missing Link
       in the Transmission Mechanism?" (2008) BIS Working Paper 268; Y Altunbas, L Gambacorta
       and D Marques-Ibanez, "Does Monetary Policy Affect Bank Risk Taking?" (2010) BIS
       Working Paper 298; De Nicolò and others, "Monetary Policy and Bank Risk-Taking" (2010)
       IMF Staff Position Note 9; T Adrian and H Shin, "Capital Flows and Risk-Taking Channel of
       Monetary Policy" (11th BIS Annual Conference, 22–23 June 2012).
       Looser monetary policy may encourage a "search for yield". R Rajan, "Has Financial
       Development Made the World Riskier?" (Greenspan Era: Lessons for the Future, Jackson
       Hole, 27 August 2005), 313; S Hason and J Stein, "Monetary Policy and Long-Term Real
       Rates" (2014) Harvard Business School Working Paper 9; P Tucker, "National Balance Sheets
       and Macro Policy: Lessons from the Past" (Business Economists Society, 28 February 2012)
       and more recently, M Neuenkirch and M Nöckel, "The Risk-taking Channel of Monetary
       Policy Transmission in the Euro Area" (2018) 93 Journal of Banking and Finance 71.

[69]   G Jiminez and others, "Hazardous Times for Monetary Policy: What Do Twenty-three Million
       Loans Say About The Effects of Monetary Policy on Credit Risk-Taking" (2008) Banco de
       Espana Working Paper 833; A Maddaloni and J Peydró, "Bank Risk-Taking, Securitisation,
       Supervision and Low Interest Rates: Evidence from Lending Standards" (2010) ECB Working
       Paper 1248; D Diamond and G Raghuram, "Illiquid Banks, Financial Stability and Interest
       Rate Policy" (2011) NEBR Working Paper 16994; D Marqués-Ibáñez and L Gambacorta,
       "The Bank Lending Channel: Lessons from the Crisis" (2011) ECB Working Paper 1335.

[70]   C Bean and others, "Low for Long? Causes and Consequences of Persistently Low Interest
       Rates" (2015) Geneva Report on the World Economies; J Taylor, "The Financial Crisis and the
       Policy Responses: An Empirical Analysis of What Went Wrong" (2009) NBER Working Paper
       14631; M Obstfeld and K Rogoff, "Global Imbalances and the Financial Crisis" (2009) CEPR
       Discussion Paper Series 7606; S Dubeck and others, "Fuzzy Capital Requirements, Risk-
       Shifting and the Risk Taking Channel of Monetary Policy" (2009) Bank of France Working
       Paper 254; P Kannan, P Rabanal and A Scott, "Macroeconomic Pattern and Monetary Policy
       in the Run-up to Asset Price Bust" (2009) IMF Working Paper 252. But see B Bernanke,
       "Monetary Policy and the Housing Market" (American Economic Association Annual
       Meeting, Atlanta, 3 January 2010).
       In the Euro area, long-term low interest rates induced banks to lend to borrowers with a poor
       or no credit history and a high probability of default. A Maddaloni and J Peydro, "Monetary
       Policy, Macroprudential Policy and Banking Stability: Evidence from the Euro Area"
       (2013) 9(1) International Journal of Central Banking 121. And in the US, M Delis, I Hasan
       and N Mylonidis, "The Risk-Taking Channel of Monetary Policy in the USA: Evidence from
       Micro-level Data" (2011) University Library of Munich MPRA Paper 34084.

[71]   These measures proved to be effective in stimulating the economy. Bean and others (2015)
       (n 70), 67–68.

[72]   IMF, "Do Central Banks Policies Since the Crisis Carry Risks to Financial Stability?"
       (April 2013) IMF Financial Stability Report, 97; H Hallett and others, "Extending Quantitative
       Easing: Are there Additional Risks for Financial Stability?" (February 2017) Monetary
       Dialogue In-Depth Analysis European Parliament PE 595.341.

Finally, the impact of central banks' activities on financial stability is not limited to periods leading up to financial crisis but may appear at the "cleaning-up" stage. Liquidity injections may relieve financial instability but can also affect the volatility of the rest of the economy.[73]

2.2.3. Yet, the Scope for Conflict between Macroprudential and Monetary Policies is Minimal

The scope for conflict between macroprudential and monetary policies is rather limited.[74] As already suggested, monetary policy setters, in ensuring their ultimate objective of price stability, have widened their perspective to include financial stability considerations. This resulted in financial stability being, to some extent, a common ground for monetary policy setters with macroprudential policy. One would, therefore, expect to encounter an overlap problem between macroprudential and monetary policies in dealing with financial imbalances. However, it is argued here, that an opposite problem of an "underlap" may occur originating from a possible incentive of each policymaker to shift the responsibility to the other policymaker. The "pass the buck" problem is not a new phenomenon and has been acknowledged in the operation of fiscal and monetary policies.[75] There are good reasons for macroprudential and monetary policies to follow suit. On the one hand, macroprudential authorities are bound to make unpopular decisions and therefore, suffer from an inherent inaction bias (Chapter 3). On the other hand, central banks will exercise caution when stepping in the "financial stability" ground. This tendency is exacerbated by the growing body of empirical research that suggests that interest rate-setting is a blunt tool to deal with credit build-up and that overall, macro-financial imbalances are better addressed by macroprudential instruments.[76] In addition,

---

[73]   G de Walque, O Pierrard and A Rouabah, "Financial (In)stability, Supervision and Liquidity Injections: a Dynamic General Equilibrium Approach" (2008) National Bank of Belgium Working Paper Research 148; E Farhi and J Tirole, "Collective Moral Hazard, Maturity Mismatch and Systemic Bailouts" (2012) 102(1) American Economic Review 60.

[74]   BIS, "Operationalising the Selection and Application of Macro-prudential Instruments" (2012) CGFS Papers 48 suggesting that under some circumstances the tension can be eased by taking a longer time perspective. Similarly see Caruana (2011) (n 16). But the tension is not completely absent. See, for instance, D Martinez-Miera and R Repullo, "Monetary Policy, Macroprudential Policy, and Financial Stability" March 2019 Voxeu.org.

[75]   A Hallett and others, "Macro-prudential Policies and Financial Stability" (2011) 87 Economic Record 277, 318.

[76]   BS Bernanke, "The Effects of the Great Recession on Central Bank Doctrine and Practice" (Federal Reserve Bank of Boston 56th Economic Conference, Boston, Massachusetts, 18 October 2011); Yellen (2014) (n 53). More recently, A Van der Ghote, "Interactions Between Monetary and Macroprudential Policies" (March 2019) ECB Research Bulletin No 56 show that the use of monetary policy to enhance financial stability generates costs in terms of increased inflation variability. But see J Stein, "Overheating in Credit Markets" ("Restoring Household Financial Stability After the Great Recession: Why Household

central banks value greatly their hard-won independence and credibility as monetary policy setters and will not hurry to jeopardise these by encroaching on other policies' territories.

Thus far, concerns over tensions between macroprudential and monetary policies seem to be more potential than real. Macroprudential instruments are generally more selective, sectoral and geographically defined than the main monetary policy tool, lowering the friction between the instruments to a minimum.[77] Nevertheless, where a macroprudential authority is pursuing its first policy pillar aimed at addressing the cyclical dimension of systemic risks (Chapter 1) the concern over tensions may become a real one.[78] Where both policies are trying to constrain the credit creation process a "push-me, pull-you" situation may occur. The macroprudential authority will tighten the availability of credit (for instance, through caps on LTV that limit loans' supply) while the monetary policy setter may offset it by measures that increase the borrowing or spending in the economy (for instance, through lowering interest rates or quantitative easing).[79] Borio has described this potential tension, as "it is a bit like driving by pressing on the accelerator and brake simultaneously – not exactly what is normally recommended."[80]

The potential friction may point to the need for central banks as monetary policy setters to take into account the macroeconomic effects of macroprudential policy and vice versa.[81] But should these policies coordinate? Here, once again there is no universal view. There is empirical evidence to support coordination,

---

Balance Sheets Matter" Federal Reserve Bank St. Louis, 7 February 2013) who highlights an important advantage of monetary policy in that "it gets in all of the cracks."

[77] I Visco, "Key Issues for the Success of Macro-prudential Policies" [2011] BIS Papers 60, 129.

[78] Hence Beau and others (n 45) chose to focus in their study exclusively on the cyclical dimension; S Ingves, "Challenges for the Design and Conduct of Macroprudential Policy" (Bank of Korea-BIS Conference on Macroprudential Reg and Policy, Seoul, 18 January 2011).

[79] Bean and others (2010) (n 52), 22–23.

[80] C Claudio, "Macroprudential Frameworks: (Too) Great Expectations?" (2017) in Schoenmaker (ed), *Macroprudentialism*, A VoxEU.org eBook, CEPR, 29, 41.

Members of the Committee of Economic and Monetary Affairs of the European Parliament (ECON) have voiced their concern, during the ESRB public hearing, regarding the potential for a systemic risk build-up due to the extended period of low interest rate coupled with quantitative easing (for instance, during the hearings on 23 March and 12 November 2015); H Hannoun, "Ultra-low or Negative Interest Rates: What they Mean for Financial Stability and Growth" (BIS, Eurofi High-Level Seminar, Riga, 22 April 2015); ESRB, "Macro-prudential Issues Arising from Low Interest Rate and Structural Changes in the EU Financial System" (November 2016), available at <https://www.esrb.europa.eu/pub/pdf/reports/161128_low_interest_rate_report.en.pdf>.

See also Schoenmaker, Gros, Langfield and Pagano (2014) (n 36), 8, which highlights that "In the euro area, monetary policy is set at the euro area level and macro-prudential policy at the country level; hence, the effects of a loosening of monetary policy may be largely undone in a specific country that chooses to tighten macro-prudential tools."

[81] JL Yellen, "Macro-prudential Supervision and Monetary Policy in the Post-crisis World" (Annual Meeting of the National Association for Business Economics, 11 October 2010).

particularly where monetary and macroprudential policies are determined by separate institutions,[82] but there is also evidence that the benefits of coordination may be very small[83] or that monetary and macroprudential policies should be conducted separately, and that explicit coordination is only warranted in rare situations.[84]

2.3. INTERACTION BETWEEN MACROPRUDENTIAL POLICY AND FISCAL POLICY

Ideally, fiscal and macroprudential policies should be mutually reinforcing. Successful macroprudential policy fosters financial stability by reducing the frequency and intensity of financial crises thus lowering the great fiscal costs associated with them. Conversely, unsustainable public finances and high levels of debt can create a vicious circle and impede the stability of the financial system. The eurozone debt crisis of 2009–2012 demonstrated how a deteriorating fiscal position in a number of Eurozone countries (Greece, Ireland, Portugal, Spain and Cyprus) could induce a re-pricing of sovereign debt and have an adverse impact on the financial system via banks' exposure to government bonds.[85] This, in turn, negatively affected the macro-economy and further weakened public finances and financial markets.[86] More generally, perceptions and expectations of large and on-going budget deficits may trigger a lack of confidence in the

---

82   Beau and others (2012) (n 45); Cecchetti and Kohler (2012) (n 42) conclude that partial harmonisation (where one policymaker moves first and the second one takes into account the policy decision of the first) is inferior to full harmonisation (each policymaker takes the other policymaker's actions into account); P Angelini, S Nicoletti-Altimari and I Visco (2012), "Macroprudential, Microprudential and Monetary Policy: Conflicts, Complimentarities and Trade-offs" [2012] Bank of Italy Occasional Paper 140; IMF (2013) (n 67); E Gerba and C Macchiarelli, "Interaction between Monetary Policy and Bank Regulation: Theory and European Practice" (2015) Systemic Risk Centre Special Paper Series 10. But there is also evidence to suggest that leadership by the macroprudential authority (i.e. it moves before monetary policy) and more frequent monetary policy decisions as follower improves overall social welfare B De Paoli and M Paustian, "Coordinating Monetary and Macroprudential Policies" (2013) Federal Reserve Bank of New York Staff Report No 653, 33.

83   Aikman and others, "Targeting Financial Stability: Macroprudential or Monetary Policy?" (May 2019) ECB Working Paper Series No 2278, 8.

84   This approach presents considerable advantages as each policy becomes more distinct, more transparent and easier to value. L Svensson, "Monetary Policy and Macroprudential Policy: Different and Separate?" (2018) CEPR Discussion Paper No 13043.

85   R Baldwin and others, "Rebooting the Eurozone: Step 1 – Agreeing a Crisis Narrative" (2015) 85 CEPR Policy Insight 1–15. Sovereign debt crises are recurring events, C Reinhart and K Rogoff, *This Time is Different: Eight Centuries of Financial Folly* (PUP, 2009).

86   ECB, "Monetary and Fiscal Policies Interactions in a Monetary Union", ECB Monthly Bulletin July 2012, P Lane, "The European Sovereign Debt Crisis" (2012) 26(3) Economic Perspectives Journal 49.

economic prospects and become a destabilising factor.[87] Furthermore, specific fiscal policy measures, such as taxes and subsidies, can affect incentives to increase leverage and therefore, could have a systemic risk implication.[88] For instance, accommodative tax treatment of mortgage rates may incentivise investments in real estate, leading to a gradual build-up of a bubble and eventually destabilise the financial system.[89] In turn, where the macroprudential toolkit includes different forms of corrective tax, such as taxes on financial institutions[90] or taxes on real estate,[91] it is advisable for the macroprudential authority to consult, prior to their implementation, with the fiscal authority.[92]

2.4. INTERACTION BETWEEN MACROPRUDENTIAL POLICY AND COMPETITION LAW

The interplay between financial stability and competition attracted considerable empirical and theoretical literature long before the emergence of macroprudential regulation and supervision as a distinct policy area. The underlying question considered by academics and policymakers is whether, as a general matter,

---

[87] ECB (July 2012) (n 86); P Hilbers, "Interaction of Monetary and Fiscal Policies: Why Central Bankers Worry About Government Budgets", Chapter 8 in IMF, *Current Developments in Monetary and Financial Law* (2005), Vol 4.

[88] By triggering a shift in financial resources between various investment types. IMF (2011) (n 16), para 82; IMF, "Debt Bias and Other Distortions: Crisis-Related Issues in Tax Policy" (June 2009) IMF Staff Paper.

On tax as a prudential tool: V Acharya and others, "A Tax on Systemic Risk" (Bank Crisis Prevention and Resolution, Duisenberg School of Finance, Amsterdam, 2–3 June 2010); H Shin, "Non-core Liabilities Taxes as a Prudential Tool" Policy Memo Princeton (Seoul Korea, 19 February 2010); B di Mauro, "Taxing Systemic Risk: Proposal for a Systemic Risk Charge and a Systemic Risk Fund" (University of Mainz and German Council of Economic Experts, Deautche Bundesbank, 25 January 2010).

See also HM Treasury, "Risk, Reward and Responsibility: The Financial Sector and Society" (December 2009); S Claessens, M Keen and C Pazarbasioglu, "Financial Sector Taxation" (September 2010) IMF Report to G20.

[89] For instance, in light of the UK buy-to-let market rapid expansion the Chancellor announced an increase in the rates of Stamp Duty Land Tax on purchase of additional residential properties, such as second homes and buy-to-let properties. HM Treasury Consultation, "FPC Powers of Directions in the Buy-to-Let Market" (17 December 2015).

[90] E Carreras, P Davis and R Piggott, "Macroprudential Tools, Transmission and Modelling" (2016) National Institute of Economic and Social Research Discussion Paper No 470; EP Carreras, P Davis and R Piggott, "Assessing Macroprudential Tools in OECD Countries within a Cointegration Framework" (2018) 37 Journal of Financial Stability 113.

[91] See, for instance, F Balfour, "How to Slow Soaring House Prices: Hong Kong and Singapore's Success", *Bloomberg* (31 July 2014); T Poghosyan, "Can Property Taxes Reduce House Price Volatility? Evidence from U.S. Regions" and J Fell, "Real Estate-Related Taxation and Macroprudential Policy: Substitutes or Complements?" Both were presented at the Bank of Lithuania Seminar "Real Estate Taxation and Macroprudential Policy", 1–2 July 2019, available at <https://www.lb.lt/en/events/macroprudential-policy-conference-2019>.

[92] C Goodhart, "The Changing Role of Central Banks" (2010) BIS Working Paper 326, 11.

strong competition between banks is inimical to financial stability.[93] Rather than pointing to a clear-cut trade-off between competition and financial stability the literature exposes complex and mixed effects.[94]

Traditionally, empirical research showed that competition can both improve financial stability and worsen it and that achieving the right balance is an elusive task.[95] Tougher competition reduces the profitability of market players and accordingly, may encourage greater risk-taking to the detriment of financial stability.[96] In addition, intense rivalry amongst banks may reduce their incentives to invest in monitoring the credit risk of their borrowers.[97] Competition may

---

[93]   J Vickers, "Central Banks and Competition Authorities: Institutional Comparisons and New Concerns" (2010) BIS Working Paper No 331.

[94]   T Beck, "Bank Competition and Financial Stability – Friends or Foes?" (2008) World Bank Policy Research Working Paper 4656; X Vives, "Competition Policy in Banking" (2011) 11(3) Oxford Review of Economic Policy 479; Independent Commission on Banking, Final Report Recommendations (London, September 2011), 159 (Box 6.1); L Papademos, "Price Stability, Financial Stability and Efficiency and Monetary Policy" (Monetary Stability Foundation Conference, "Challenges to the Financial System-Ageing and Low Growth", Frankfurt, 7 July 2006).

See also E Carletti and P Hartmann, "Competition and Stability: What Special about Banking?" (2002) ECB Working Paper 146; F Allen and D Gale, "Competition and Financial Stability" (2004) 36(3) Money, Credit and Banking Journal 453; A Berger, L Klapper and R Ariss, "Bank Competition and Financial Stability" (2008) World Bank Working Paper 4696. More recently, see A Kanas, "Bank Competition, Stability, and Intervention Quality" (2019) 24(1) International Journal of Finance and Economics 568; SJA de-Ramon, WB Francis and M Straughan, "Bank Competition and Stability in the United Kingdom" (August 2018) Bank of England Staff Working Paper No 748 show that competition may lower bank stability though overall, the economic significance of such effects is modest. The authors also show that facilitating effective competition may drive improvements in the stability of those firms that are already closer to default but lower the stability of relatively safe firms.

[95]   OECD, "Bank Competition and Financial Stability" (2011), available at <http://www.oecd. org>; Independent Commission on Banking, Final Report Recommendations (London, September 2011), 159; F Allen and D Gale, "Competition and Financial Stability" (2004) 36(3) Journal of Money, Credit and Banking 453.

[96]   A Marcus, "Deregulation and Bank Financial Policy" (1984) 8 Journal of Banking and Finance 557; M Keeley, "Deposit Insurance, Risk and Market Power in Banking" (1990) 80 American Economic Review 1183; E Carletti, P Hartmann and G Spagnolo, "Implications of the Bank Merger Wave for Competition and Stability" (Risk Measurement and Systemic Risk, Third Joint Central Bank Conference, 2002), 38–50; G Jimenez, J Lopez and J Saurina, "How does Competition Impact Bank Risk Taking?" (2007) Bank of Spain Working Paper 1005; Beck (2008) (n 94), 7; M Amidu and S Wolfe, "Bank Competition, Diversification and Financial Stability" (2013) 3(3) Review of Development Finance 152.

Known as the "Competition-Fragility" scholars, e.g. G Dell'Ariccia, D Igan and L Laeven, "Credit Booms and Lending Standards: Evidence from the Sub-prime Mortgage Market" (2008) IMF Working Paper 106 provide evidence that new entrants in the sub-prime market lowered lending standards. For a more recent empirical study, see D Corbae and R Levine, "Competition, Stability, and Efficiency in Financial Markets" ("Changing Market Structure and Implications for Monetary Policy", Jackson Hole, 25 August 2018).

[97]   A Boot and S Greenbaum, "Bank Regulation, Reputation and Rents: Theory and Policy Implications" in C Mayer and X Vives (eds), Capital Markets and Financial Intermediation (Cambridge University Press, 1993), 292–318.

compel banks to pursue aggressive strategies in the hope of achieving good-looking short-term results and attract investors. Excessive competition can, therefore, lead to fragility and restraints on competition may be necessary to preserve the stability of the banking system.[98]

Weak competition, on the other hand, may negatively affect financial stability.[99] With fewer rivals in the market, interconnectedness increases, and each player is more likely to be systemically important, hence increasing the "too-big-to-fail" or "too-important-to-fail" phenomenon. Where market power leads to higher borrowing rates, customers might pursue riskier but more profitable strategies and migrate financial activity to less regulated or unregulated channels resulting in increased systemic risk in the financial system. These observations have led to the conclusion that "both very concentrated markets and very strong competition can be tied to systemic risks, through either concentration risks or a weakening of lending standards".[100]

The entrance of large, well-established technology firms (BigTechs) into the financial services space is probably the most topical example for the potential tension between competition and financial stability. In a recent report, the FSB draws attention to the changes that BigTech companies bring to market structure, the impact on competition and the need to monitor financial stability implications in that sector.[101] The report suggests that BigTechs benefit from established networks and accumulated big data and are, therefore, a significant source of competition with other financial institutions. At the same time, the report warns that this heightened competition could also put pressure on financial institutions' profitability leading to "an inappropriate loosening of lending standards by banks and more risk-taking by other financial institutions in order to maintain margins."[102] Similarly to other interactions discussed earlier in this chapter, a solution for the tension can be found in the form of consultation of the

---

[98]   For instance, Beck (2008) (n 94), 7.

[99]   Known as the "Competition-Stability" view. J Boyd and G De Nicolo, "The Theory of Bank Risk Taking and Competition Revisited" 60(3) (2005) Journal of Finance 1329; J Boyd, G De Nicolo and A Jalal, "Banking Risk-Taking and Competition Revisited: New Theory and New Evidence" (2006) IMF Working Paper 297; M Schaeck and others, "Are More Competitive Banking Systems More Stable?" (2006) IMF Working Paper 143 present evidence that more competitive banking systems are less prone to systemic crises.

[100] FSB, "Fintech and Market Structure in Financial Services Market Developments and Potential Financial Stability Implications" (February 2019), available at <https://www.fsb.org/2019/02/fintech-and-market-structure-in-financial-services-market-developments-and-potential-financial-stability-implications/>, 4.
See also BIS, "Big Tech in Finance: Opportunities and Risks", Chapter 3 in BIS Annual Economic Report, June 2019, 73.

[101] BIS (2019) (n 100), 73.

[102] FSB (2019) (n 100), 18–19.
See also FSB, "BigTech in Finance Market Developments and Potential Financial Stability Implications" (December 2019), available at <https://www.fsb.org/wp-content/uploads/P091219-1.pdf>.

competition authority with the macroprudential authority, where its decision may affect the structure of the financial industry and vice versa.[103] Coordination will ensure the systemic implications, as well as competition implications, are being factored in the policy decisions of the respective authorities.

2.5. INTERACTION BETWEEN MACROPRUDENTIAL POLICY AND CONDUCT-OF-BUSINESS

Conduct-of-business supervision is an independent policy alongside micro and macroprudential policies.[104] It focuses on how financial institutions conduct business with their customers and how they behave in markets, by prescribing rules about appropriate behaviour and monitoring behaviour that can be harmful to customers and to the functioning of markets.[105]

Despite their differing rationales, macroprudential policy and conduct-of-business policy may intersect. The way financial institutions conduct their business has the potential to impact the stability of the financial system from a system-wide view. In other words, where prevailing practices in the conduct-of-business or with consumer protection concerns result in negative externalities to the system as a whole, they may require the intervention of a macroprudential authority. As such, mis-selling of financial products on a large scale (e.g. the Payment Protection Insurance mis-sold in the UK)[106] can lead to a suboptimal allocation of investments and risks and manipulation of financial markets (e.g. the manipulation of LIBOR and foreign exchange benchmark rates)[107] can

---

[103] E Carletti and A Smolenska, "10 Years on From the Financial Crisis: Co-operation Between Competition Agencies and Regulators in the Financial Sector" (December 2017) OECD Working Party No 2 on Competition and Regulation, 10–11.

[104] R Herring and J Carmassi, "The Structure of Cross-Sector Financial Supervision" (2008) 17(1) Financial Markets, Institutions and Instruments 51. This general taxonomy can be broken down to further detailed classification as in D Llewellyn, "Integrated Agencies and the Role of Central Banks" in D Masciandaro (ed), *Handbook of Central banking and Financial Authorities in Europe: New Architectures in the Supervision of Financial Markets* (E Elgar Pub, 2005), 109; J Kremers and D Schoenmaker, "Twin Peaks: Experiences in the Netherlands" (2010) LSE Financial Markets Group Special Paper 196.
The International Organisation of Securities Commissions (IOSCO) defines conduct of business as "principles of conduct which govern the activities of those who provide financial services and which have the objective of protection of the interests of their customers and the integrity of the markets". IOSCO, "International Conduct of Business Principles" (9 July 1990).

[105] D Schoenmaker, "Financial Supervision in the EU" in G Caprio (ed), *Encyclopaedia of Financial Globalization* (Elsevier Amsterdam, 2011); D Llewellyn, "The Economic Rationale for Financial Regulation" (1999) Financial Services Authority Occasional Paper Series in Financial Regulation 1.

[106] EIOPA, "Background Note on Payment Protection Insurance" (28 June 2013).

[107] W Dudley, "Restoring Confidence in Reference Rates" (Salomon Center for the Study of Financial Institutions, NYU Stern School of Business, 2 October 2014).

weaken markets' confidence and impair their functioning.[108] Furthermore, the magnitude of the resulting litigation costs and fines for the misconduct of financial institutions can transform a typical firm-specific risk to a systemic one thus bringing it under the umbrella of the macroprudential authority.[109]

Nonetheless, given their different objectives, the scope for conflict between macroprudential and conduct-of-business policies is limited. It could potentially emerge where the objective of orderly markets and fair treatment of consumers may not coincide with the objective of ensuring the financial stability of the system as a whole. For instance, at times of crisis and in order to preserve public confidence, the macroprudential authority may require lifting certain disclosure requirements imposed on financial institutions. This may be counterproductive to the transparency requirements imposed on these institutions when dealing with their customers as an integral part of the conduct-of-business policy.

The real estate market and the conduct of mortgage business within banks in the UK can provide another constructive example for the potential conflict between macroprudential and conduct-of-business policies. In 2014, the FPC recommended that the PRA and FCA ensure that mortgage lenders limit the issuance of high Loan-to-Income (LTI) mortgage loans.[110] This limitation on borrowing was necessary from a system-wide perspective to contain the build-up of a housing bubble in the UK. However, from a consumer protection point of view, the limitation has the potential to deny responsible borrowers' access to mortgage finance.[111] Indeed, the far-reaching social and political implications of limitations on lending was already discussed in Chapter 6.

3. COORDINATION MECHANISMS: UK, US AND THE EU

3.1. UK: COORDINATION THROUGH HIERARCHY OR COHERENCE?

Prior to the establishment of the FPC, the PRA[112] and the FCA, legislators were mindful of the importance of effective coordination between these new regulatory authorities, observing that "There is a concern that having a

---

[108] M Carney, Opening Statement at the European Parliament's ECON Committee, 7 December 2015.

[109] ESRB, "Report on Misconduct Risk in the Banking Sector", June 2015; A Minto, "Misconduct in Banks: Approaching the Issue from a Systemic Perspective" (2016) 31(2) JIBLR 94.

[110] FPC Recommendation on Loan-To-Income Ratios in Mortgage Lending, 25 June 2014.

[111] The Financial Services Consumer Panel Response to the Consultation of the FPC's Housing Market Tools, 27 November 2014, available at <http://www.fs-cp.org.uk>.

[112] The Bank of England and Financial Services Act 2016, section 13 inserted section 30A BEA 1998 and created the Prudential Regulation Committee (PRC) and integrated the PRA into the Bank of England thus ending the PRA's legal status as a subsidiary company. This brought the PRC onto the same legal footing as the MPC and the FPC.

regulatory structure made up of three separate bodies (FCA, PRA and FPC) will not be efficient and it may be difficult to maintain strong relationships among different bodies".[113] Cross-membership was accordingly designed as a key mechanism to anchoring coordination amongst the FPC and the other regulators. It is to be recalled that within the FPC, six members are from the Bank of England: The Governor and four Deputy Governors for financial stability, markets and banking, monetary policy and prudential regulation (who are also members of the MPC) and the Executive Director for Financial Stability Strategy and Risk.[114] The Chief Executive of the FCA is also a member of the FPC.[115] The members of the PRC include the Governor of the Bank of England; Deputy Governors for Financial Stability, Markets and Banking, Prudential Regulation and Monetary Policy[116] and the Chief Executive of the FCA.[117] In turn, the Bank of England's Deputy Governor for Prudential Regulation (who is also the CEO of the PRA) is a member of the FCA.[118]

The cross-memberships are reinforced by several other coordination mechanisms, as discussed in the following sub-sections.

3.1.1. Coordination of the FPC with the MPC

During the legislative process, the UK Government highlighted that "some macroprudential interventions have a long-time horizon and may be adjusted infrequently, whereas the MPC meets much more regularly".[119] It expected that the MPC would be a "last mover" and adjust its analysis to take account of the likely impact of the most recent action taken by the FPC.[120] Therefore, careful sequencing of FPC and MPC meetings alongside an overlap between the membership of the MPC and the FPC was seen sufficient to manage interactions between monetary and macroprudential policies and avoid any potential conflicts.[121] In addition, in practice, there are established mechanisms to foster

---

[113] The Treasury Select Committee, Twenty-Sixth Report, 10 January 2012, The Financial Conduct Authority, para 81, available at <https://publications.parliament.uk/pa/cm201012/cmselect/cmtreasy/1574/157406.htm>.

[114] Section 9B(1) BEA 1998. The latter as a member appointed by the Governor with the approval of the Chancellor.

[115] Section 9B(1)(c) BEA 1998. For full details of membership and governance of the FPC see Chapter 3.

[116] Section 30A(2) of the BEA 1998. The latter as a member appointed by the Governor of the Bank with the approval of the Chancellor of the Exchequer.

[117] Section 30A(2) (e) BEA 1998. The PRC also consists of at least six members appointed by the Chancellor of the Exchequer. Section 30A(2)(g) BEA 1998.

[118] Section 2(2) of Schedule 1ZA Financial Services Act 2000.

[119] HM Treasury, "A New Approach to Financial Regulation – Building a Stronger System", February 2011, Cm 8012 2.103–2.105.

[120] Ibid.

[121] Ibid.

sharing of relevant information, briefing and analysis across the FPC and MPC. The FPC and MPC members are free to attend the other committee's briefing meetings and have joint discussions on topics of mutual interest.[122]

Most importantly, the FPC and the MPC have regard to the actions of the other committee[123] and their coordination is judged to be performing well "through testing times and is well equipped to address future challenges".[124] In particular, when giving forward guidance on monetary policy, the MPC includes a financial stability "knockout", in which it acknowledges that there might be circumstances when monetary policy settings have to reflect risks to financial stability.[125] To that end, the FPC is committed to alerting the MPC publicly "if the stance of monetary policy poses a significant threat to financial stability that cannot be contained by the substantial range of mitigating policy actions available to the FPC, the FCA and the PRA in a way consistent with their objectives."[126] This approach recognises the important role that monetary policy has to play in mitigating financial stability risks, but only as a last line of defence.[127]

Ensuring that these coordination efforts are open and transparent is also vital. The Chancellor of the Exchequer recommended to the FPC that

> where appropriate, the FPC should note in the records of its meetings, its policy statements and its Financial Stability Reports how it has had regard to the policy

---

[122] Such as the effect of low long-term interest rates and the channels through which adverse economic shocks could arise as a result of Brexit. HM Treasury Remit and Recommendations for the FPC, 29 October 2018, Recommendations as to the Interaction Between Monetary Policy and Macroprudential Policy, available at <https://www.bankofengland.co.uk/-/media/boe/files/letter/2018/governor-letter-051218>.

[123] D Kohn, "Cooperation and Coordination Across Policy Domains" (The Joint Financial Stability Institute and Bank for International Settlements Conference on Supervisory Policy Implementation in the Current Macro-Financial Environment, Basel, 19 September 2017). For instance, Record of the 17 and 25 June 2014 meetings of the FPC: "The Committee also discussed how this package of macroprudential measures (limits on high loan-to income ratio) could be considered to interact with monetary policy. They were intended to act as a complement to monetary policy by insuring against risks arising in specific sectors and therefore seeking to make the central projection in the MPC forecast more precisely".

[124] HM Treasury, Remit for the Monetary Policy Committee, 22 November 2017, available at <https://www.gov.uk/government/uploads/system/uploads/attachment_data/file/661066/PU2118_MPC_Remit_Autumn_Budget_2017_WEB.pdf>.
See also A Spicer and others, "Cultural change in the FCA, PRA and Bank of England: Practising What they Preach", New City Agenda and Cass Business School, August 2016, available at <http://newcityagenda.co.uk/wp-content/uploads/2016/10/NCA-Cultural_Change_in_regulators_report.pdf>, 36.

[125] P Fisher, "Microprudential, Macroprudential and Monetary Policy: Conflict, Compromise or Co-ordination?" (Richmond University, 1 October 2014), available at <https://www.bankofengland.co.uk/-/media/boe/files/news/2014/october/microprudential-macroprudential-and-monetary-policy-conflict-compromise-or-co-ordination>.

[126] Bank of England, "Monetary Policy Trade-offs and Forward Guidance", August 2013, available at <https://www.bankofengland.co.uk/-/media/boe/files/inflation-report/2013/monetary-policy-trade-offs-and-forward-guidance>, 34.

[127] FPC Response to HM Treasury Remit and Recommendations to the FPC, 26 March 2015.

settings and forecasts of the MPC. In the same way, the government remit to the MPC requires it to reflect in any statements on its decisions, the minutes of its meetings and its inflation reports how it has had regard to the policy actions of the FPC.[128]

3.1.2. Coordination of the FPC with the FCA and PRA/PRC

During the legislative process, it was envisaged that the relationship between the FPC and the regulators (FCA and PRA) will take the form of "a collaborative two-way exchange of information, advice and expertise relevant to financial stability."[129] To ensure shared understanding, the PRA and FCA's mandates are aligned with the Bank of England's financial stability objective[130] and the FCA is subject to a requirement to take steps as it considers appropriate to cooperate with the Bank of England in connection with the pursuit by the Bank of its Financial Stability Objective.[131]

The FPC, in turn, is under a duty, so far as it is possible while complying with its objectives, to avoid exercising its functions in a way which would prejudice the advancement by the FCA of any of its operational objectives or the advancement by the PRA of any of its objectives.[132] More generally, the Bank of England, in pursuing the Financial Stability Objective, must aim to work with other relevant bodies including the Treasury and the FCA.[133]

There is also a frequent exchange of information to enhance coordination between the authorities. Staff from the PRA and the FCA brief the FPC on developments that are relevant to financial stability including, as appropriate,

---

[128]   HM Treasury, Recommendations for the FPC as to the Interactions Between Monetary Policy and Macroprudential Policy (2018) (n 122); HM Treasury, Remit to the MPC, 29 October 2018.

[129]   HM Treasury, "A New Approach to Financial Regulation" (n 119), para 2.106.

[130]   One of the operational objectives of the FCA is the integrity objective (section 1B(3)(b) FSMA 2000, as amended by FSMA 2012) and the "integrity" of the UK financial system includes its soundness, stability and resilience (section 1D(2)(1) FSMA 2000, as inserted by FSMA 2012).

With regard to the PRA, according to section 2B(2)–(3) FSMA 2000 its general objective is: promoting the safety and soundness of PRA-authorised persons and this is to be advanced primarily by (a) seeking to ensure that the business of PRA-authorised persons is carried on in a way which avoids any adverse effect on the stability of the UK financial system, and (b) seeking to minimise the adverse effect that the failure of a PRA-authorised person could be expected to have on the stability of the UK financial system.

This similarity is due to recognising the overriding importance of financial stability as a goal of the regulatory system. See HM Treasury, "A New Approach to Financial Regulation" (n 119), para 3.7.

[131]   Section 3Q FSMA 2000. According to section 3Q(2) FSMA 2000, cooperation includes the sharing of information that the FCA is not prevented from disclosing. It is to be noted that the Financial Services Act 2016 amended the section so that it only applies to the FCA.

[132]   Section 9F(2) BEA 1998

[133]   Section 2A(2) BEA 1998.

the position of individual financial institutions[134] and the FPC has asked the PRC, on many occasions, to gather added information on particular activities that could pose a risk to financial stability.[135] Communication also flows in the other direction, with the FPC to provide the PRA and the FCA with advice and expertise on all matters relating to systemic risks to financial stability.[136]

Overall, the UK financial supervisory framework aims to achieve coordination via encouraging a common understanding, coherence and better communication.[137] This is particularly exemplified in the "One Bank, One Mission" strategy, launched in March 2014, which is aimed at creating "a single, unified institution better able to exploit the synergies and complementarities across its policy functions and promoting increased connectivity within the Bank of England.[138]

It is to be recalled that the FPC is a policy committee and as such, it does not have a role in firm-specific regulation of firms and does not act as an arbiter for firm-specific disputes within the system of financial regulation. Similarly, there is no bureaucratic statutory process such as an automatic requirement for the PRA and FCA to consult the FPC on rules.[139] Nonetheless, there is a certain degree of a hierarchy in the institutional framework, with the FPC having powers of recommendations and directions to the FCA and PRA (Chapter 4). Furthermore, the PRA has the power to require the FCA to refrain from a specified action that would threaten the stability of the UK financial system or lead to a disorderly failure of a firm or firms that would adversely affect the UK financial system.[140] The legal framework recognises the primacy of financial stability, in some circumstances but it is emphasised that the FCA should not be seen as subordinate to the PRA.[141]

---

134 HM Treasury, Remit and Recommendations to the FPC June 2013.
135 For example, information about commercial real estate lending helped the FPC judge whether action is needed to preserve resilience, see Kohn (2017) (n 123).
136 HM Treasury, "A New Approach to Financial Regulation" (n 119), para 2.108.
137 Fisher (2014) (n 125).
138 The Bank of England Annual Report 2014, available at <https://www.bankofengland. co.uk/-/media/boe/files/annual-report/2014/boe-2014>, 14; M Carney, "One Mission One Bank Promoting the Good of the People of the United Kingdom" (The 30th Mais Lecture, Cass Business School, City University, London, 18 March 2014); IMF, "Macroprudential Institutional Framework – Technical Note" (June 2016), 4, available at <https://www.imf.org/ external/pubs/ft/scr/2016/cr16160.pdf>.
139 HM Treasury, "A New Approach to Financial Regulation" (n 119), para 2.110.
140 Section 3I FSMA 2000, as inserted by FSMA 2012; section 72 in the Memorandum of Understanding between the FCA and the Bank of England (exercising its prudential regulation powers), July 2019, available at <https://www.fca.org.uk/publication/mou/mou-bank-of-england.pdf>.
141 HM Treasury, "A New Approach to Financial Regulation" (n 119), para 1.48. Interestingly, the Treasury Committee was concerned that this will result in the FCA being seen as subordinate to the PRA and recommended that the veto should be given to the FPC and applied only in exceptional circumstances. Treasury Committee, Financial Conduct Authority Twenty-Sixth Report of Session 2010–12, HC 1574, paras 91–97.

3.1.3. FPC and the Treasury

As discussed in Chapter 3, a representative of HM Treasury is a non-voting member of the FPC.[142] The Treasury (on the one hand) and the Bank of England and the PRA (on the other) have a duty to co-ordinate the discharge of their respective functions so far as they relate to the stability of the UK financial system, and affect the public interest.[143] The Bank of England must consult both the Treasury and the FPC in drawing up its financial stability strategy[144] and after each Financial Stability Report is published, there must be meetings between the Governor of the Bank of England (who is also the chair of the FPC) and the Chancellor.[145]

During the legislative process, the Treasury Committee recommended reserving the Treasury a veto power over the FPC.[146] The compromise was found in the form of a power of the Treasury to issue remit letters, similar to the ones addressed to the MPC, specifying what the economic policy of the government is taken to be.[147] The BEA 1998 also allows the Treasury to make recommendations to the FPC on matters that the FPC should regard as relevant to its understanding of the Bank of England's Financial Stability Objective and the FPC's responsibility in relation to the achievement of that objective.[148] The Treasury is required to specify the economic policy of the government and make recommendations to the FPC at least once in every calendar year.[149] In addition, the Treasury is empowered at any time to make recommendations to the FPC about the responsibility of the FPC in relation to support for the economic policy of Her Majesty's Government, including its objectives for growth and employment and matters to which the FPC should have regard in exercising its functions.[150] Consideration of wider economic and fiscal implications are

---

[142]   Section 9B(1)(f) and section 11(7) Schedule 2A BEA 1998.

[143]   Section 64 Financial Services Act 2012. According to section 64(2) Financial Services Act 2012, in complying with the duty to coordinate, the Treasury, the Bank of England and the PRA must have regard in particular to the importance of co-ordination in circumstances where the Bank has given, or is considering the giving of, a public funds notification. The Bank of England has a duty to notify Treasury of a possible need for public funds under section 58 Financial Services Act 2012.

[144]   Section 9A(2) BEA 1998. The FPC may make at any time recommendations to the BoE Court of Directors as to the provisions of the financial stability strategy (section 9A(3)).

[145]   Section 9X BEA 1998. The Treasury is required to publish a record of the meeting by the end of six weeks beginning with the day of the meeting, unless in the opinion of the Treasury, after consulting with the Bank of England, it would be against the public interest.

[146]   Treasury Committee, "Financial Regulation: A Preliminary Consideration of the Government's Proposals", Seventh Report of Session 2010–11, HC 430, para 184.

[147]   Section 9D(1) BEA 1998.

[148]   Section 9E(1) BEA 1998.

[149]   Sections 9D(2) and 9E(2) BEA 1998. The remit and recommendations are issued in the form of a letter of the Chancellor addressed to the Governor of the Bank of England and are issued alongside autumn Budgets. See Remit and Recommendations for the FPC, 8 March 2017.

[150]   Section 9E(1) BEA 1998.

therefore incorporated within this remit.[151] For instance, according to the 2018 remit, one of the elements of the government's economic strategy is "a credible fiscal policy, returning the public finances to health, while providing the flexibility to support the economy."[152] and in the 2013 remit, it included "deficit reduction, returning the public finances to a sustainable position and ensuring that fiscal credibility underpins low long-term interest rates".[153]

Given the relatively short timeframe of the regime, it is too early to determine the effectiveness of these coordination mechanisms. To that end, HM Treasury has recently opened a public consultation to examine the processes for coordination between regulatory authorities[154] and it remains to be seen whether it will expose any tensions that are currently not in the public eye.

3.2. THE FSOC AND THE FEDERAL FINANCIAL REGULATORS

The FSOC was designed to assume a coordinating role among its member agencies and other Federal and State agencies regarding domestic financial services policy development, rulemaking, examinations, reporting requirements and enforcement actions.[155] Yet, as discussed in Chapter 4, the FSOC confronts many challenges as a meta-agency consisted of existing agencies that are each tied to its particular mission. Lack of coherence and common objectives often result in turf wars and ultimately, inhibit coordination amongst the agencies, potentially inhibiting the effectiveness of the macroprudential regime. It comes as no surprise that in its recent 2019 Report, the US Government Accountability Office suggested that: "Under their authority, FSOC should work with federal financial regulators to establish formal coordination policies that clarify issues such as when interagency coordination should occur around rulemakings and the role FSOC should play in facilitating that coordination."[156]

---

[151] R Barwell, "Macroprudential Policy Practice Ahead of Theory and a Clear Remit" in P Mizen, M Rubio and P Turner, *Macroprudential Policy and Practice* (Cambridge University Press, 2018), 275, 285–286 suggests that the FPC has been willing to interpret its remit in a flexible fashion and that this was particularly evident in the FPC decision in June 2014 to impose limit on loan-to-income ratio basing the decision on an intermediate objective of economic stability (which might then pose an ultimate risk to financial stability).

[152] Remit to the MPC 2018 (n 128).

[153] Chancellor of the Exchequer, Remit and Recommendations for the FPC, April 2013.

[154] HM Treasury, "Financial Services Future Regulatory Framework Review Call for Evidence: Regulatory Coordination" (July 2019), available at <https://assets.publishing.service.gov.uk/government/uploads/system/uploads/attachment_data/file/819025/Future_Regulatory_Framework_Review_Call_for_Evidence.pdf>.

[155] Section 112(a)(2)(E) Dodd-Frank Act. This was an alternative to centralisation that was not a politically viable solution. A Camacho and R Glicksman, *Reorganizing Government: A Functional and Dimensional Framework* (NYU, 2019), 182 arguing that the coordination role of the FSOC is unlikely to significantly reduce inefficient and inconsistent regulation (p 190).

[156] US Government Accountability Office, "Modernizing the U.S. Financial Regulatory System in High-Risk Series" GAO-19-157SP (March 2019), 91, 93.

Coordination cannot be said to be fully based on a hierarchy since the FSOC powers are soft/semi-soft and allow for each prudential regulator to remain relatively unconstrained.[157] This is not to say that a hierarchy across policies is completely absent from the Dodd-Frank Act. On a petition of a member agency, the FSOC has an authority to issue a stay or set aside regulations prescribed by the Consumer Financial Protection Bureau by a two-thirds vote of the FSOC members if it "would put the safety and soundness of the United States banking system or the stability of the financial system of the United States at risk."[158] Thus, to some extent, the superiority of financial stability objective over consumer protection is recognised in the Dodd-Frank Act.[159] As discussed in Chapter 4, the FSOC also plays a role in facilitating the resolution of jurisdictional issues among member agencies.[160]

3.3. COORDINATION MECHANISMS IN THE EU

3.3.1. Coordination between the ESRB and the ECB (Monetary Policy)

As discussed in Chapter 3, the ECB plays a leading role in the EU macroprudential oversight primarily through cross-membership and strong internal governance ties with the ESRB.[161] In addition, the ECB is tasked with ensuring the provision of a Secretariat for the ESRB, thereby providing it with analytical, statistical, logistical and administrative support.[162] The head of the Secretariat of the ESRB is to be appointed by the ECB, in consultation with the General Board of the ESRB.[163] These channels promote mutual internalisation of policy actions and effective coordination between macroprudential policy and monetary policy.[164] Coordination is further promoted by the symmetry of

---

[157] Ibid, 190.

[158] Section 1023 Dodd-Frank Act.

[159] AJ Levitin, "The Consumer Financial Protection Bureau: An Introduction" (2013) 32 Review of Banking and Financial Law 321, 354, available at SSRN <https://ssrn.com/abstract=2199678> or <http://dx.doi.org/10.2139/ssrn.2199678>, 354 argues that this is a unique provision in federal legislation, which raises separation of powers concerns.

[160] Section 119 Dodd-Frank Act. The powers of the FSOC are discussed in length in Chapter 4.

[161] The ESRB Regulation, Preamble para 24 – in light of the ECB expertise and existing responsibilities in the area of financial stability; The de Larosière Report, paras 174–178; S Mckphilmey, "Integrating Macro-prudential Policy: Central Banks as the 'Third force' in EU Financial Reform" (2016) 39(3) West European Politics 526. But, as discussed in Chapter 3, this relative closeness of the ECB to the ESRB is not without criticism.

[162] ESRB Regulation, article 4(4). The Secretariat is responsible for the day-to-day business of the ESRB; Council Regulation (EU) 1096/2010 of 17 November 2010 conferring Specific Tasks upon the ECB concerning the Functioning of the ESRB L331/162, articles 2 and 3.

[163] Article 4(2) and 4(2a) ESRB Regulation, as amended. The Regulation Amending the ESRB Regulation, Preamble 11 adds a requirement for the ECB to consider to systematically open the selection procedure to external candidates.

[164] IMF, "Macro-prudential Supervision: An Organising Framework" (2011) (n 16), 42.

the ESRB and the ECB's respective objectives. Maintaining price stability in the euro area as a whole is the primary objective of the ECB but it is also entrusted, without prejudice to the price stability, to support the general economic policies in the Union with a view to contributing to the achievement of the objectives of the Union.[165] In addition, the ECB is tasked with contributing to policies pursued by the competent authorities relating to the stability of the financial system and promoting the smooth functioning of payment systems.[166] The ECB's legitimate interest in financial stability is thus embedded in its objective reinforcing the notion that in the long-run financial stability supports sustainable price stability.[167]

Despite these close governance links, the role of the ECB in setting monetary policy is expected to remain independent of the role of the ESRB as a macroprudential authority. This autonomy is frequently emphasised in the ESRB communications and parliamentary hearings.[168] But theory and practice are often far apart. Chapter 7 suggested that, in practice, the distinction between the two ECB "hats" is often blurred during the ESRB parliamentary hearings.[169] This blur could potentially impede the quality of the ESRB policy advice, particularly where the ECB's direct interests are at stake.[170]

---

[165] Consolidated version of the Treaty on the European Union and the Treaty on the Functioning of the EU, 26 October 2012 OJ C 326 (TFEU), article 127(1) refers to the ESCB (which includes all the NCBs in the EU), however it should be read as a reference to the Eurosystem (i.e. the ECB and the NCBs of the Member States that have adopted the euro). D Gluch, L Škovranová and M Stenström, "Central Bank Involvement in Macro-prudential Oversight" (2013) ECB Legal Working Paper Series 14, 10.

[166] Ibid, articles 127 (1), 127(2) and 127(5) TFEU.

[167] Accordingly, the ECB has been involved from the outset in systemic risk analysis and almost a decade ago started publishing a biannual Financial Stability Report (FSR) with the aim of identifying potential vulnerabilities in the financial system at an early stage. L Papademos, "Price Stability, Financial Stability and Efficiency and Monetary Policy" (Third Conference of the Monetary Stability Foundation, "Challenges to the Financial System – Ageing and Low Growth", Frankfurt am Main, 7 July 2006) BIS Review 64.

[168] ESRB, "The ESRB at Work: Its role, Organisation, and Functioning", Macro-prudential Commentaries Issue 1, February 2012; see, A Keller, "Independence, Accountability and Transparency: Are the Conventional Accountability Mechanisms Suitable For the European Systemic Risk Board?" (2017) 28(5) International Company and Commercial Law Review 176.

[169] Chapter 7 suggested that during ESRB parliamentary hearings questions are frequently answered in the monetary policy capacity rather than the macroprudential capacity.

[170] E.g. where low interest and quantitative easing can be considered as giving hand to unsustainable credit expansion and systemic risk build-up. On the importance of reassuring stakeholders of absence of conflict see High-Level Group on the ESRB Review (March 2013), available at <http://www.esrb.europa.eu/pub/pdf/other/130708_highlevelgroupreport.pdf>, 31. The risk to the ESRB/ECB respective autonomy may also exist where the ECB has no direct interest in the ESRB decision. For instance, the ESRB may be required to assess risks associated with sovereign lending in the banking sector, a sensitive area in political terms that involves a judgment on national fiscal sustainability.
The SSM may add another layer of complexity given that the ECB in its supervisory capacity is a potential addressee of the ESRB recommendations and the Chair of the

As the ESRB gains its own distinct credibility, there is a strong case to slightly loosen these ties. However, the recent Regulation Amending the ESRB Regulation seems to be moving away from previous suggestions that would have slightly loosened the ties between the ESRB and the ECB.[171] As such, the amendment maintains the President of the ECB as the Chair of the ESRB on a permanent basis[172] and discards the idea presented during the initial stages of the legislative process of adding a role of a full-time managing director from outside the ECB.[173]

3.3.2. ESRB and the ECB (SSM)

Under the Single Supervisory Mechanism (SSM),[174] the ECB has direct supervisory competence in respect of credit institutions, financial holding companies, mixed financial holding companies established in participating Member States, and branches in participating Member States of credit institutions established in non-participating Member States that are significant.[175] The National

---

Supervisory Board of the ECB is a member without voting rights of the General Board of the ESRB (Regulation Amending the ESRB Regulation amending articles 16 and 6 of the ESRB Regulation.

See also ASC, "The Consequences of the Single Supervisory Mechanism for Europe's Macro-prudential Framework" (September 2013) Report No 3, 7.

[171] Indeed, the 2013 Review of the ESRB Mission and Organisation (in accordance with article 20 ESRB Regulation) suggested, for instance, that the ESRB chair should be an independent and dedicated one (i.e. not the ECB president) appointed by the ESRB General Board and approved by the European Parliament. S Macphilemy and J Roche, Study commissioned by the ECON, "Review of the New ESFS, Part 2: The Work of the ESRB-The ESFS'S Macro-Prudential Pillar" (2013), 9.

[172] Regulation Amending the ESRB Regulation, Preamble para 4 and amending article 5(1) ESRB Regulation.

[173] High-Level Group on the ESRB Review (n 170); Commission Report on the Mission and Organisation of the ESRB of 8 August 2014 COM (2014) 508 final, 8, para 3.2.1 that received the support of the ECB in ECB Opinion of the 4 February 2015 on the Review of the Mission and Organisation of the ESRB OJ C192/1 and Summery of Responses, Feedback Statement on the Consultation Review of the EU Macro-prudential Framework, available at <https://ec.europa.eu/finance/consultations/2016/macroprudential-framework/index_en.htm>, 19.

See Chapter 3 on further adjustment that effectively means slightly looser ties between the ESRB and ECB/national central banks.

[174] Council Regulation (EU) No 1024/2013 Conferring Specific Tasks on the European Central Bank Concerning the Policies Relating to Prudential Supervision of Credit Institutions [2013] OJ L 287/63 (SSM Regulation); Regulation of the ECB of 16 April 2014 Establishing the Framework for Cooperation within the Single Supervisory Mechanism between the European Central Bank and National Competent Authorities and with National Designated Authorities (ECB/2014/17).

[175] Articles 4 and 6 SSM Regulation. According to article 2 SSM Regulation "participating Member State" means a Member State whose currency is the euro or a Member State whose currency is not the euro which has established a close cooperation in accordance with article 7 SSM Regulation.

For classification of significant and less significant, see article 6(4) SSM Regulation.

Competent Authorities (NCAs) continue to conduct the direct supervision of entities that are less significant.[176] In addition, the SSM Regulation confers specific macroprudential supervision powers on NCAs or national designated authorities (NDAs) in participating Member States[177] and on the ECB.[178]

Naturally, there is an inherent overlap between the roles of the ESRB and the SSM.[179] Nevertheless, the overlap is confined since the SSM macroprudential responsibilities are more limited than the ESRB ones. First, the scope of the SSM supervisory tasks is limited to the prudential supervision of the banking sector[180] and applies to the euro area as well as other Member States wishing to participate.[181] In contrast, as discussed in Chapter 2, the ESRB mandate goes beyond the banking sector and covers the entire financial system, including other financial institutions, markets and products and applies to all EU Member States. Second, the macroprudential tools available as part of the SSM are more limited compared to the macroprudential toolkit of the national supervisors (and accordingly, the purview of the ESRB). Macroprudential instruments under the SSM are outlined in the Capital Requirement Directive[182] or in the Capital Requirement Regulation.[183] Either at the request of the national authorities

---

See also ECB, "Guide To Banking Supervision", September 2014, available at <https://www.bankingsupervision.europa.eu/ecb/pub/pdf/ssmguidebankingsupervision201409en.pdf>; the ECB publishes a list of supervised institutions that includes the reasons why each institution is classified as significant.

[176] Though the ECB has the power to decide in specific cases to directly supervise such entities where this is necessary for the consistent application of supervisory standards.

[177] Article 5(1) SSM Regulation. For definitions of NCAs and NDAs see SSM Regulation, article 2. The establishment of the national macroprudential supervisors (either as a separate authority or conferring macro-prudential powers on existing national authorities) was partially triggered by the ESRB Recommendation of 22 December 2011 on the Macro-prudential Mandate of National Authorities (ESRB/2011/3) OJ C 41 p 1.

[178] Article 5(2) SSM Regulation. If deemed necessary, the ECB, instead of the NCA or NDA of the participating Member State, apply higher requirements for capital buffers than applied by these authorities.

[179] SSM Regulation, article 25(2) clarifies that the tasks conferred on the ECB by the SSM Regulation will not interfere with its tasks in relation to the ESRB or any other tasks.
For different views on the consequences of the creation of the SSM for the ESRB see ASC Report (September 2013) (n 170), 5–7.
See also IMF, "European Union: Publication of Financial Sector Assessment Program – Technical Note on Macroprudential Oversight and the Role of the ESRB" (March 2013) IMF Country Report No 70, 22 observing that the role of the ESRB will be complemented and enhanced by the SSM and that coordination between the two bodies is warranted.

[180] SSM Regulation, article 1.

[181] SSM Regulation, Preamble para 10.

[182] Directive 2013/36/EU of 26 June 2013 on Access to the Activity of Credit Institutions and the Prudential Supervision of Credit Institutions and Investment Firms, OJ L 176/338 (CRD IV).

[183] Council Regulation (EU) No 575/2013 of 26 June 2013 on Prudential Requirements for Credit Institutions and Investment Firms [2013] OJ L 321/6 (CRR IV).
It is to be recalled, as discussed in Chapter 4, that the ESRB also plays a role under the CRR IV and CRD IV including delivering opinions and recommendations on envisaged activation

---

or by its own initiative, the ECB can decide to adopt stricter measures than the ones adopted at the national level.[184] The set of macroprudential tools in CRR/CRD IV is broad and includes both mandatory and optional instruments, such as the Counter-Cyclical Buffer (articles 130 and 135–140 of CRD IV) and the Systemic Risk Buffer (articles 133–134 of CRD IV).[185] Nevertheless, tools that are not harmonised under EU law, such as, borrower-based lending limits, are outside the remit of the SSM.[186]

The Regulation amending the ESRB Regulation, which was drafted prior to the creation of the SSM, now explicitly takes account of the SSM. As such, the SSM is represented in the ESRB board, though in practice, an SSM representative was invited to the ESRB meetings as an observer prior to the amendment.[187] In order for the ECB and the ESRB to act as complementarities rather than overlapping institutions, it is essential to ensure that coordination takes place.[188] The ECB is required to cooperate closely with the ESRB and other authorities which form part of the ESFS[189] and not to interfere with the ESRB's tasks.[190] In practical terms, this means taking into account the ESRB recommendations before deciding on macroprudential measures.[191]

Overall, a Report from the Commission on the SSM observed that – "the interaction and cooperation between the ESRB and SSM technical committees

---

of specific macroprudential tools at the national level (articles 133 CRD IV and 458 CRR IV) and providing guidance (article 135 CRD IV).

[184] Article 5(2) and (3) SSM Regulation.

[185] Commission Consultation Document, "Review of the Macro-prudential Policy Framework" (from 1 August to 24 October 2016), 6–7 (Table 1), available at <http://ec.europa.eu/finance/consultations/2016/macroprudential-framework/docs/consultation-document_en.pdf>. The activation of most macro-prudential tools under the CRR/CRD IV has to be notified to the ESRB (articles 129(2), 130(2), 131(2), 133, 134(2), 136(7) and 160 CRD IV and articles 99(7) and 458 CRR IV). In addition, there is a mandatory sequencing for the activation of macroprudential instruments (the so-called pecking order). This means that instruments in the hands of micro-prudential supervisors (articles 124 and 164 CRR, Pillar 2) and macroprudential instruments with less discretion (CCyB, G-SII and O-SII buffer) are considered for application first, before more discretionary macro-prudential tools (SRB, article 458 CRR) can be used. This sequencing inhibits the needed national flexibility in macroprudential policy making. See, ESRB Response to the European Commission Consultation Document on "Review of the EU Macro-prudential Policy Framework" (24 October 2016). The Consultation Document (August 2016) is available at <https://ec.europa.eu/finance/consultations/2016/macroprudential-framework/docs/consultation-document_en.pdf>.

[186] ESRB, "Flagship Report on Macro-prudential Policy in the Banking Sector", March 2014, Table 5, 21; Summary of Responses to Consultation on EU Macro-prudential Framework, available at <https://ec.europa.eu/finance/consultations/2016/macroprudential-framework/docs/summary-of-responses_en.pdf>, 15–16.

[187] ESRB (2016) (n 185), 4. Regulation amending the ESRB Regulation adding article 6(2)(c).

[188] V Constâncio, "Implications of the SSM on the ESFS" (Public Hearing on Financial Supervision in the EU, Brussels, 24 May 2013).

[189] Which would now include national macroprudential authorities.

[190] SSM Regulation, Preamble para 31 and articles 3(1), 3(3) and 25.

[191] ECB, "Guide to Banking Supervision", November 2014, 20.

has improved over time, notably as regards information sharing and the avoidance of work duplication ..."[192] The recent changes in the Regulation amending the ESRB Regulation formalise the institutional representation of the ECB in its supervisory capacity in the ESRB governance structure. The Chair of the Supervisory Board will become a member of the ESRB General Board without voting rights and a representative of the SSM will sit on the ATC.[193] It is suggested that in order to facilitate a two-way interaction, a representative of the ESRB could participate as an observer in the SSM Supervisory Board[194] when macroprudential issues are being discussed.

3.3.3. ESRB and Fiscal Policy

In contrast to the intensive interaction between macroprudential policy and monetary policy, the mechanisms in the ESRB Regulation that provide for coordination with fiscal policies are very modest. The President of the EFC is a member of the ESRB General Board but without a voting right;[195] there is a representative of the EFC in the ATC[196] and the president of the EFC is a member of the Steering Committee.[197] In addition, the ESRB Regulation requires the ESRB to inform the EFC regularly and send the texts of any warnings and recommendations as soon as they have been adopted.[198] To enhance coordination and a two-way exchange of information there may be room to enable the ESRB chair to attend meetings without the right to vote in the Eurogroup similar to the arrangement adopted in the monetary-fiscal

---

[192] Report from the Commission to the European Parliament and Council on the SSM Established Pursuant to Regulation (EU) No 1024/2013 COM (2017) 591 final, 16.
[193] Regulation Amending the ESRB Regulation, inserting article 6(2)(c) and 13(1)(fa), respectively.
[194] SSM Regulation, article 26.
[195] Article 6(2)(b) ESRB Regulation. Nonetheless, it is to be noted that whilst the ESRB Regulation did not envisage that national macroprudential authorities will be formed, some of these authorities are directly answerable to the finance ministry (as in Germany, Austria, Bulgaria, France and Luxembourg). C Noyer, "Macro-prudential Policy: From Theory to Implementation" (April 2014) Banque de France Financial Stability Review 18, 9. It is to be noted that the Regulation amending the ESRB Regulation (2019) amends article 7 ESRB Regulation and adds a requirement that "No member of the General Board (whether voting or non-voting) shall have a function in the central government of a Member State."
[196] ESRB Regulation, article 13(1)(g).
[197] ESRB Regulation, article 11(1)(h).
[198] ESRB Regulation, Recital 19. The De Larosiere Report highlighted the importance of informing the EFC where there are concerns related to fiscal matters (e.g. excessive deficits or the accumulation of debt), 46. It envisaged a bigger role to the EFC and recommended that the ESRC not only inform the EFC when risks are of a serious nature but also that the EFC, working with the Commission, will then implement a strategy ensuring that the risks are effectively addressed (Recommendation 17, p 46).

dialogue.[199] In turn, the president of the Eurogroup will have a statutory right to attend the meetings of the ESRB.

3.3.4. ESRB and the ESAs

Cross-membership in the governing bodies of the ESAs and the ESRB ensure close interaction and exchange of information. The chairpersons of the ESAs are members of the ESRB with voting rights[200] and sits on the Steering Committee and the ATC.[201] A representative of the ESRB is a non-voting member of the Board of Supervisors of the ESAs.[202] The requirement for coordination between the ESRB and the ESAs is embedded in the ESAs Regulations. The ESAs are given the objective of protecting the stability of the financial system aligning it with the ESRB's main objective.[203] They are explicitly required to cooperate, closely and on a regular basis, with the ESRB.[204] More generally, the ESAs and the ESRB are required to cooperate with trust and full mutual respect and to ensure the flow of appropriate and reliable information between them.[205] Other areas of coordination include the development by the EBA, in collaboration with the ESRB, of a common set of quantitative and qualitative indicators (risk dashboard) to identify and measure systemic risk[206] the development by the ESAs, in consultation with the ESRB, of criteria and adequate stress-testing regime which includes an evaluation of the potential for systemic risk posed by financial institutions to increase in situations of stress.[207]

The Joint Committee is the principal forum for coordination between the ESAs and the ESRB.[208] It is composed of the chairpersons of the ESAs[209] and meets at least once every three months.[210] A representative of the ESRB is invited

---

[199] Though with lower frequency. G Galati and R Moessner, "Macro-prudential Policy: A Literature Review" (December 2010) DNB Working Paper 267, 24.

[200] ESRB Regulation, article 6(1)(d)–(f).

[201] ESRB Regulation, articles 11(1)(e)–(g) and 13(1)(c)–(e) respectively.

[202] ESAs Regulations, article 40(1)(e).

[203] EBA Regulations and ESMA Regulation, articles 1(5), as amended; EIOPA Regulation, article 1(6), as amended.

[204] ESAs Regulations, article 36(1).

[205] And from the ESAs to the European Parliament, to the Council and to the Commission. In accordance with the principle of sincere cooperation pursuant to TFEU, article 4(3); ESRB Regulation, article 1(4); ESAs Regulations, article 2(4), as amended.
See also ESRB Regulation, article 15(1).

[206] EBA Regulation, article 22(2), as amended.

[207] ESAs Regulations, article 23, as amended. The Regulations amending the ESAs Regulations clarifies that these include potential environmental-related systemic risk. See also ESAs Regulations, article 32, as amended.

[208] ESAs Regulations, article 54(1)–(2).

[209] ESAs Regulations, articles 55(1); where applicable, the joint committee will also compose of the Chairperson of any Sub-Committee established pursuant to article 57.

[210] Article 55(4) ESAs Regulations, as amended.

to attend meetings of the Joint Committee as an observer and the chairperson of the Joint Committee acts as the second Vice-Chair of the ESRB.[211]

A careful examination of those arrangements, however, reveals that the requirement to coordinate is mostly one-sided, flowing from and initiated by the ESAs. The ESRB is under no explicit obligation when making policy decisions, to have regard to the responsibilities of the ESAs, giving way to possible conflicts with micro-prudential concerns, when recommending the implementation of macroprudential tools.[212]

4.   CONCLUSION

Taming systemic risk is an intractable policy problem which necessitates reaching out beyond the strict boundaries of the macroprudential mandate. The main thesis of this chapter is the acknowledgment that macroprudential policy cannot be conducted in silos and that in ensuring financial stability, the macroprudential authority must take a holistic view, considering a wide range of policy areas, including monetary policy, fiscal policy and structural and social policies. The design of macroprudential frameworks must therefore acknowledge the possible trade-offs and interlinkages with other policy areas and provide a satisfactory institutional infrastructure through which coordination can take place. Without coordination, there is a risk that policies will point in opposite directions. Yet, coordination could also blur the respective objectives of policymakers and weaken the independence and accountability of the macroprudential authority. This trade-off between coordination and indistinct mandate with vague accountability is not unique to macroprudential policy, but it is certainly more acute in that sphere. Much therefore depends on the methods and degree of coordination and the institutional setting within which the macroprudential authority operates in. Albeit, the debate on the effectiveness and suitability of coordination mechanism is still in its infancy and the empirical basis for policy coordination of macroprudential policy with other policy areas has not yet produced a clear-cut guidance to allow for drawing generalised conclusions.

With these hurdles in mind, the chapter brought to light important questions such as should coordination be horizontal and based on a clear hierarchy with financial stability and price stability at the top? Or would it be better to emphasise a shared objective and horizontal coordination through cross-membership,

---

[211]   ESAs Regulation, article 55(2)–(3), as amended.

[212]   The ESRB Regulation, Preamble para 30 however acknowledges that "Only with arrangements in place that properly acknowledge the interdependence of micro and macro-prudential risks can all stakeholders have sufficient confidence to engage in cross-border financial activities."

exchange of information and consultation without risking blurred objectives and diluted accountability?

It may be that in practical terms, coordination between macroprudential policy and other policy areas essentially requires "a degree of humility" of the respective authorities.[213] This means that the macroprudential authority should aim to ensure financial stability but should not seek the "stability of the graveyard"; the micro-prudential authority should seek to ensure the safety and stability of individual institutions but should not seek to implement a "zero failure regime" and allow financial institutions to fail where this will not cause a disruption to the rest of the financial system and finally, monetary policy setters should follow, when pursuing their price stability objective, a more flexible approach taking into account, to a certain degree, financial stability considerations.

---

[213] P Fischer, "Microprudential, Macroprudential and Monetary Policy: Conflict, Compromise or Co-ordination?" (Richmond University, London, 1 October 2014), 4.

CHAPTER 9

DATA COLLECTION AND ANALYSIS
IN MACROPRUDENTIAL POLICY

An Epistemic View

1. DATA GAPS AS AN ANCILLARY CULPRIT

The 2007–2009 global financial crisis revealed that regulators, supervisors and market players lacked data needed to fully assess risks in financial markets and monitor the financial system.[1] Accordingly, it was observed that "The crisis has reaffirmed an old lesson – good data and good analysis are the lifeblood of effective surveillance and policy responses both at national and international levels."[2] Financial data collected were too aggregated, limited in scope, out of date and incomplete.[3]

To support the development of robust macroprudential frameworks at the national and global levels further work to enhance data for financial stability was needed. This included efforts to repurpose existing datasets that were already being collected by central banks and prudential supervisors and collecting new data sets where data gaps exist. Despite significant progress, some data gaps remain in place and hinder both the ability of macroprudential authorities to construct and use indicators for systemic risk analysis, implement appropriate macroprudential measures and analyse their effectiveness. Most importantly, it is evident that "a fully detailed, real-time heat-map of financial system risks is still far out of reach."[4]

---

[1]   FSB and IMF, "The Financial Crisis and Information Gaps" (November 2009) Report to the G20 Finance Ministers and Central Bank Governors, available at <https://www.fsb.org/wp-content/uploads/r_091029.pdf>, 9–10.

[2]   Ibid, 4.
       See also J Black, "Restructuring Global and EU Financial Regulation: Character, Capacities, and Learning" in E Wymeersch, KJ Hopt and G Ferrarini (eds) *Financial Regulation and Supervision: A Post Crisis Analysis in Restructuring Global and EU Financial Regulation* (Oxford University Press, 2012).

[3]   Office of Financial Research 2012 Annual Report, preface, 3.

[4]   JM Serena and B Tissot, "Data Needs and Statistics Compilation for Macroprudential Analysis", Overview of Proceedings of the IFC–National Bank of Belgium Workshop in Brussels on 18–19 May 2017 Irving Fisher Committee Bulletin No 46, 4.

The chapter is structured as follows. Section 1 outlines the post-crisis key initiatives to close data gaps and underlines the remaining data gaps needed to conduct effective macroprudential policy. Section 2 explores the types of data needed for macroprudential purposes and suggests key features of data quality in the macroprudential context. Section 3 explores the institutional and governance aspects of data collection in the EU and the UK and critically analyses the unique setting in the US, which separates the macroprudential mandate from the task of data collection and analysis. Section 4 explores two emerging challenges that macroprudential authorities are facing in data collection and analysis. The first is the use of big data and machine learning and the second, the design and use of stress tests to generate data. Section 5 moves away from the particularities of the data collection task of macroprudential authorities and delves deeper into its theoretical foundations. It borrows from the literature in Organisational Studies[5] and in particular, knowledge management and suggests that knowledge and expertise are critical to understanding the role that macroprudential authorities play in the realm of data collection and analysis. The section exposes the multi-layered nature and the unique features of expertise in macroprudential policymaking and the myriad of hurdles these present to macroprudential authorities. Finally, Section 6 suggests that the preceding analysis yields two key observations. The first is related to the limitations of data collection for macroprudential purposes. Closing data gaps can assist macroprudential authorities in addressing the known knowns (by, for instance, identifying the magnitude or likelihood of known risks) and the unknown knowns (by bringing it within the regulatory perimeter, it can become "known known"). Yet, data collection is virtually powerless with regards to "unknown unknowns". Expertise is perhaps the only way to overcome this gap. But expertise in macroprudential policy is still scarce and fraught with many problems. Its nature is multidisciplinary, "one that combines the skills of economists, financial experts, payments systems analysts, and other specialists"[6] and therefore, it is also fragmented, shared with other prudential supervisors, external experts and financial markets. Asymmetries of expertise arise between macroprudential authorities and other prudential authorities that have close contact with regulatees. Asymmetries also emerge between macroprudential authorities and financial markets[7] that

---

5   Organisational studies borrowed ideas from philosophical and psychological interpretations of wisdom. See, for instance, N Dalal and D Pauleen, "The Wisdom Nexus: Guiding Information Systems Research, Practice, and Education" (2019) 29 Information Systems Journal 224.

6   BS Bernanke, "Implementing a Macroprudential Approach to Supervision and Regulation" (The 47th Annual Conference on Bank Structure and Competition, Chicago, Illinois 5 May 2011).

7   K Bamberger, "Technologies of Compliance: Risk and Regulation in a Digital Age" (2009) 88 Texas Law Review 669, 673 contends that "Regulated firms have far better information than the agencies who oversee them regarding firm organization as well as the sources of risk and capacity for risk mitigation."

utilise the complexity and opaqueness of financial products and regulation and engage in regulatory arbitrage.[8] This creates a never-ending spiral of closing data gaps and rule evading that opens new gaps. The legal framework should, therefore, nurture and enhance the accumulation of expertise and utilise the complementarities of its sources.

2. POST-CRISIS KEY INITIATIVES TO CLOSE DATA GAPS AND REMAINING DATA GAPS

2.1. TYPES OF DATA NEEDED TO SUPPORT A MACROPRUDENTIAL MANDATE

Data collected for macroeconomic and monetary policy purposes as well as data collected by micro-prudential supervisors is also utilised for macroprudential analysis.[9] In addition, macroprudential authorities need aggregate data that will help in identifying a build-up of risk in the financial system as a whole such as, aggregate balance sheet; broad macro indicators, most notably ratios of Credit-to-GDP; data on markets including price trend and volatility and data on individual institutions to gauge their behaviour under stress and likely contagion effect on other parts of the financial system.[10] Macroprudential authorities also incorporate qualitative data into their systemic risks analysis including assessments of credit underwriting standards and the adequacy of banks' risk management processes.[11]

2.2. DATA SOURCES

Data sources for macroprudential analysis can fall into five key categories: data released by international organisations; data released by national agencies; data from commercial data providers,[12] market intelligence and stress testing.

---

8   F Partnoy, "Financial Derivatives and the Costs of Regulatory Arbitrage" (1997) 22 Journal of Corporate Law 211, 227 defines regulatory arbitrage as "those financial transactions designed specifically to reduce costs or capture profit opportunities created by different regulations or laws."

9   A Clark and A Large, "Macroprudential Policy: Addressing the things We Don't Know" (2011) Group of 30 Occasional Paper No 87.
    See also P Korhonen, "Do Macroprudential Tools Require Micro-Data?" IFC Bulletin No 37, 187, available at <https://www.bis.org/ifc/publ/ifcb37zo.pdf>.

10 IMF, "Financial Soundness Indicators and Macroprudential Analysis" in Financial Soundness Indicators Compilation Guide 2019, 171.

11 Ibid.

12 C Carini, "SYRTO (Systemic Risk Tomography) Project – Data and Quality Framework" Technical Report, available at <http://syrtoproject.eu/wp-content/uploads/2016/03/dataquality.pdf>, 4.

While these sources can potentially entail a rich source of information for macroprudential authorities several reservations are warranted. To begin with, as the data may be privately owned, it may only be accessible at a cost and its integrity and security can be put into question.[13] In addition, data might be available only with significant lags and they do not necessarily contain sufficient detail on essential items for macroprudential analysis.[14] Finally, data from these different sources may not be standardised and thus lack comparability, making it more difficult for macroprudential authorities to "connect the dots".

Macro-stress testing is an additional quantitative and qualitative source of data used to inform macroprudential authorities. For instance, a stress test can be used to assess the impact of a macroprudential instrument or determine the resilience of the banking system to some common economic or financial risks.[15] In macro-stress testing, financial institutions are simultaneously subjected to the same stress scenario. Macroprudential authorities can extract quantitative data on losses from systemic risk amplification as well as qualitative information on the "reactions of the system" in periods of stress.[16] Specifications of scenarios in macro-stress tests are chosen to explore system-wide vulnerabilities that can be either cyclical or structural in nature.[17] For instance, recently, the FPC and the PRC announced that macro-stress tests are planned to be used to stress test the UK financial system for resilience to climate change risks, arising from the increased frequency of weather events and the transition to a carbon-neutral emission economy.[18] It is hoped that this, first of its kind, stress test will motivate

---

"Commercial data providers" include trade repositories (collect data on trades in OTC derivatives), credit registers (private or public), cheque and securities clearing systems and stock, futures and options exchanges. See G Murphy and R Westwood, "Data Gaps in the UK Financial Sector: Some Lessons Learned from the Recent Crisis" (IFC on Data Gaps, Basel, 25–26 August 2010).

[13]   For instance, voluntary reporting of hedge funds to commercial data providers may give rise to a selection bias. The Centre of Hedge Fund Research, Imperial College, "The Value of the Hedge Fund Industry to Investors, Markets and the Broader Economy", 2012, available at <https://home.kpmg.com/ru/en/home/insights/2012/06/hedge-fund-value.html>; AL Aiken, CP Clifford and J Ellis, "Out of the Dark: Hedge Fund Reporting Biases and Commercial Databases" (2013) 26(1) The Review of Financial Studies 208.

[14]   J Henry and C Kok, "A Macro Stress Testing Framework for Assessing Systemic Risk in the Banking Sector" ECB (October 2013) Occasional Paper Series 152, 65.

[15]   B Baudino and others, "Stress-testing Banks – A Comparative Analysis" (November 2018) BIS Financial Stability Institute Insights on Policy Implementation No 12, 3.

[16]   R Anderson and others, "Macroprudential Stress Tests and Policies: Searching for Robust and Implementable Frameworks" (2018) IMF Working Paper No 197, 9–10.

[17]   Chapter 1 in RW Anderson (ed), *Stress Testing and Macroprudential Regulation: A Transatlantic Assessment* (CEPR Press, 2016), 13.

[18]   M Carney, "A New Horizon" (The European Commission Conference: "A Global Approach to Sustainable Finance", 21 March 2019).
        See also the Bank of England's Response to the Van Steenis Review on the Future of Finance, "New Economy, New Finance, New Bank", June 2019, available at <https://www.bankofengland.co.uk/-/media/boe/files/report/2019/response-to-the-future-of-finance-report>.

firms to address data gaps as well as develop cutting-edge risk management consistent with a range of possible climate pathways.[19]

Another important source of data is network analysis. Network analysis models the interlinking exposures between financial institutions, across sectors of the economy or in a cross-border network analysis, the relationships between national financial systems.[20] It is crucial for the identification of systemically important financial institutions and markets and can assist macroprudential authorities in detecting spillovers that are likely to arise from interlinkages in the system.[21]

2.3. DATA GAPS INITIATIVE: PHASES 1 AND 2

The experience of the 2007–2009 financial crisis led the G20 finance ministers and central bank governors, in November 2009, to call for the IMF and the FSB (at the time, the Financial Stability Forum) "to explore gaps and provide appropriate proposals for strengthening data collection before the next meeting of the G-20 Finance Ministers and Central Bank Governors."[22] The joint IMF-FSB report, *The Financial Crisis and Information Gaps*, was published in October 2009 and set out a series of recommendations to address identified data gaps launching the G20 Data Gaps Initiative (DGI).[23] Following several progress reports,[24] in September 2015, the G20 concluded the first phase of the DGI and endorsed the launch of its second phase.[25] The five-year horizon DGI-2

---

[19] Summary and Record of the Financial Policy Committee Meetings on 13 June and 4 July 2019.

[20] ECB, "Recent Advances in Modelling Systemic Risk Using Network Analysis" (January 2010), Preface, available at <https://www.ecb.europa.eu/pub/pdf/other/modellingsystemic risk012010en.pdf>. It therefore requires detailed information on bilateral exposures.
    See also "The Network Analysis Approach" Part 1 Section B in L Ong (ed), *A Guide to IMF Stress Testing: Models and Methods* (IMF, 2014).

[21] Gertrude Tumpel Gugerell, Introductory remarks in ECB (2010) (n 20), 8. The primary criticism on network analysis is the lack of a behavioural aspect (ibid, 10).
    For a recent paper, see, for instance, S Avdjiev, P Giudici and A Spelta, "Measuring Contagion Risk in International Banking" (2019) BIS Working Papers No 796.

[22] G20 Finance Ministers and Central Bank Governors Working Group on Reinforcing International Co-operation and Promoting Integrity in Financial Markets, London, 2 April 2009.
    See also Articles of Agreement of the IMF article VIII, section 5 "… act as a centre for the collection and exchange of information on monetary and financial problems …".

[23] IMF-FSB, "The Financial Crisis and Information Gaps" (October 2009) Report to the G-20 Finance Ministries and Central Bank Governors, available at <https://www.imf.org/external/np/g20/pdf/102909.pdf>.

[24] Most recently, Sixth Progress Report on the Implementation of the G-20 Data Gaps Initiative (September 2015), 6.

[25] FSB and IMF, Second Phase of the G-20 Data Gaps Initiative Fourth Progress Report – Countdown to 2021, October 2019, available at <https://www.fsb.org/2019/10/fsb-and-imf-publish-2019-progress-report-on-g20-data-gaps-initiative/>.

focused on "compiling and disseminating increasingly consistent datasets across the G-20 economies" with "an increased emphasis to the inter-linkages across the economic and financial system reflecting the evolving policy needs."[26] Its 20 new or revised recommendations focus on datasets that support monitoring of risk in the financial sector and analysis of vulnerabilities, interconnections and spillovers, not least cross-border.[27] Considerable progress has been made to-date by the participating economies[28] including in shadow banking monitoring and reporting of data on Global Systemically Important Banks (G-SIBs).[29] The impact of the recommendations goes beyond the G-20, with templates for collecting and compiling internationally comparable data becoming a worldwide standard.[30] Still, as will be discussed in length in Section 2.4 below, significant data gaps persist.[31]

2.4. OTHER GLOBAL AND REGIONAL DATA INITIATIVES

The DGI-2 is conducted in parallel to other workstreams at the global level (such as the IMF Financial Soundness Indicators and the Legal Identity Identifier) and at the regional level (for instance, AnaCredit).

The IMF Financial Soundness Indicators (FSIs) was the first database specifically tailored to macroprudential needs.[32] The database currently has over 50 indicators that focus on the financial system as a whole and its interaction

---

[26] Meeting of G20 Finance Ministers and Central Bank Governors, Cairns, 21 September 2014 Communiqué, Brisbane Summit; see proposal in the DGI Sixth Progress Report (September 2015) (n 24), 21.

[27] Annex 1 of the DGI Sixth Progress Report (September 2015) (n 24).

[28] The G20 economies and five non-G20 FSB member economies (Hong Kong, the Netherlands, Singapore, Spain and Switzerland).

[29] The Third Progress Report of DGI-2 (September 2018). The Fourth Progress Report on DGI-2 (October 2019) (n 25) also noted that "Overall improvements were noted in coverage, timeliness, or periodicity of: securities statistics, derivatives data, sectoral accounts, international investment position, international banking statistics, and government finance statistics." However, "challenges remain in fully implementing the DGI-2 recommendations by 2021."

  See also FSB Global Shadow Banking Monitoring Report 2018 pointing out that the "coverage and consistency of data provided by jurisdictions for the calculation of risk metrics has continued to improve" (p 4), and that "Chinese authorities are now fully contributing to the FSB monitoring exercise" (p 7); B Tissot and E Bese, "Monitoring Systemic Institutions for the Analysis of Micro-Macro Linkages and Networks Effects" International Statistical Institute 61st World Statistics Congress July 2017.

[30] P de Ven and D Fano, *Understanding Financial Accounts* (OECD Publishing, 2017), 373.

[31] Main Takeaways and Concluding Comments FSB/IMF Global Conference on the Second Phase of the G-20 DGI-2, Washington DC, USA, 12–13 June 2019.

[32] S Boh and others, "European Macroprudential Database" (IFC-National Bank of Belgium Workshop on "Data Needs and Statistics Compilation for Macroprudential Analysis", Brussels, Belgium, 18–19 May 2017), Box 1 on p 21.

with the real economy as well as monitoring the condition of households and corporate sectors. These include financial market data and macro indicators (such as the difference between Credit-to-GDP ratio) and other variables such as real estate prices and growth of credit to the private sector.[33] Nevertheless, FSIs have a limited role in several other aspects of analysis for macroprudential purposes. In particular, FSIs may not assist in the analysis of macro-financial linkages (i.e. how shocks to the financial sector result in a feedback loop to the real sector as well as contagion effects within the financial system) and the impact of these linkages on broader macroeconomic conditions.[34] Areas of improvement include the need to better the periodicity and timeliness of FSIs, most importantly for residential real estate prices.[35]

In the EU, the Macroprudential Database, launched in 2015, includes a relatively large number of country-level public indicators related to the macroeconomy and financial markets, debt and credit, residential and commercial real estate, the banking sector, the non-banking sector and interconnectedness.[36] In the euro area, Analytical credit data standards (AnaCredit) is a dataset containing detailed harmonised information on individual bank loans.[37] It covers various aspects of credit exposure, such as the outstanding amount, interest rate, maturity, collateral or guarantee and information on the counterparty.[38] However, since data collection only started

---

[33] The IMF 2019 Financial Soundness Indicators Compilation Guide, 169. The guide includes new indicators to expand the coverage of the financial sector, including other financial intermediaries, money market funds, insurance corporations, pension funds, non-financial corporations, and households.

[34] Ibid, 170.

[35] Main Takeaways and Concluding Comments FSB/IMF Global Conference DGI-2 (2019) (n 31).

[36] It is accessible via the ECB Statistical Data Warehouse and includes around 370 indicators in the internal version. For a detailed account of this dataset see S Boh and others (2017) (n 32).

[37] Decision of the ECB of 24 February 2014 on the Organisation of Preparatory Measures for the Collection of Granular Credit Data by the European System of Central Banks ECB/2014/6 OJ L 104/72; Regulation (EU) 2016/867 of the European Central Bank of 18 May 2016 on the Collection of Granular Credit and Credit Risk Data ECB/2016/13 (AnaCredit Regulation). Outside the Euro Area participation is on a voluntary basis (Preamble, section 7).
    See also OC Brananova and G Watfre, "Use of AnaCredit Granular Data for Macroprudential Analysis" (Irving Fisher Committee – National Bank of Belgium Workshop on "Data Need and Statistics Compilation for Macroprudential Analysis", Brussels, 18–19 May 2017).
    On the limitations of this dataset see F Dierick, E Point, W Cornacchia and M Pirovano, "Closing Real Estate Data Gaps for Financial Stability Monitoring and Macroprudential Policy in the EU" (2017) IFC Bulletin 46 (Proceedings of the IFC-National Bank of Belgium Workshop on "Data Need and Statistics Compilation for Macroprudential Analysis", Brussels, 18–19 May 2017).

[38] ECB, "Explanatory Note on the AnaCredit Regulation", available at <https://www.ecb.europa. eu/stats/money/aggregates/anacredit/shared/pdf/explanatorynoteanacreditregulation. en.pdf>.

---

in 2018, AnaCredit does not cover a long historical series, which is a necessary feature for the assessment of risk development over time.[39]

Another important initiative in improving global data collection and comparability is the Legal Entity Identifier (LEI).[40] The LEI was originally an initiative launched by the OFR in 2010.[41] It then shifted to the global scene and in 2012, the FSB published *A Global Legal Entity Identifier for Financial Markets* setting out 15 high-level Principles and 35 recommendations for the development of a unique identification system for parties to financial transactions.[42] The FSB recommendations were endorsed by the G20 in June 2012, highlighting the importance of worldwide adoption of the LEI "to support authorities and market participants in identifying and managing financial risks".[43]

The LEI is a 20-character, alpha-numeric code, used to uniquely identify legally distinct entities that engage in financial transactions.[44] Each entity is associated with a reference data, which currently includes core identification information, such as the official name of the legal entity, the address of its headquarters and address of legal formation.[45] By standardising the identification of legal entities at the global level, the LEI supports the management and analysis of large datasets and can assist macroprudential authorities in aggregation[46] and

---

[39] Serena and Tissot (2017) (n 4). Therefore, data from AnaCredit should be complemented with data from national central credit registers, though these data sources are not harmonised and differ, amongst other things, in data coverage.

[40] FSB, "Global Legal Entity Identifier for Financial Markets" (June 2012), available at <http://www.financialstabilityboard.org/publications/r_120608.pdf>; FSB, "Thematic Peer Review on Implementation of the Legal Entity Identifier, Summary Terms of Reference" (August 2018), available at <https://www.fsb.org/wp-content/uploads/P160818.pdf>.

[41] Department of US Treasury, "Statement on Legal Entity Identification for Financial Contracts" (2010) Federal Register 75, available at <https://www.federalregister.gov/documents/2010/11/30/2010-30018/office-of-financial-research-statement-on-legal-entity-identification-for-financial-contracts>, 74146–74148.

[42] FSB, A Global Legal Entity Identifier for Financial Markets (2012) (n 40).

[43] G-20 Leaders Declaration Los Cabos, Mexico, 19 June 2012, para 44.

[44] The Legal Entity Identifier Regulatory Oversight Committee (LEI ROC), available at <https://www.leiroc.org/>.

[45] Ibid. Since 9 May 2017 LEI also includes parent information. LEI ROC, "Launch of the Data Collection on Parent Entities in the Global LEI System" (May 2017), available at <https://www.leiroc.org/publications/gls/roc_20170509-1.pdf>.

[46] See also BCBS, "Principles for Effective Risk Data Aggregation and Risk Reporting" (January 2013), Preamble section 7. Evidence show the industry have been slow to meet those principles. BCBS, "Progress in Adopting the Principles for Effective Risk Data Aggregation and Risk Reporting" (June 2018) concluding that "G-SIBs have found it challenging to comply with the Principles, due mainly to the complexity and interdependence of IT improvement projects. As a result, the expected date of compliance has slipped back for many banks."
See also C Crowley, "Setting Standards for Microdata when Industry and Regulators Work Together, All Can Benefit from Improved Data Quality" (Eight ECB Conference on Statistics, July 2016).

a more flexible retrieval of granular data on entities from multiple sources as well as in the analysis of their interconnectedness.[47]

To promote the implementation of the global LEI initiative, the FSB established in 2013 the Regulatory Oversight Committee (ROC), now encompassing members from 71 public authorities and 19 observers from more than 50 countries.[48] Despite its swift launch and impressive implementation with over 1.4 million entities uniquely identified by an LEI in more than 200 countries,[49] the LEI is lacking in coverage. In particular, its coverage is too low outside securities and derivatives markets to effectively support regulatory and supervisory uses.[50] It should be broadened to cover non-financial corporations' sector, particularly small and medium-sized companies (SMEs)[51] and identification of consolidated group-level structures.[52]

2.5. REMAINING DATA GAPS

Despite the progress made in closing data gaps and many positive developments in data collection and analysis for macroprudential purposes, blind spots remain a concern.[53] Data gaps can impede timely and pre-emptive macroprudential policymaking and hinder the ability of macroprudential authorities to assess the effectiveness of macroprudential tools. Closing data gaps is far from being a one-off exercise.[54] It is a dynamic process which has to respond to

---

47   However, the LEI was established for a large range of potential uses, including, for instance, by private sector to support improved risk management. Preamble of the Charter of the LEI ROC, endorsed by the G20 Finance Ministers and Central Bank Governors on 5 November 2012; LEI ROC, "Progress Report The Global LEI System and Regulatory Uses of LEI" (April 2018), available at <https://www.leiroc.org/publications/gls/roc_20180502-1.pdf/>.

48   Available at <https://www.leiroc.org/>.

49   Letter of RK Quarles, the FSB's Chair to G20 Leader Meeting in Osaka, 24 June 2019, available at <https://www.fsb.org/wp-content/uploads/P250619-1.pdf>.

50   FSB, "Peer Review of Implementation of the Legal Entity Identifier" (May 2019), available at <https://www.fsb.org/2019/05/fsb-publishes-peer-review-of-implementation-of-the-legal-entity-identifier/>.

51   Committee on Monetary, Financial and Balance of Payments Statistics, "Opinion on Business Identifiers and Business Registers: Recommendations for Statistical Production" (December 2016), available at <https://www.cmfb.org/opinions>.

52   C Buch, "Data Needs and Statistics Compilation" (IFC-National Bank of Belgium Workshop on "Data needs and Statistics Compilation for Macroprudential Analysis", Brussels, 18–19 May 2017), available at <https://www.bis.org/ifc/publ/ifcb46_keynote.pdf>.

53   Serena and Tissot (2017) (n 4).

54   "The Great Unknown: Can Policymakers Fill the Gaps in Their Knowledge About the Financial System?" The Economist (13 January 2011), available at <http://www.economist.com/node/17900268?story_id=17900268&fsrc=rss>.
      See also B Tunç and B Tisso, "Statistical Implications of the New Financial Landscape – Conference Overview" (The Eighth IFC Conference "Statistical Implications of the New Financial Landscape". Basel, 8–9 September 2016) IFC Bulletin No 43.

emerging technological developments, innovations and regulatory initiatives. Macroprudential authorities should aim to adapt their data collection efforts rapidly and identify new areas where data is needed, needed more frequently or needed in a different form.[55] The importance of certain data sets will, accordingly, change over time and there will be a need to introduce new data sets.

At the time of writing, there are several remaining data gaps that have been identified:

1. Information on commercial property is an important input for macroprudential policy given that it can play a major role in driving booms and busts in the financial cycle.[56] Currently, data coverage of commercial property price indicators (CPPIs) is partial, with only a handful of countries publishing such a data set and there is a weak comparability across countries.[57]

2. Data from trade repositories on transaction-level derivatives data are useful in the area of macroprudential policymaking, in particular in assessing concentration or interconnections.[58] Following the 2007–2009 global financial crisis, the coverage of the global derivatives market has improved but significant data gaps remain, such as missing details on notional value, counterparty and termination date and data on transactions between unregulated entities.[59] There is also a difficulty in aggregating the data given the lack of common identifiers for products, trades and counterparties which are involved in the over-the-counter derivatives transactions.[60] The adoption of a global unique product identifier (UPI) as a key harmonised

---

[55] FSB, IMF and BIS, "Macroprudential Policy Tools and Frameworks: Update to G-20 Finance Ministers and Central Bank Governors" (14 November 2011).

[56] For instance, BIS, "When the Financial Becomes Real" (2015) Chapter III in BIS 85th Annual Economic Report; L Onorante, M Lozej and A Rannenberg, "Countercyclical Capital Regulation in a Small Open Economy DSGE Model" (IFC–National Bank of Belgium Workshop, "Data Needs and Statistics Compilation for Macroprudential Analysis", Brussels, 18–19 May 2017) show that property market indicators are useful in guiding the activation or deactivation of CCyBs in small open economies and are more useful than the popular Credit-to-GDP indicator.

[57] IFC, "Mind the Data Gap: Commercial Property Prices for Policy" (March 2019), available at <https://www.bis.org/ifc/publ/ifc_report_cppis.pdf>. This gap is apparent even after the recent expansion of indicators disseminated by the BIS on prices for residential properties and commercial properties, available at <http://www.bis.org/statistics/pp.htm>.

[58] IFC, "Central banks and Trade Repositories Derivatives Data 2018 Survey" (October 2018), available at <https://www.bis.org/ifc/publ/ifc_report_cb_trade_rep_deriv_data.pdf>, 5.

[59] Ibid.

[60] Serena and Tissot (2017) (n 4), 11.

identifier will hopefully facilitate effective aggregation of data on these transactions.[61]

3. Data on cross-border linkages and activities of global corporations is still lagging behind.[62] For instance, only a limited number of countries report the sectoral identities of international investors and even in those cases, the sectoral identities of the cross-border counterparts are typically not reported.[63]

4. The rapidly growing digital sector, which comprises online platforms, platform-enabled services and suppliers of information and communication technology goods and services, created new data needs.[64] Improved data coverage is needed, for instance, for marketplace lending platforms[65] that facilitate peer-to-peer credit transactions[66] or extend credit from their own funds. These platforms are less regulated than conventional financial intermediaries and may not be subject to reporting requirements.[67] Their data coverage, particularly of platforms that lend their own funds and act as intermediaries, is important for macroprudential purposes as these platforms may generate credit and liquidity risks. Moreover, the digitisation of the economy could also affect the quality and relevance of the available data, which is utilised for macroprudential surveillance. For instance, the growth of the digital sector can affect the

---

[61]   FSB, "Governance Arrangements for the Unique Product Identifier (UPI) Second Consultation Document" (April 2018), available at <https://www.fsb.org/2018/04/governance-arrangements-for-the-unique-product-identifier-upi-second-consultation-document/>.
See also BIS, Committee on Payments and Market Infrastructures Board of the International Organisation of Securities Commission, "Consultative Report: Harmonisation of the Unique Product Identifier" (December 2015).

[62]   On gaps in cross-border data see P Lane, "Cross-Border Financial Linkages: Identifying and Measuring Vulnerabilities" (2015) available at Vox CEPR Policy Portal, available at <https://voxeu.org/article/cross-border-financial-linkages-identifying-and-measuring-vulnerabilities>; on group-level data see Task Force of the Inter-Agency Group on Economic and Financial Statistics, "Consolidation and Corporate Groups: An Overview of Methodological and Practical Issues" (October 2015), available at <https://www.bis.org/ifc/publ/iagrefdoc-oct15.pdf>.

[63]   Lane (2015) (n 62).

[64]   IMF, "Measuring the Digital Economy" (2018) IMF Policy Paper, 7 and 36.

[65]   Ibid, 33; Main Takeaways and Concluding Comments FSB/IMF Global Conference DGI-2 (2019) (n 31) noting the Fintech and digital economy are, unfortunately, only partially covered in the DGI-2.

[66]   Through matching borrowers with individual investors. They may also allow banks and other institutional investors to invest in loans and securitise the loans.

[67]   IMF Measuring the Digital Economy (2018) (n 64), 32.
See also J Younker, "Peer-to-peer Lending: An Emerging Shadow Banking Data Gap" (2017) IFC Bulletin No 46 (The IFC–National Bank of Belgium Workshop "Data Needs and Statistics Compilation for Macroprudential Analysis" Proceedings, Brussels, 18–19 May 2017).

accuracy of estimates of nominal GDP, which is used to gauge the build-up of imbalances,[68] and the national accounts benchmark,[69] which is used as an indicator for setting the CCyB. Closing data gaps on marketplace lending platforms that lend their own funds and on peer-to-peer lending is, therefore, a matter of urgency.[70]

Further challenges for effective data collection for macroprudential purposes, other than specific data gaps, include lack of sufficient resource allocation (skills and IT) and infrastructure to support data access and sharing.[71] Finally, improvement is needed in the level of coordination among statistical agencies, at both the national level and the international level.[72]

3. DATA QUALITY FEATURES FOR MACROPRUDENTIAL ANALYSIS

3.1. WHAT IS DATA QUALITY?

Data quality (or lack thereof) can have far-reaching implications on the quality of policy decisions and accordingly, on the credibility of the supervisory authority. There are numerous international and European frameworks which set out the main quality principles and elements guiding the production and use of data. These include, for instance, the European Statistics Code of Practice,[73] the Bank of England Data Quality Framework[74] and the IMF's Data Quality Assessment Framework (IMF DQAF).[75] The current quality frameworks, however, are not tailored to the purpose of macroprudential analysis and

---

[68] Since survey data used to compile GDP does not always record digital sector output. IMF, "Measuring the Digital Economy" (2018) (n 64), 6; IMF and G20, "Future of Work: Measurement and Policy Challenges" (2018), available at <https://www.imf.org/external/np/g20/pdf/2018/071818a.pdf>, 9.

[69] IMF (2018) (n 64), 26. The benchmark is updated only every five years and does not reflect the size of the sector.

[70] IMF (2018) (n 64), 38.

[71] IMF and FSB, Third Progress Report on G-20 Second Phase of the Data Gaps Initiative (September 2018), 5.

[72] Main Takeaways and Concluding Comments FSB/IMF Global Conference on DGI-2 (2019) (n 31).

[73] European Statistical System Committee, the European Statistics Code of Practice, last updated on 16 November 2017, available <https://ec.europa.eu/eurostat/documents/4031688/8971242/KS-02-18-142-EN-N.pdf/>.

[74] Bank of England, "Data Quality Framework" (March 2014), available at <https://www.bankofengland.co.uk/-/media/boe/files/statistics/data-quality-framework> (DQF).

[75] IMF, "Data Quality Assessment Framework" (May 2012), available at <https://dsbb.imf.org/content/pdfs/dqrs_Genframework.pdf>.

policy implementation. This brought the Bank of England to observe that "The development of statistics for financial stability is in its infancy, and presents a fresh set of challenges, including devising and implementing appropriate quality standards."[76]

Generally, the quality of statistical data is defined in terms of how well outputs meet user needs, or whether they are "fit for purpose".[77] Two important observations can be made at this juncture.

First, in the macroprudential setting, "fit for purpose" would naturally mean collecting data that is relevant and necessary to achieving the macroprudential authority's objective(s) but could be widely interpreted to also mean meeting the expectations of the key stakeholders. Key stakeholders could include "outsiders", such as the various data sources through which data is being transferred to the macroprudential authority and reporting agents from which data is being collected. Accordingly, safeguarding confidentiality and minimising the burden on reporting agents should form part of the quality principles for data collection.

Second, a macroprudential authority is a data consumer from the various data sources outlined above. It can, however, also act as a data producer, as is the case in the US with the FSOC and the OFR. As shall be seen in Section 4.1 below, the purpose of the data collected by the OFR is to support the FSOC in fulfilling its duties and monitoring changes in system-wide risks.[78] In addition, the OFR is tasked with maintaining "expertise in such areas as may be necessary to support specific requests for advice and assistance from financial regulators".[79] Data collected for macroprudential purposes can also be used by micro-prudential authorities and other agencies to fulfil their respective objectives.[80] Thus, the meaning of "fit for purpose" is specificities-dependent.

---

[76] DQF (n 74), 14.

[77] Office of National Statistics, "Guidelines for Measuring Statistical Output Quality" (2013), section A3; or "fitness for use" see OECD, "Quality Framework and Guidelines for OECD Statistical Activities" (17 January 2012), available at <http://www.oecd.org/std/qualityframeworkforoecdstatisticalactivities.htm>, 7.
See also GK Tayi and DP Ballou, "Examining Data Quality" (1998) 41(2) Communications of Association for Computing Machinery 54.

[78] Sections 153(a) and 154(c)(1); 112(a)(2)(A)–(B) and 112(d)(1) Dodd-Frank Act.
See also article 3(2)(a) ESRB Regulation.

[79] Article 154 (c)(1)(E) Dodd-Frank Act.

[80] The purpose of the OFR is also to support member agencies by collecting data on behalf of the FSOC and sharing it with member agencies (section 153(a) Dodd-Frank Act); the OFR is required to share data and information, including software that it develops, with the FSOC, member agencies, and the Bureau of Economic Analysis subject to the approval of the Treasury secretary (as chairperson of the FSOC) (section 153(b) Dodd-Frank Act).
In addition, one of the duties of the FSOC is to facilitate information sharing and coordination among the member agencies and other Federal and State agencies (section 112(a)(2)(E) Dodd-Frank Act).

3.2. ANALYSIS OF QUALITY FEATURES FOR MACROPRUDENTIAL PURPOSES

In broad terms, data quality for macroprudential purposes should include, but are not limited to, the following features.

3.2.1. *Accessibility and Completeness but not Excessiveness*

Accessibility reflects how readily the data can be accessed by the macroprudential authority. This element largely depends on any remaining data gaps as well as the scope and strength of data collection powers of the macroprudential authority (Chapter 4).[81] Macroprudential authorities, however, need to avoid the pitfall of collecting too much information. "Over collecting" data inhibits the effectiveness and quality of the decision-making process and may result in missing the forest for the trees[82] or in "poverty of attention".[83] In addition, a cost-effective approach should be taken to avoid duplication of efforts and utilising, whenever possible, existing sources of data. Ensuring non-excessive data collection will result in a reduced burden on reporting agents and accordingly, will be aligned with the "fit for purpose" requirement.

As shall be seen in Section 5 below, data collection is only the first (necessary but not sufficient) stage in the macroprudential policymaking. To monitor financial instability macroprudential authorities need to process this data through an analytical lens and take the necessary action. Therefore, "As much as collecting dots is necessary, connecting the dots is of critical importance".[84]

---

[81] See, for instance, OFR, "Developing Best Practices For Regulatory Data Collections" (10 May 2016) OFR Viewpoint, available at <https://www.financialresearch.gov/viewpoint-papers/files/OFRvp-2016-01_Best-Practices-Data-Collection.pdf> emphasising accuracy, timeliness, and completeness.

[82] M Ramaswamy, "On the Phenomenon of Information Dilution" (2006) 7 Issues in Information Systems 289 suggest that "information explosion has also made it harder to get the relevant and accurate information needed for good decision-making."

[83] H Simon, "Designing Organizations for an Information-rich World" in M Greenberger (ed), *Computers, Communications, and the Public Interest* (Johns Hopkins Press, 1971), 40–41.

[84] L Awazu, P da Silva and G von Peter, "Financial Instability: Can Big Data Help Connect the Dots?" (The Ninth European Central Bank Statistics Conference on "20 years of ESCB Statistics: What's Next?", Frankfurt am Main, 11 July 2018), available at <https://www.bis.org/speeches/sp181203.pdf>.
In the EU, the recent ESFS Review emphasised that "While improvements in the ability to collect data are to be encouraged, it is not clear that 'more data' should be an end in itself, nor that access to more data would necessarily help the ESRB to identify and assess systemic risks". S McPhilemy and J Roche, "Review of the New European System of Financial Supervision (ESFS) Part 2: The Work of the European Systemic Risk Board – The ESFS's Macro-Prudential Pillar" (October 2013) Report to the ECON PE 507.490, available at <http://www.europarl.europa.eu/RegData/etudes/etudes/join/2013/507490/IPOL-ECON_ET(2013)507490_EN.pdf>, 32.

3.2.2. Timeliness and Accuracy

Timeliness of data refers to the length of time between the availability of data and the event or phenomenon they describe.[85] There may also be an additional reporting lag referring to the length of time between the availability of data to the data sources (such as micro-prudential supervisors) and the availability to the macroprudential authority. Timeliness is a particularly pertinent feature of data collection for macroprudential purposes given that assets of financial institutions are highly liquid and can be shifted quickly into higher, excessive risk. Timely data would ensure that vulnerabilities are detected early and that policy measures are deployed in time. To achieve that, macroprudential authorities should have the power to regularly collect data at short intervals and, where necessary, and in particular, during times of crisis, collect data on an *ad hoc* basis. Furthermore, macroprudential authorities should be cognisant of the potential trade-off between timeliness and accuracy of data[86] and accordingly, prioritise the various data sources. On the one hand, rushed false alarms will damage the credibility of the macroprudential authority and jeopardise its effective operation and on the other hand, tardy responses will defeat the purpose of establishing such a macroprudential authority.

3.2.3. Comparability

Comparability is the degree to which data may be compared over time and/ or across domains. In order to establish comparability across time and adequately assess developments throughout the financial cycle, macroprudential authorities need historical statistical series.[87] Longer time-series data enables macroprudential authorities to corroborate their initial assessment and confirm the causal relationships identified thus enhancing the ability to assess the effectiveness of policy measures.[88] Moreover, comparability across domains

---

[85]   European Statistical System Definitions of Quality Dimensions.

[86]   ECB, "Trade-off between Timeliness and Accuracy, ECB Requirements for General Economic Statistics" (15 March 2001). Accuracy refers to the closeness between the estimated value and the (unknown) true value.

[87]   Serena and Tissot (2017) (n 4), 5.
       See also OFR, "Developing Best Practices for Regulatory Data Collections" OFR Viewpoint 16-01, 10 May 2016 refers to interoperability of data.

[88]   C Lim and others, "Macroprudential Policy: What Instruments and How to Use Them? Lessons from Country Experiences" (2011) IMF Working Paper 238, available at <https://www.imf.org/external/pubs/ft/wp/2011/wp11238.pdf>; M Flood, H Jagadish and A Kyle, "Using Data for Systemic Financial Risk Management" (Conference on "Innovative Data systems Research", California, 9–12 January 2011).

in the macroprudential sphere is multifaceted: it could refer to comparability across sectors, across financial products and ultimately across global markets.[89]

Both the de Larosière High-Level Group and the Issing Committee recommended the creation of an international risk map that will include a common database with data on all major international financial institutions and all major financial products in order to identify systemic risks on a global scale.[90] Until such a utopia is reached, initiatives such as the global LEI are welcomed.

3.2.4. Aggregated and Granular Data

There is no consensus on how detailed the data collected for the purpose of conducting macroprudential analysis needs to be. Generally, macroprudential authorities cannot solely rely on aggregate statistics in order to assess effectively vulnerabilities. To form a nuanced view of the financial system and reveal underlying developments and distribution of risks, macroprudential authorities need to "drill-down" to the granular level.[91] More granular data enables macroprudential policymakers to identify the specific mechanism(s) underlying the build-up of systemic risk and implement targeted measures to address the specific source that is causing it.[92] For example, where a macroprudential authority flags out, based on aggregated data, acceleration of credit to businesses in a specific country, the data will not point to the underlying sources or nature of that development.[93] Is it because of a better access to credit and a greater appetite for investment? Or alternatively, is it triggered by fragile and highly indebted companies increasing their borrowing, accompanied by deterioration of credit standards?[94] The two options signify the difference between a healthy growth that will not result in materialisation of systemic risks and a credit boom that requires policy intervention and timely implementation of macroprudential measures. Granular loan-by-loan data can reveal the characteristics of specific

---

[89]   IMF, BIS and FSB, "The Financial Crisis and Information Gaps" Report to G20 (October 2009); IMF, BIS and FSB, "The Financial Crisis and Information Gaps" Second Progress Report (June 2011).

[90]   The High-Level Group on Financial Supervision in the EU (February 2009) (the de Larosière Report), Recommendation 27; The Issing Committee, "New Financial Order" (London, 2 April 2009), para 2.

[91]   Buch (2017) (n 52); K Knot, "Granular Data and Macroprudential Policy: Examples and Challenges" (8th ECB Statistics Conference on "Central Bank Statistics: Moving Beyond the Aggregates", Frankfurt am Main, 6 July 2016).

[92]   JL Peydro, L Laeven and X Frixas, *Systemic Risk, Crises and Macroprudential Regulation* (MIT Press, 2015), 167.

[93]   Indeed, only one in three credit booms are followed by a crisis. Dell'Ariccia and others, "Credit Booms and Macrofinancial Stability in Economic Policy" (CEPR, 2016), 299, 304.

[94]   S Lautenschläger, "Central Bank Statistics: Moving Beyond the Aggregates" (The Eighth ECB Statistics Conference, Frankfurt am Main, 5 July 2016), available at <https://www.ecb.europa.eu/press/key/date/2016/html/sp160705_1.en.html>.

groups of counterparties and enable the macroprudential authority to assess the "driving forces" behind the aggregate picture.[95]

Another example of the importance of the granularity of data is in the context of data needs on the shadow banking sector. Whilst global and national aggregated figures of shadow banking is vital, granular data is needed to identify particular sources of systemic risks arising from the shadow banking sector and answering questions such as

> how do shocks hitting individual institutions propagate through the system? How important are linkages between different sectors, including between the shadow banking sector and the traditional banking sector, for the propagation of shocks? Has the strength of cross-border channels of contagion increased or decreased and how relevant are common exposures?[96]

More granular data raises, however, concerns over lack of comparability and difficulty in compilation and sharing of data[97] as well as meeting confidentiality restrictions.[98] The legal framework or the decision-making process underlying the macroprudential authority's data collection task should, therefore, put in place safeguards to protect firm-level data and identification of specific institutions from the disclosed data. This is a salient issue particularly in a regional macroprudential authority, such as the ESRB. Without satisfactory confidentiality arrangements, member countries will not be willing to share data about local institutions that are experiencing difficulties for fear that the data could be leaked and negatively affect market confidence and even precipitate a crisis. Therefore, when collecting data from the various data sources (such as the ESAs and the ECB) the ESRB uses a granularity rule of thumb. According to the rule, aggregated data comprises data on at least three legal persons, none of which represents 85 per cent or more of the relevant market, whether it consists of one or more Member States or the Union as a whole.[99] This rule, however, is

---

[95] B Coeuré, "Policy Analysis with Big Data" (Conference on "Economic and Financial Regulation in the Era of Big Data" organised by the Banque de France, Paris, 24 November 2017).

[96] Buch (2017) (n 52).

[97] S Cecchetti, I Fender and P McGuire, "Toward a Global Risk Map" (2010) BIS Working Paper 309.

[98] IMF, BIS and FSB, Information Gaps Progress Report (June 2011) (n 89), 24.

[99] Decision of the ESRB of 21 July 2015 on the Provision and Collection of Information for the Macro-prudential Oversight of the Financial System within the Union repealing Decision ESRB/2015/2 OJ C 394/4 (ESRB Data Collection Decision). However, if dispersion measures are disclosed to the ESRB in addition to the aggregated information, the information is more granular. In that case, the aggregated information will comprise data on at least five legal persons when referring to publicly available data and on at least six legal persons when there is a need to protect confidential firm-level data (Annex II of the ESRB Data Collection Decision) Dispersion measures are not defined in the Decision. Measures of dispersion are the quantities that characterise the "spread" of the data (<Unesco.org>).

disposed of when it comes to collecting data on an *ad hoc* basis. Here, the ESRB General Board has more flexibility, particularly useful in times of crisis, and is able to collect more granular data.[100]

4. INSTITUTIONAL STRUCTURE: DATA COLLECTION AND ANALYSIS TASKS

4.1. FSOC AND OFR

The US is an interesting example of an institutional structure that partly outsources the function of data collection and analysis and separates it from the macroprudential authority. The FSOC is empowered to collect data from its member agencies, other federal and state financial regulatory agencies, and the Federal Insurance Office.[101] The FSOC can also provide direction and request data and analysis from the Office of Financial Research (OFR) to support its work.[102] If necessary to assess risks to the US financial system, the FSOC may also direct the OFR to collect information from bank holding companies and non-bank financial companies.[103] The OFR is therefore designed to support the FSOC in fulfilling its purposes and duties.[104] This includes collecting data on behalf of the FSOC and providing such data to the FSOC and member agencies, standardising the types and formats of data reported and collected, performing applied and essential long-term research, and developing new tools for measuring and monitoring risk in the financial system.[105] As to be expected, the FSOC and the OFR and the other member agencies are subject to confidentiality of any data, information, and reports.[106]

The Dodd-Frank Act mandated the establishment of two separate units within the OFR: a Data Center and a Research and Analysis Center.[107] The Data Center Analysis is responsible to collect, validate, and maintain data obtained from "member agencies, commercial data providers, publicly available data sources, and financial entities".[108] To that end, the OFR is empowered to "require the submission of periodic and other reports from any financial company for the purpose of assessing the extent to which a financial activity or financial

---

100   Annex III of the ESRB Data Collection Decision (n 99).
101   Sections 112(a)(2)(A) and 112(d)(1), (2) Dodd-Frank Act.
102   Section 112(a)(2)(B) Dodd-Frank Act.
103   Section 112(a)(2)(A) Dodd-Frank Act.
      See also sections 112(d)(3)(A) and 116 Dodd-Frank Act.
104   Section 153(a) Dodd-Frank Act.
105   Ibid.
106   Sections 112(d)(5) and 154(b)(2)(B) Dodd-Frank Act.
107   Section 154(a) Dodd-Frank Act.
108   Section 154(b)(1)(A) Dodd-Frank Act.

market in which the financial company participates, or the financial company itself, poses a threat to the financial stability of the United States"[109] and collect, in consultation with the FSOC, financial transaction data and position data from financial companies.[110] However, to mitigate reporting burdens, before requiring the submission of a report from any financial company, the OFR has to coordinate with the relevant member agency, primary financial regulatory agency, a foreign supervisory authority and whenever possible, rely on information available from such agencies or authority.[111] The OFR may share data and information with the FSOC, the public, its member agencies, and the Bureau of Economic Analysis.[112]

The Research and Analysis Center is responsible to "conduct, coordinate and sponsor research to support and improve regulation of financial entities and markets", "maintain expertise in such areas as may be necessary to support specific requests for advice and assistance from financial regulators" and "conduct studies and provide advice on the impact of policies related to systemic risk".[113]

The OFR is an office within the Treasury, albeit it is designed to be independent from both the FSOC and the Treasury.[114] Its Director is appointed for a six-year term by the President and with the advice and consent of the Senate.[115] The independence of the OFR is also in terms of funding. Its expenses[116] are ensured

---

[109] Section 154(b)(1)(B)(1) Dodd-Frank Act.

[110] Section 154(b)(1)(B)(3) Dodd-Frank Act. For definition of Financial transaction data and position data see section 151 Dodd-Frank Act. "Financial transaction data" is defined as "the structure and legal description of a financial contract, with sufficient detail to describe the rights and obligations between counterparties and make possible an independent valuation." "Position data" includes: (1) "data on financial assets or liabilities held on the balance sheet of a financial company, where positions are created or changed by the execution of a financial transaction"; and (2) "information that identifies counterparties, the valuation by the financial company of the position, and information that makes possible an independent valuation of the position."

[111] Section 154(b)(1)(B)(2) Dodd-Frank Act.

[112] Note the distinction here between data and information as discussed below. Sections 153(b)(1) and 154(b)(5) Dodd-Frank Act. The OFR can, after consultation with the member agencies, provide certain data to financial industry participants and to the general public subject to confidentiality requirements and where it poses no significant threats to the financial system of the United States. Section 154(b)(6) Dodd-Frank Act.
AL Nazareth and ME Tahyar, "Transparency and Confidentiality in the Post Financial Crisis World – Where to Strike the Balance?" (2011) 1 Harvard Business Law Review 145.

[113] Section 154(c) Dodd-Frank Act.

[114] Section 152(a) Dodd-Frank Act. The independence of the OFR is evident in section 153(d)(2) Dodd-Frank Act that ensures that no officer or agency of the US can require the OFR Director to submit congressional testimony to any officer or agency of the US for approval, comment or review prior to the submission of such testimony.

[115] Section 152(b)(1)–(2) Dodd-Frank Act.

[116] This includes expenses of the FSOC (section 118 Dodd-Frank Act) and certain expenses of the FDIC (section 210 Dodd-Frank Act).

through the "Financial Research Fund" in the Treasury[117] and collected from non-bank financial companies with total consolidated assets of $250 billion or greater, G-SIB and non-bank financial companies supervised by the Board of Governors of the Federal Reserve.[118]

The independence of the OFR is intended to ensure a high degree of insularity from political and industry pressure.[119] Nonetheless, in practice, the independence of the OFR has been frequently questioned, arguably given its subordinate position within Treasury.[120] Moreover, the separation of regulation and supervision from data collection and analysis tasks may come with a risk of an informational disadvantage of the OFR. As such, the OFR

> would not be involved directly in supervision or market monitoring, such an agency would be hampered in its ability to understand the types of information needed to effectively monitor systemic risks and conduct macroprudential supervision. Data collection and analysis are not done in a vacuum; an agency's duties will inevitably reflect the priorities, experience, and interests of the collecting entity. Even regular arms-length consultations among agencies might not be effective, because detailed

---

[117] Section 155 Dodd-Frank Act, as amended by section 401 Economic, Growth Regulatory Relief and Consumer Protection Act Public Law No 115–174 115th Congress. Section 401(c)(1)(d) Economic Growth Act replaced the $50 billion reference in section 155(d) Dodd-Frank Act with $250 billion. In addition, section 401(f)(2) of the Economic Growth Act required for the purposes of section 155(d) Dodd-Frank Act any bank holding company, regardless of assets size, that was identified as a G-SIB (under section 217.402 of title 12, Code of Federal Regulation) to be considered a bank holding company with total consolidated assets equal to or greater than $250 billion.

[118] The US Treasury Department, "Assessment of Fees on Large Bank Holding Companies and Nonbank Financial Companies Supervised by the Federal Reserve Board to Cover the Expenses of the Financial Research Fund" 21 May 2012, 77 FR 29884.
      A proposed rule is currently open to public comments. The US Treasury Department Proposed Rule, "Assessment of Fees on Certain Bank Holding Companies and Nonbank Financial Companies Supervised by the Federal Reserve Board to Cover the expenses of the Financial Research Fund" 4 November 2019, 84 FR 59320.

[119] MS Barr, "Comment: Accountability and Independence in Financial Regulation: Checks and Balances, Public Engagement and Other Innovations" (2015) 78 Law and Contemporary Problems 119, 125 observing that "The OFR can act as an independent voice regarding financial stability, serving as a counterweight to the Fed and other supervisory agencies".

[120] V Finkle, "The Most Important Agency You've Never Heard of the Office of Financial Research is meant to be the early-warning system for the next financial crisis. Is it Doing its Job?", *Washington Monthly* (12 June 2016); S Johnson, "The Disappointing Office of Financial Research", *The New York Times* (30 January 2014) a former Chief Economist of the IMF observed that "The Office of Financial Research could have been set up to be more independent of Treasury – and this was part of the original intent. It has an independent budget, but appears to operate very much under Treasury's wing."
      See also EA Ludwig, "Assessment of Dodd-Frank Financial Regulatory Reform: Strengths, Challenges and Opportunities for a Stronger Regulatory System" (2012) 29 Yale Journal 181, 185 questioning "… whether, in a presidential election year, the OFR will be able to express its views freely as to the dangers ahead, particularly if those dangers may have been caused by a president's policies".

appreciation of the regulatory context within which financial activities that generate data and risks is needed.[121]

The OFR data collection authority is also armed with strong teeth. The OFR Director can require from a financial company, by subpoena, the production of the data under its power of data collection, following a written finding that such data is required to carry out the OFR data collection functions and that the OFR has coordinated with the relevant primary financial regulatory agency.[122] In the case of contumacy or failure to obey a subpoena, it is enforceable by order of the court.[123]

To date, however, the OFR subpoena power has not been used and the OFR has been able to accomplish much of its work "relying on data already collected by other regulators, or voluntarily provided by industry, rather than undertaking compulsory measures."[124]

Nevertheless, there is much room to improve the effectiveness of the OFR's data collection process from the relevant agencies as "procuring such data takes months or years, and many requests remain under discussion among legal teams."[125] In addition, while the OFR has been mandated to standardise the types and format of data reported and collected on behalf of the FSOC,[126] standardisation of data is lagging behind, and agencies have been slow to abandon their individual data identification systems.[127] Recently, however, the OFR has signed bilateral memoranda of understanding with various financial agencies and thus gained access, for instance, to data which the SEC collects

---

[121]   Testimony of DK Tarullo, "Equipping Financial Regulators with Tools Necessary to Monitor Systemic Risk", 12 February 2010, Hearing Before the Subcommittee on Security and International Trade and Finance, 42. Also suggesting that the separation of data collection and regulation could also dilute accountability if supervisors did not have authority to shape the form and scope of reporting requirements by regulated entities in accordance with supervisory needs.

[122]   Section 153(f)(1) Dodd-Frank Act. Coordination is required under section 154(b)(1)(B)(2) Dodd-Frank Act.

[123]   Section 153(f)(3) Dodd-Frank Act.

[124]   Testimony of OFR Director Richard Berner before the US House Financial Services Subcommittee on Oversight and Investigations, Hearing on "Examining the OFR", 7 December 2017.

[125]   Ibid.

[126]   Section 153(a)(2) Dodd-Frank Act.

[127]   Testimony of OFR Director Richard Berner (2017) (n 124); A Grody, "The House Gives Data Standardisation Another Go", The Hill (12 May 2019) agencies are reluctant to make changes to their internal systems. Perhaps reflecting "a lack of regulatory understanding regarding the benefits or a failure to adequately value gains that accrue outside a particular regulator's mandate."
See also R Berner and K Judge, "The Data Standardization Standard" (2019) European Corporate Governance Institute Working Paper No 438; Columbia Law and Economics Working Paper No 598 Forthcoming in DW Arner, E Avgouleas, D Busch and SL Schwarcz (eds), Systemic Risk in the Financial Sector: Ten Years After the Great Crash (CIGI Press, 2019).

from hedge funds and data which the Federal Reserve collects from banks for its annual stress tests.[128]

4.2.　ESRB

The ESRB is tasked with determining and/or collecting and analysing all relevant and necessary information for the macroprudential oversight of the financial system within the EU in order to contribute to the prevention or mitigation of systemic risks to financial stability in the EU.[129]

Article 15 entrusts the ESRB with the powers to perform this task. The ESAs, the ESCB, the European Commission, the national supervisory authorities and national statistics authorities are all required to cooperate closely with the ESRB and provide it with all the information necessary for the fulfilment of its tasks in accordance with EU legislation.[130] The ESRB is empowered to request information from the ESAs, as a rule, in a summary or aggregate form, such that individual financial institutions cannot be identified.[131] Similarly to the OFR's framework, existing data has to be utilised before requesting to collect other data. As such, the ESRB first has to take account of the existing statistics produced, disseminated and developed by the European Statistical System (ESS) and the ESCB.[132] If the requested information is not available or is not available in a timely manner, the ESRB may request it from the ESCB, the national supervisory authorities or the national statistics authorities and if the

---

[128]　G Feldberg, "Don't Dismantle the Post-Crisis Early Warning System", Brookings, November 2018, available at <https://www.brookings.edu/research/dont-dismantle-the-post-crisis-early-warning-system/>.

[129]　Article 3(2) ESRB Regulation. The mechanism and guiding principles of the ESRB's data collection exercises are set out in the ESRB Data Collection Decision (n 99). Articles 2 and 3 of that decision refer to both ongoing data collection and *ad hoc* requests of aggregated information.

[130]　Article 15(2) ESRB Regulation.

[131]　Article 15(3) ESRB Regulation.

[132]　Article 15(4) ESRB Regulation. The order of these subsections is somewhat cumbersome as the ESRB will receive the necessary information first under article 15(4) of the ESRB Regulation (from the ESS and the ESCB) and only then will it receive information under article 15(3) (from the ESAs).
　　The ESS is the partnership between the Community Statistical Authority (Eurostat), the national statistical institutes and other national authorities responsible in each Member State for the development, production and dissemination of European statistics. Council Regulation (EC) 223/2009 of 11 March 2009 on European Statistics [2009] OJ L 87; Council Regulation (EC) 2533/98 of 23 November 1998 concerning the Collection of Statistical Information by the ECB [1998] OJ L 318, 8; Council Regulation (EU) 2015/373 of 5 March 2015 amended Regulation (EC) No 2533/98 Concerning the Collection of Statistical Information by the ECB OJ L 64/6 to enable the transmission and use, by ESCB Members and the relevant authorities (including the ESRB) of the statistical information collected by the ESCB (preamble para 3).

information remains unavailable the ESRB may request the information from the Member State concerned.[133]

The ESRB Regulation includes a specific provision for requesting information of a supervisory nature which is not in summary or aggregate form.[134] The ESRB is required to submit, after consulting with the relevant ESA, a justified and proportionate request, explaining why the data is deemed to be systemically relevant and necessary, considering the prevailing market situation.[135] If the relevant ESA does not consider the request to be justified and proportionate, it will send the request back to the ESRB and ask for additional justification.[136] The ESRB Regulation, however, does not clarify what the procedure will be in case the additional justification provided by the ESRB does not convince the relevant ESA that the request is justified and proportionate.[137]

Preventing identification of individual financial institutions is a critical issue in the ESRB data collection process particularly due to the sensitivity of a micro-data and the broad range of parties involved in the ESRB's governance structure that arguably increases the risk of leakages. Thus, confidential information, obtained while performing the ESRB tasks, cannot be divulged to any person or authority whatsoever, except in summary or aggregate form.[138] This sweeping restriction may inhibit the ability of the ESRB to issue appropriate warnings and recommendations, where it identifies an individual institution as posing a systemic risk for the financial system and perhaps there is room to relax it.[139] The Regulation amending the ESRB Regulation now permits members of the ESRB from national central banks, national supervisory and macroprudential authorities to provide, subject to certain safeguards, to national authorities or to bodies responsible for the stability of the financial systems information which is necessary for the exercise of their tasks.[140] However, it seems that this new

---

[133] Article 15(5) ESRB Regulation.

[134] Articles 15(6)–(7) ESRB Regulation.

[135] Article 15(7) ESRB Regulation, as amended. The Regulation amending the ESRB Regulation clarified that such information will be of a supervisory nature.

[136] Ibid.

[137] IMF, "Lessons from the European Financial Stability Framework Exercise" (2011) Country Report No 186, available at <http://www.imf.org/external/pubs/ft/scr/2011/cr11186.pdf>. In order to ensure a smooth exchange of non-aggregate information the report suggests establishing guidelines with the ESAs outlining criteria for handling such "reasoned" requests.

[138] ESRB Regulation, article 8(3).

[139] It is to be noted that to be differentiated from the FSOC, the ESRB does not have designation powers.

[140] Regulation amending the ESRB Regulation inserting article 8(2a). According to the new article 8(2b) where information originates from other authorities that those referred to in paragraph 2a, members of the ESRB from national central banks, national supervisory authorities and national authorities entrusted with the conduct of macroprudential policy may use the information for the exercise of their statutory tasks with explicit agreement with those authorities.

provision is still subject to the sweeping restriction with regard to disclosure to any authority in summary or aggregate form.

Overall, the ESRB data collection process is comprehensive but has proved to be particularly cumbersome and lengthy.[141] Moreover, it lacks any teeth, with no method whereby the rights of access to information may be enforced or any procedure whereby disagreements are to be resolved.[142]

5. CHALLENGES FOR THE FUTURE: THE USE OF BIG DATA AND MACHINE LEARNING FOR MACROPRUDENTIAL ANALYSIS

Big data could be an effective tool in supporting analysis for macroprudential purposes and holds the promise to improve the accuracy and timeliness of policy decisions.[143]

The conventional understanding of big data refers to "bigginess" in terms of the scale of the data (high-volume); the speed at which data is created, processed and stored (high-velocity); diversity and complexity of the data types and sources (high-variety).[144] Over time, the list of Vs have expanded and now

---

[141] Report from the Commission to the European Parliament and the Council on the Mission and Organisation of the ESRB COM (2014) 508 final, 10 "Stakeholders have identified a need to improve the processes for dealing with the exchange of data between the ESRB and ESAs within the ESFS. There is a detailed and lengthy approval process through which the ESRB receives data, which can affect the timeliness and impact of its output."

[142] A provision referring to the enforcement of the ESRB right to collect information was suggested in the European Parliament's Report on the Proposal for a Regulation on Community Macroprudential Oversight of the Financial System and Establishing the ESRB 2009/0140 (COD), amendment 79 proposing a new para 4a as follows: "If information referred to in this Article is not made available or in the event of an emergency, the General Board may call on the European Parliament and the Council to act in an appropriate way." This was not included in the final version of article 15 ESRB Regulation.

[143] B Tissot, "Big Data and Central Banking" (2017) IFC Bulletin 44 (IF Satellite Meeting, ISI Regional Statistics Conference, "Big Data", Bali, 21 March 2017), available at <https://www.bis.org/ifc/publ/ifcb44_overview_rh.pdf>; C Hammer, D Kostroch and G Quiros, "Big Data: Potential, Challenges, and Statistical Implications" (2017) IMF Staff Discussion Note 6.

[144] D Laney, "3D Data Management: Controlling Data Volume, Velocity and Variety" (February 2001), available at <https://blogs.gartner.com/doug-laney/files/2012/01/ad949-3D-Data-Management-Controlling-Data-Volume-Velocity-and-Variety.pdf>. But R Kitchin and G McArdle, "What Makes Big Data, Big Data? Exploring the Ontological Characteristics of 26 Datasets" (2016) 3(1) Big Data and Society that the 3Vs meme is actually false and misleading. See also Survey conducted by IFC, "Central Banks' Use of and Interest in 'Big Data'" (2015), available at <https://www.bis.org/ifc/publ/ifc-report-bigdata.pdf> Annex 2 for a comprehensive list of definitions; A Katal, M Wazid and R Goudar, "Big Data: Issues, Challenges, Tools and Good Practices" (2013) (Proceedings of the Sixth International Conference on Contemporary Computing, Noida: IEEE, 2013) 404–409, available at <https://www.ibmbigdatahub.com/infographic/four-vs-big-data>; PN Andersen, "Big data – the Hunt for Timely Insights and Decision Certainty: Central Banking Reflections on the Use of Big Data for Policy Purposes" (2016) IFC Working Paper No 14.

includes many other Vs, for instance, the uncertainty of data, i.e. noise and bias (high-veracity)[145] but at times, it is difficult to distinguish between Vs that signify the defining features of big data and the challenges it presents.

The interest in utilising big data to benefit macroeconomic and financial statistics and accordingly, macroprudential analysis is gaining momentum. A recent survey shows that big data is a mainstream activity for central banks and increasingly plays a significant role in policymaking and supervisory processes,[146] particularly for monetary and macroprudential purposes.[147]

Big data can be used to produce new (and more accurate) risk indicators and establish a more comprehensive early warning system to monitor the build-up of systemic risks.[148] Big data offers faster insights to macroprudential authorities since key variables, such as financial and price data can be observed almost instantaneously.[149] By providing more granular data, big data can also assist in exposing and assessing the effects of macroprudential policy measures and consequently generate and produce more data. Moreover, there is a myriad of innovative ways to utilise big data for macroprudential policy analysis such as, to construct a sentiment-based early-warning system[150] and use of SWIFT data

---

[145] B Marr, "Big data: The 5 Vs Everyone Must Know" (6 March 2014), available at <https://www.linkedin.com/pulse/20140306073407-64875646-big-data-the-5-vs-everyone-must-know>; E Uprichard, "Big Data, Little Questions", *Discover Society* (1 October 2013), available at <http://discoversociety.org/2013/10/01/focus-big-data-little-questions/>. More recently, T Shafer, "The 42 V's of Big Data and Data Science" (2017) Elder Research Inc, available at <https://www.kdnuggets.com/2017/04/42-vs-big-data-data-science.html>.
See also D Lupton, "The Thirteen Ps of Big Data", *The Sociological Life* (13 May 2015), available at <https://simplysociology.wordpress.com/2015/05/11/the-thirteen-ps-of-big-data/> suggests swapping the Vs of big data with Ps words but Kitchin and McArdle (2016) (n 143) contend that "While useful entry points into thinking critically about Big Data, these additional v-words and new p-words are often descriptive of a broad set of issues associated with Big Data, rather than characterising the ontological traits of the data themselves".

[146] Central Banking in association with BaeringPoint, "Big Data in Central Banks Survey 2018", available at <https://www.centralbanking.com/central-banks/economics/data/3661931/big-data-in-central-banks-2018-survey-results>.

[147] Ibid. Around 90 per cent of respondents to the 2018 Big Data in Central Banks Survey prioritised macroprudential policy first or second and the importance of big data for macroprudential policy was particularly evident in emerging market central banks.
See also IFC, "Central banks' Use of and Interest in 'big data'" Survey (2015) (n 142); AG Haldane, "Will Big Data Keep Its Promise?" (Data Analytics for Finance and Macro Research Centre, King's Business School, 19 April 2018).

[148] R Kitchin, "Big Data and Official Statistics: Opportunities, Challenges and Risks" (2015) 31(3) Statistical Journal of the International Association of Official Statistics 471; V Mayer-Schonberger and K Cukier, *A Revolution that Will Transform How We Live* (John Murray, 2013), 52 contend that big data shows policymakers what is happening rather than why it is happening.

[149] Hammer and others (2017) (n 143), 15.

[150] For instance, R Nyman and others, "News and Narratives in Financial Systems: Exploiting Big Data for Systemic Risk Assessment" (January 2018) Bank of England Staff Working Paper No 704 apply algorithmic analysis to large amounts of financial market text-based data and show the formation of very high levels of sentiment (excitement) prior to the global financial crisis.

to monitor global financial flows thus assisting macroprudential supervisors in early identification of movements and trends and assessment of concentration and cross-border transactions.[151] In the UK, the FPC used the FCA's Product Sales Database to inform and calibrate its decisions on setting macroprudential restrictions on high LTI mortgages to households.[152]

Difficulties in accessing and processing big data and ensuring its quality are seen, however, as significant challenges.[153] To begin with, while partnership between the private sector can improve access to data[154] it may become increasingly more difficult to do so with the transition of big data from being a by-product to an asset generated by the private sector.[155] In addition, big data is "complex, incomplete and noisy and can contain outliers and extreme events"[156] and thus its quality becomes a central concern when used to inform policy decisions. The perceived accuracy of big data can also generate a false sense of certainty and precision and potentially lead to misguided policy decisions.[157] Furthermore, big data can be unstructured[158] and can originate from diversified sources ranging from public and official sources, databases of financial institutions and data vendors and to a lesser extent, internet-based data.[159] Therefore, integration, processing and extracting insights from such data become harder,[160] particularly in the absence of a tailored best practice or

---

[151]   These are insights and correlations to be differentiated from actual information (such as positions of outstanding debt). Hammers and others (2017) (n 143), 17.
    See, for instance, P Cerchiello and P Giudici, "Big Data Analysis for Financial Risk Management" (2016) 3(1) Journal of Big Data 1 using big data of financial tweets.

[152]   FPC, Financial Stability Report, June 2014.

[153]   Hammer and others (2017) (n 143), 11. As well as new required skills and technologies. IMF and FSB DGI-2 Third Progress Report, September 2018 (n 71).

[154]   IMF, "Measuring the Digital Economy" (2018) (n 64), 37.

[155]   Hammer and others (2017) (n 143), 22.

[156]   Ibid, 21.

[157]   Tissot (2017) (n 143), 3.

[158]   E Baldacci and others, "Big Data and Macroeconomic Nowcasting: From Data Access to Modelling" (2016) Eurostat Statistical Books, available at <https://ec.europa.eu/eurostat/documents/3888793/7753027/KS-TC-16-024-EN-N.pdf>; Coeuré, "Policy Analysis with Big Data" (2017) (n 95). Though the use of unstructured big data relatively limited, often targeted at methodological improvements, reducing reporting lags and revisions. B Tissot, "How Can Big Data Support Financial Stability Work?" (Workshop on "Big Data for Economic Statistics: Challenges and Opportunities", Rio de Janeiro, 11 September 2018).
    On the use of unstructured data for macroeconomic and microeconomic analysis by the Bank of Italy see D Broeders and J Prenio, "Innovative Technology in Financial Supervision (Suptech) – The Experience of Early Users" (2018) BIS Financial Stability Institute Insights No 9, 15.

[159]   Hammer and others (2017) (n 143), 9.

[160]   L Cai and Y Zhu, "The Challenges of Data Quality and Data Quality Assessment in the Big Data Era" (2015) Data Science Journal 14, 2; Flood and others, "Big Data Challenges and Opportunities in Financial Stability Monitoring" (April 2016) 20 Financial Stability Review, Banque de France 129–142.
    See also L Alexander and others, "Research Challenges in Financial Data Modelling and Analysis" (2017) 5(3) Big Data 177.

methodological guidance for the use of big data.[161] Finally, since the source of big data is often in the private sector, the availability and comparability of data over time and across countries is problematic and uncertain.[162]

Machine learning algorithms are also increasingly used in macroprudential policymaking.[163] The technology entails a great potential in improving systemic risks surveillance by automating macroprudential analysis and data quality assurance.[164] Machine learning algorithms are "capable of learning from massive amounts of data, and once that data is internalised, they are capable of making decisions experientially or intuitively like humans."[165]

The use of machine learning for macroprudential analysis, however, comes with a price. It might lead to costly misguided policy decisions and thus, undermine the credibility of macroprudential authorities.[166] Still, rather than being unique to the use of machine learning this danger may be inherent in the introduction of new technological advancements. On the dangers of using novel technology in financial regulation, Kenneth Bamberger explained that:

> Technology systems are not merely tools for implementing the goals of those who employ them; they shape the meaning of those goals themselves ... they create ... world view, that alters the perceptions of the decisionmakers they inform. In the context of risk, they privilege the measurable and mask uncertainty, obscuring the very hazards with which policymakers are concerned and clouding the judgment

---

[161] Tissot (2017) (n 143), 5.

[162] R Kitchin, "Big Data and Official Statistics: Opportunities Challenges and Risks" (2015) 31(3) Journal of the International Association of Official Statistics 471.
See also Baldacci and others (2016) (n 158).

[163] Including for network analysis, sentiment analysis and big data analysis. See G Kou and others, "Machine Learning Methods for Systemic Risk Analysis in Financial Sectors" (2019) 25(2) Technological and Economic Development of Economy 716.
On the use of Artificial Intelligence in macroprudential policymaking see J Danielsson, A Macrae and A Uthemann, "Artificial Intelligence, Financial Risk Management and Systemic Risk" (2017) Systemic Risk Center Special Paper No 17.
See also "Future of Finance Report, Review on the Outlook for the UK Financial System: What It Means For the Bank of England" Chaired by Huw van Steenis, June 2019, 14 and 20 emphasise that "Machine learning and new data sets can strengthen the Bank's armoury to spot irregularities and get a better picture of the system's overall health and emerging risks" and advocated to "develop principles, and share best practice, for the responsible, explainable and accountable use of machine learning in finance".

[164] FSB, "Artificial Intelligence and Machine Learning in Financial Services Market Developments and Financial Stability Implications" (November 2017), available at <https://www.fsb.org/wp-content/uploads/P011117.pdf>, 21; T Cagala, "Improving Data Quality and Closing Data Gaps with Machine Learning" (IFC-National Bank of Belgium Workshop on "Data Needs and Statistics Compilation for Macroprudential Analysis", Brussels, 18–19 May 2017).

[165] Y Bathaee, "The Artificial Intelligence Black Box and the Failure of Intent and Causation" (2018) 31(2) Harvard Journal of Law and Technology 889, 891.

[166] B Tissot, "Financial Big Data and Policy Work: Opportunities and Challenges" (2019) Eurostat Statistical Working Papers, available at <https://ec.europa.eu/eurostat/documents/3888793/9545860/KS-TC-19-001-EN-N.pdf>, 13.

of users upon whom risk regulation relies. Moreover, they create automation biases-decision pathologies that hinder careful review of automated outcomes ...[167]

One of these biases is a "bias towards the knowable and measurable-or at least towards those types of risks that risk culture believes can be known and measured ... As such, the process tends to exclude from automation those things that cannot be automated".[168] This bias can be most notable in data analysis in the macroprudential sphere, where initial inputs, patterns and indicators are shaped by humans (often homogenised group of central banks) who may naturally have a narrow and perhaps backwards-looking view of sources of systemic risks. There is a risk, therefore, that uncertainty will be left "off-screen".[169]

These concerns resulted in a rather extreme reaction of some scholars who contend that the use of AI in macroprudential policymaking is dangerous and even has the potential to destabilise the financial system:

> ... the systemic danger emanating from an AI engine working for the financial authorities is that it will focus on the least important types of risk, those that are readily measured while missing out on the more dangerous endogenous risk. In effect, it will automate and reinforce the adoption of mistaken assumptions that are already a central part of current crises. In doing so, it will make the resulting complacency even more likely to build up over time.[170]

In addition, and related to that, machine learning algorithms can be "black boxes, even to their creators",[171] and is "as difficult to understand as the human brain".[172] Where macroprudential authorities cannot fully understand how the model is arriving at its decisions or predictions, their transparency and accountability are accordingly diluted. After all, reasons for policy decisions cannot be communicated to the public or parliament, simply because they are absent from the decision-making process.

As shall be seen in Section 6 below, understanding these gaps and biases and the way to overcome them is rooted in the difference between data, knowledge

---

[167] KA Bamberger, "Technologies of Compliance: Risk and Regulation in a Digital Age" (2009/10) 88 Texas Law Review 669.

[168] Ibid, 707.

[169] Ibid, 712. Therefore, Danielsson and others (2017) (n 163) suggest that prior to the 2007–2009 financial crisis regulators missed the danger of CDOs and that AI analysis probably would not have done any better given that "If there are no observations on the consequences of subprime mortgages put into CDOs with liquidity guarantees, there is nothing to train on".

[170] Danielsson and others (2017) (n 163), 9. Also suggesting that because AI favours best practice and standardised best-of-breed models that closely resemble each other, it increases pro-cyclicality and hence systemic risk. In addition, the scholars contend that, being removed from human understanding, AI analysis and conclusions might not coincide with our human objectives.

[171] Bathaee (2018) (n 165), 891.

[172] D Castelvecchi, "Can We Open the Black Box of AI?", *Nature* (5 October 2016).

and expertise. In particular, to ensure expertise is strengthened and tailored to the macroprudential policymaking, it is vital to embed, in the data collection and analysis process, collaboration with the financial industry and other market players.[173]

6. CONNECTING THE DOTS OR CLOSING THE EXPERTISE GAP

Empowering macroprudential authorities with data collection powers and ability to influence the regulatory perimeter, ensuring data qualities and closing data gaps are only the first premises. These elements should not detract from the importance of building up a pool of knowledge and expertise in this relatively new policy area.[174] To fully understand the gravity of this contention, an explanation of the distinction between data gaps and expertise gaps in the macroprudential sphere is warranted.

The knowledge management literature sets out a hierarchy of the data, information, knowledge and wisdom notions (DIKW) where "Wisdom is located at the top of a hierarchy [...] Descending from wisdom there are ... knowledge, information, and, at the bottom, data. Each of these [categories – author's addition] includes the categories that fall below."[175] The DIKW hierarchy has become "one of the fundamental, widely recognized and 'taken-for-granted' models in the information and knowledge literatures".[176] At the most basic level, data is the essential raw material for the creation of information,[177] or

---

[173]   Ibid, 677 and 684 suggesting that the regulated should be viewed as partners of regulators and regulators should be "drawing both on the granular expertise of firms and on the broader vantage of the administrative agency".

[174]   E Becker, *Knowledge Capture in Financial Regulation, Data, Information and Knowledge Asymmetries in the US Financial Crisis* (Springer, 2014), 22. Of course, there is nothing new in this idea that expertise is at the core of policymaking, The international organisation literature, for instance, has long recognised that epistemic communities, defined as a "network of professionals with recognised expertise and competence in a particular domain and an authoritative claim to policy-relevant knowledge within that domain" influence state interests. PM Haas, "Knowledge, Power, and International Policy Coordination" (1992) 46(1) International Organization 1. More generally on the role of expertise in governance, see H Wilke, *Governance in a Disenchanted World* (Cheltenham: Edward Elgar 2009).

[175]   RL Ackoff, "From Data to Wisdom" (1989) 16 Journal of Applied Systems Analysis 3–9 adds another layer of understanding defined as the ability to increase efficiency; M Zeleny, "Management Support Systems: Towards Integrated Knowledge Management" (1987) 7(1) Human Systems Management 59–70 proposes enlightenment at the top of the hierarchy that includes the attainment of sense of truth, and right and wrong.
          See also J Rowley, "The Wisdom Hierarchy: Representations of the DIKW Hierarchy" (2007) 33(2) Journal of Information Science 163.

[176]   Rowley (2007) (n 175), 163–164

[177]   Becker (2014) (n 174), 163.

"symbols that represent the properties of objects and events".[178] Information is processed from data and has a meaning or value for the recipient and knowledge makes possible the transformation of information into instructions. As such, "the value of information is intangible, unless it is translated into knowledge and thus into measurable action."[179] Knowledge is the aggregation of related information that forms a set of expectations or rules providing a clearer understanding of information[180] and enabling humans to make "distinctions, choices and decisions".[181] Accordingly, while information contributes to the production of knowledge as one of the inputs, knowledge requires human judgements and experience. Humans "do not compute the world" of data rather they "use their subjectively perceived world of turbulent circumstances to bring forth (create, recreate and adapt), again and again, knowledge as an autopoietic network of relations through which they coordinate their actions."[182] In the macroprudential sphere, data and information are often lacking, and experience on the use of tools is very limited. Hence, by and large, knowledge-building will be gradual and based on experimentation and trial and error.[183]

This hierarchical structure of the DKIW was subject to criticism. For instance, data often emerges only after information is available, and that information emerges only after there is knowledge.[184] "Blind" data collection, without advanced use of knowledge, is therefore problematic and might result in very costly and ineffective policymaking.

---

178   Rowley (2007) (n 175), 166; M Boisot and A Canals, "Data, Information and Knowledge: Have We Got It Right?" (2004) 14(1) Journal of Evolutionary Economics 43 explain that "Data can be treated as originating in discernible differences in physical states-of-the-world".

179   M Zelany, "Production of Knowledge: Moving from Data and Information to Knowledge and Wisdom", Chapter 1 in M Zelany, *Human Systems Management: Integrating Knowledge, Management and Systems* (Scientific World, 2005), 18.

180   RP Schumaker, "From Data to Wisdom: The Progression of Computational Learning in Text Mining" (2011) 11(1) Communications of the IIMA Article 4.

181   M Zeleny, "Management Support Systems: Towards Integrated Knowledge Management" (1987) 7(1) Human Systems Management 59, 63.

182   Ibid, 59.

183   A Baker, "The Gradual Transformation? The Incremental Dynamics of Macroprudential Regulation" in M Moschella and E Tsingou (eds), Regulating Finance After the Crisis: Unveiling the Different Dynamics of the Regulatory Process (Wiley, 2013); A Haldane and R May, "Systemic Risk in the Banking Ecosystems" (2011) 469 Nature 351; A Baker, "Political Economy and the Paradoxes of Macroprudential Regulation" (2017) Sheffield Political Economy Research Institute Paper No 40, 4.

       See also D Aikman and others, "Rethinking Financial Stability" (2018) Bank of England Staff Working Paper No 712, available at <https://www.bankofengland.co.uk/-/media/boe/files/working-paper/2018/rethinking-financial-stability.pdf> referring to "learning by doing".

184   I Tuomi, "Data Is More than Knowledge: Implications of the Reversed Knowledge Hierarchy for Knowledge Management and Organizational Memory" (1999) 16(3) Journal of Management Information Systems 103.

Next, at the pinnacle of the DKIW hierarchy is wisdom. Wisdom transcends knowledge in its reflective and prudent practice.[185] It is "the judgement, selection and use of specific knowledge for a specific context".[186] It signifies the "ways that organizations might rise above the mere development and leveraging of knowledge and focus on the higher-order objective of using knowledge in efficient and effective ways. It reflects the realities of a business climate that is increasingly complex, diverse, fluid, and interdependent ..."[187]

Whilst not forming part of the DIKW hierarchy, the notion of expertise encompasses both data and the knowledge of what to do with it and how to obtain specific outcomes.[188] It is viewed as a particular type of knowledge which provides the ability to reflect upon the rules with respect to their improvement or change and the ability to change the rules.[189] These characteristics of expertise bring knowledge closer to the pinnacle of the pyramid, i.e. to the notion of wisdom.

What are the insights that can be drawn from distinctions and understandings on the design of a legal framework for data collection and analysis in the macroprudential policy sphere?

A famous observation on policymaking in an uncertain environment can assist in understanding the importance of framing macroprudential policymaking in terms of expertise. It is generally agreed that "There are known knowns; there are things we know that we know. There are known unknowns; that is to say, there are things that we now know we don't know. But there are also unknown unknowns – there are things we do not know we don't know."[190]

Collecting data, as a first step, may assist macroprudential authorities in addressing known knowns (by, for instance, identifying magnitude or likelihood of known risks). Closing data gaps will assist macroprudential authorities

---

[185] EH Kessler, "Organizational Wisdom Human, Managerial and Strategic Implications" (2006) 31(3) Groups and Organisation Management 296, 296.

[186] EH Kessler and EW Christensen, "Organizational Learning, Knowledge and Wisdom" (2000) 13(6) Journal of Organizational Change Management 595–618.

[187] Kessler (2006) (n 185), 297. Wisdom, however, is a diverse concept with several different strands. Therefore, a wise person "... needs to have an understanding of the epistemic status of what he or she knows, i.e. they have to be a fallibilist ... Then a wise person has to know, fallibly, plenty ... Then this wide knowledge has to be of a certain kind, a kind that applies to the many and varied problems of life ... The wide knowledge has to be applicable to tricky problems of an ethical and practical kind, of how to act ... The wise person must not only have wide appropriate knowledge, but they must act in accordance with the knowledge they have." M Frické, "The Knowledge Pyramid: a Critique of the DIKW Hierarchy" (2009) 35(2) Journal of Information Science 131, 140.

[188] N McCarty, "Complexity, Capacity, and Capture", Chapter 5 in D Carpenter and D Moss (eds), *Preventing Regulatory Capture: Special Interest Influence and How to Limit It* (Cambridge University Press, 2014), 102.

[189] M Zeleny, "Knowledge-information Autopoietic Cycle: Towards the Wisdom Systems" (2006) 7(1) International Journal Management and Decision Making 3.

[190] D Rumsfeld, 12 February 2002 Press Conference of Secretary of Defense.

in addressing "known unknowns" by bringing these known risks within the regulatory perimeter and transforming them into "known known". Yet, collecting data and closing data gaps may not do much for the unknown unknown. How would macroprudential authorities collect data when they are "completely in the dark" and yet to become knowledgeable about the need to do so? Here, expertise comes into play and is needed.

Indeed, as discussed in Chapter 7, academic and policy literature heavily relies on expertise as a source of authority and legitimacy to macroprudential policy.[191] Accumulating expertise is, therefore, an integral component in any data collection and analysis frameworks of macroprudential authorities[192] and should follow, build upon and reinforce data, information and knowledge. Nonetheless, macroprudential authorities face several hurdles in accumulating the necessary expertise to meet their mandate.

First, macroprudential authorities are caught in a chasing game: financial markets – constantly try to avoid regulation through utilising complexity and opacity, and macroprudential supervisors – attempt to keep up the pace and tame the build-up of systemic risk. Becker describes this chasing game between macroprudential authorities and financial markets as a paradox ("data paradox") suggesting that: "confronted with an increasingly complex financial system their knowledge is necessarily limited. Yet given the fact that complexity has become an industry strategy to circumvent regulation they must strive to address dark and unknown areas of the market."[193] Therefore, it can be argued

---

[191] D Lombardi and M Moschella, "The Symbolic Politics of Delegation: Macroprudential Policy and Independent Regulatory Authorities" (2017) 22(1) New Political Economy 92; A Baker, "Macroprudential Regimes and the Politics of Social Purpose" (2018) 25(3) Review of International political Economy 293.
See also BS Bernanke, "Financial Reform to Address Systemic Risk", Speech Delivered at the Council on Foreign Relations, Washington, DC, 10 March 2009; S Claessens and L Kodres, "The Regulatory Responses to the Global Financial Crisis: Some Uncomfortable Questions" (2014) IMF Working Paper 46.
More generally, on the increasing reliance on experts see S Brint, "Rethinking the Policy Influence of Experts: From General Characterizations to Analysis of Variation" (1990) 5 Sociological Forum 361.
In central banking see M Marcussen, "Institutional Transformation? The Scientization of Central Banking as a Case Study" in T Christensen and P Leagreid (eds), *Autonomy and Regulation: Coping with Agencies in the Modern State* (Edward Elgar, 2006), 81–109.

[192] Becker (2014) (n 174), 170 therefore views data collection as "just the starting point."

[193] Ibid, 210.
See also ST Omarova, "Wall Street as Community of Fate: Toward Financial Industry Self-Regulation" (2011) 159 University of Pennsylvania Law Review 411, 416 suggesting that "Given the complexity and global nature of the modern financial market, any government's attempt to regulate it in a purely unilateral command-and-control manner will inevitably encounter the fundamental problem of regulatory arbitrage, whereby financial institutions find new ways to get around government rules, thus creating a never-ending spiral of rulemaking and rule evading".

that the expertise of a macroprudential authority may be lagging behind the market and the industry as the latter have the advantage of a "first mover". This phenomenon and the nature of financial innovation, continuously create new "unknown unknowns" for the macroprudential authority[194] and set practical limits on the capacity of experts to understand and manage systemic risk, even with new data.[195]

The "expertise gap" or "expertise asymmetry" can be addressed by bringing the private sector into the process of accumulating expertise. Yet, looking through the prism of the profit-seeking private sector may prove to be dangerous, impeding on the legitimacy of the macroprudential authority[196] and reinforcing supervisory inaction bias.

Second, knowledge in the macroprudential sphere is specialised and thus its base is fragmented and dispersed, making broad integrated understanding difficult.[197] To gain an understanding of the financial system as a whole, macroprudential authorities need to have a clear view of developments within key firms and markets.[198] This creates, in turn, challenges for these authorities that lack direct contacts with the regulatees. Of course, there are institutional ways to alleviate this "expertise gap", primarily via membership of prudential authorities in the governance of the macroprudential authority. The effectiveness of this mechanism, however, depends on strong coordination mechanisms and the absence of any disruptive turf-wars (Chapters 4 and 8).

In addition, the increasing use of big data to inform macroprudential decisions would require multidisciplinary expertise from different professional backgrounds[199] and from national and international institutions in order "to break silos."[200]

Third, in the macroprudential setting, accountability mechanisms often rely on external scrutiny of macroprudential decisions by the courts or

---

[194] McCarty (2014) (n 188), 102.

[195] E Engelen and others, "Misrule of Experts? The Financial Crisis as Elite Debacle" (2012) 41(3) Economy and Society 360, 377–378 suggesting greater public engagement and representation on bodies with financial system oversight responsibilities.

[196] Arguing along these lines in the context of global financial regulation L Mosley, "Private Governance for the Private Good? Exploring Private Sector Participation in Global Financial Regulation" Chapter 7 in HV Milner and A Moravcsik (eds), *Power, Interdependence, and Nonstate Actors in World Politics* (Princeton University Press, 2009).

[197] D Foray, "Optimising the Use of Knowledge" Chapter 2 in B Kahin and D Foray (eds), *Advancing Knowledge and the Knowledge Economy* (MIT Press, 2006), 9, 13.

[198] BS Bernanke, "Implementing a Macroprudential Approach to Supervision and Regulation" (The 47th Annual Conference on Bank Structure and Competition, Chicago, Illinois, 5 May 2011).

[199] Hammer and others (2017) (n 143), 23. Expertise is spanning over programming, applied mathematics and statistics, economics and finance and project management.

[200] Ibid, 28.

democratic/parliamentary committees.[201] These external counterforces will also suffer from an "expertise gap" that can diminish the effectiveness of these accountability mechanisms. This gap is evident, for instance, in the ESRB hearings before the European Parliament that are used as a key accountability mechanism. As discussed in Chapter 7, the questions presented during the hearings are often of an "informational nature", rather than questions that have the potential to challenge the ESRB's performance towards achieving its statutory mandate. The nature of these parliamentary hearings can be (at least in part) attributed to the fact that MEPs may not have the required expertise to ask the ESRB Chair challenging questions.[202]

Judicial accountability of macroprudential authorities may also suffer from an expertise gap. Similar to financial regulation,

> … the discretion conferred on a supervisor is typically broad. Courts, in practice, exercise restraint and defer to the expert knowledge of the supervisor, given that they do not normally possess the expertise in financial matters. Substantive accountability is, therefore, of less significance, and judicial review is generally limited to review of legality with a view to ensuring that discretion is not exercised in bad faith or for improper purposes.[203]

Again, the concern of a weak judicial counterweight to the supervisors' expertise will be even more acute in the very technical macroprudential sphere. The limitations of a judicial review in a complex and technical policy were discussed in length in Chapter 7. The resulting guiding principle is that courts cannot supplant or replace the policy decision "venturing into a highly technical terrain in often which it is necessary to have an expertise and experience".[204] Their scrutiny can only extend to the parameters and legal frameworks that surround the policy decision (rather than its content) in order to determine whether the mandate has been exceeded.[205]

---

[201]   Parliamentary committees in many jurisdictions are used as a way to address the fact that "Politicians rarely have the time and expertise to absorb the information and make detailed judgments on the complex financial and technical issues …" M Taylor, M Quintyn and EHG Hüpkes, "The Accountability of Financial Sector Supervisors: Principles and Practice" (2005) IMF Working Paper 52.

[202]   This weakness of parliamentary accountability mechanisms may not be unique to the macroprudential setting. In relation to monetary policymaking, it has been observed that "neither the general public nor the even arguably its elected representatives have the necessary expertise and information to monitor central bankers' decisions in a rigorous way." N Jabko, "Democracy in the Age of the Euro" (2003) 10 Journal of European Public Policy 710, 728.

[203]   Taylor and others (2005) (n 201), 27.

[204]   C Goodhart and R Lastra, "Central Bank Accountability and Judicial Review" (2018) SUERF Policy Note 2585, available at <https://www.suerf.org/policynotes/2585/central-bank-accountability-and-judicial-review/html#f1>.

[205]   Opinion of Advocate General Cruz Villalón in *Peter Gauweiler and others v Deuscher Bundestag* Case C- 62/14, delivered on 14 January 2015, available at <http://eur-lex.europa.eu/legal-content/EN/TXT/?uri=CELEX%3A62014CC0062>, para 111.

Finally, a macroprudential authority can be described as a knowledge-based authority since it heavily relies on a "professional power" as a basis for its delegated authority.[206] However, putting expertise at the centre also creates new risks and doubts over the democratic legitimacy of technocrats (Chapter 7)[207] and the risk of experts becoming subject to groupthink (Chapter 3)[208] or overconfident in their ability to control risks.[209] Dissent is thus valuable in accumulating expertise (Chapters 3 and 7), without which particular and valuable knowledge may be overlooked.[210] As such, the best collective policy decisions, including those of experts, are "the product of disagreement and contest, not consensus or compromise."[211]

To address these challenges and expertise-gaps, the legal system and the institutional and governance frameworks should be designed and deployed:

1. To provide a clear mechanism to expanding the reporting and data collection perimeter and broaden the macroprudential data-field. This will allow macroprudential policymaking to be dynamic and move in pace alongside the moving targets of financial activity and risks.

2. To "favorably influence processes of transferring, sharing, integrating, using, and creating knowledge."[212] This could be achieved through coordination with other prudential regulators and utilising their "added-value expertise" which they gain through a direct contact with regulatees. This process may be fraught not only with legal impediments but also with practical difficulties. Literature in Information Technology demonstrates how social factors and policies, such as culture and practices of the relevant agencies, trust amongst agencies and goal alignment, may all influence the effectiveness of this sharing and integration process.[213] Agencies, therefore,

---

[206] S Brint, "Rethinking the Policy Influence of Experts: From General Characterizations to Analysis of Variation" (1990) 5 Sociological Forum 361, 376.

[207] Ibid, 365. Technocrats are "thought to exercise authority by virtue of trained competence in an applied scientific field, a stance of objectivity above the contest of ideology and interest, an orientation to problem solving, rather than to interest or value representation" (at 365).

[208] M Solomon, "Groupthink versus the Wisdom of Crowds: The Social Epistemology of Deliberation and Dissent" (2006) 44 (S1) The Southern Journal of Philosophy 28.

[209] JV Rizzi, "Behavioural Basis of Financial Crisis" in RW Kolb (ed), *Lessons from the Financial Crisis* (Hoboken, NJ: John Wiley 2010), 277.

[210] Solomon (2006) (n 208).

[211] JS Wiecki, *The Wisdom of the Crowd* (Anchor Books, 2005), 19.

[212] Based on the "knowledge governance approach" which advocates choosing governance structures to promote these aspects. These governance structures include not only legal frameworks but also informal mechanisms such as trust, organisational cultures and communication flows, NJ Foss and S Michailova, "Knowledge Governance: Themes and Questions" in S Michailova and NJ Foss (eds), *Knowledge Governance: Processes and Perspectives* (Oxford Scholarship Online, 2009).

[213] TA Pardo and others, "Modelling the Social and Technical Processes of Interorganizational Information Integration" (37th Hawaii International Conference on System Sciences, Hawaii, 31 January 2004).

"often focus on their own programs rather than on cross-boundary issues or linkages with outside organisations".[214] Aligning the mandates of these agencies (for instance, micro-prudential supervisors and conduct of business) with the mandate of the macroprudential authority could assist in establishing strong institutional coordination.

3. To avoid experts ignoring the benefits of alternatives,[215] particularly where there is no single course of policy action, the legal framework should incorporate and incentivise diversity in the macroprudential decision-making process (Chapter 3).[216]

4. View market players as partners and cautiously utilise their expertise as an integral part of a dynamic expertise-accumulation process of the macroprudential authority.[217] Such collaboration could promote a better understanding of market behaviour and dynamics[218] and strengthen the achievement of the macroprudential mandate. Macroprudential authorities already engage in such collaboration through integrating market-intelligence in their data collection process.[219] In the future, the importance of this collaboration will intensify, with the transition of data

---

[214] Ibid, 4.

[215] Rizzi (2010) (n 209), 8.

[216] This can be achieved, for instance, via external members who "will provide vital expertise and challenge to the Committee's [FPC – author's addition] deliberations." HM Treasury, "A New Approach to Financial Regulation: Building a Stronger System" (February 2011) Cm 8012, 35.

[217] On the role of civil society in influencing the behaviour of banks (in contrast to regulators) see R McCormick, "Towards a More Sustainable Financial System: The Regulators, The Banks and Civil Society" (2011) 5(2) Law and Financial Markets Review 129.
More specifically, see J Black, "Enrolling Actors in Regulatory Systems: Examples from UK Financial Services Regulation" (2003) Public Law 63 highlights that "any single actor is likely to have only part of the information necessary for the performance of any one of the regulatory functions" and suggests that "Specialist 'infomediaries', companies whose business is information provision, may here play a potentially valuable role or example in the financial services context information services such as Reuters and other 'aggregators' who collect and publish market information on a range of products (such as prices, interest rates), credit rating agencies, and the media."
See also I Chiu, "Enhancing Responsibility in Financial Regulation – Critically Examining the Future of Public-Private Governance: Part 1" (2010) 4(2) Law and Financial Markets Review 170 and I Chiu, "Enhancing Responsibility in Financial Regulation – Critically Examining the Future of Public-Private Governance: Part 2" (2010) 4(3) Law and Financial Markets Review 286.

[218] For instance, the FSOC supports the creation of a private sector council of senior executives "that would focus specifically on ways that cyber incidents could impact business operations and market functioning and liaise with principal-level government counterparts on cybersecurity issues. This council could help identify specific vulnerabilities in the sector's ability to provide critical products and services and propose standards for cybersecurity and operational resilience." FSOC 2017 Annual Report, 7.

[219] For instance, R Jeffery and others, "The Bank's Market Intelligence Function" (2017) Bank of England Quarterly Bulletin Q1. Though in a recent BIS paper, only a small percentage of central banks viewed market intelligence as extremely important for macroprudential policymaking. BIS, "Market Intelligence Gathering at Central Banks" (2016) Markets Committee Papers No 8, available at <https://www.bis.org/publ/mktc08.pdf>.

from solely being a "by-product" to being an asset, generated and owned by the private sector.[220] In particular, BigTechs are increasingly providing financial services and gain a competitive advantage of data over banks.[221] The advantage originates from the nature of their business model that relies on the "data-network-activity-loop".[222] As such, BigTechs have direct interactions among a large number of users and accordingly, own a large stock of user data. This data is then utilised as input to offer further services (including financial services), generating further user activity and in turn, generating more data.[223] Consequently, the dependence of macroprudential authorities on external private data resources will gradually increase. Legislators must, therefore, ensure that the legal framework facilitates the sharing of information and in time, integrate these sources within the data collection and analysis phase of macroprudential authorities.

5. Finally, data collection for systemic risks regulation and supervision should be a global effort, underpinned by strong international standards and deep supervisory cooperation. The necessity for such an integrated framework will only grow in light of the rise in the use of national data localisation rules that restrict the transfer of data across borders.[224]

To conclude, Claudio Borio emphasised that data collection is just the first steppingstone in the macroprudential supervisory cycle, suggesting that "The main reason why crises occur is not lack of statistics but the failure to interpret them correctly and to take remedial action."[225]

---

[220]   B Schmarzo and M Sidaoui, "Applying Economic Concepts to Big Data To Determine The Financial Value of the Organization's Data And Analytics, and Understanding the Ramifications on the Organizations' Financial Statements And IT Operations and Business" (2017), available at <https://infocus.dellemc.com/wp-content/uploads/2017/04/USF_The_Economics_of_Data_and_Analytics-Final3.pdf>.

[221]   BIS, "Big Tech in Finance: Opportunities and Risk" BIS 2019 Annual Report, 55.

[222]   Ibid.

[223]   Ibid.
        See also FSB, "BigTech in Finance Market Developments and Potential Financial Stability Implications" (December 2019), available at <https://www.fsb.org/wp-content/uploads/P091219-1.pdf>.

[224]   Deutsche Bank, "Regulation Driving Banking Transformation Insights into the Key Regulatory Developments Shaping the Data Economy, FinTech and BigTech Companies in the Financial Industry and Crypto-assets", available at <https://cib.db.com/docs_new/Regulation_driving_banking_transformation_second_edition.pdf>, 14.
        See also Future of Finance Review on the Outlook for the UK Financial System: What It Means for the Bank of England Chaired by Huw van Steenis, June 2019, available at <https://www.bankofengland.co.uk/-/media/boe/files/report/2019/future-of-finance-report>, 75; Institute of International Finance, "Data Flows Across Borders Overcoming Data Localization Restrictions", March 2019, available at <https://www.iif.com/Portals/0/Files/32370132_iif_data_flows_across_borders_march2019.pdf>, 5–6.

[225]   "The Great Unknown: Can Policymakers Fill the Gaps in Their Knowledge About the Financial System?", The Economist (13 January 2011), available at <http://www.economist.com/node/17900268?story_id=17900268&fsrc=rss>.

The resurgence of data collection powers and closing data gaps will not in themselves bring the needed transformation in the data and analysis premises of macroprudential policy. A fundamental change in this area can be better achieved by stimulating expertise within a macroprudential authority through a diversity of viewpoints, facilitating collaboration with the industry and other agencies and ensuring the regulatory perimeter is dynamic. These efforts should be complemented by a strong "outside" or "counter-expertise" with the capability of holding the macroprudential authority accountable. As seen in Chapter 7, this was largely achieved in the US with active judicial review as well as in the UK, with the dominant ECON parliamentary committee.

CHAPTER 10

THE GLOBAL ARCHITECTURE OF SYSTEMIC RISK REGULATION AND SUPERVISION

This chapter moves away from the domestic and regional legal and institutional macroprudential arrangements to the emerging global regulatory architecture for the regulation and supervision of systemic risk. The 2007–2009 global financial crisis, as well as the sovereign debt crisis in the euro area that began in 2009, strongly demonstrated how systemic risks are not contained within borders and how imbalances can easily spill over from one jurisdiction to another. Therefore, the reforms that took place in recent years in this sphere, both in expanding the corpus of international financial standards and changes in membership, governance and monitoring by international institutions, is natural. Whilst some scholars suggest that a more homogenised and centralised international regulatory order is needed to effectively prevent or mitigate systemic risk, this chapter suggests that the incremental and depolarised structure of the global architecture of systemic risk regulation and supervision is not the crux of the problem. Still, there are areas that call for improvements such as enhancing inclusiveness, legitimacy and accountability of these international institutions. In particular, the political character of the FSB that is accountable to the G-20 does not go hand in hand with the nature of macroprudential regulation and supervision given the need to have a certain degree of autonomy to sound the sirens of systemic risk.

The aim of this chapter is to connect the scholarly literature on the adoption and development of global financial standards with the insights gathered so far in the book on macroprudential policy.

It shows that the unique nature of the macroprudential perspective, being context-dependent and often, unpopular, and the changing nature of globalisation brings about the need to tailor specific governance and accountability arrangements to enhance the effectiveness of any global regime.

This chapter proceeds as follows. Section 1 begins by briefly tracing the development of the global financial regulatory architecture and its components (agenda setters, standards setters and institutions promoting compliance) and introduces the reforms that took place following the 2007–2009 financial crisis.

The crisis exposed the international dimension of systemic risk and the urgent need to effectively frame and govern it at that level. Section 2 discusses recent changes in the nature of globalisation and their potential implications on the manner in which the global architecture of systemic risk regulation and supervision is shaped and complied with. Section 3 explores the three strands of the scholarly literature that provides a theoretical foundation for the creation and adoption of international financial standards: the interstate, the domestic, and the transnational approaches. Section 4 draws on this scholarship and analyses how it applies, in practice, to the global architecture of systemic risk regulation and supervision. Section 5 moves on to specificities and analyses the roles of the FSB and the IMF in shaping the global macroprudential oversight and the challenges these institutions face. In particular, the section explores the political nature of the FSB and the division of roles between the FSB and the IMF. It also presents the urgent need for inclusiveness that goes much beyond broader membership and extends to a more inclusive interpretation of a macroprudential perspective and reaching out to a wider circle of stakeholders including non-member jurisdictions and a broader set of regulators and stakeholders. Section 6 maps the way forward and Section 7 concludes.

There are three principal takeaways from this chapter.

First, the global financial architecture remains decentralised and fragmented. This, however, does not mean that the cogs in the machine are not working well. On the contrary, the multi-layered nature of the global institutional setting for macroprudential regulation and supervision introduces dynamism, diversity of perspectives and expertise and form a beneficial system of checks and balances. Still, a more integrated and coordinated approach should be introduced to ensure that no significant vulnerabilities and regulatory gaps "fall between the stools". Moreover, despite reforms that expanded the membership of the FSB and broadened its mandate to reflect the macroprudential perspective, it remains ascendant to the G20 and largely reactive to its agenda and priorities. While the political underpinning of the FSB has its benefits, it does not go hand in hand with the need for autonomy and insularity from political pressures in the macroprudential sphere.

Second, there are limits to global macroprudential regulatory and supervisory convergence. Difficulties in reaching consensus and 'mock' compliance with soft law will only grow stronger in the face of shifting trends in globalisation and the realisation of emerging and developing economies that the 'western' one-dimensional macroprudential perspective may not be synonymous to their perspective. This is particularly evident in the oversight of the shadow banking sector, where the "Western" macroprudential perspective focuses solely on "financial stability" and thus largely differ from emerging and developing countries' view and the need to balance financial stability with other social goals such as financial inclusion.

Third, the solution to many of these challenges can be found in the genuine inclusiveness of "new" market power as well as in the enhancement of the legitimacy of institutions with global financial stability roles.

1. THE INTERNATIONAL DOMAIN OF FINANCIAL REGULATION: FRAGMENTED BUT STRUCTURED

The international domain of financial regulation (including macroprudential regulation and supervision) is fragmented but as shall be seen, the division of roles amongst its components is clear overall. Several regulatory networks are involved in setting agenda, promulgating international financial standards, including in the macroprudential domain and facilitating their compliance. The G-20 and the FSB determine policy direction and are thus considered agenda setters; In order of their establishment, the Basel Committee on Banking Supervision (BCBS), the International Organisation of Securities Commissions (IOSCO), the International Association of Insurance Supervisors (IAIS), the Committee on Payments and Market Infrastructures and the International Association of Deposit Insurers are the sectoral standard setters and finally, the IMF and World Bank play a key role in monitoring domestic compliance with international financial standards and emerging best practices in macroprudential frameworks, standards and tools.

The first wave of the global financial regulatory regime began over two decades ago and its development was described as incremental and reactive.[1] In 1974, following the failure of Bankhaus Herstatt, the central bank Governors of the Group of Ten countries established the BCBS.[2] The membership has since been expanded twice, in 2009 and 2014 and now includes 45 institutions from 28 jurisdictions. The members of the BCBS include organisations with direct banking supervisory authority and central banks.[3] The BCBS's charter states that "The BCBS is the primary global standard-setter for the prudential regulation of banks and provides a forum for cooperation on banking supervisory matters. Its mandate is to strengthen the regulation, supervision and practices of banks worldwide with the purpose of enhancing financial stability."[4]

---

[1]   J Liberi, "The Financial Stability Forum A Step on the Right Direction: Not Far Enough" (2003) 24 University of Pennsylvania Journal of International Law 549; E Helleiner, "What Role for the New Financial Stability Board? The Politics of International Standards After the Crisis" (2010) 1(3) Global Policy 282.
       See also M Moschella, "Designing the Financial Stability Board: A Theoretical Investigation of Mandate, Discretion, and Membership" (2013) 16(3) Journal of International Relations and Development 380.

[2]   Initially named the Committee on Banking Regulations and Supervisory Practices.

[3]   Article 4, BCBS Charter.

[4]   Article 1, BCBS Charter.

The BCBS's decisions do not have legal force and it relies on member jurisdictions' commitment to work together to achieve its mandate and promote financial stability.[5] The same year that the BCBS held its first meeting, the Group of Seven major industrial countries (G7)[6] started to hold annual economic summits at the level of head of state or government as a forum for discussion of economic and financial issues.

In 1999, in the wake of the East Asian financial crisis, the Group of 20 (G20)[7] was established to promote open and constructive discussion between industrial and emerging-market countries on key issues related to global economic stability. It was designed as an enlargement of the G7 and intended to be a broader forum for informal discussion of Finance Ministers and Central Bank Governors from developed and emerging economies with systemic significance for the international financial system. While the G20 remained rather dormant after its inception, following the 2007–2009 financial crisis it re-emerged as the main forum to inspire the reformed agenda and standards for international financial regulation.[8]

The FSB was established in April 2009 as a successor to the Financial Stability Forum (FSF). The FSF was created in 1999 by the Finance Ministers and Central Bank Governors of the G7 "to promote international financial stability through information exchange and international cooperation in financial supervision and surveillance."[9] The FSF, however, was "a relatively small and unmuscular group"[10] limited to 11 advanced economies members[11] and a number of international regulatory groups.[12] In comparison to its predecessor, the FSB had a broader mandate and expanded membership.[13] To begin with, its membership included the original members of the FSF and the G20, Spain and the European Commission. Since then, the FSB's membership has been further expanded and now includes 72 members from 25 jurisdictions.

---

5   Article 5, BCBS Charter.
6   Canada, France, Germany, Italy, Japan, UK and the US.
7   Argentina, Australia, Brazil, Canada, China, France, Germany, India, Indonesia, Italy, Japan, Korea, Mexico, Russia, Saudi Arabia, South Africa, Turkey, UK, US and EU.
8   M Callaghan, "Overview: Refining the Role of the G20 in Strengthening Financial Regulation"; H Jorgensen, "A Stocktake of Global Financial Reform Five Years After the Collapse of Lehman Brothers" (July 2013) both in G20 Monitor Financial Regulation and the G20 No 4, G20 Studies Centre and the Lowy Institute for International Policy. In November 2008, the G-20 was elevated to the Heads of States level.
9   G7 Finance Ministers, 20 February 1999, Bonn.
10 RK Quarles, "Ideas of Order: Charting a Course for the Financial Stability Board" (BIS Special Governors Meeting Hong Kong, 10 February 2019). See also Liberi (2003) (n 1), 572.
11 Canada, France, Germany, Italy, Japan, the US and the UK and at a later date, Australia, Hong Kong, the Netherlands, and Switzerland, along with the ECB.
12 Including the BCBS, IASB, IOSCO, IMF and the World Bank.
13 G20, "Declaration on Strengthening the Financial System", London Summit, 2 April 2009.

Other international organisations and standard setters such as BIS, the World Bank and the IMF are also members of the FSB. Members of the FSB are represented through independent domestic regulators, such as central banks and securities regulators as well as government representatives such as finance ministers.[14] It is accountable and reports to the G20 leaders but lacks any formal legal power. The FSB's original Charter of 25 September 2009 was amended in June 2012,[15] inter alia, with the aim of reinforcing its role in reducing the likelihood of financial crises, including reviewing regulatory policy within a macroprudential perspective. As shall be seen in Section 3 of this chapter, the FSB is working in coordination with the IMF and the division of their tasks and areas of expertise is by and large clear. The FSB – tasked with developing regulatory standards and the IMF – with ensuring their consistent implementation and their global compliance. But, as will be discussed further down, this division is subject to spontaneous developments[16] thus contributing to the dynamism of the global architecture.

The 2007–2009 financial crisis has led to a radical shift in the conception of financial regulation with the emergence of a macroprudential perspective. The priority given to developing macroprudential frameworks and policies is reflected in the 2009 declaration of the G20: "we will amend our regulatory systems to ensure authorities are able to identify and take account of macroprudential risks across the financial system including in the case of regulated banks, shadow banks, and private pools of capital to limit the build-up of systemic risk …".[17] The growing intensity of global financial regulation, designed to match the borderless nature of systemic risk, was quick to follow. Efforts at the global domain, included, to name a few, the development of the macroprudential overlay under Basel III;[18] papers documenting the

---

[14]   The organisational structure of the FSB is simple. The Plenary is the FSB's main decision-making authority (article 9 FSB Charter). The Steering Committee supports the Plenary through preparatory work and monitoring the progress of the Plenary decisions (article 12 FSB Charter).

[15]   FSB, Report to the G20 on Strengthening FSB Capacity, Resources and Governance, Los Cabos Summit, 18–19 June 2012. The Charter does not have a legal effect (article 23 FSB Charter).

[16]   A-M Slaughter, "The Accountability of Government Networks" (2001) 8(2) Indiana Journal of Global Legal Studies 347. One example of this fluidity is that recently, the IMF has become the hub for global data on macroprudential tools and institutional arrangement supporting macroprudential policy, based on responses on survey received from more than 140 jurisdictions.

[17]   Statement issued by G20 leaders, "Declaration on Strengthening the Financial System", London, 2 April 2009.

[18]   BCBS, Basel III: International Framework for Liquidity Risk Measurement, Standards and Monitoring (December 2010); BCBS, Basel III: A Global Regulatory Framework for More Resilient Banks and Banking System (June 2011), available at <https://www.bis.org/publ/bcbs189.htm> and the December 2017 reforms <https://www.bis.org/bcbs/publ/d424.htm>.

development and implementation of macroprudential policies;[19] establishing new frameworks for identifying SIFIs[20] and cross-border resolution[21] and enhancing data collection and analysis for macroprudential purposes.[22] Even a cursory view would suggest that the prominence of global market players, be it agenda or standard-setters or international institutions promoting compliance with the standards, is, perhaps by inertia, increasing. But is there a different engagement and commitment across countries? What are the driving forces behind the development of the global financial architecture?

2. THE CHANGING FACE OF GLOBALISATION AND THE MOVEMENT TO A DEPOLARISED WORLD

The spur of globalisation over recent decades in the form of greater volumes of cross-border finance is often attributed to three key dynamics: deregulation, technology and innovation.[23] In broad terms, the first contributor to globalisation involved the easing of regulation over capital and financial products that generated incentives to engage in cross-border complex financial transactions. Simultaneously, advances in technology and the digitisation of information simplified the process of cross-border transactions, bringing real-time transmission and interconnectivity to financial markets.[24] Finally, financial innovation, such as innovations in derivative instruments, was a key driver of financial liberalisation and enabled the transfer of risks across the globe thus accelerating the rise of cross-border financial flows.[25]

The benefits of globalisation are sizable. Primarily, it allows for "world savings to be directed to the world's most productive investment opportunities"[26] thus

---

[19] For instance, IMF, FSB and BIS, "Elements of Effective Macroprudential Policies" (August 2016), available at <https://www.fsb.org/2016/08/elements-of-effective-macroprudential-policies/>.

[20] For instance, BCBS, "Global Systemically Important Banks: Assessment Methodology and the Additional Loss Absorbency Requirement" (July 2013).

[21] FSB, "Key Attributes of Effective Resolution Regimes for Financial Institutions" (2011, 2014).

[22] G20 Data Gaps Initiative and the following joint FSB and IMF progress reports (see Chapter 8); IMF, Global Survey of Macroprudential Measures in the Integrated Macroprudential Policy (iMaPP) Database.

[23] C Brummer, *Soft Law and the Global Financial System Rule Making in the 21st Century* (Cambridge University Press, 2012), 10–11.

[24] Ibid; O Issing, "The Globalisation of Financial Markets" (12 September 2000, Ottobeuren), available at <https://www.ecb.europa.eu/press/key/date/2000/html/sp000912_2.en.html>.

[25] For a comprehensive overview of the nature, origins and consequences of financial globalisation see A Walter, "Understanding Financial Globalization" (2002) 25 S Rajaratnam School of International Studies Working Papers.

[26] M Obstfeld, "International Capital Mobility in the 1990s" (1994) CEPR Discussion Paper No 902, 1.

increasing development and economic growth. Globalisation also deepens liquidity in financial markets and enables rapid spreading of technological advances and financial innovation around the globe irrespective of location. But globalisation naturally also results in enhanced interconnectedness amongst financial institutions and may expose financial markets to the build-up of systemic risks.[27] Risks to financial stability have, therefore, been the key drivers behind the development of international financial standards and agenda and standards setters.

In recent years, in the face of populist nationalism and protectionism, many predicted that globalisation is on the verge of coming to a halt.[28] Despite these gloomy predictions, globalisation persists though there is evidence to suggest that it is changing form and shifting from developed countries to emerging economies.[29] As such, financial markets in China, the biggest emerging economy, have gone through rapid expansion and cross-border integration[30] and four of the largest banks in China are on the 2018 FSB Global Systemically Important Banks list.[31] As shall be seen in Section 3, this shift may soon affect the way international financial standards, in general, and global systemic risk regulation and supervision, in particular, are shaped and complied with.

3. TAXONOMY OF LITERATURE FOR SHAPING INTERNATIONAL FINANCIAL STANDARDS: INTERSTATE, DOMESTIC, AND TRANSNATIONAL

With the increasing dominance of the global regulatory players and the changing forces that guide it, it is useful to revisit scholarly literature developed to explain the reasons for the creation and strengthening of international

---

[27] J Lipsky, "Through the Looking Glass: The Links Between Financial Globalization and Systemic Risk" (The Joint IMF/Chicago Federal Reserve Conference, 27 September 2007).

[28] For instance, N Saval, "The Rise and Fall of an Idea that Swept the World", *Guardian* (14 July 2017); R Sharma, "Globalisation as We Know It Is Over – and Brexit is the Biggest Sign Yet", *Guardian* (28 July 2016); I Lakshmanan, "Trump Won. Globalization Lost. Now What?", *Boston Globe* (10 November 2016); SD King, *Grave New World: The End of Globalisation, The Return of History* (Yale University Press, 2017) contending that globalisation can all too easily go into reverse and that global institutions that have assisted in governing globalisation's advance are losing their credibility.

[29] "Globalisation Has Faltered", *Economist* (24 January 2019); M Wolf, "Manufacturing at Risk from Global Shift to Asia", *Financial Times* (20 May 2011).
   See also M wolf, "Davos 2019: Globalisation Faces Bumpy Road Ahead", *Financial Times* (20 January 2019); W Wen, "Emerging Markets are Set to Lead Globalisation", *Financial Times* (10 April 2017).

[30] McKinsey Report, *The New Dynamics of Financial Globalisation*, August 2017.

[31] FSB, 2018 List of Systemically Important Banks, available at <https://www.fsb.org/2018/11/2018-list-of-global-systemically-important-banks-g-sibs/>.

financial standards. The taxonomy of the scholarly strands is three-pronged: the interstate, the domestic and the transnational.[32]

The first strand of scholarship, the interstate approach, focuses on the exercise of power by dominant states as a key factor in shaping international financial standards. The interstate approach suggests that market size is the determinative source of international power and accordingly, that the international regulatory landscape is dominated and driven by "the Euro-American condominium".[33]

The "domestic approach" complements the interstate approach and attempts to explain the variation in preferences of regulators towards international standards, where some regulators are strong supporters and others adamantly resist them. The domestic approach suggests that the study of the preferences of regulators that drive the initiatives in this global sphere is also essential to understanding the reasons behind creating international financial standards. Regulators must engage in a careful balance between financial stability and competitiveness. Costly regulation may be necessary to ensure financial stability, but it can also be inimical to the global competitiveness of the domestic market. Thus, regulators are more likely to press for enhanced international standards when domestically they are in a precarious position – there are risks to financial stability and there is a rising competitive threat from foreign financial institutions. Attempting to tighten regulation domestically will only intensify the rising threat to the competitiveness of domestic players but doing nothing may result in materialisation of risks. Regulators' preferences to international standards are therefore generally driven by domestic constraints and their inability to unilaterally balance financial stability and competitiveness by domestic regulation.[34] According to the domestic approach, these preferences are also dictated by domestic politics and the influence of domestic private actors on the regulatory agenda.[35] The epicentre of this approach is thus the interaction between regulators and domestic industry groups[36] and potentially a wider range of actors.[37]

---

[32] E Helleiner and S Pagliari, "The End of an Era in International Financial Regulation? A Post-crisis Research Agenda" (2011) 65(1) International Organisation 169.

[33] L Newman and E Posner, *Voluntary Disruptions International Soft Law, Finance and Powers* (Oxford University Press, 2018), in particular Chapter 3; E Posner, "Making Rules for Global Finance: Transatlantic Regulatory Cooperation at the Turn of the Millennium" (2009) 63(4) International Organization 665.

[34] D Singer, *Regulating Capital: Setting Standards for the International Financial System* (Cornell University Press, 2007), 20–30.

[35] Ibid; D Drezner, *All Politics Is Global: Explaining International Regulatory Regime* (Princeton University Press, 2007), 32.

[36] Helleiner and Pagliari (2011) (n 32), 173.

[37] Even taxpayers, A Walter, *Governing Finance: East Asia's Adoption of International Standards* (Cornell University Press, 2008).

The third strand of scholarship, the transnational approach, offers an alternative to the paradigm that the emergence of international financial standards is based on states and other domestic players' interests and powers. This approach attributes the creation and development of international financial standards to trans-governmental networks and transnational non-state actors that work together to address common problems.[38] Rather than driven by interests of powerful actors, these networks form "institutionalized technical collaboration" and are removed from the interests of the powerful.[39]

The agreements reached and the policies formulated within these networks are not the result of national bargains and compromise but rather "debates over best practices for obtaining the broader goal of financial stability or the specific shared purposes of the regulatory grouping."[40] The collaboration in the transnational approach is, therefore, based on "loosely structured, peer-to-peer ties developed through frequent interaction rather than formal negotiation".[41] These regulatory networks are perceived to be "fast, flexible and decentralised" allowing them to function particularly well in a rapidly changing environment.[42]

The transfer of decisions on global financial issues to depoliticised, technocratic officials, however, is a two-edged sword. The very informality and lack of transparency of these networks and their technocratic de-politicisation bring about questions of legitimacy and accountability.[43] It can also be attacked for masking elitism, exclusions and inequality. Do these standards and the interpretation of their compliance promote the interest of more powerful states and thus reinforce the prevailing conception of financial stability and its acceptable balance with innovation and financial inclusion?

---

[38] A-M Slaughter, *A New World Order* (Princeton University Press, 2004), 45; A Slaughter and D Zaring, "Networking Goes International: An Update" (2006) 2(1) Annual Review of Law and Social Science, available at SSRN <https://ssrn.com/abstract=960484>.
See also K Raustiala, "The Architecture of International Cooperation: Transgovernmental Networks and the Future of International Law" (2002) 43(1) Virginia Journal of International Law 1.

[39] T Porter, "Technical Collaboration and Political Conflict in the Emerging Regime for international Financial Regulation" (2010) 10(3) Review of International Political Economy 520, 544–545 presents a Technical Systems Approach to be contrasted from approaches that focus on the role of states.

[40] T Porter, "Public and Private Authority in the Transnational Response to the 2008 Financial Crisis" (2011) 30(3) Policy and Society 175.

[41] Raustiala (2002) (n 38), 5.

[42] A-M Slaughter, "The Accountability of Government Networks" (2001) 8(2) Indiana Journal of Global Legal Studies 347.

[43] Ibid, 363; S Picciotto, "Networks in International Economic Integration: Fragmented States and the Dilemmas of Neo-Liberalism" (1996–1997) 17(1) Northwestern Journal of International Law and Business 1014, 1027.

4. THEORY IN PRACTICE: GLOBAL SYSTEMIC RISK REGULATION AND THE INTERSTATE, DOMESTIC AND TRANSNATIONAL APPROACHES

Global systemic risk regulation provides a useful laboratory for exploring the application of these theories. The transnational approach may fit well with the realisation that the sole prominence of the US and Europe as the dominant powers in shaping international financial standards no longer prevails. As shall be seen in Section 5, "new powers", including China and other emerging and developing economies, are increasingly taking an active part in shaping international financial standards. In addition, market power is emerging as a multifaceted concept, which relates not only to market size but also to the location of international important investors and institutions.[44] International standards and practices within international institutions may, therefore, shift away from polarised state-power to a more even and balanced transnational system where common goals and technical deliberation are the basis for policy formation. Still, it can be argued that the change in powers may not necessarily signal a shift in conception but rather a change of form. Market power, on its various facets, remains the determinative factor in forming standards and thus will fit in well with the interstate approach. Alternatively, changes in globalisation may encourage the emergence of a new "power-as-autonomy".[45] Instead of striving to influence the behaviours of other countries through international rulemaking, "power as autonomy" lessens the dependence of domestic financial markets on other markets. It thus increases the capacity "to exercise policy independence – i.e. to act freely, insulated from outside pressure in policy formulation and implementation. In this sense, power does not mean influencing others; rather, it means not allowing others to influence you".[46] Regionalism may be viewed as an exercise of "power-as-autonomy". In East Asia, for instance, regionalism in financial regulation is taking place through the Association of Southeast Asian Nations +3 that engages, inter alia, in macroeconomic surveillance for the region.[47] Regionalism may have good qualities in addressing the specific needs of

---

44 Helleiner and Pagliari (2011) (n 32), 169–200.
45 Borrowed from the international relations, in particular in the realm of monetary affairs. See BJ Cohen, "The Macrofoundations of Monetary Power" in D Andrews (ed), *International Monetary Power* (NY: Cornell University Press, 2006), 31–50.
46 Ibid, 42.
47 ASEAN + 3 is committed to a macroprudential perspective and the use of policy actions, where needed. The Joint Statement of the 20th ASEAN+3 Finance Ministers' and Central Bank Governors' Meeting (Yokohama, 4 May 2018).
    But for a gloomier outlook of the chances of a substantial coordination in East Asia in the absence of real commonalities see WW Grimes, "Financial Regionalism after the Global Financial Crisis: Regionalist Impulses and National Strategies" Chapter 6 in W Grant and GK Wilson (eds), *The Consequences of the Global Financial Crisis: The Rhetoric of Reform and Regulation* (Oxford University Press, 2012), 88.

countries, but it may also result in a dangerous global regulatory fragmentation[48] and impinge on the ability to regulate and supervise systemic risk.

In turn, the domestic approach is also far from being an abstract and theoretical explanation for the involvement of countries in formulating international financial standards. The impact that the balance between competitiveness and financial stability has on international standard-setting still resonates nowadays. This is evident, for instance, in a recent letter sent by Congressman Patrick McHenry to the Federal Reserve's Chair, Janet Yellen, calling to stop its participation in international forums on financial regulation. The letter expresses dissatisfaction with the legitimacy and transparency of international financial regulatory institutions: "It appears that the Federal Reserve continues negotiating international regulatory standards for financial institutions among global bureaucrats in foreign lands without transparency, accountability ... It is incumbent upon all regulators to support the US economy, and scrutinize international agreements that are killing American jobs".[49]

Similarly, in a meeting between the US Treasury Secretary, Steven Mnuchin and a former FSB's chair, Mark Carney, emphasised the US commitment to cooperate with other G20 and FSB members "To achieve our common goals of addressing financial stability risks, fostering efficient global financial markets, and promoting a global level playing field" but also noting that "one of the Administration's core principles for financial regulation is to promote American interests in international financial regulatory negotiations and meetings".[50]

These extracts demonstrate the influence of domestic forces (including domestic politics) on the willingness or reluctance to take an active part in shaping global financial regulation and the balancing act involved between financial stability and competitiveness.

The applicability of these three approaches in inquiring about the current nature of global macroprudential regulatory and supervisory frameworks means that they are not mutually exclusive and directs to a more integrative approach which puts together insights from all three strands.[51] In practical terms, this means that both the power of states, stakeholders and transnational networks have an important role to play in the development and deployment of standards in the macroprudential sphere.

See also S Chutikamoltham, "Effectiveness of Regional Mechanisms for Multilateral and Regional Governance" (April 2017) Asian Development Bank Institute No 719, available at <https://think-asia.org/handle/11540/7297>.

[48]   K Suominen, "Lessons in Regionalism: What can the WTO Teach the IMF?", 3 November 2010, available at <https://voxeu.org/article/lessons-regionalism-what-can-wto-teach-imf>.

[49]   Letter from Rep. Patrick McHenry to Janet Yellen, 31 January 2017, available at <https://ftalphaville-cdn.ft.com/wp-content/uploads/2017/02/02104940/McHenry-letter-to-Yellen.pdf>.

[50]   US Department of the Treasury, Press Release 23 February 2017, Meeting Between Treasury Secretary Steven Mnuchin and FSB Chair Carney, available at <https://www.treasury.gov/press-center/press-releases/Pages/sm0013.aspx>.

[51]   See also Helliener and Pagliari (2011) (n 32).

5. FSB: ONE PAWN IN THE GLOBAL MACROPRUDENTIAL REGULATORY NETWORK

5.1. THE FSB'S MACROPRUDENTIAL MANDATE

The FSB is tasked with identifying new and emerging vulnerabilities in the financial systems; completing the remaining elements of post-crisis reforms, supporting their consistent implementation and evaluating the effects of these reforms.[52]

Article 1 of the FSB's Charter sets out its objectives, as follows:

> The Financial Stability Board (FSB) is established to coordinate at the international level the work of national financial authorities and international standard-setting bodies (SSBs) in order to develop and promote the implementation of effective regulatory, supervisory and other financial sector policies. In collaboration with international financial institutions, the FSB will address vulnerabilities affecting financial systems in the interest of global financial stability.

Article 2 of the Charter outlines the FSB's mandate and tasks and adds specific references to a macroprudential perspective in subsection 1(a):

> (1) As part of its mandate, the FSB will:

> (a) assess vulnerabilities affecting the global financial system and identify and review on a timely and ongoing basis *within a macroprudential perspective* [author's emphasis], the regulatory, supervisory and related actions needed to address them, and their outcomes;

> (b) promote coordination and information exchange among authorities responsible for financial stability;

> (c) monitor and advise on market developments and their implications for regulatory policy;

> (d) advise on and monitor best practice in meeting regulatory standards;

> (e) undertake joint strategic reviews of and coordinate the policy development work of the international standard-setting bodies to ensure their work is timely, coordinated, focused on priorities and addressing gaps;

> (f) set guidelines for and support the establishment of supervisory colleges;

> (g) support contingency planning for cross-border crisis management, particularly with respect to systemically important firms;

---

[52] FSB Chair's letter to the G-20 Finance Ministers and Central Bank Governors, April 2019, available at <https://www.fsb.org/2019/04/fsb-chairs-letter-to-g20-finance-ministers-and-central-bank-governors-april-2019/>.

(h) collaborate with the International Monetary Fund (IMF) to conduct Early Warning Exercises;

(i) promote member jurisdictions' implementation of agreed commitments, standards and policy recommendations through monitoring of implementation, peer review and disclosure; and

(j) undertake any other tasks agreed by its Members in the course of its activities and within the framework of this Charter.

(2) The FSB will promote and help coordinate the alignment of the activities of the SSBs to address any overlaps or gaps and clarify demarcations in light of changes in national and regional regulatory structures relating to prudential and systemic risk, market integrity and investor and consumer protection, infrastructure, as well as accounting and auditing.

(3) The FSB should, as needed to address regulatory gaps that pose risk to financial stability, develop or coordinate development of standards and principles, in collaboration with the SSBs and others, as warranted, in areas which do not fall within the functional domain of another international standard-setting body, or on issues that have cross-sectoral implications.

5.2. THE POLITICAL CHARACTER OF THE FSB DOES NOT GO HAND IN HAND WITH SYSTEMIC RISK REGULATION AND SUPERVISION

Despite the expanded membership and broader mandate, the FSB is still criticised as a non-inclusive institution and labelled the "technocratic extension of the more political G20",[53] "a permanent secretariat or working group whose priorities and agenda are set by the G20"[54] and "the G20's handmaiden in global financial regulatory reform".[55] The direct participation of political representatives in the FSB demarcates it from other international bodies in financial regulation.[56] Finance ministers and treasury secretaries have a strong position in shaping the

---

[53] Brummer (2012) (n 23), 72.

[54] A Baker, "Mandate, Accountability and Decision-Making Issues to be Faced by the FSB" in S Griffith-Jones, E Helleiner and N Woods (eds), *Special Report: The Financial Stability Board: An Effective Fourth Pillar of Global Economic Governance* (The Centre for International Governance Innovation, 2010), 19 refers to the FSB as "a knowledge generation function as directed by the G20".

[55] A Persaud, "The Locus of Financial Regulation: Home Versus Host" (2010) 86(3) International Affairs 637, 643.

[56] S Gadinis, "The Financial Stability Board: The New Politics of International Financial Regulation" (2013) 48 Texas International Law Journal 157, 159 suggests that the political underpinning of the FSB through its composition is an attribute that enabled better coordination.

agenda since they constitute a significant block in the FSB's Plenary.[57] Moreover, the links between the FSB and the G20 are overpowering. The FSB submits to the G20 annual reports on progress made on financial regulatory reforms, their implementation by FSB members and an assessment of the effects of the reforms on the global financial system.[58] At the request of the G20, the FSB prepares specialised reports on various themes, its Chairman sends letters to the G20 providing an update on the FSB's work and there are frequent progress reports on specific regulatory initiatives.

The political underpinning of the FSB signals a shift in paradigm from regulatory networks that are based on the technocratic and independent decision-making process, isolated (at least, on paper) from political pressures to involvement of politicians in setting financial regulatory agenda.[59]

Clearly, there are advantages in a multidisciplinary forum that includes finance ministries and is almost attached to G20. Where the implementation of a reform is particularly reliant on adequate resource allocation and political support, such as in the case of closing data gaps, political underpinning is beneficial.[60] Nevertheless, it can be argued that the political nature of the FSB does not go hand in hand with regulation in the macroprudential realm. As suggested in Chapter 7, identification of systemic risk in prevalent practices, products or markets is generally an unpopular exercise. A certain degree of independence and insularity from domestic powers and interstate powers is therefore warranted. In addition, the scrutiny of the FSB work is limited. The G20 tends to act as "an uncritical rubber stamp of the FSB's work."[61] and there is no Independent Evaluation Office (IEO) (similar to the IMF's IEO) that can provide a mechanism of checks and balances and challenge the work of the FSB.

The complete ascendancy of the FSB to the G20 and the reactive nature of its operation, being confined to the G20 priorities, is, however, not grounded in the FSB Charter. In fact, according to article 2 of the Charter, the FSB will "undertake any other tasks agreed by its Members in the course of its activities and within the framework of this Charter." Therefore, to identify vulnerabilities in financial markets and areas where further research and regulation is needed, the FSB

---

57   Approximately a third are political representatives – a ministry of finance or treasury totals 19, plus the heads of monetary authorities in authoritarian regimes – Hong Kong, Singapore and Saudi Arabia.

58   Article 4 of the FSB Charter.

59   S Cho and C Kelly, "Promises and Perils of New Global Governance: The Case of the G20", (2012) 12(2) Chicago Journal of International Law 491, 516 refer to the G20 as an "executive coordinator". Slaughter (2004) (n 38), 135 referred to the FSB predecessor, the FSF, as a "networks of networks".

60   FSB and IMF, "Second Phase of the G20 Data Gaps Initiatives Third Progress Report" September 2018, available at <https://www.imf.org/external/np/g20/pdf/2018/092518.pdf>, 5.

61   S Bardy, "Whither the G20 and the FSB? The 2014 Agenda" in Callaghan and others (eds), *Financial Regulation and the G20* No 4 (Lowy Institute for International Policy and G20 Studies Centre, July 2013), 44.

should be proactive rather than reactive to the G20's recommendations and build its autonomy from the political agenda. This, in turn, will expand the FSB's "out of the box" thinking and enhance the effectiveness of its macroprudential regulatory efforts.

More recently, there are small signs that the FSB is willing to take a more proactive approach that is independent from the agenda set by politicians.[62] For instance, the FSB 2019 Working Plan indicates that the FSB intends to extend the traditional perimeter of regulation to include large, well-established technology firms that provide financial services (BigTechs) and assess their financial stability implications.[63]

5.3. BROADER MEMBERSHIP – GENUINE INCLUSIVENESS OR LIP SERVICE?: AN INCLUSIVE APPROACH TO "FINANCIAL STABILITY"

In November 2008, the G20 called to broaden the FSB membership.[64] This could have originated from the need to enhance the FSB's legitimacy; from a genuine acknowledgement of the importance of diverse views to ensuring financial stability or perhaps, it was simply part of a more general idea that China and other emerging economies are becoming "responsible stakeholders" of the international system.[65]

To be differentiated from the almost universal membership of the IMF, the FSB membership is still exclusive. The number of representatives per member jurisdiction in the Plenary, the FSB's decision-making body, varies from one to three and reflects the changing size of the national economy, financial market activity and national financial stability arrangement of the member jurisdiction.[66] In 2014, the FSB acknowledged the need to strengthen the voice of markets and

---

[62] By slightly detaching itself from the G20, the FSB will be able to overt the concern that G20 leaders will not have the same magnitude of influence once the 2007–2009 global financial crisis and its impact have subsided and the discussion will shift to more technical matters unsuitable for discussion at the G20 leadership level. See CI Bradford and W Lim, "Towards the Consolidation of G20 Summits: From Crisis Committee to Global Steering Committee" in CI Bradford and W Lim (eds), *Global Leadership in Transition: Making the G20 More Effective and Responsive* (The Brookings Institute Press, 2011).

[63] FSB Work Programme for 2019 (February 2019), available at <https://www.fsb.org/wp-content/uploads/P120219.pdf>.
See also FSB, "FinTech and Market Structure in Financial Services: Market Developments and Potential Financial Stability Implications" (February 2019), available at <https://www.fsb.org/2019/02/fintech-and-market-structure-in-financial-services-market-developments-and-potential-financial-stability-implications/>.

[64] G20, "Declaration of the Summit on Financial Markets and the World Economy", Washington DC, 15 November 2008.

[65] A Etzioni, "Is China a Responsible Stakeholder?" (2011) 87(3) International Affairs 539.

[66] The number of representatives is periodically reviewed. FSB Charter, article 11.

economies outside developed countries in its governance and agreed to allocate to five emerging and developing economies a second Plenary seat each.[67]

But does the broader membership of the FSB that extends beyond developed countries and also includes developing and emerging countries translate into genuine attainment of inclusiveness?[68] Does it mean that the specific and unique needs and priorities of these countries, in particular in the design and implementation of macroprudential policies, are taken into account? It seems that despite the efforts to broaden membership and increase representation, in practice, genuine inclusiveness in the formation of the global architecture is still absent. The role that China, the world's largest developing country,[69] plays in the FSB is perhaps a testimony to the lack of genuine inclusiveness. China became a formal member of the FSB in 2010 and fully supports the FSB's work[70] but there is a growing dissatisfaction with the actual influence it wields in FSB negotiations.[71] Either due to its relatively low degree of interconnectedness or lack of regulatory experience and expertise,[72] China seems to have stayed out of the limelight and there is little evidence to suggest that to date it has exercised any significant influence within the FSB.[73]

---

[67]   FSB, "Report to the G20 Brisbane Summit on the FSB's Review of the Structure of its Representation", 15–16, November 2014, available at <https://www.fsb.org/wp-content/uploads/Report-to-the-G20-Brisbane-Summit-on-the-FSB's-Review-of-the-Structure-of-its-Representation.pdf>.
The seats of international organisations the BCBS, IAIS, IOSCO, the IMF and the World Bank were accordingly reduced to one Plenary seat each.

[68]   Concerns over representation is not coming solely from emerging and developing countries. There is also a perception that Europe has the upper hand during negotiations. N Sheets, "Race to the Top: The Case of the Financial Stability Board" (April 2017) Peterson Institute for International Economics Policy Brief.

[69]   Regular Press Conference of the Ministry of Commerce with Gao Feng (1 August 2019), available at <http://english.mofcom.gov.cn/article/newsrelease/press/201908/20190802894334.shtml>.

[70]   Chinese Government and World Bank and other international organisations, Joint Press Release on the Second "1+6" Roundtable, ("Promoting an Open, Invigorated and Inclusive World Economy", Beijing, 12 September 2017) declare that "China applauds and supports the FSB's work in building a safer, simpler, fairer financial system and improving the financial regulation coordination framework."

[71]   P Knaack, "An Unlikely Champion of Global Finance: Why Is China Exceeding International Banking Standards?" (2017) 46(2) Journal of Current Chinese Affairs 41, 44–45.

[72]   Ibid; A Walter, "Emerging Countries and Basel III: Why is Engagement Still Low?" in CR Henning and A Walter (eds), *Global Financial Governance Confronts the Rising Powers* (Waterloo: Centre for International Governance Innovation, 2016), 179–210. But there is some evidence to suggest that this is no longer the case on both accounts. See E Jones and P Knaack, "Global Financial Regulation: Shortcomings and Reform Options" (2019) 10(2) Global Policy 193; CGFS and FSB, "FinTech Credit: Market Structure, Business Models and Financial Stability Implications" (May 2017), available at <https://www.bis.org/publ/cgfs_fsb1.pdf>.

[73]   In particular, China has not played a leading role in any of the four standing committees nor has it to date led the Regional Consultative Group (RCG) for Asia or led the drafting of any of FSB documents for China and International Financial Standards. H Wang, "From 'Rule Taker' to 'Rule Maker'?" (August 2018) Centre for International Governance Innovation Papers No 182, 2 also observed that China had little input in the deliberation of Basel III.

In addition, broader membership does not necessarily address the differing views and approaches to macroprudential regulation and supervision across member jurisdictions. After all, what it means to be "responsible" can be interpreted differently by states.[74] The regulation of non-banks provides a constructive example of the intricacies and tensions between FSB members from developed economies and FSB members from emerging and developing economies. In 2010, the G20 "called on the FSB to work in collaboration with other international standard-setting bodies to develop recommendations to strengthen the regulation and oversight of the shadow banking system …".[75] The dedicated Task Force published in 2011 a report titled *Shadow Banking: Strengthening Oversight and Regulation: Recommendations of the FSB* setting out the definition of shadow banking and the measures needed to ensure prevention and mitigation of systemic risks in that sector.[76] It has been suggested, however, that the FSB shadow banking framework focuses on one aspect – systemic risks to financial stability, at the expense of other valuable goals – economic development and financial inclusion. The pursuit of financial stability and inclusive growth simultaneously is particularly important to financial development in emerging and developing countries.[77] The FSB's approach to the regulation of shadow banking was thus perceived to be

> … rooted in the experience of developed economies and lessons from the financial crisis that had its epicenter in the United States. Notions of shadow banking as a vehicle for financial inclusion, efficient credit allocation, and diversification of investment channels are of marginal relevance to this frame. While the FSB acknowledges the need to balance costs and benefits in designing proportionate regulation, it precludes the notion of outright promoting the shadow banking sector for the sake of greater economic development.[78]

---

[74] W Grimes, "Financial Regionalism After the Global Financial Crisis: Regionalist Impulses and National Strategies" in W Grant and GK Wilson (eds), *The Consequences of Global Financial Crisis: The Rhetoric of Reform and Regulation* (Oxford University Press, 2012).

[75] G20 Declaration in Seoul Summit, 11–12 November 2010, available at <https://www.fsb.org/wp-content/uploads/g20_leaders_declaration_seoul_summit_2010.pdf>, 10.

[76] FSB, "Shadow Banking: Strengthening Oversight and Regulation: Recommendations of the FSB" (October 2011), available at <https://www.fsb.org/wp-content/uploads/r_111027a.pdf>, 3. Shadow banking is broadly defined as "the system of credit intermediation that involves entities and activities outside the regular banking system". This report was the basis for subsequent FSB work on shadow banking.

[77] Jones and Knaack (2019) (n 72), 199.

[78] P Knaack and J Gruin, "From Shadow Banking to Digital Financial Inclusion: Regulatory Framework Contestation between China and the FSB" (2017) University of Oxford, Global Economic Governance Programme Working Paper 134; in its last Peer Review of China (August 2015), available at <https://www.fsb.org/wp-content/uploads/China-peer-review-report.pdf>, 9 the FSB stated that: "A non-bank sector that provides sound and sustainable finance is an essential part of a developed financial system. In that sense, the growth of non-bank credit intermediation in China in part reflects a welcome deepening of the financial system and an alternative source of finance to the real economy" but then moved on to discuss the risks and the need to strengthen regulation of that sector."

The dissatisfaction from the FSB single-dimensional approach to shadow banking became publicly evident, during the regional Asian consultative groups (RCG) meeting in 2014.[79] The RCG comprises both FSB-Member authorities and non-FSB member authorities and reaches its decisions by consensus. It critically noted that:

> All members expressed the view that shadow banking risks faced by Asia are different to those in the US or EU, consequently, while the risks identified for NBFIs [non-bank financial intermediaries – author's addition] in these markets may be a useful reference for Asia, they are not as relevant to Asia to warrant similar policy responses … In Asia, banks remain the dominant providers and facilitators of credit-intermediation. NBFIs do not play a primary or systemic role in credit intermediation. In most jurisdictions, there are a large number of very small NBFIs which provide financial services to specific sectors often populated by small domestic companies, to fill the credit void as these sectors may not have access to bank finance.[80]

The RCG further exclaimed that:

> in order for members to be able to effectively implement the FSB's policy framework, it is important that this is tailored to the unique features of the financial markets in Asia, taking into account the varying stages of economic development in the jurisdictions, differing socio-economic characteristics and the unique roles played by NBFIs [non-bank financial institutions – author's addition] in Asia.[81]

It comes as no surprise that China (and other emerging or developing jurisdictions) chose to frame non-bank financial institutions under the label of financial inclusion and financial technology (Fintech) rather than "shadow banking".[82] China is not an outlier in that respect. The view that "financial stability-maximising approach may be at odds with developing country needs and preferences" is gaining support.[83] The discontent with the prevailing

---

On the role of shadow banking in promoting growth see R Buckley, DW Arner and M Panton, "Financial Innovation in East Asia" (2014) 37 Seattle University Law Review 307.

The importance of financial inclusion was also evident in other FSB Regional Consultative Group (RCG) meetings for instance, at the meeting of the FSB RCG Consultative Group for sub-Saharan Africa, 4 December 2015, available at <https://www.fsb.org/2015/12/meeting-of-the-financial-stability-board-regional-consultative-group-for-sub-saharan-africa-2/>.

[79] FSB RCG Asia, "Report on Shadow Banking" (August 2014), available at <http://www.fsb.org/wp-content/uploads/r_140822c.pdf>.

[80] Ibid, 54.

[81] Ibid, 5.

[82] Ibid, 6; Knaack and Gruin (2017) (n 78), 4.

[83] Jones and Knaack, (2019) (n 72), 199. It is also important to integrate inclusion into financial sector assessments. See A Barkawi and JS Serrate, "Central Banks and the G20 Agenda: Ensuring Policy Coherence" (International Financial Architecture for Stability and Development/Crypto-assets and Fintech, G20 Japan and Think 20 Japan, March 2019), 5, available at <https://t20japan.org/wp-content/uploads/2019/03/t20-japan-tf2-12-central-banks-g20-agenda-policy-coherence.pdf>.

"Western" view of shadow banking, however, is not just on paper. There are worrying signs that it may also negatively affect the way in which developing and emerging countries engage with, cooperate and share information with the FSB.[84]

Interestingly, despite being directed by and accountable to the G20, there is a striking misalignment between the FSB and the G20 when it comes to advancing "financial inclusion". Financial inclusion generally means the access to and use of formal financial services by households and firms.[85] In its 2010 Seoul Summit's declaration, the G20 reiterated its strong commitment to financial inclusion and recognised "the benefits of improved access to finance to lift the lives of the poor and to support the contribution of SMEs to economic development." Following the declaration, the G20 set out the Financial Inclusion Action Plan,[86] established the Global Partnership for Financial Inclusion (GPFI), inter alia, to implement this plan[87] and endorsed the Principles for Digital Financial Inclusion.[88] The GPFI explicitly acknowledged the potential tension between developed and developing countries in that respect:[89] "... SSB [standard-setting bodies, author's addition] guidance needs to accommodate widely varying financial market structures (especially with the advent of digital financial inclusion, introducing new non-bank actors including non-financial firms) as well as varying levels of policymaking, regulatory, and supervisory capacity".[90] Nonetheless, in contrast to the prominence of financial inclusion in the G20 agenda, it is almost entirely absent from the FSB's discourse and in particular in its approach to the regulation of shadow banking. The FSB clearly focuses on achieving financial stability and the risks involved in non-bank activities, largely overlooking the potential trade-offs with financial inclusion.[91] This is not

---

[84] For instance, it has been suggested that the Chinese regulatory authorities have recently limited their degree of cooperation with the FSB and are only partially sharing information with their peers. This is also the case with India. FSB, "Thematic Review on the Implementation of the FSB Policy Framework for Shadow Banking Entities" (May 2016) Peer Review Report, available at <http://www.fsb.org/wp-content/uploads/Shadow-banking-peer-review.pdf>.

[85] R Sahay and others, "Financial Inclusion: Can it Meet Multiple Macroeconomic Goals?" (2015) IMF Discussion Note 17, available at <https://www.imf.org/external/pubs/ft/sdn/2015/sdn1517.pdf>, 16.

[86] The original 2010 version has been revised twice: in 2014 and more recently, in 2017. G20 leaders welcomed the new version in the 2017 G20 Summit held on 7–8 July 2017 in Hamburg, Germany.

[87] The GPFI was launched at the G20 Summit on 10 December 2010 in Seoul.

[88] Developed by the GPFI, the Chinese Central Bank and the World Bank.
G20 High Level Principles for Digital Financial Inclusion endorsed in G20 Summit 4–5 September 2016, Hangzhou, China.

[89] GPFI White Paper, "Global Standard-Setting Bodies and Financial Inclusion The Evolving Landscape" (March 2016), available at <https://www.gpfi.org/sites/gpfi/files/documents/GPFI_WhitePaper_Mar2016.pdf>.

[90] Ibid, 17.

[91] Sahay and others (2015) (n 85), 18–19.

to say that the FSB should overreach its mandate or ignore the risks involved in irresponsible credit extension through non-bank financial institutions.[92] Rather, within its mandate, the FSB should acknowledge and consider potential trade-offs with other social goods. The challenge in creating a regulatory framework that is strong enough to ensure financial stability, yet not so severe that the costs of regulatory compliance inhibit innovation can be achieved, for instance, through the concept of proportionality.[93]

Most importantly, perhaps emerging and developing countries are now more readily willing to challenge the ideas and knowledge developed by advanced industrial states within the FSB. This resonance is particularly acute in the sphere of macroprudential regulation that cannot take a "one size fits all" approach (Chapter 1). Voicing their concerns, developing and emerging countries will bring in new viewpoints and preferences to the FSB thus minimising scope for groupthink.[94] At the same time, this heterogeneity could inhibit the ability of the FSB to reach a consensus[95] or could eventually result in a moderate and compromised policy agenda and action.

---

[92] Ibid. On the implication of innovation on financial stability see, for instance, FSB, FinTech and Market Structure (2019) (n 63); BCBS, "Sound Practices, Implications of FinTech Developments for Banks and Bank Supervisors" (2018), available at <https://www.bis.org/bcbs/publ/d431.pdf>; United Nations Secretary-General's Special Advocate for Inclusive Finance for Development (UNSGS) FinTech Working Group and Cambridge Centre for Alternative Finance (CCAF), "Early Lessons on Regulatory Innovations to Enable Inclusive FinTech: Innovation Offices, Regulatory Sandboxes, and RegTech" (New York and Cambridge, UK, 2019); CGAP (Consultative Group to Assist the Poor), "Financial Inclusion – Linkages to Stability Integrity and Protection" (Washington, DC, 2019), available at <http://www.cgap.org/research/publication/financial-inclusion-linkages-stability-integrity-and-protection>.

[93] The G20 High-Level Principles for Digital Financial Inclusion Principle 3; Communiqué of the G20 Finance Ministers and Central Bank Governors Meeting 23–24 July 2016, Chengdu, China, para 9 encourages countries to consider these principles in devising their broader financial inclusion plans, particularly in the area of digital financial inclusion.

[94] See, for instance, IMF Independent Evaluation Office, "IMF Performance in the Run Up to the Financial and Economic Crisis" (2011) Evaluation Report, 17.

[95] Baker (2010) (n 54), 22 suggests that reaching decisions via consensus effectively provides a right of veto to any member and accordingly, may hamper the effectiveness, 23; E Helleiner and S Pagliari, "The End of an Era in International Financial Regulation? A Post-crisis Research Agenda" (2011) 65(1) International Organization 169; M Levinson, "Faulty Basel: Why More Diplomacy Won't Keep the Financial System Safe" (2010) 89(3) Foreign Affairs 76, 85 suggest that in light of the failure of the US–UK dominant thinking to bring financial stability, it has become more difficult to agree on a focal point around which convergence can be reached.
This is not a theoretical concern. See, for instance, Transcript of a Press Conference by IMF Managing Director Dominique Strauss-Kahn following the Group of 20 Finance Ministers and Central Bank Governors Meeting, Paris, 20 February 2011: "What I was worried about – I'm sorry to say – materialized: which is that it's more difficult than it was before to have people agree … When they were really scared, they were happy to find a consensus. Now … many believe – wrongly-the crisis is behind us and they have domestic concerns."

5.4. INCLUSIVENESS BEYOND THE MEMBERSHIP'S PERIMETER

While the FSB's 24 members represent over 80 per cent of the global GDP,[96] financial system vulnerabilities are global and clearly transcend much beyond the G20 member jurisdictions. To identify these vulnerabilities and enhance the FSB's legitimacy, it is therefore vital for the FSB to reach out beyond its membership perimeter.[97]

Under article 3 of the FSB's Charter, the private sector and non-member authorities may be consulted in the development of the FSB's strategic plans and standards. For that purpose, the FSB established in 2011 six consultative groups representing large regions of the globe – the Americas, Asia, Europe, the Middle East and North Africa, Sub-Saharan Africa and the Commonwealth of Independent States. In practical terms, this means that the FSB receives input to its policy formulation from approximately 70 non-member jurisdictions, though, formally, their consent is not needed to reach a consensus in the decision-making process. These consultative groups, however, are viewed as having only "an ancillary role"[98] and they "struggled in practice".[99]

A change in approach may be on the horizon. In 2019, the FSB has prioritised the need to strengthen and widen its outreach beyond its member jurisdictions and acknowledged the importance of this aspect to maintaining its legitimacy.[100] This is also evident in the recent speech of Randal K Quarles, Vice Chair for Supervision Board of Governors of the Federal Reserve System Chair Financial Stability Board

> While we are directly accountable to the G20, we are, through the G20, accountable to all of the people affected by our actions. In my view, that means we must engage in genuine, substantial dialogue with all of these stakeholders, to a greater and more effective degree than we have in the past.[101]

The FSB also engages with other external stakeholders, inter alia, through conducting public consultations on its policy recommendations. The period for

---

[96] SG Cecchetti, "Collaboration in Financial Regulatory Reform: The IMF, the Financial Stability Board, and the Standard Setting Bodies" (2018) IMF Independent Evaluation Office Background Paper 18-02/04.

[97] RK Quarles, "The Financial Stability Board: Beyond the Fog of Battle" (European Bank Executive Committee Forum, "The Future of Banking: The Human Factor", Brussels, Belgium, 2 April 2019).

[98] Cecchetti (2018) (n 96), 18.

[99] RK Quarles, "Ideas of Order: Charting a Course for the Financial Stability Board" (BIS Special Governors Meeting, Hong Kong, 10 February 2019). The FSB has also begun a review of the effectiveness of the regional consultative groups, but this will not change the matter of fact that their voice is not needed to reach a consensus, 2.

[100] FSB Work Programme for 2019, available at <https://www.fsb.org/wp-content/uploads/P120219.pdf>.

[101] Quarles (2019) (n 99).

consultations has recently been extended to 60 days to enable true dialogue with stakeholders and the FSB has committed to publishing reports that summarise the comments and how they have been addressed.[102]

A final note on inclusiveness is warranted. In the macroprudential sphere, the meaning of diversity and inclusiveness should not be limited to geographical representation[103] but also include diversified areas of expertise and access to non-financial stakeholders. The FSB's strength emanates from its multidisciplinary being a unique forum drawn from senior policymakers from finance ministries, central banks and supervisors to discuss and address financial stability risks.[104] However, in light of the potential trade-offs between macroprudential policy and other policy areas, systemic risk surveillance and agenda-setting should be drawn from a much wider set of regulators and stakeholders, such as competition regulators, consumer protection and data protection regulators (Chapter 8).[105] Such collaboration may not be an easy task. These policy areas have been traditionally the province of national regulators and may have limited or no authority to engage with counterparts at the international level.[106]

Engagement with regulators and stakeholders, traditionally thought to have nothing to do with a system-wide stability, should take first priority as the FSB enters the "unknown" territory of regulating FinTech. Potentially overlapping groups at the international arena in this area are already emerging. In January 2019, an international group of 35 financial regulators (including the UK's FCA) and other organisations from 26 jurisdictions have launched the Global Financial Innovation Network (GFIN). The GFIN is "a collaborative knowledge sharing initiative aimed at advancing areas including financial integrity, consumer wellbeing and protection, financial inclusion, competition and financial stability through innovation in financial services, by sharing experiences, working jointly on lessons learned and facilitating responsible cross-border experimentation

---

[102] FSB Procedural Guidelines, as amended, article 88. The amendment was following a review in 2018 of the FSB's processes and transparency. The key recommendations of the review are available at FSB Press, FSB Completes a Review of its Processes and Transparency to Maximise its Effectiveness, 27 November 2018, available at <http://www.fsb.org/2018/11/fsb-completes-a-review-of-its-processes-and-transparency-to-maximise-its-effectiveness/>.

[103] I.e. the weight given to geographic areas. There is, for instance, a perception that the US is underrepresented compared to the EU. See Sheets (2017) (n 68).

[104] Mark Carney's comments on the FSB Review of its Processes and Transparency to Maximise its Effectiveness (2018) (n 100). Indeed, the diversified views and experiences is one of the qualities of the FSB in comparison to the IMF. Cecchetti (n 96), 18.

[105] Recently, the FSB initiated an evaluation of the Too-Big-To-Fail reforms and "Stakeholder outreach will be an important aspect of the evaluation". Terms of Reference, Evaluation of the Tool-Big-To-Fail, 23 May 2019, available at <https://www.fsb.org/wp-content/uploads/P230519.pdf>. These stakeholders include academics, think tanks and consumer associations.

[106] BC Matthews, "Big Tech – Financial Regulators Are Heading Your Way", *Medium* (2 April 2019), available at <https://medium.com/@BCMstrategy/big-tech-financial-regulators-are-heading-your-way-1f480e79c1be>.

of new ideas".[107] Members and observers include central banks, consumer protection regulators, securities regulators, development banks, NGOs, the World Bank and the IMF.[108] On the one hand, this collaborative network introduces another layer to an already crowded financial regulatory domain. On the other hand, it can provide a vehicle for the FSB to gather information and widen its interaction with a wider range of regulators.

5.5. TOO MANY COOKS?: THE IMF AND THE FSB – DIVISION AND INTERACTION IN THE MACROPRUDENTIAL SPHERE

5.5.1. The IMF and the FSB – Membership and Collaboration

The IMF was founded in 1944 at the United Nations Bretton Woods conference in New Hampshire, US to oversee the international monetary system and monitor the economic and financial policies. It plays a role in the surveillance of the financial sector and strengthening the global financial stability. This latter role is exercised through initiatives such as the Financial Stability Assessment Program (FSAP), collection and dissemination of the IMF's Financial Soundness Indicators (FSIs), encouraging greater disclosure of FSIs through the Co-ordinated Compilation Exercise (CCE) and regular bilateral and multilateral surveillance often reported in the IMF's Global Financial Stability Report (GFSR). The IMF takes an active part in developing and helping national authorities operationalise macroprudential frameworks[109] and sharpening its risk assessments to identify the build-up of vulnerabilities.[110] The introduction of the Consolidated Spillover Report in 2012 signalled the efforts of the IMF to focus on linkages between sectors and countries making its surveillance as interconnected as the global economy.[111]

In 2011, an external report stated that the IMF is a "global financial stability adviser" and that:

> ... The Fund is the only organization with the potential to carry out the overarching role [in ensuring global financial stability author's comment], working hand-in-hand

---

[107] Terms of Reference for Membership and Governance of the Global Financial Innovation Network (GFIN), available at <https://www.fca.org.uk/publication/mou/gfin-terms-of-reference.pdf>.

[108] Information on GFIN is available at <https://www.fca.org.uk/firms/global-financial-innovation-network>.

[109] IMF, "Key aspects Macroprudential Policy" (June 2013), 38.

[110] As assessed and identified in the IMF Global Financial Stability Reports.

[111] IMF Independent Evaluation Office, "Report on the Evaluation of the Financial Sector Assessment Program" (5 January 2006); O Evans and others, "Macro Prudential Indicators of Financial Soundness" (2000) IMF Occasional Paper 192; IMF, "Consolidated Spillover Report – Implications from the Analysis of the Systemic-5" (11 July 2011), available at <http://www.imf.org/external/np/pp/eng/2011/071111.pdf>.

with other bodies, such as the FSB, BIS, OECD, national/regional risk boards and national authorities. Only the Fund has a truly multilateral and universal perspective – one that encompasses countries at different stages of development and one that cuts across borders, markets and sectors.[112]

Further, in 2013, the IMF declared that it "can play the role of a global macroprudential facilitator."[113]

However, in 2018, a report of the IMF Independent Evaluation Office observed that:

> The creation of the FSB put the IMF in an awkward position. Why hadn't the G20 leaders asked the Fund to spearhead the global financial regulatory reform process?[114] Despite it being a universal institution with currently 180-member countries[115] *the IMF was denied a leading role in coordinating the global response to the 2007–2009 financial crisis* [author's emphasis][116]

Is there a way to reconcile these views as to the prominence of the IMF in leading the global post-crisis macroprudential response?

At first glance, these inconsistencies may signify a turf battle between the IMF and the FSB. However, another way to reconcile these views is to reinforce the observation that the global architecture in financial regulation, in general, and in macroprudential oversight, in particular is multi-layered and develops incrementally. Indeed, at the outset, there was an attempt to clarify the division

---

[112]   J Palmer and Y Tok, "The Triennial Surveillance Review (TSR)-External Study-IMF and Global Financial Stability" (July 2011), para 15.

[113]   J Viñals, "Making Macroprudential Policy Work" (Brookings, 16 September 2013).

[114]   Cecchetti (2018) (n 96), 6.

[115]   Founded at the United Nations Monetary and Financial Conference, Bretton Woods, New Hampshire, 1–22 July 1944. See, for instance, JM Boughaton, "Becoming a Universal Institution: Expansion of Membership" Chapter 2 in *Tearing Down the Walls The IMF 1990–1999* (IMF, 2012), available at <https://www.imf.org/external/pubs/ft/history/2012/pdf/c2.pdf>.

[116]   Shying away from the IMF as a global regulator can be attributed to its failure to provide adequate warnings prior to the crisis. IMF, "Initial Lessons of the Crisis" (Washington, February 2009), 9 suggesting that "in general the warnings were too scattered and unspecific to attract even domestic – let alone collective – policy reaction." This has been followed by criticism on the IMF's failure in highlighting the magnitude of the risks in Greece Portugal and Ireland. IMF Independent Evaluation Office, "The IMF and the Crises in Greece, Ireland and Portugal" (2016) Evaluation Report, available at <https://ieo.imf.org/en/our-work/Evaluations/Completed/2016-0728-the-imf-and-the-crises-in-greece-ireland-and-portugal>.
There were other legal and operational limitations. IMF, "The Fund's Mandate-An Overview" (January 2010), IMF Policy Paper, available at <https://www.imf.org/external/np/pp/eng/2010/012210a.pdf>; on data limitation in the IMF see J Black, "Restructuring Global and EU Financial Regulation: Capacities, Coordination and Learning" (2010) LSE Law, Society and Economy Working Paper 18.

of roles between the FSB and the IMF. In a letter of Dominque Strauss-Kahn (then IMF Managing Director) and Mario Draghi (then the Chair of the FSF) to the G20 Ministers and Governors. The IMF was to be taking the lead on the surveillance of the global financial system and provide a global perspective on macroeconomic and macrofinancial risks and analysis of emerging issues, and the FSB was to take the lead on regulatory and supervisory matters.[117] After the establishment of the FSB, some saw the merit in revisiting the joint letter[118] but instead, it was again clarified that while the FSB was created to be the key forum for the advancement of the G20 agenda, the IMF was tasked with monitoring the implementation of the standards developed by the standard setters.[119]

In September 2010, the IMF accepted membership in the FSB and after long deliberation, it was approved by the IMF Executive Board in March 2013.[120] Since then, the IMF has been actively supportive of the FSB and there is clear evidence of effective collaboration between the two institutions.[121] The IMF openly accepts and respects "the lead role of the FSB and SSBs in developing new rules and regulatory frameworks."[122]

At the FSB, the IMF provides an overview of global financial risks and shares views on the regulatory reform process. But perhaps the most interesting role that the IMF attributes to itself is that of promoting inclusiveness and protection against unequal market power: "as a global institution with universal membership, it speaks for those who are not present" and "… it helps FSB member countries reach consensus, particularly when some advanced country delegation is pushing towards diluting and weakening standards."[123] Being an organisation of 189 countries with national representatives who are removed from the regulated institutions[124] and independent from the G20, the IMF is

---

[117] Joint Letter of the FSF Chairman and the IMF Managing Director to G20 Ministers and Governors, 13 November 2008, available at <https://www.fsb.org/2008/11/r_081113/>.

[118] IMF, "IMF Membership in the FSB" (August 2010), available at <https://www.imf.org/external/np/pp/eng/2010/081010.pdf>; "IMF Executive Board Approves Fund Membership in the Financial Stability Board" (September 2010) Public Information Notice No 10/133, available at <http://www.imf.org/external/np/sec/pn/2010/pn10133.htm>.

[119] Cecchetti (2018) (n 96), 3 referring to a presentation by the IMF Financial Counsellor to the Executive Board in March 2010.

[120] IMF, "IMF Membership in the Financial Stability Board" (March 2013) Public Information Notice No 33.

[121] IMF Independent Evaluation Office, "IMF Response to the Financial and Economic Crisis" (2015) Chapter 2 on p 6 discussing the concern that membership will impinge on the independence of the IMF given its role in conducting article IV surveillance (see Section 5.5.2.1. below).

[122] IMF Independent Evaluation Office, Financial Surveillance Evaluation Report 2019, 3.

[123] Ibid, 25.
See also Cecchetti (2018) (n 96), 19.

[124] Normally the country representative is the minister of finance or the head of the central bank.

---

bringing an independent view to the discussions on standards, highlighting the concerns of non-FSB members and at times, helping in reaching a consensus.[125]

Overall, the IMF and the FSB play complementary roles and work in conjunction to monitor and address global risks to financial systems.[126] The following sections demonstrate the added value of having such a multi-layered architecture.

5.5.2. *The IMF's Financial Surveillance: Key Diagnostic Tool for Identifying Vulnerabilities and Risks*

5.5.2.1. Bilateral Surveillance

Financial surveillance is a central element of the IMF work and includes both bilateral surveillance that focuses on activities and products in a single country and multilateral surveillance that examines the global financial system. Both levels are vital to the identification of potential sources of financial instability and macroprudential surveillance.

The two key vehicles for the IMF bilateral surveillance are the Financial Sector Assessment Program (FSAP) and the IMF article IV consultations.

The FSAP, launched in 1999, is conducted jointly with the World Bank as a voluntary exercise. Following the 2007–2009 financial crisis, it became a mandatory exercise, at least every five years, for the 29 jurisdictions with systemically important financial sectors (S29) and voluntary for the rest of the member countries (non-S29). The FSAPs include three standard components: assessment of the main risks to financial and macrofinancial stability; the country's financial stability oversight framework; and the authorities' capacity to manage and resolve a financial crisis.[127] The conclusions are summarised in the Financial System Stability Assessment (FSSA), which includes recommendations (of a micro-prudential and macroprudential nature) to be followed up by a subsequent article IV consultation.[128]

The IMF article IV consultation is a periodical (normally annual) assessment of a country's financial sector concerns. Since 2014, it integrates a macrofinancial

---

[125] Nevertheless, the IMF Independent Evaluation Office has recently suggested that some view the G20's influence on the IMF excessive and overshadowing. See IMF Independent Evaluation Office, Evaluation Update 2018 "Current State of the IMF Governance", 20.

[126] House of Lords, European Union Committee, "The Future of EU Financial Regulation and Supervision" (June 2009), Chapter 8: The Role of the EU in Global Supervision and Regulation, para 203.

[127] The FSAPs also include reports on the Observance of Standards and Codes (on compliance with international standards) and for Low- and middle-income countries, an assessment of financial development and inclusion.

[128] The publication of the FSAPs is voluntary but the majority of them are published. Independent Evaluation Office of the IMF, IMF Financial Surveillance 2019, available at <https://ieo.imf.org/en/our-work/Evaluations/Completed/2019-0115-fis-evaluation>, 12.

analysis,[129] including systemic risks, analysis of cross-border spillovers and coverage of oversight institutions and macroprudential policies.[130]

These exercises are a valuable source of information on financial systems as well as an oversight of institutions around the globe. However, given that it takes around 18 to 24 months to conduct an FSAP, fast-evolving threats to financial stability can become outdated and there is demand particularly from non-S29 countries for more frequent exercises.[131] Moreover, the integration between the FSAPs and article IV consultations is lacking: The 2019 Evaluation Report of the IMF's Independent Evaluation Office noted that "FSAPs are too infrequent to be relied upon to detect fast-developing financial stability risks; while Article IV consultations typically do not have the breadth and depth of skills and resources to adequately identify and warn about financial stability risks."[132]

In addition to the IMF bilateral surveillance, FSB member counties also commit to undergo periodic peer reviews, approximately two to three years following an FSAP,[133] and the macroprudential element is a key part of them. These reviews are a powerful tool in strengthening the financial regulatory and supervisory framework. For instance, the most recent FSB's peer review of China indicated a high degree of compliance with international standards but noted that there is an urgent need to better integrate macroprudential management across sectors and that "relevant bodies with a system-wide remit ... to be used more formally as a coordination mechanism".[134] Following

---

[129] Which examines the connection between financial factors and the real economy.

[130] The IMF 2014 Triennial Surveillance Review (TSR) recommended that macrofinancial analysis becomes an integral part of article IV consultations and that steps be taken to strengthen the IMF's focus on macroprudential policies and how they complement other economic policies. More recently, it was observed that coverage of macroprudential policies in article IV has improved, but that there is scope to strengthen links to underlying risks. IMF, "Approaches to Macrofinancial Surveillance in Article IV Reports" (February 2017) IMF Policy Paper, 25–26.
Prior to the main work in the FSAP the teams also prepare a preliminary assessment of systemic risks and the financial oversight frameworks in the country (Financial Stability Note).

[131] In 2017, the IMF has launched a new surveillance tool, the Financial System Stability Review (FSSRs) which is directed to low and lower-middle income countries. The IMF Independent Evaluation Office recently suggested in its "IMF Financial Surveillance" Report, December 2018 suggested to expand this new diagnostic tool (on p 40).

[132] The IMF Independent Evaluation Office, 2019 Evaluation Report of the IMF Financial Surveillance, Section 3 Bilateral Surveillance, 19.

[133] Article 6.1 of the FSB Charter. It consists of Thematic reviews (focusing on the implementation and effectiveness across FSB members of international financial standards in a particular area important to global financial stability) and country reviews (which focus on the implementation and effectiveness of regulatory, supervisory or other financial sector policies in a specific FSB member jurisdiction). Handbook of FSB Peer Reviews, 31 March 2017, available at <https://www.fsb.org/wp-content/uploads/Handbook-for-FSB-Peer-Reviews.pdf>.

[134] FSB Peer Review of China (August 2015) (n 78), 7–8.

this recommendation, several reforms have taken place, inter alia, the creation of the Financial Stability and Development Committee (FSDC) and granting the People's Bank of China a more central role in financial stability.[135]

The quality of the peer country reviews, however, is subject to criticism: "The very nature of the exercise carried out by FSB members on their peers, encourages logrolling. Regulators that participated in peer reviews acknowledge that they are lenient in their assessments, based on an understanding that when their turn comes, they will receive similarly lenient treatment."[136]

5.5.2.2. Multilateral Surveillance

The multilateral surveillance that examines the global economy is largely based on the Global Financial Stability Report (GFSR) and the Early Warning Exercises (EWA).[137]

The IMF publishes biannually the GFSR highlighting and assessing vulnerabilities and key risks (imminent and over the medium term) to the global financial system. The GFSR is, however, not the only report on global risks in the scene. The BIS Annual Report analyses economic and financial developments, focusing on monetary policy and financial stability policies; the BIS Quarterly Reviews provide analysis on financial market development and international banking and the IMF World Economic Outlook analyses global economic developments and describe a wide array of risks.[138] In addition, a recent review highlights several drawbacks of GFSR, including that instead of being forward-looking it relates to risks that have recently been realised.[139] Doubts have also been raised as to whether GFSRs are subject to "type 1 errors" (failing to warn about a potential crisis event before it occurred or failing to discuss in-depth its financial stability implications)[140] as well as "type 2 errors" (warning excessively on too-minor risks in terms of probability and/or consequence).[141]

---

[135] L Zheng, "The Macro Prudential Assessment Framework of China: Background, Evaluation and Current and Future Policy" (2018) CIGI Papers No 164.
See also "China's PBOC Sets Up Bureau to Improve Financial Oversight", *Bloomberg News* (2 February 2019).

[136] Cecchetti (2018) (n 96), 11 recommending that "the IMF should ensure that the timing and the substance of the FSAPs and peer reviews work in a way that benefits the member country in question."

[137] Article IV consultations that include analysis of cross-border spillovers are also a tool for multilateral surveillance.

[138] The GFSR and World Outlook are generally consistent in the identified risks and often cross-referenced each other. J Zettelmeyer, "IMF Multilateral Financial Surveillance" (2018) Independent Evaluation Office Background Paper, 19.

[139] For many other weaknesses such as narratives which are not always supported by empirical evidence, lack of data transparency and presentation see Zettelmeyer (2018) (n 138), 27.

[140] Most importantly, the failure to warn about the sharp decline in commodity prices in 2014 and 2015 which led to recessions in several emerging economies. Ibid, 14.

[141] IEO, IMF Financial Surveillance (2019) (n 128), 11–12.

With regard to the EWA, both the IMF and the FSB prepare a confidential presentation to around 50 governors and ministers at the IMF's Annual and Spring Meetings.[142] In several instances, the EWE succeeded in identifying risks that later materialised, but the transparency of the presentations is limited as "Less than one-third of member countries have direct access to the EWE presentations. Even in those countries whose high-level officials attend the EWE session, most senior officials do not know what was discussed in that restricted meeting."[143] Clearly, keeping the attendance at the EWE meeting very limited allows for a discussion of particularly sensitive issues and open exchange of views.[144] Nevertheless, the lack of transparency could inhibit accountability and create an uneven level playing field, where information-"weak" countries are kept in the dark and disadvantaged in identifying or mitigating systemic risks. Data should be disseminated to all member jurisdictions in a manner that does not compromise confidentiality and risks a "self-fulfilling prophecy" scenario.

It is important to note that the nature of the FSB and IMF respective presentations differ:

"The IMF presentation is thought-provoking and generates lively discussions by taking on outside-the-box issues[145] ... the parallel FSB presentation has consistently focused more strictly on regulatory issues and financial risks and seems to prompt less discussion from the audience ...".[146]

While the respective presentations bring different insights to the table, a better synergy is needed to ensure a thorough assessment of vulnerabilities and build-up of systemic risk.[147] Integration will also prevent gaps in the system to emerge. For instance, in recent years, the EWE has focused on new vulnerabilities emerging from political and technological development and became less

---

[142]   Ibid, 23.

[143]   Ibid, 24.

[144]   Ibid.

[145]   Partly this can be attributed to the increasing focus on longer term structural changes and risks at the expense of narrower set of macrofinancial risks. Zettelmeyer (2018) (n 138), 2.

[146]   Independent Evaluation Office, IMF Financial Surveillance (2019) (n 128), 24. The explanation for this gap is at least in part grounded in the extent of the independence from national regulators and political agenda-setters: "While the IMF's EWE is prepared by an independent staff team, the FSB's presentation is rooted in the views and analysis of its members." Zettelmeyer (2018) (n 138) also note that "The IMF's contribution to the EWE has been of high quality, often raising risks and policy challenges long before they were discussed in the WEO and GFSR and by the broader public".

See also S Fischer, "Preparing for Future Crises" (2009) BIS Review No 107, 13, available at <http://www.kansascityfed.org> observed that "By making an organization of typically collegial national supervisors [FSB – author's addition] responsible for international surveillance of financial systems, the G-20 injected a potential weakness into the proposed system of global financial surveillance."

[147]   The FSB Charter makes no specific reference to its relationship with the IMF. The IMF Articles of Agreement's provision on commitment to cooperation with international organisations is of a general nature.

interested in macrofinancial risks, thus leaving this area unaddressed at the higher-level of policymakers.[148]

These observations are in line with the recommendations of the G20 Eminent Persons Group on Global Financial Governance that called for a more integrated global system of risk surveillance while maintaining the independence of perspectives of the current international financial institutions.[149] In other words, it is vital to preserve the current diversity in the institutional setting of systemic risk regulation so as to avoid a dangerous convergence on a diluted consensus.[150] While the IMF gives particular attention to economic and macro-financial risks and sovereign vulnerabilities, the FSB focuses on financial risks and the BIS – on global flows and market infrastructure risks.[151]

Overall, rather than converging into a single lead institution, the regulation of global architecture of systemic risk regulation and supervision is diffused and dynamic. That way, it can meet the fast-changing demands of market practises and trends and provide a kaleidoscope of insights on potential vulnerabilities threating global financial stability. The following section will suggest that enhancing the effectiveness of the global architecture in regulating systemic risks can be achieved through coordination and enhancing legitimacy between the participating actors in the global arena.

5.6. COMPLIANCE CHALLENGES WITH MACROPRUDENTIAL STANDARDS: IS "MOCK" COMPLIANCE PREVALENT?

In addition to surveillance tools discussed above, market pressure is often regarded as a key tool for enhancing compliance with soft law. There is an expectation that market players will take into account in their credit and pricing decisions the degree and quality of implementation of international financial standards in a given jurisdiction.[152] The threat of market exclusion from financial centres when failing to implement standards and the complementing incentive that implementation will come with a greater access to these markets could potentially enhance compliance.[153] Nonetheless, it has long been suggested that developing countries often resist international compliance pressures through

---

[148]   Zettelmeyer (2018) (n 138), 21–22.

[149]   G20 Eminent Persons Group on Global Financial Governance Report, "Making the Global Financial System Work for All" (October 2018).

[150]   Ibid, 21.

[151]   Ibid.

[152]   M Giovanoli, "The Reform of the International Financial Architecture After the Global Crisis" (2009) 42(81) New York University Journal International Law and Politics 111.

[153]   BA Simmons, "The International Politics of Harmonization: The Case of Capital Market Regulation" (2001) 55(3) International Organization 589.

cosmetic or "mock" compliance.[154] This is not unique to macroprudential standards but is particularly acute where standards are complex and thus difficult to follow and monitor.[155] Mock compliance can also result from the limited timely data that is available to supervisors, the persistent gaps in infrastructure and weak supervisory capacity to support the implementation of policies.[156]

Since data challenges are pertinent in the macroprudential domain (Chapter 9) and there is a dearth in research on the use of macroprudential tools (Chapter 6) it comes as no surprise that the implementation of Basel III's macroprudential overlay has been adopted less frequently than other components of Basel III.[157] Moreover, given that in developing countries improving inequality is one of the most important macroeconomic policy objectives, policymakers tend to attach considerable weight to distributional effects of policy measures.[158] It has already been seen in Chapter 6 that macroprudential measures may have an immediate distributional effect and can inhibit, in the short term, economic growth. Therefore, a macroprudential authority in these countries may be particularly deterred from implementing macroprudential measures with hard-to-measure and long-term benefits.[159]

6. THE WAY FORWARD

The need for international institutions with a global financial stability role to have a degree of autonomy and insulation from political pressure is key to timely identification of vulnerabilities to global stability. Naturally, there is a risk that sounding the early warning siren and curtailing procyclicality may not always be compatible with political plans at the national level.[160] Therefore, while there are clear benefits for political backing of regulatory reforms, there is a risk that institutions such as the FSB would be subject to demands to mute or tone down any politically unpopular messages or findings.[161] Therefore, the FSB should

---

[154] A Walter, *Governing Finance: East Asia's Adoption of International Standards* (Cornell University Press 2008), Chapter 7, 166–184.

[155] Helleiner (2010) (n 1), 286.

[156] M Rubio and DE Unsal, "Macroprudential Policy, Incomplete Information and Inequality: The Case of Low-Income and Developing Countries" (2017) IMF Working Paper 59, 6.

[157] E Jones and AO Zeitz, "The Limits of Globalizing Basel Banking Standards" (2017) 3(1) Journal of Financial Regulation 89.

[158] R Buckley, D Arner and M Panton, "Financial Innovation in East Asia" (2014) 37(2) Seattle University Law Review 307. There is a concern that since macroprudential measures in Basel III were designed with banking structures in developed counties in mind, they may significantly constrain the ability of banks in developing countries to provide financing to small and medium-size companies.

[159] Rubio and Unsal (2017) (n 156), 8.

[160] Baker (2010) (n 54), 21.

[161] Ibid.

make greater use of the breadth of its mandate and strengthen the forward-looking and proactive nature of its activities expanding beyond the restrictive role as the "G-20 executive arm".[162] Similarly, the IMF should maintain its independence from the G20 to preserve its unique "out of the box thinking". It should also continue representing countries outside the FSB's perimeter to enhance the overall legitimacy of the global institutions and standards and in turn, strengthen compliance. In addition, the nature of macroprudential policy necessitates pre-emptive measures and a long-term vision. This can only be assured by a proactive approach to identifying vulnerabilities and gaps in the global regulatory and supervisory macroprudential frameworks.

The acknowledgement of the need for inclusiveness in global financial architecture has been almost an integral part of its design and development. However, gaps remain, and genuine inclusiveness is still absent. This is reflected for instance, in the manner in which shadow banking is interpreted in the FSB policy documents and the one-dimensional consideration of financial stability. Inclusiveness should expand beyond which countries participate in the dialogue; it should also be about engaging with non-member countries, external stakeholders and a wide range of regulators that may not have an official role but can offer a contrarian view or bring in relevant expertise from other policy areas. Inclusiveness also includes accepting a different conception of financial stability and acknowledging its potential trade-offs with financial development and inclusion. Inclusiveness, on its myriad of aspects, will not only be a source of data for trends and practices that may materialise into systemic risks but also a mechanism to enhance the legitimacy of international regulatory and supervisory institutions.[163]

Finally, the multi-layered nature of global institutional setting for macroprudential regulation and oversight should not be seen as a negative element of the current architecture. Rather, it introduces to the structure diversity of perspectives, expertise and a balance between independence and political support that is beneficial when a timely system-wide overview is sought. Still, a more integrated and coordinated approach should be introduced to ensure that no significant vulnerabilities and regulatory gaps "fall between the stools". This can be achieved through a Memorandum of Understanding or an updated joint letter setting out the areas of responsibilities and ways of coordination across the institutions. On the one hand, it will not impinge on the dynamic nature of the architecture and allow for the utilisation of expertise

---

[162] Article 2 of the FSB Charter permits the FSB to "undertake any other tasks agreed by its Members in the course of its activities and within the framework of this Charter."

[163] Much of the legitimacy challenges resemble the ones discussed in Chapter 7 and evolve around the reliance on technocratic expertise as a solid justification for international regulatory institutions in their exercises of power and anchoring their legitimacy.

in new areas that need attention.[164] On the other hand, it will ensure that some order in the somewhat overcrowded scene of institutions involved in systemic risks regulation is achieved and that there are complementarities in their work and recommendations. The global regulatory and supervisory architecture of systemic risk can also be strengthened by greater transparency of planned work and focus. Recently, the FSB has taken a step in the right direction and publicly released, for the first time, its annual work programme detailing its work priorities and expected publications for the year to come.[165]

7. CONCLUSION

In order to explain the development of international financial standards and institutions a combination of interstate, domestic and transnational theories is needed. The interstate approach – given that the power of states (in its various forms) is still an influencing factor in the development of global financial standards and commitment to the work of international institutions; the domestic approach – given that preferences of regulators to international standards remain driven by domestic constraints of politics and private stakeholders; and finally, the transnational approach explains the nature of these soft law institutions that share a common goal of global financial stability and which are thriving to be detached, to varying degrees, from politicians. The application of these theories in the macroprudential sphere exposed the challenges in compliance and the differing approaches of countries with varying stages of economic development.

The incremental and piecemeal development of a distinctive international financial architecture took place alongside the consistent trend of globalisation of financial markets. The face of globalisation is changing and with it there is an increased need to focus on inclusiveness of developing and emerging economies and their different conception of "financial stability" that is not considered in isolation from financial development and inclusion. As themes move on from banking to BigTech, global agenda and standards setters will have to enhance their interaction with supervisors from policies such as consumer protection and competition. While these policies were traditionally perceived to be national and thus completely detached from the global financial architecture, they are essential to identifying vulnerabilities and risks to global stability.

This chapter uncovered the multi-layered and dynamic nature of the global financial architecture that often produces parallel reports and surveillance tools.

---

[164] For instance, it is suggested that the IMF should, in the future, be more involved in the analysis of cross-border interconnectedness and spillovers and in ex-post impact assessment of reforms that took place following the 2007–2009 financial crisis.

[165] FSB Work Programme for 2019 (February 2019), available at <http://www.fsb.org/2019/02/fsb-work-programme-for-2019/>.

The added value of this structure is in bringing diversity in expertise, approaches and coverage in systemic risk surveillance and regulation. But it could also create a fragmented framework that risks concerns falling between the stools. A more integrated approach with a clear division of work is necessary to prevent uncoordinated changes in the focus of these institutions and from regulatory gaps to materialise.

INDEX

ABOUT THE AUTHOR

Dr. Anat Keller is a Lecturer in law at the Dickson Poon School of Law, King's College London, and a Research Fellow at the Centre for Data Analytics for Finance and Macroeconomics (DAFM) at King's Business School. She was previously a Teaching Fellow and a Visiting Lecturer in law at University College London (2007–2016). She is also a qualified solicitor and serves as a Deputy Chief Examiner of the University of London. She is co-author of the book 'Law Relating to Financial Services' now in its 8th edition and has published numerous articles and chapters in peer-reviewed journals and edited collections focusing on macroprudential policy.